About Island Press

Island Press is the only nonprofit organization in the United States whose principal purpose is the publication of books on environmental issues and natural resource management. We provide solutions-oriented information to professionals, public officials, business and community leaders, and concerned citizens who are shaping responses to environmental problems.

In 2003, Island Press celebrates its nineteenth anniversary as the leading provider of timely and practical books that take a multidisciplinary approach to critical environmental concerns. Our growing list of titles reflects our commitment to bringing the best of an expanding body of literature to the environmental community throughout North America and the world.

Support for Island Press is provided by The Nathan Cummings Foundation, Geraldine R. Dodge Foundation, Doris Duke Charitable Foundation, Educational Foundation of America, The Charles Engelhard Foundation, The Ford Foundation, The George Gund Foundation, The Vira I. Heinz Endowment, The William and Flora Hewlett Foundation, Henry Luce Foundation, The John D. and Catherine T. MacArthur Foundation, The Andrew W. Mellon Foundation, The Moriah Fund, The Curtis and Edith Munson Foundation, National Fish and Wildlife Foundation, The New-Land Foundation, Oak Foundation, The Overbrook Foundation, The David and Lucile Packard Foundation, The Pew Charitable Trusts, The Rockefeller Foundation, The Winslow Foundation, and other generous donors.

The opinions expressed in this book are those of the author(s) and do not necessarily reflect the views of these foundations.

ACHIEVING SUSTAINABLE FRESHWATER SYSTEMS

ACHIEVING SUSTAINABLE FRESHWATER SYSTEMS

A WEB OF CONNECTIONS

Edited by
MARJORIE M. HOLLAND, ELIZABETH R. BLOOD,
and LAWRENCE R. SHAFFER

ISLAND PRESS
Washington • Covelo • London

Library of Congress Cataloging-in-Publication Data

Achieving sustainable freshwater systems : a web of connections / edited by Marjorie M. Holland, Elizabeth R. Blood, and Lawrence R. Shaffer.
     p. cm.
  ISBN 1-55963-928-8 (hardcover : alk. paper) — ISBN 1-55963-929-6 (pbk. : alk. paper)
  1. Freshwater ecology. 2. Ecosystem management. I. Holland, Marjorie M. II. Blood, Elizabeth R. III. Shaffer, Lawrence R.
  QH541.5.F7 A34 2003
  333.91—dc21

                                 2002155341

No copyright claim is made in the work of Paul B. Rodrigue, John A. Stanturf, Emile S. Gardiner, Melvin L. Warren Jr., Charles M. Cooper, and Matthew T. Moore, employees of the federal government.

British Cataloguing-in-Publication Data available.

Book design by Brighid Willson.

Printed on recycled, acid-free paper

09 08 07 06 05 04 03   10 9 8 7 6 5 4 3 2 1

Contents

Preface

One of the challenges facing the editors of a volume such as this is to present a unified and cohesive book, while also presenting perspectives from authors trained in many different disciplines. Nevertheless, these differing, sometimes far ranging, perspectives may well represent the key to achieving sustainability in the twenty-first century. The editors wish to celebrate the many perspectives presented in this volume. We believe the goal of achieving sustainability in the twenty-first century will be served by a synthesis of many viewpoints.

An international, multidisciplinary conference entitled "Sustainability of Wetlands and Water Resources: How Well Can Riverine Wetlands Continue to Support Society into the Twenty-first Century?" was held in May 2000 to honor the opening of The University of Mississippi's Center for Water and Wetland Resources. The focus of the conference was on recent work in freshwater wetlands (both natural and constructed) with a view toward understanding wetland processes in a watershed context. Because Oxford, home to The University of Mississippi, is uniquely located in the lower Mississippi River drainage basin, it seemed an ideal place to host such a conference, and conference participants were able to share with colleagues their experiences with a variety of river systems.

The mission of the Center for Water and Wetland Resources at The University of Mississippi Field Station is to undertake research, education, and service related to water and wetlands of the mid-South region of the United States. The conference assembled public and private-sector leaders and eminent researchers from around the world to address the most recent research and conservation work involving water and wetlands. Presentations were sorted into several sessions, and the results of those separate sessions have been summarized in various ways. For authors of some papers, their work is available through the conference proceedings (Holland et al. 2002). For others, such as Chapter 7 in this volume prepared by Nagle et al., the goal of the session was to convene an expert panel from diverse scientific disciplines to produce a synthesis of current thinking on a particular topic. An objective of the conference was to build partnerships promoting integrated approaches to urgent national and global concerns for environmental protection, human health, quality of life, economic vitality, and agricultural and aquacultural productivity.

This volume emerged in part from the dynamic May 2000 conference and attempts to capture and synthesize the integrative, cross-disciplinary interactions of the diverse groups who participated. It will be useful in a variety of applications: as a university textbook, as a scientific resource for researchers in the public and private sectors, and as a source for local, national, and international leaders and organizations. In addition, new materials have been added and the concluding section of the book reconfigured to provide additional environmental insights and to encourage public policy action.

In writing this book, our objectives are (1) to be visionary yet practical; (2) to be applicable to both developed and developing countries; (3) to be understandable to scientifically and technically oriented individuals but also to policy-makers and managers; and (4) to be useful in as many environmental settings as possible. We would like to provide information on ways to enhance the sustainability of wetlands and other freshwater resources for ecosystem conservation and for the benefit of society. We also wish to advance scholarship, research, and teaching focused on sustainability of watershed and aquifer systems. It is our desire to encourage public and private-sector partnerships to achieve interdisciplinary solutions to critical environmental and societal issues related to water and wetland resources. Our more specific goal is to promote effective, strategically targeted conservation activities and public policy development through the exchange of understandable ecological knowledge among nongovernmental organizations and educational, scientific, corporate, agricultural, and governmental constituencies. The interrelated challenges—to effectively promote research and data collection, interdisciplinary collaboration, clear communication of research findings to policy-makers and involved constituencies, leadership for consensus building, and communication of lessons learned to a broader public—are crucial to the goal of conserving critical freshwater and associated wetland ecosystems. It is the pressing need for an integrated, equitable, and sustainable approach to these environmental and societal challenges that this volume addresses.

Acknowledgments

We greatly appreciate the financial support of the Phil Hardin Foundation and the Henry L. and Grace Doherty Charitable Foundation to the Center for Water and Wetland Resources, the National Science Foundation grant DEB 00-0003056 to Marjorie M. Holland, and conference support from the U.S. Department of Agriculture, Natural Resources Conservation Service, Wildlife Habitat Management Institute, and the Wetlands Science Institute. We would like to thank the Joseph W. Jones Ecological Research Center and the Robert W. Woodruff Foundation for their financial support of one of the editors (Elizabeth R. Blood) and their institutional implementation of the resource conservation ethic articulated in this book. We are most grateful to each chapter author for the professionalism and patience with which they handled the various comments and recommendations received along the way. The persistence and attention to detail of the following staff and student workers in The University of Mississippi Field Station office is gratefully recognized: Justin Ainsworth, Brad Babb, Jason Beadle, Sherry Blount, Julie Chambers, Matt Dugas, Daniel Flint, Leili Gordji, Rachel Harris, Maureen Kent, Bounthanom Munxayaphom, Chris Patton, Dezra Peltier, Jamie Posey, Dinesh Talreja, Justin Wilkins, and Katie Winsett. We also extend our appreciation to Barbara Dean, Laura Carrithers, Barbara Youngblood, Chace Caven, and the other talented and dedicated staff of Island Press for their involvement in the myriad details necessary to bring this book to press.

References

Holland, M. M., M. Warren, and J. Stanturf, editors. 2002. *Proceedings from a Conference on Sustainability of Wetlands and Water Resources: How Well Can Riverine Wetlands Continue to Support Society into the 21st Century?* USDA Forest Service, Asheville, North Carolina. General Technical Report SRS 50.

Introduction

As the twenty-first century begins, the issue of sustainable water supplies is providing humanity with one of its greatest challenges. The problem is complex. We must figure out how to satisfy the water demands of an ever-expanding human population while at the same time protecting the aquatic ecosystems and ecological services upon which all life depends. Our relationship with our water supplies over the past 150 years has left us a legacy of damaged wetland ecosystems and ingrained water-use practices that are not sustainable. Human water demands have tripled in the past fifty years. We use approximately 4,000 cubic kilometers of water per year from rivers, streams, lakes, and aquifers. Irrigated agricultural land, which encompasses over 270 million hectares, accounts for about 70 percent of global water use. Industry accounts for approximately 20 percent, and cities and towns for about 10 percent (Brown and Flavin 1999).

At current rates, the world's human population uses about half of all the available freshwater, and the rate of water use continues to rise. Much of our current water allocation is at the expense of other species (see Chap. 4), ecosystem function (see Chap. 1), and, if we are not careful, future generations (see Chap. 5). The world's hydrological patterns have been greatly altered by our activities. We have fragmented our rivers with dams, for example, to the point that many of them run dry for parts of the year. Freshwater species are threatened with extinction across the planet. Our relationship with groundwater should also be cause for concern. Water tables are falling in many places around the world because the volume of water withdrawn for human uses greatly exceeds the ability of nature to replenish it. This problem is also one of global scale, and can be found in, to cite only a few examples, the Punjab of India, the north plain of China, and the Great Plains of the United States (Postel 2002).

Wetlands perform crucial services to humans and the other species to which we are inextricably linked. In humid regions of the world, wetlands often serve as the interface between precipitation events and groundwater recharge. In their absence, water does not stay in a given area but instead rushes away downstream.

1

Despite their importance to the local ecology, economies, and the hydrologic cycle, half of the world's wetlands have been lost during the twentieth century as a result of land conversion to agricultural and urban uses, cutting off of rivers from their floodplains and deltas, and overpumping of groundwater aquifers (Postel 2002).

It is not difficult to imagine the problems that humanity might experience in the absence of sustainable water use. For example, an increasing percentage of the world's agricultural production relies on groundwater, with the result that it is overpumped in many places. As these aquifers fail, food production could become erratic, which, in turn, could easily lead to domestic upheavals and international tensions. In addition, unsustainable water use practices will continue to put additional pressure on surface sources of fresh water, which will further exacerbate the high rate of species decline that became a hallmark of the twentieth century (Minkoff and Baker 2001).

Thus, we acknowledge the reality that one of the greatest natural resource challenges faced by humans around the world is the management of fresh water and the systems it supports. This book serves educators, scientists, engineers, advocates, business leaders, lawyers, members of nongovernmental organizations, watershed associations, citizens groups, and policy-makers by examining three fundamental components: (1) a cross-disciplinary knowledge base for prioritizing and conducting conservation activities; (2) the integrative scientific foundation and crucial common ground essential for development and implementation of judicious public policy for water and wetlands conservation; and (3) networks of collaborations and partnerships that can strengthen the environmental community, including nongovernmental organizations.

Within the context of freshwater management, one section of this volume examines recent work in freshwater wetlands (both natural and constructed) with a view toward understanding wetland processes in a watershed context. Our focus on wetlands stems from our location in the traditionally humid mid-South and southeastern regions of the United States. A wetland definition that would prove satisfactory to all users has not yet been developed, partly because the definition of wetlands depends on the objectives of wetland users and the users' fields of interest (Mitsch and Gosselink 2000). However, most wetland definitions include three main characteristics: (1) wetlands are distinguished by the presence of water, either at the surface or within the root zone; (2) wetlands often have unique soil conditions that differ from adjacent uplands; and (3) wetlands support vegetation adapted to wet conditions (hydrophytes) and, conversely, are characterized by an absence of flooding-intolerant vegetation (Mitsch and Gosselink 2000). The Convention on Wetlands of International Importance Especially as Waterfowl Habitat, also known as the Ramsar Convention from its place of adoption in 1971 in Iran, is an international treaty that provides a framework for international cooperation for the conservation of wetland habitats. The Convention takes an extremely broad approach to identifying the "wetlands" that come under its purview. It defines wetlands as "areas of marsh, fen, peatland, or water, whether natural or artificial, permanent or temporary, with water that is static or flowing, fresh, brackish or salt, including areas of marine waters, the depth of which at low tide does not exceed six metres." As a result of these provisions, the coverage of the Convention extends to a wide variety of habitat types including rivers, coastal areas, and, even, coral reefs (Ramsar Convention Bureau 1987). A variety of wetlands are used as examples throughout this book, and chapter authors adhere closely to the Mitsch and Gosselink (2000) definition presented above. For example, in Chapter 2, Fletcher uses a wetland definition from the U.S. Army Corps of Engineers, which refers to the three elements of the Mitsch and Gosselink definition. We hope that the wetland examples presented will provide useful insights for similar humid locations around the globe.

Part of what gives a wetland its characteristics is its location in the drainage basin or watershed; thus, it is important to take note of its elevation, surrounding land use, upstream or upslope characteristics, and the cultural value placed on any goods and services derived from it. Taking a holistic or whole system view of a wetland, including water sources and flow (quantity) and duration, is considered in these examples. Today, wetlands are acknowledged to be important components of watersheds, often serving as critical connections between land and open-water systems (Holland et al. 1990). Many wetland scientists have worked to understand the goods and services wetlands provide for humans, and they agree that wetlands serve as sinks, pathways, buffers, producers, and stores (Hollis et al. 1988). Wetlands function as "sinks" when sediment is deposited in floodplains along river channels. They serve as "pathways" when they host migratory waterfowl along journeys north or south. Wetlands function as "buffers" when floods are attenuated by riparian marshes and oxbow lakes. They serve as "producers" of timber from bottomland hardwood forests, and adjacent marshes support the young of various freshwater fish species. Last, but certainly not least, wetlands serve as a "store" of genetic diversity and allow recolonization after major storm events (Hollis et al. 1988). Thus, natural wetland systems provide numerous goods and services crucial to supporting human economic and social systems.

Five characteristics of watersheds or drainage basins underlie the discussions presented throughout this book. First, a watershed includes the entire physical area or basin drained by a distinct stream or riverine system, physically separated from other watersheds by ridgetop boundaries (Fig. I.1). Second, a watershed is an area with four-dimensional processes that connect the longitudinal (upstream-downstream), lateral (floodplains-upland), and vertical (hyporheic or

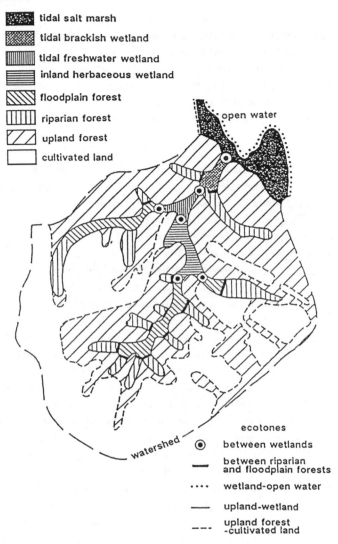

tidal salt marsh
tidal brackish wetland
tidal freshwater wetland
inland herbaceous wetland
floodplain forest
riparian forest
upland forest
cultivated land

open water

watershed

ecotones
between wetlands
between riparian and floodplain forests
wetland-open water
upland-wetland
upland forest-cultivated land

Figure I.1. Overview of various wetland types within a single watershed (from Holland et al. 1990)

groundwater zone-stream channel) dimensions, each differing temporally (Holland et al. 1990). Third, a watershed is an area composed of a mosaic of different land or terrestrial habitats connected or drained by a network of streams. Fourth, the flowing-water environment of a watershed is composed of a mosaic of habitats in which materials and energy are transferred and, therefore, connected through biologically diverse food webs. Fifth, human activities can fragment and disconnect watershed habitat patches if their management is not planned and implemented from an ecosystem and watershed perspective (Doppelt et al. 1993).

Our view of sustainability implies that resource management should at least facilitate continuation of the quality or quantity of freshwater resources, as characterized by residents of the drainage basin, for many, many years. A definition specific to fresh water has recently been provided as part of the Georgia Comprehensive State Water Management Plan (Georgia Joint Comprehensive Water Plan Study Committee 2002), which suggests that water resources are to be used and managed "so that economic, environmental, social, and cultural values can be supported indefinitely." The Georgia perspective is useful because it includes financial, social, and natural science components, and effectively blends current thinking from these disciplines (Costanza 1991; Heal 1998; Chichilnisky and Heal 2000; Agar 2001).

Role of Stakeholders

Management of human activities and impacts at regional and watershed scales as a means of ensuring sustainable freshwater resources presents a continuing dilemma. Because of the large scale of regional considerations and the environmental problems associated with them, environmental management decisions in some cases may best be coordinated or directed by one or more entities with a large purview. In fact, experience suggests that invariably effective and efficient solutions to environmental problems are developed by involving local stakeholders who often best understand the resources and the resource users. Therefore, a general model of interactions needed to support sustainable regional resource management has been described as resembling a wheel, with components of a management plan providing connections between stakeholder groups, similar to the spokes of a wheel keeping the parts of a wheel together. As seen in Figure I.2, the spokes actually fortify the rim and provide a way for each individual to contribute to and enhance the whole (Holland 1996; Barnthouse et al. 1998). Whatever the stakeholder group is called (e.g., Advisory Board, citizens committee), the availability of a mechanism for promoting dialog among diverse interest groups can be extremely beneficial to the final project outcome. The more "buy in" the members of a group feel, the better the possibility that the final plan will be implemented. In this book, we provide examples of sustainable environmental management that clearly illustrate each of the six spokes of a wheel. In particular, readers are encouraged to act on our recommendations for "education" and "implementation,"—spokes that have not been addressed adequately in the past.

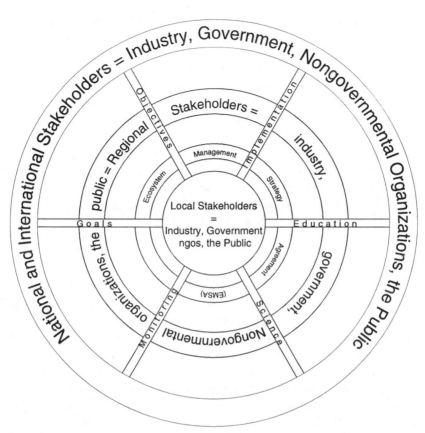

Figure I.2. A general strategy for sustainable management of regional ecosystems where the Ecosystem Management Strategy Agreement (EMSA) operates close to the local stakeholders (from Holland 1996)

About This Book

This book reviews present and past knowledge about the assessment and maintenance of sustainable freshwater systems, and it brings together this knowledge in a form that is useful for both scientific and management purposes. Indeed, the term "sustainability" is best captured in the message attributed to the Great Law of the Iroquois Confederacy: "In our every deliberation, we must consider the impact of our decisions on the next seven generations." This message alludes to the value of viewing situations at the right scale, and it suggests that individuals should consider the context of time and place when making personal and societal decisions about the use of natural resources. We agree with others (Naiman et al. 1995; Postel 1999; Natural Resources Law Center 2000; World Resources Institute 2000) that water resources management is at a critical stage, and we would hope that this volume complements and supports other recent voices (Vitousek et al. 1997; Burger et al. 2000; Jensen 2000) that urge comprehensive, effective, and vigorous action(s) to minimize or prevent further degradation and to restore functionality where possible.

Three themes appear throughout the chapters, weaving them into a cohesive whole. The first theme provides readers with an understanding of the intrinsic links between human infrastructure and natural areas that foster sustainable freshwater systems. It is critical to consider the ecological, geographical, and societal dimensions when formulating solutions to problems of sustainable water use. Natural systems provide goods and services essential for supporting human systems. The needs of humans cannot be considered on their own. Rather, sustainable freshwater systems are only fostered when the needs of the other organisms they support are also considered.

The second theme urges readers to adopt a holistic approach to developing solutions for achieving sustainable freshwater systems. There is a need, for example, to look both upstream and downstream of a project in order to truly appreciate the possible impacts of what is being proposed.

The third and last theme urges persons striving to forge sustainable solutions to promote action through effective networks. Too often we work solely within our own associations or social groups. In contrast, effective networks can be useful tools, enabling us to derive more benefit from life, socially, professionally, personally, and so forth. It is important to share these tools and to forge associations with other groups with whom we may not have previously worked. Today, we hear much emphasis on "partnerships," whether at the local, state, regional, national, or international level. These partnerships can include collaborations between industry and government, between government and academia, between academia and nongovernmental organizations, or in some cases among them all. Partnerships allow us to share the burden, the responsibility, the credit, and the pleasure of watching something develop, grow, and work well. Several successful partnerships are presented and discussed in different chapters throughout the book.

This book is not meant to be an extensive technical treatise on the topic of sustainable systems but rather is intended to provide sufficient information to allow interested persons to acquire a broad, general knowledge of background issues leading to the current situation and to provide the steps needed to achieve and maintain sustainable freshwater wetlands and water resources. In this way, both decision makers and technical staff can diagnose and formulate site-specific solutions.

The reader will find over 100 water-related organizations mentioned throughout the text. Virtually all have Web pages that offer additional information, suggestions, examples, and resources. Individual Web pages can be located by typing an organization's name in an Internet search engine. Much information can be gained through Internet searches for organizations as diverse as, for example, the American Cancer Society, the Flint River Drought Protection Act, or the Zambezi Action Plan.

Chapters have been organized using the "hourglass" approach, first describing broad, global topics, narrowing the view using examples from the mid-South and southeastern region of the United States, and then looking outward again at the bigger issues. This approach allows us to provide a global overview of critical issues, discuss them in the context of wetlands with which we are familiar, and then present some overall thoughts and conclusions.

We've grouped the book's chapters into four parts: Part I defines key aquatic resource issues facing the world today and describes the history of wetland laws in the United States. Examples of contamination and mismanagement of freshwater resources are also found in Part I, along with a history of wetland and watershed disruption in the United States.

Part II offers the perspectives of the scientific community and describes research efforts that investigate the importance of wetlands as a link between upland and open water systems. This section will be of particular interest to more technically inclined readers, including freshwater biologists, ecologists, students of biogeochemical cycling, and pharmacologists.

Part III emphasizes the positive relationships that exist between humans and the environment by using examples of recently developed restoration techniques. This section will be of interest to resource managers, including those charged with wetland restoration.

In Part IV, we hope to encourage readers to think creatively about opportunities for the future. In this section we ask the question, "Can we achieve sustainable freshwater systems in the future?" In the concluding chapter, the editors focus on the book's global utility. While numerous local and regional case studies are presented throughout the book, they provide the examples for specific points, which the editors reformulate into global implications and global challenges.

References

Agar, N. 2001. *Life's intrinsic value: Science, ethics, and nature.* New York: Columbia University Press.

Barnthouse, L. W., G. R. Biddinger, W. E. Cooper, J. A. Fava, J. W. Gillett, M. M. Holland, and T. F. Yosie. 1998. *Sustainable environmental management: Proceedings of the Pellston Workshop on Sustainability-Based Environmental Management, 25–31 August 1993, Pellston, Michigan.* Pensacola, Fla.: Society of Environmental Toxicology and Chemistry.

Brown, L. R., and C. Flavin. 1999. A new economy for a new century. Pp. 3–21 in *State of the World 1999*, edited by Linda Starke. New York: W. W. Norton.

Burger, J., E. Ostrom, R. B. Norgaard, D. Policansky, and B. D. Goldstein, eds. 2001.

Protecting the commons: A framework for resource management in the Americas. Washington, D.C.: Island Press.

Chichilnisky, G., and G. Heal, eds. 1998. *Environmental markets: Equity and efficiency.* New York: Columbia University Press.

Costanza, R., ed. 1991. *Ecological economics: The science and management of sustainability.* New York: Columbia University Press.

Doppelt, B., M. Scurlock, C. Frissell, and J. Karr. 1993. *Entering the watershed: A new approach to save America's river ecosystems.* Washington, D.C.: Island Press.

Firth, P. 1999. The importance of water resources education for the next century. *Journal of the American Water Resources Association* 35 (3):487–492.

Georgia Joint Comprehensive Water Plan Study Committee. 2002. *Final report of the Joint Comprehensive Water Plan Study Committee.* A report to the Governor and to the General Assembly. Carl Vinson Institute of Government, University of Georgia, Athens, Ga.

Griffin, C. B. 1999. Watershed Councils: An emerging form of public participation in natural resource management. *Journal of the American Water Resources Association* 35 (3):505–518.

Harrington, K. W., T. D. Feather, and G. R. Clark. 1999. State water law reform: Identifying legal and managerial issues and options. *Journal of the American Water Resources Association* 35 (3):545–553.

Heal, G. 1998. *Valuing the future: Economic theory and sustainability.* New York: Columbia University Press.

Holland, M. M. 1996. Ensuring sustainability of natural resources: Focus on institutional arrangements. *Canadian Journal of Fisheries and Aquatic Sciences* 53 (Supplement 1):432–439.

Holland, M. M., D. Whigham, and B. Gopal. 1990. The characteristics of wetland ecotones. Pp. 171–198 in *Land/inland water ecotones,* edited by R. J. Naiman and H. Decamps. London: Parthenon Publishing Group.

Hollis, G. E., M. M. Holland, E. Maltby, and J. S. Larson. 1988. Wise use of wetlands. *Nature and Resources* 24, (1):2–13.

Jensen, M. N. 2000. Common sense and common-pool resources. *BioScience* 50 (8):638–644.

Michelsen, A. M., J. T. McGuckin, and D. Stumpf. 1999. Nonprice water conservation programs as a demand management tool. *Journal of the American Water Resources Association* 35 (3):593–602.

Minkoff, E. C., and P. J. Baker. 2001. *Biology today: An issues approach.* 2d ed. New York: Garland Publishing.

Mitsch, W. J., and J. G. Gosselink. 2000. *Wetlands.* 3d ed. New York: John Wiley and Sons.

Naiman, R. J., J. J. Magnuson, D. M. McKnight, and J. A. Stanford. 1995. *The freshwater imperative: A research agenda.* Washington, D.C.: Island Press.

Natural Resources Law Center. 2000. *The new watershed source book.* www.colorado.edu/Law/NRLC/recentpubs.html. University of Colorado, Boulder.

Postel, S. 1999. *Pillar of sand: Can the irrigation miracle last?* New York: W. W. Norton.

———. 2002. Human alterations of earth's fresh water: Scale, consequences, and a call to action. Pp. 1–3 in *Proceedings of a Conference on Sustainability of Wetlands and*

Water Resources, edited by M. M. Holland, M. L. Warren Jr., and J. A. Stanturf. USDA Forest Service, Southern Research Station, General Technical Report SRS-50.

Ramsar Convention Bureau. 1987. *Convention on wetlands of international importance especially as waterfowl habitat.* Gland, Switzerland: International Union for Conservation of Nature and Natural Resources.

Ruhl, J. B. 1999. The (political) science of watershed management in the ecosystem age. *Journal of the American Water Resources Association* 35 (3):519–526.

Vitousek, P. M., H. A. Mooney, J. Lubchenco, and J. M. Melillo. 1997. Human domination of earth's ecosystems. *Science* 227:494–504.

World Resources Institute, United Nations Development Programme, United Nations Environment Programme, and World Bank. 2000. *People and ecosystems: The fraying web of life.* Washington, D.C.: World Resources Institute.

Chapter 1

Sustainable Freshwater Resources: The Promise and the Reality

Walter Rast

Economic development as a means of improving human well-being and living standards is a goal of virtually all governments on our planet. Until about twenty years ago, the general belief was that all economic development carried with it an environmental price tag in the form of natural resource exploitation and environmental degradation. There are numerous examples of the uncontrolled environmental exploitation and degradation around the world, one being the industrial regions of many parts of Eastern Europe. The blighted countryside and polluted water, land, and air resources in some of these regions clearly illustrate the problems of economic development carried out with little or no consideration of the long-term environmental, human, or ecosystem impacts of such activities.

It has become increasingly clear over the last several decades, however, that economic development cannot be sustained without proper regard for the environmentally sound management and use of natural resources. The notion that development and environment are interdependent forms the basis for "sustainable development" (Laszlo et al. 1988). Sustainable development is not a form of government or politics, nor a regulatory process meant to eliminate specific industrial activities or rigorously dictate land-use activities or patterns. Rather, this notion marks a fundamental change in how we must view the relation between the economic growth and development desired by humans on the one hand, and the natural resources needed to sustain it on the other hand. An analogy would be to view our physical environment as a kind of natural resources "bank." As long as we do not spend our environmental

11

currency (minerals, water, biodiversity, etc.) at a faster rate than nature can replenish it, we are "living within our means." The same analogy applies to our not depleting our resources faster than nature can supply them, nor degrading our environment faster than nature has the ability to clean it, or otherwise assimilate the wastes and pollutants we discharge. Only by accepting such realities can we ensure that the natural environment will provide its resources and services to us indefinitely. If we exceed nature's capacities, in the form of unbridled natural resource exploitation or uncontrolled pollution, we ensure that we will eventually overwhelm nature's ability to provide the needed resource base and assimilative capacity for our well-being and economic advancement. Under this condition, our desired economic development will no longer be sustainable, with potentially dire consequences over the long term.

Many tribal societies, in fact, do live in relative harmony with nature in their subsistence cultures. Nevertheless, experience suggests that some basic level of economic development appears to be necessary to foster environmental concern. This is because the very poor must do what is necessary to survive, without the option of being able to worry about the environmental consequences of their actions. Only when our basic survival needs are met can we readily expand our horizons to consider the state of the world around us.

This is not to suggest that the best solution to any human problem is to mimic the natural world, or that the key to achieving sustainable development is to protect the environment at all costs. Conversely, it does not mean that humans should engage in the uncontrolled exploitation of natural resources. Rather, the key to sustainable development is to balance the resource needs of economic growth and the ability of nature to provide them while also preserving environmental quality (Rast 1999). Basic tenets underlying the goals of sustainable development (Laszlo et al. 1988) include the following:

- Economic development must occur within the constraints of the natural resource base
- Development must be cost effective, and may require nontraditional economic criteria
- Development should not result in environmental degradation nor reduce environmental productivity over the long term
- The needs of the very poor must be addressed, because their quest for survival may leave them with no options other than to degrade or destroy their own environment
- Issues of health control, appropriate technologies, self-reliance in food, clean water, and shelter for all citizens must be considered
- Environmental systems at the greatest risk require first consideration.

Sustainable Development and Agenda 21

The interdependence of development and environment was at the core of the governmental deliberations and conclusions at the United Nations Conference on Environment and Development (also known as the Rio Summit), held in Rio de Janeiro in 1992. One significant outcome of this international conference was the Rio Declaration on Environment and Development, the first principle of which states that "human beings are at the centre of concerns for sustainable development. They are entitled to a healthy and productive life in harmony with nature."

The other significant outcome from the Rio Summit was Agenda 21 (United Nations 1992). This was a major governmental commitment to sustainable development on a global scale, identifying thirty-eight major interrelated environmental and economic policy goals. The goals were to be tackled through 131 priority programs addressing a range of diverse environmental issues, including atmosphere, land resources, deforestation, desertification and drought, mountain ecosystems, agriculture and rural development, biological diversity, biotechnology, marine and coastal resources, freshwater resources, toxic chemicals, and hazardous, solid, and radioactive wastes. Agenda 21 contains more than 2,500 individual recommendations for national and inte national actions, all based on the goal of facilitating sustainable development at the global, regional, and local levels.

Freshwater Resources and Agenda 21

The notion of sustainability applies equally well to freshwater resources. As long as nature can supply water for human activities and ecosystem maintenance at a rate greater than humans withdraw the water, the water supply can be sustained indefinitely. Once this capacity is exceeded, however, the water supply will eventually be depleted. It is analogous to a bathtub full of water, representing the available water resources. Water can be added to the tub through a faucet, and will exit the tub via a drain at the bottom. As long as the volume of water entering the tub through the faucet (i.e., precipitation) is greater than the volume of water draining from the tub (i.e., human water demands), the tub will not empty. If the volume of drainage water exceeds the water entering the tub, however, the water in the tub will eventually be depleted. Water pollution also represents a form of water scarcity in that the range of possible water uses is reduced without pretreatment, which can be costly and time consuming. Although extraordinary measures can be undertaken to augment existing water supplies (e.g., transfer of water between drainage basins), such measures are

Table 1.1. River water resources by continent

Continent	Land area (million km²)	Population (in millions)	Water resources (km³/year) Average	Maximum	Minimum
Europe	10.46	685.0	2,900	3,210	2,442
North America	24.25	448.0	7,770	8,820	6,660
Africa	30.10	708.0	4,040	5,080	3,070
Asia	43.48	3,403.0	13,508	15,010	11,800
South America	17.86	315.0	12,030	14,350	10,330
Australia and Oceania	8.95	28.7	2,400	2,880	1,890
Global total	135.00	5,588.0	42,659	44,460	39,660

Source: Shiklomanov 1997.

typically very expensive, require major constructions, and may themselves be unsustainable over the long term.

Human water demands have changed significantly over the last century. Between 1940 and 1990, for example, the world's population doubled. The per capita water use also doubled, meaning that human water consumption on a global scale increased by more than four times during this fifty-year period. With a relatively constant supply of freshwater on a global scale, coupled with an increasing population, the maximum per capita availability of water has decreased. It is estimated that approximately one-third of the global population already lives under conditions of water stress (defined as 1,700 cubic meters or less per person annually), with the problem being most severe in the developing countries. It is further predicted that this fraction will increase to two-thirds of the global population by the year 2025, *if present water use trends continue* (WMO 1997). Water shortages are already a major problem in the Middle East, North Africa, and sub-Saharan Africa. China, with a population of more than one billion, only has about 8 percent of the world's renewable water resources. It is estimated that India's water demands will reach 92 percent of its total annual freshwater resources by the year 2025. The available water resources expressed by continent and major river basin are identified in Tables 1.1 and 1.2 respectively (Shiklomanov 1997).

The global pattern of water use also has changed over time. At the beginning of the last century, agricultural water use represented about 90 percent of total global water use. At the beginning of the twenty-first century, however, global agricultural water use is estimated to be only about 65 percent of total water use. In contrast, industrial water use, estimated to be only about 6 percent of total water use in 1900, has now increased to about 24 percent on a global scale. With increasing industrialization and urbanization, water pollution

Table 1.2. Water resources in major rivers of the world

River	Watershed land area (million km²)	Population (in millions)	Water runoff volume (km³/year)		
			Average	Maximum	Minimum
Amazon	6.92	14.30	6,920.0	8,510.0	5,790.00
Ganges (including Brahmaputra and Meghna Rivers)	1.75	439.00	1,389.0	1,690.0	1,220.00
Congo	3.50	48.30	1,300.0	1,775.0	1,050.00
Orinoco	1.00	22.40	1,010.0	1,380.0	706.00
Yangtze	1.81	346.00	1,003.0	1,410.0	700.00
La Plata	3.10	98.40	811.0	1,860.0	453.00
Yenisey	2.58	4.77	618.0	729.0	531.00
Mississippi	3.21	72.50	573.0	880.0	280.00
Lena	2.49	1.87	539.0	670.0	424.00
Ob	2.99	22.50	404.0	567.0	270.00
Mekong	0.79	75.00	505.0	610.0	376.00
Mackenzie	1.75	0.35	333.0	420.0	281.00
Amur	1.86	4.46	328.0	483.0	187.00
Niger	2.09	131.00	303.0	482.0	163.00
Volga	1.38	43.30	255.0	390.0	161.00
Danube	0.82	85.10	225.0	321.0	137.00
Indus	0.96	150.00	220.0	359.0	126.00
Nile	2.87	89.00	161.0	248.0	94.80
Amu Darya	0.31	15.50	77.1	118.0	56.70
Hwang Ho	0.75	82.00	66.1	97.0	22.10
Dnieper	0.50	36.60	53.3	95.0	21.70
Syr Darya	0.22	13.40	38.3	75.0	26.20
Don	0.42	17.50	26.9	52.0	11.90
Murray	1.07	2.10	24.0	129.0	1.16

Source: Shiklomanov 1997.

from point and nonpoint sources also is increasing in both developed and developing countries. Another complicating factor is that the world is undergoing an "urban revolution." The United Nations Population Fund estimates that approximately 77 percent of the population of Latin America, 41 percent of Africa's population, and 35 percent of Asia's population now live in cities. Further, there are now twenty-three cities with populations exceeding 10 million people. About eighteen of these twenty-three "mega-cities" are located in developing countries, which are usually least able to address their natural resource requirements and the accompanying environmental degradation problems (WMO 1997).

These hydrologic and environmental realities dictate that the interdependence of development and environment embodied in the notion of sustainable development applies equally well to freshwater resources. To this end, the International Conference on Water and the Environment, held in Dublin in early 1992, provided some significant guiding principles for achieving sustainable water resources. These principles, listed below, are meant as a basis of action at the local, national, and international levels (WMO 1992):

• Freshwater is a finite and vulnerable resource, essential to sustain life, development, and the environment
• Water development and management should be based on a participatory approach, involving users, planners, and policy-makers at all levels
• Women play a central role in the provision, management, and safeguarding of water
• Water has an economic value in all its competing uses and should be recognized as an economic good.

Chapter 18, the largest chapter of Agenda 21, is directed to the goal of sustainable freshwater resources. In addressing protection of the quality and supply of freshwater resources, Chapter 18 emphasizes the integrated development, management, and use of these resources (United Nations 1992). Its general objectives are (1) to ensure that adequate supplies of clean, safe water are maintained for the entire population of the planet; (2) to preserve the hydrological, biological, and chemical functions of ecosystems; (3) to adapt human activities within the capacity limits of nature; and (4) to combat vectors of water-related diseases.

To facilitate achievement of these water objectives by governments and other major stakeholders, Chapter 18 of Agenda 21 identified seven major program areas focusing on freshwater resources (United Nations 1992):

• Integrated water resource development and management
• Water resources assessment
• Protection of water resources, water quality, and aquatic ecosystems
• Drinking-water supply and sanitation
• Water and sustainable urban development
• Water for sustainable food production and rural development
• Impacts of climate change on water resources.

Continuing experience on a regional and global scale suggests that successful achievement of integrated freshwater resource management, the first of the above-noted program areas, is the most rational and feasible means to ensure achievement of the other program areas of Chapter 18 as well. The approach also provides a rational basis for efforts by governments and other major stakeholders to pursue the goal of sustainable freshwater resources.

Implementation of Freshwater Objectives in Different Regions of the World

Agenda 21 contains 270 individual recommendations directed to achievement of sustainable freshwater resources. Given their greater financial and human resources, and their enhanced ability to implement regulatory and institutional approaches, the developed countries of the world should be most capable of implementing these recommendations, on both national and international scales. Nevertheless, water quantity and quality issues remain major concerns in developed countries as well. Even more problematic, however, is the very slow pace of implementation (see Chap. 13) of these recommendations in developing countries.

To assess the progress made in implementing the freshwater objectives of Agenda 21, the United Nations Environment Programme (UNEP), in cooperation with its regional offices and the United Nations Regional Economic Commissions, convened a series of regional workshops during 1995–1996. Because these areas were expected to have the most difficulty implementing the freshwater objectives, the workshops focused on developing regions of the world, or regions with economies in transition, as follows: (1) Asia and Pacific Region (Bangkok, Thailand), (2) West Asia Region (Amman, Jordan), (3) Africa Region (Nairobi, Kenya), (4) Latin America and Caribbean Region (Santiago, Chile), and (5) Eastern European Region (Minsk, Belarus).

The basic objective of the workshops was to provide government officials and other stakeholders with a forum to discuss progress made, and problems encountered, in achieving the freshwater objectives of Agenda 21. A particular goal was to determine *if*, and *how*, countries were addressing freshwater issues in their national development plans and actions within the context of Agenda 21. This information would provide an indication of the extent to which the objectives were guiding or influencing national and regional economic development plans.

The conclusions arising from UNEP's regional workshops are summarized in the following sections and reflect the order in which the regional meetings were held. Because it is ultimately the responsibility of individual governments to set their priorities for addressing their freshwater resources, the following sections provide (1) an overview of the problems and perspectives regarding freshwater resources in different regions of the world, (2) the extent to which the freshwater objectives of Agenda 21 were being implemented (or not) in these regions, and (3) the constraints to their timely implementation. It is emphasized that these overviews do not reflect the opinions of this author, but rather summarize the comments and conclusions expressed by the regional workshop governmental representatives and experts participating in the meetings.

Asia and Pacific Region

This region covers a vast area, extending north and south from Mongolia to New Zealand and east to west from the Cook Islands to Iran. It contains the world's largest and third-largest oceans and three of the largest and most populous countries (China, India, and Indonesia). Comprising only about 23 percent of the world's total land area, it contains about 58 percent of the world's population. Individual economies in the region have exhibited high growth rates in the past. At the same time, however, more than two-thirds of the world's 1.2 billion people living in absolute poverty (i.e., less than U.S.$1 per day) are found in this region. The region's environment and natural resource base is under significant stress from high population growth, urbanization, and industrialization. The region contains both arid/semi-arid and humid tropical areas. It has some of the world's largest rivers (e.g., Ganges-Brahmaputra, Mekong, Yangtze) and a substantial number of lakes. It also has extensive groundwater resources, the primary freshwater source for many of the region's small island states (UNEP 1997, 1999).

Water use is increasing rapidly in virtually all the countries of the region. The rapid expansion of many Asian economies in recent decades, accompanied by accelerated population growth, has raised the standards of living throughout the region, while at the same time creating problems of unsustainable water resource development. A number of countries are already facing serious seasonal water shortages, as well as heavily contaminated and depleted surface and groundwater supplies. Afghanistan and Iran, for example, suffer chronic water shortages because of aridity. China and India experience the same problem because of their high population densities.

The renewable water resources and water withdrawals for selected countries in the Asia-Pacific region are summarized in Table 1.3. Many countries in the region have reached the end of an era when water was considered a virtually unlimited resource. Many are now entering an era in which water is becoming recognized as an economic commodity, to be used in a more rational manner and to be protected from degradation.

Agriculture currently accounts for 60–90 percent of annual water withdrawal in most of the countries of the region. Although the water withdrawal for industrial use currently represents only a fraction of the region's total water abstraction, water demands for energy production, manufacturing, mining, and material processing are rapidly increasing in those countries on an industrialization path. At the same time, many industries have few controls on their wastewater discharges.

Table 1.3. Renewable water resources and withdrawals for selected countries in the Asia-Pacific region

Country	Annual renewable water resources[a]		Annual water withdrawals			Sectoral water withdrawals (%)		
	Total (km^3)	1995 per capita (m^3)	Year of data	% of annual water resources	Per capita (m^3)	Domestic	Industry	Agriculture
Afghanistan	50.0	2,482	1987	52	1,830	1	0	99
Bhutan	95.0	57,998	1987	0	14	36	10	54
China	2,800.0	2,292	1980	16	461	6	7	87
India	2,085.0	2,228	1975	18	612	3	4	93
Indonesia	2,530.0	12,804	1987	1	96	13	11	76
Iran	117.5	1,746	1975	39	1,362	4	9	87
Japan	547.0	4,373	1990	17	735	17	33	50
Rep. Korea	66.1	1,469	1992	42	632	19	35	46
Malaysia	456.0	22,642	1975	2	768	23	30	47
Papua New Guinea	801.0	186,192	1987	0	28	29	22	49
Singapore	0.6	211	1975	32	84	45	51	4

Source: UNEP 1997.

[a]Including river inflows from other countries.

There is a fundamental need for improved and more efficient management of water resources of the entire Asia and Pacific region. In fact, many countries have formulated national water policies, some of which have also been translated into national master water plans. What has not yet been done, however, is to translate these policies into real actions, with the development of realistic implementation plans and programs for water resources development and protection.

WEST ASIA REGION

This largely arid region comprises Bahrain, Iraq, Jordan, Kuwait, Lebanon, Oman, Qatar, Saudi Arabia, Syria, United Arab Emirates, Palestine, and Yemen. These countries are characterized by major differences in their surface areas, natural resources endowment, population, income, and levels of socioeconomic development.

Fresh water is the region's most precious and limited natural resource. More than 70 percent of the region is arid, with low, unpredictable and variable rainfall, accompanied by high evaporation rates. Most rainfall occurs during winter, with the summer lasting between five and nine months each year. Only Iraq, Syria, and Lebanon have relatively dependable surface water sources. Groundwater is the major freshwater source for the remaining countries in the region (UNEP 1997, 1999). The conventional and nonconventional water resources, and sectoral water withdrawals, for the West Asia region are summarized in Table 1.4.

High population growth, coupled with inadequate distribution of the region's scarce water resources, constitutes basic riparian problems. Because more than 80 percent of the region's freshwater withdrawals are for agricultural irrigation, achieving more efficient irrigation water use is a major requirement for sustainable water resources.

There is a serious and increasing gap between the readily available freshwater supplies and the human demands for them, which is affecting both the quality and quantity of the region's water resources. The use, protection, and management of the available freshwater resources, therefore, are crucial regional issues. Due to the scarce conventional freshwater sources, some countries have been forced to use expensive, nonconventional sources (Table 1.4), including (1) desalination of brackish water and seawater; and (2) reuse of domestic treatment plant effluents for irrigation. As a result, this region leads the world in the development and use of such nonconventional water sources.

The current approach to economic and regulatory aspects of water use and protection is largely inadequate throughout the region. There are inadequate pricing structures, resulting in limited cost-recovery in the water sector. The regulatory environment is generally weak. Freshwater allocation, use, and preservation

Table 1.4. Water resources and sectoral water withdrawals for the West Asia region for the early 1990s

Country	Conventional water resources (million m³)		Non-conventional water resources (million m³)		Total (million m³)	Sectoral water withdrawals (million m³)		
	Surface water[a]	Ground water[c]	Desalinization	Waste-water reuse		Domestic	Agriculture	Industry
Bahrain	0.2	90	75.0	9.5	174.7	86	120	17
Iraq	76,880.0	1,500	7.4	—	78,387.4	3,800	40,000	5,600
Jordan	660.0	275	2.5	52.0	989.5	190	650	43
Kuwait	0.1	182	240.0	83.0	505.1	295	80	8
Lebanon	2,500.0	12,000	1.7	—	14,501.7	310	750	60
Oman	918.0	10,500	32.0	25.0	11,475.0	81	1,150	5
Qatar	1.4	2,500	92.0	25.0	2,618.4	76	109	9
Saudi Arabia	2,230.0	84,000	795.0	217.0	87,242.0	1,508	14,600	192
Syria	22,688.0	3,000	2.0	50.0	25,740.0	650	6,930	146
United Arab Emirates	125.0	20,000	385.0	110.0	20,620.0	513	950	27
Palestine[b]	30.0	150	—	—	180.0	78	140	7
Yemen	2,000.0	13,500	9.0	9.1	15,518.1	168	2,700	31

Source: UNEP 1997.

[a]The Tigris and Euphrates river flows will be reduced by upstream withdrawals in Turkey.

[b]West Bank and Gaza.

[c]Shallow aquifer ground water reserve with varying water quality.

efforts in most countries also suffer from a lack of inter- and intrabasin cooperation, poor data, and uncoordinated piecemeal approaches, resulting in fragmented policies and actions.

Given the high per-capita consumption and limited freshwater resources, the growing pressure on water resources is becoming increasingly more serious in this region, dictating an urgent need for long-term solutions. In the absence of such actions, the increasing pressure on the region's water resources will lead to even more serious water shortages in the future.

AFRICA REGION

Africa has experienced serious and persistent economic and environmental problems over the past four decades, and many African countries are continuing to experience political and social turmoil. The continent has the highest overall population growth rate in the world, and poverty has perpetuated underdevelopment and mismanagement of natural resources. Although economic reform measures and political liberalization are occurring in many countries, corruption and mismanagement still play a major role in exacerbating the environmental and economic stresses facing the continent. Alleviating the poverty of the majority of the over 660 million Africans remains the overriding regional priority (UNEP 1997, 1999).

A major problem for many African countries is an unbalanced use of their resources. Soil and vegetation are being overexploited, for example, while water, energy, mineral, and organic resources are underdeveloped, even in the same areas.

Water availability is highly variable, both in time and space, and Africa often is described in terms of its Saharan and sub-Saharan components. The rainfall varies from essentially zero in the Horn of Africa, to more than 4,000 millimeters per year in the western equatorial region. A large proportion of the African continent is semiarid in character, receiving between 200 and 400 millimeters of rainfall per year. The freshwater supply is particularly limited in the Sudano-Sahelian belt and parts of southern Africa. At the same time, the continent has a large number of rivers and lakes (e.g., Congo, Nile, and Zambezi Rivers; Lake Victoria). Although about 4 trillion cubic meters of renewable water are available annually, only about 4 percent of it is currently being used, due primarily to inadequate infrastructure development. As a result, Africa contains nineteen of the world's twenty-five countries with the highest percentage of their population lacking access to safe drinking water (UNEP 1999). Table 1.5 summarizes the renewable water resources and water withdrawals for some selected African countries. For crucial water supply and sanitation services, as well as for a range of key economic, health, and human development indicators, most African countries and sub-regions, as well as the continent as a whole, fall significantly below the averages for all developing countries and for the world. Thus, the

Table 1.5. Renewable water resources and withdrawals for selected African countries

Country	Annual renewable water resources[a]		Annual water withdrawals			Sectoral water withdrawals (%)		
	Total (km³)	1995 per capita (m³)	Year of data	% of annual water resources	Per capita (m³)	Domestic	Industry	Agriculture
Algeria	14.8	528	1990	30	180	25	15	60
Burundi	3.6	563	1987	3	20	36	0	64
Congo	832.0	321,236	1987	0	20	62	27	11
Egypt	58.1	923	1992	97	956	6	9	85
Ethiopia	110.0	1,998	1987	2	51	11	3	86
Kenya	30.2	1,069	1990	7	87	20	4	76
Libya	0.6	111	1994	767	880	11	2	87
Morocco	30.0	1,110	1992	36	427	5	3	92
Nigeria	280.0	2,506	1987	1	41	31	15	54
Tunisia	3.9	443	1990	78	381	9	3	89
Zaire	1,019.0	23,211	1990	0	10	61	16	23

Source: UNEP 1997.

[a]Including river inflows from other countries.

priority for water resource management throughout most of Africa continues to be provision of safe drinking water supplies and adequate sanitation.

Over 50 percent of Africa's land area is either covered by desert or prone to desertification because of intensive cultivation of marginal lands and severe drought. Practices such as rainfed agriculture and raising livestock, therefore, are difficult to carry out. Agricultural water use dominates the water sector in Africa. Thus, more efficient agricultural water use is a priority. Ironically, although unevenly distributed by nature, freshwater resources are abundant on a continental scale. Africa contains more than fifty international river basins, more than any other continent. At the same time, however, there are no international agreements in place for the sustainable and equitable use of most of these shared transboundary water resources, making their rational development and sound management very difficult.

The low quality of potable water, coupled with poor environmental sanitation conditions, has reduced the possibility of eliminating endemic waterborne diseases and improving the population's general health. There is a serious need, therefore, to facilitate national freshwater development efforts and water-related environmental management programs, including institutional, scientific, technology, and manpower capabilities. There also is a need to accelerate the decentralization of planning, decision making, and resource management to local authorities and to facilitate greater involvement of local communities, organizations, and water users.

Government capabilities for systematically monitoring and assessing freshwater resources are generally inadequate throughout much of Africa, resulting in significant knowledge gaps regarding water quality and sustainable supplies.

The element of "equity" also must be added to "environment" and "development," in order to make Agenda 21 more operational in Africa. The dominant challenge for African policy-makers and planners for the next decade, therefore, is to ensure that everyone, including the poor majority, competing water users, and the environment, enjoy the benefits to be derived from their "fair share" of safe water at the national and sub-regional level.

LATIN AMERICA AND CARIBBEAN REGION

The countries in this region exhibit economic, social, and environmental diversity. At the same time, the region has several environmental characteristics distinguishing it from other regions of the world, including immense river systems (e.g., Amazon, Orinoco, and La Plata Rivers) and vast and unique biological diversity and ecosystem heterogeneity. Most countries in the region are generally characterized by high proportions of urban populations, high ethnic diversity (including native indigenous populations), clearcutting of forests and rapidly expanding agricultural areas, an emerging active civil society, and increasing inequality and poverty (UNEP 1997, 1999).

Although the region contains some of the world's largest rivers, it also

Table 1.6. Renewable water resources and withdrawals for selected Latin American and Caribbean countries

Country	Annual renewable water resources[a] Total (km³)	1995 per capita (m³)	Annual water withdrawals Year of data	% of annual water resources	Per capita (m³)	Sectoral water withdrawals (%) Domestic	Industry	Agriculture
Argentina	994.0	28,739	1976	4	1,043	9	18	73
Brazil	6,950.0	42,957	1990	1	246	22	19	59
Chile	468.0	32,814	1975	4	1,626	6	5	89
Colombia	1,070.0	30,483	1987	0	174	41	16	43
Cuba	34.5	3,125	1975	23	870	9	2	89
Ecuador	314.0	27,400	1987	2	581	7	3	90
Haiti	11.0	1,532	1987	0	7	24	8	68
Mexico	357.4	3,815	1991[b]	22	899	6	8	86
Peru	40.0	1,682	1987	15	300	19	9	72
Venezuela	1,317.0	60,291	1970	0	382	43	11	46

Source: UNEP 1997.

[a]Including river inflows from other countries.

[b]Data are from early 1990s.

exhibits enormous variation in the regional distribution of its water resources. Further, even though about 13 percent of the world's continental waters are found in the Latin American and Caribbean region, about two-thirds of this region is arid or semiarid in character, including portions of Argentina, Chile, Bolivia, Peru, northeastern Brazil, Ecuador, Colombia, and central and northern Mexico. Ironically, the average rainfall in the Latin American and Caribbean region as a whole is estimated to be more than 50 percent greater than the global average. More than 90 percent of the population in the region lives in areas receiving between 500 and 2,000 millimeters of rainfall annually.

The regional view of water as a perpetually abundant resource, however, is misleading when attempting to address problems of growing water demands, increasing competition between water users, and increasing water pollution. In fact, the spatial distribution of rainfall and rivers is diverse. Some areas with serious flooding problems are located near areas of water scarcity (where irrigation is the only way to maintain viable social systems). In other areas, a destructive cycle of prolonged droughts and destructive floods renders large-scale agricultural activities impractical. Clearing of forests for agriculture and raising livestock has increased surface water runoff and associated soil erosion. The renewable water resources and water withdrawals for selected countries in this region are summarized in Table 1.6.

Over the past decade, many countries in the region have suffered setbacks in their economic and social spheres as a result of living beyond their economic means. There also is a notable absence of an institutional framework for facilitating integrated management of water resources, although some efforts are being made in this direction. The most dramatic consequence of a lack of integrated management is its effects on the least-protected element, namely, the region's freshwater resources. Even though political authorities do not doubt either the wisdom or urgency of change, a number of countries in the region have not yet achieved the institutional or social conditions to enable them to more effectively cope with prevailing regional trends. At the same time, it is recognized that the needed change must also be feasible from a social perspective.

EASTERN EUROPEAN REGION

This meeting included both the Eastern European region and the Russian Federation. Most Eastern European countries were devastated by the dramatic industrial development of the 1950s and 1960s, during which short-term economic benefits were pursued without consideration of their environmental consequences. As a result, a large portion of the region's national and transboundary waters was severely polluted. However, even though high water consumption, mismanagement of water resources, and water pollution are major problems, water scarcity per se is not the region's main water problem. The renewal of water resources and water withdrawals for selected countries in the eastern European region are summarized in Table 1.7.

Table 1.7. Renewable water resources and withdrawals for selected Eastern European countries

Country	Annual renewable water resources[a]		Annual water withdrawals			Sectoral water withdrawals (%)		
	Total (km³)	1995 per capita (m³)	Year of data	% of annual water resources	Per capita (m³)	Domestic	Industry	Agriculture
Albania	21.3	6,190	1970	1	94	6	18	76
Estonia	17.6	11,490	1989	21	2,097	5	92	3
Romania	208.0	9,109	1994	13	1,134	8	60	59
Russian Fed.	4,498.0	30,599	1991	3	790	17	26	23

Source: UNEP 1997.

[a]Including river inflows from other countries.

The main objective for almost all the countries in this region is the provision of good-quality, safe drinking-water supply and sanitation. Groundwater is a very important regional source of drinking water. Pollution of surface and underground waters from point and nonpoint sources throughout the region, however, is very high. A ten-year study in the Russian Federation, for example, indicated that only 21 percent of 245 rivers were acceptable in terms of bacteriological pollution (UNEP 1997). Ironically, pollution concerns were somewhat reduced during the 1990s because of perestroika and the temporal economic recession and associated decline of wastewater discharges during this period. Insufficient funds for maintaining water systems, sewage, and waste collection systems have led to numerous malfunctions, causing serious declines in sanitation standards and increases in water-related illnesses (UNEP 1997, 1999).

Eastern European countries must review their traditional centrally managed approach, legislation, and institutional framework, and adjust them to accommodate the changes required to achieve an integrated approach for the efficient and holistic management of their water resources. Countries currently in transition from a centrally managed economy to one of free market forces and democracy require a totally new approach addressing the issues of development, management, and use of water resources in an environmentally sound and integrated manner.

The region's water priorities include the (1) design and implementation of national action programs, with defined goals and costs; (2) establishment of appropriate institutional structures and legal instruments; and (3) implementation of efficient water-use programs for achieving sustainable schemes of water resources development. These actions must be undertaken within the prevailing conditions in the different countries, characterized by extremely diverse cultural, social, economic, and structural backgrounds and circumstances.

Although serious efforts are being made in all Eastern European countries to achieve the objectives of Agenda 21, the substantial political changes in this region in recent years suggests that the abandonment of traditional procedures, and the development and implementation of new mechanisms, will take additional time.

Integrated Freshwater Resource Management

The conclusions and recommendations arising from UNEP's regional meetings differed between the various regions. Nevertheless, a general consensus on the major factors constraining implementation of the freshwater objectives of Agenda 21 became evident throughout all the developing regions. Equally interesting is the observation that these constraints appear to be applicable to many of the water-related problems of the developed world as well.

As noted below, factors constraining the implementation of the freshwater objectives can be traced to inadequate monetary and intellectual resources, fragmentation of authority and responsibility, and inadequate public awareness and involvement (Rast 1999). The list includes:

• Lack of proper coordination of management activities
• Lack of appropriate management tools
• Inability to integrate water resource policies
• Institutional fragmentation
• Insufficiently trained and qualified workforce
• Shortfalls in funding (for most countries, the objectives of Chapter 18 cannot be achieved without significant additional resources, even greater than the initial estimates provided in Agenda 21)
• Inadequate public awareness
• A low level of community involvement, nongovernmental organizations, and the private sectors in water management activities.

Fortunately, just as humans create problems, they also have the capacity to solve them. This possibility is also recognized in the freshwater recommendations in Agenda 21, and it is becoming more and more accepted that an integrated, multidisciplinary approach is necessary to achieve a sustainable freshwater supply to satisfy present and future human and ecosystem water needs. This approach requires consideration of the physical, chemical, and biological realities that define the quantity and condition of freshwater resources, as well as the social and economic factors that fundamentally control how humans use them.

Because the watershed or drainage basin is the basic water planning and management unit, an integrated approach must focus on this unit. Depending on the geographic area in which they are located, and the prevailing climatic and hydrologic conditions, drainage basins can contain a variety of waterbodies and water sources, including rivers, lakes, wetlands, and groundwater aquifers. Further, our individual and collective actions within drainage basins are not isolated; rather, they are interconnected in both cause and effect. An integrated approach recognizes the interlinkages between human activities in one part of a watershed and their impacts in other parts of the watershed. People live downstream, for example, from agricultural lands or factories. Farmers live downstream from industrial complexes. Industries are located downstream from cities. Cities are located downstream from other cities. Fishes live downstream from cities. Ecosystems (e.g., wetlands) can exist both upstream and downstream from all of them. Indeed, the hydrologic cycle ensures that virtually all of us live downstream from some entity that can affect us. Our actions, in turn, can significantly affect those that live downstream from us (Rast 1999; PLUARG 1978).

The physical environment is the source of all freshwater via nature's hydrologic cycle. Thus, ensuring a sustainable freshwater supply necessarily includes a comprehensive assessment of the magnitude of the readily available water supply, and the human and ecosystem demands placed on it, as well as the natural and anthropogenic factors affecting both the supply and the demands. These factors include the hydrology, geology, physiography, flora, fauna, land usage and trends, types and sources of pollution, human settlements and land-based activities in the drainage basin, and so forth (Rast 1996). The environmental linkages *between* these various components also must be identified and factored into the sustainable management equation.

Perhaps even more important, and certainly more difficult to identify and integrate into the sustainable water resource equation than the purely scientific and technical factors, are the social and economic elements. They include the types and adequacy of existing institutional structures, the type of regulatory frameworks, the state of the monitoring and assessment systems, the economic conditions and general health of the drainage basin inhabitants, demographics, cultural habits and mores, and political structure. Although most of these elements are not amenable to the quantitative evaluation possible with the scientific and technical elements, they are important components to be addressed. Are the existing institutional frameworks, for example, adequate to ensure sustainable freshwater resources? What are the criteria for deciding whether or not the legal framework is sufficient to address human water needs? How can the cultural mores and political realities be integrated into a comprehensive river basin management plan? How should competing water uses be considered? How should the international dimensions of transboundary freshwater resources be factored into the equation? Although admittedly difficult elements to evaluate, and even though many are subjective in nature, we are now beginning to develop techniques and approaches to answer such questions, and the answers are beginning to be integrated into national development plans (Rast 1996 and Chap. 13). Elements to be considered in integrated management plans for sustainable freshwater supplies include the following (Laszlo et al. 1988):

- Recognizing the fundamental role of water in economic and social development, and the well-being of drainage basin citizens
- Facilitating the goal of maximizing the benefits of the available water resources for all drainage basin inhabitants (i.e., the notion of equity)
- Recognizing the fundamental multifaceted environmental challenges emerging from water scarcity, water pollution, and related land degradation
- Acknowledging regional differences in the sensitivity of the natural environment to human influences

- Recognizing the complex mix of water-related social, economic, legal, and institutional issues to be addressed
- Appreciating the necessary balance between short-term needs and the long-term perspective for protecting available freshwater resources
- Addressing also the water needs of nature.

Facilitating Sustainable Use of Freshwater Resources

Some elements to facilitate integrated freshwater resource management for sustainable use of national and transboundary waterbodies have been identified (Rast 1996).

Accurate Assessment of Water Problems

Development of solutions to ensure sustainable water supplies requires realistic consideration of social, economic, legal, and political issues. Nevertheless, the fundamental environmental problem(s) to be addressed must be identified and accurately defined on the basis of sound scientific and technical knowledge. Such knowledge requires accurate information and data on the available water sources and systems of concern (rivers, lakes, wetlands, groundwater aquifers, etc.), and their linkages to other technical and nontechnical components influencing or controlling sustainable water supplies. Further, the knowledge, information, and data must be conveyed to policy-makers, decision makers, the public, the media, and other stakeholders in a form that all can readily understand and use. For transboundary water systems, sharing of relevant data and information between the riparian countries is a fundamental requirement for ensuring their sustainable use and provides a basis for engendering trust between them.

The possible consequences of a wrong decision also should be considered in such efforts. In the absence of sufficient information and data, for example, opponents of a program or plan for addressing sustainable water resources may argue that we simply don't know enough about the problem to justify its implementation. This can be an especially compelling argument if implementation of a project will be very costly. If an implemented project is ultimately found not to be necessary, it will result in an unnecessary expenditure of public or private funds. On the other hand, not implementing a project when it is actually needed can result in serious environmental and social consequences over the long term and will almost certainly be more expensive if implemented at a later date. Both possibilities must be realistically considered, therefore, from both a scientific and a socioeconomic perspective.

Maximizing Water–Related Benefits on a Drainage Basin Scale

The overall goal of integrated management for sustainable water resources is to maximize the benefits of the water resources for the greatest number of people in the drainage basin, while at the same time maintaining beneficial ecosystem services. For transboundary waterbodies, this goal may sometimes be contrary to the national interest of states with riparian water rights, and can enhance competition between water users and uses within and among the states. However, if individual countries utilizing a transboundary waterbody base their development plans solely on national interests, without consideration of how these plans may affect other upstream or downstream riparian countries, the sustainable use of the waterbody and its accompanying socioeconomic and ecosystem benefits may be lost. The possibility of water-related tensions and conflicts also will be increased.

Maximizing water-related benefits within a drainage basin should not be taken literally to mean the equal distribution of the available water resources among all the basin's inhabitants, but rather the equal distribution of the benefits to be derived from using these resources. It may make more sense from a hydrologic perspective, for example, for countries in arid regions to use their limited water resources to manufacture products of high economic value rather than for agricultural irrigation, which typically requires large quantities of water in a consumptive manner. The higher-valued products could, in turn, be traded or sold for food produced in countries or regions with water supplies more suitable for agricultural activities, as well as for other products with large water requirements. This was, in fact, one of the conclusions reached in a United Nations interagency assessment of the state of the world's freshwater resources (WMO 1997). Implementation of such actions, however, particularly for countries in arid or semiarid regions with a major dependence on transboundary water sources, would require some countries to rely on the good will of other countries in regard to their food security. Unfortunately, although a logical suggestion from a hydrologic perspective, such reliance is a difficult leap of faith for many countries, particularly in regions characterized by a history of distrust or previous conflicts.

Incorporating Appropriate Technologies

In pursuing the goal of sustainable water resources, attention also must be given to identifying and implementing appropriate technologies for a given situation or region. In developed countries, for example, governments and other major water stakeholders typically employ high-tech solutions to address water problems. Experience suggests that the use of high-tech equipment and structures to address water problems is often more efficient and cost effective over the long term in these countries. In contrast, developing countries often lack the financial resources required for capital-intensive, high-tech solutions to water problems, and many lack the trained personnel necessary for their sustained implementation and operation. At the same time, however, developing countries often have a large, cheap labor force available to them. Thus, even though they may be less efficient than high-tech solutions, labor-intensive approaches may be more appropriate for many developing countries. Indigenous methods (e.g., rainwater and fog harvesting) also merit serious consideration for these latter situations.

Public Awareness, Education, and Participation

Involvement of the public can be very beneficial in identifying and addressing water-related problems. The inhabitants in a given drainage basin, for example, may have little knowledge or understanding of their role, either individually or collectively, in *causing* a water problem, including unsustainable water use. They also typically have little or no understanding of what they can do to help *solve* the problem. Indeed, often the only role for the public envisioned by many governments in such matters is to provide the required funds for the programs and activities necessary to address the problems, rather than working with the public to reduce current problems and avoid similar problems in the future. Enhancing opportunities for public awareness and participation can go far to address this deficiency. In some cases, such activities can be as simple as educating the inhabitants in a drainage basin regarding how they can change their work routines or personal habits to alleviate water scarcity or pollution problems. The education system, the media, and the religious community can be especially helpful in this regard, providing information, guidance, and inspiration regarding the protection and sustainable use of available water resources, as well as helping shape positive public attitudes about water-related problems and the need for solutions.

Considering the Water Needs of Nature

In allocating freshwater resources among competing users, we often forget to consider the basic water needs of terrestrial and aquatic ecosystems and their living organisms. This is due partly to inadequate understanding of the complex interlinkages between and within ecosystems, and between their living and nonliving components, including their relation to human needs and activities. Many aquatic ecosystems perform important services for humanity without which our well-being would be drastically reduced. Further, most of these services are provided to humanity free of charge. If important aquatic ecosystems are destroyed or degraded, therefore, humans will have to pay for these previously free services. Accordingly, better identification and quantification of the basic water needs of aquatic ecosystems also is essential in the pursuit of sustainable freshwater supplies (e.g., a wetland needs a certain minimum quantity of freshwater inflow to remain a wetland). Further, nature's water needs must be incorporated into national and international development plans, and the associated allocation of water supplies, at an early stage rather than as an afterthought.

As an illustration of the importance of maintaining aquatic and terrestrial ecosystems, Costanza et al. (1997) analyzed the direct and indirect contributions of ecological systems to human welfare. All ecosystems require varying quantities of water to perform their natural functions, with or without the presence of humans. The work of Costanza and his co-workers, however, focused on identifying the benefits of ecosystem services to humans, and expressing them in monetary terms. Although acknowledging some assumptions in their calculations, this group of ecologists and economists estimated conservatively that the total economic value of seventeen ecosystem services (regulating climate, purifying air and water, decomposing wastes, preventing erosion, pollinating food crops, etc.) provided by sixteen types of ecosystems (open ocean, estuaries, forests, rangelands, wetlands, river and lakes, deserts, etc.) averaged $33 trillion a year. This was equivalent to approximately twice the total annual gross national product of all the countries in the world. Water-based ecosystems, including oceans, estuaries, rivers, lakes, and wetlands, comprised nearly $28 trillion of the total. Further, some aquatic ecosystems have extremely high individual values. The estimated value of the ecosystem services provided to humanity by wetlands, for example, averaged approximately $15,000 per hectare of wetland area, with the values of swamps and floodplains being even higher at more than $19,500 per hectare. These results offer compelling rationale for greater attention directed to the protection and conservation of aquatic ecosystems as a fundamental component of programs directed to the goal of sustainable freshwater resources.

Proactive Approach to Water Issues

We have been faced with the problem of providing adequate freshwater supplies for drinking, growing food, and sanitation since ancient times, and this requirement persists to the present. We continue to use our freshwater resources in a continuing cycle of water withdrawal—treatment—use—pollution—discharge, often with little thought of the consequences or unsustainable nature of this cycle. And the unfortunate reality is that humans tend to respond to crises rather than trying to identify and address problems in a proactive manner. Experiences around the world, however, have repeatedly demonstrated that the *prevention* of water problems is inevitably less expensive than *correcting* them after they have become major environmental and/or socioeconomic problems. In other words, the most prudent approach to water-related problems (as well as other environmental problems) is to consider them at the earliest possible stage. The significant growth of megacities (populations greater than 10 million) and the associated water and other natural resource needs, particularly in the developing world, provide a significant example of an environmental issue requiring proactive attention.

Accurate Identification of, and Honest Brokerage Between, Competing Water Users

The need for honest brokerage between states with riparian water rights is fundamental for sustainable use of internationally shared, transboundary water resources. Unfortunately, this goal is very difficult to achieve in many cases. Many riparian countries may be reluctant to give up any degree of national sovereignty or interest regarding their use of transboundary water systems. Fragmentation of responsibilities for management and allocation of water resources between many ministries or departments within riparian countries (including developed countries) also inhibits international cooperation. There is a fundamental need, therefore, for riparian countries to be forthright about their water needs and uses at an early stage. The relevant parties must appreciate that their shared water resources are finite, irreplaceable, and sensitive to human impacts, and that impacts in one part of a drainage basin can significantly affect water uses and needs in other parts of the basin. Further, many freshwater systems, particularly rivers and wetlands, are part of a larger land-freshwater-coastal hydrologic linkage that must be considered in addressing the sustainability of all the systems. Thus, it is inherently beneficial for decision makers and policy-makers to identify major water issues in a comprehensive, honest, and forthright manner and to determine collectively how to resolve the relevant issues, never losing sight of the ultimate goal of sustainable water resources. Neutral "referees" (e.g., United Nations or other international agencies) can be very useful in such situations. On a smaller scale, this consideration can be applied to sustainable water resources at the local level.

An Ecosystem Approach and the North American Great Lakes Water Quality Agreement

Although the process can be visualized on a conceptual level, effective implementation of integrated water resources management for sustainable use is continuing to be an elusive goal, whether on a local, national or international scale. The United Nations Environmental Programme (UNEP), for expample, has worked to develop drainage-basin scale water resource management programs for a number of international water systems, including the Zambezi River and Lack Chad drainage basin in Southeast Asia (see Chpt. 13). The United Nations Development Programme (UNDP) and the World Bank have attempted similar programs for other international waterbodies. Unfortunately, no unequivocal example of the successful application of integrated water resource management yet exits. Accordingly, governments, agencies and other major water stakeholders must continue to refine and apply this concept as the logical basis for addressing the complex issue of sustainable freshwater resources.

There are, however, some successful examples of international cooperation within the spirit of integrated water management for sustainable use and ecosystem maintenance. One example is provided by the Laurentian American Great Lakes of North America, a transboundary water system shared by the United States and Canada (also see Chpt. 13). To address transboundary water problems, the International Joint Commission (IJC) was established under the Boundary Waters Treaty of 1909 between the two countries. The stated purpose of the Treaty was "to prevent disputes regarding the use of boundary waters and to settle all questions which are now pending between the U.S. and the Dominion of Canada involving the rights, obligations, or interests of either in relation to the other or to the inhabitants of the other, along their common frontier, and to make provision for the adjustment and settlement of all such questions as may hereafter arise" (IJC 1998).

The water quality of the Great Lakes, one of the major transboundary freshwater systems in the world, is a primary IJC concern. Although occupying a large surface area, and having an enormous volume, the Great Lakes are nevertheless sensitive to a wide range of water pollutants. Major pollutant sources include effluent discharges from industrial factories and municipal plants, storm-induced runoff from agricultural and urban areas, seepage from waste disposal sites, and atmospheric deposition from the long-range transport of airborne pollutants.

The U.S. and Canadian governments signed the Great Lakes Water Quality Agreement in 1972 (IJC 1994). The purpose of the Agreement was "to restore and maintain the chemical, physical, and biological integrity of the Great Lakes Basin Ecosystem." To facilitate achievement of this goal, the two governments agreed to "make a maximum effort to develop programs, practices and technology necessary for a better understanding of the Great Lakes Basin Ecosystem and to eliminate or reduce to the maximum extent practicable the discharge of pollutants into the Great Lakes System." The Agreement also endorsed the benefits of an ecosystem approach for addressing Great Lakes Basin Ecosystem water quality issues (PLUARG 1978; IJC 1998).

The continuing goal of the Water Quality Agreement is to enhance the ability of the United States and Canada to address the many complex water quality issues facing the Great Lakes Basin Ecosystem. Accordingly, the Agreement contains annexes addressing a range of water pollution issues, as well as annexes dealing with surveillance and monitoring, contingency plans for spills or accidental discharges of hazardous polluting substances, and research needs.

To facilitate an ecosystem approach for addressing water quality degradation in the Great Lakes Basin Ecosystem, the Agreement calls for development of comprehensive management plans to restore local degraded areas in the basin exhibiting significant impairment of beneficial water uses, as well as lakewide management plans dealing with critical or hazardous pollutants affecting whole lakes. Development of ecosystem objectives for measuring the degree of restoration of the lake ecosystem integrity also was mandated in the Agreement (IJC 1994).

Because solutions to Great Lakes' water quality problems involve two nations, two Canadian provinces and eight U.S. states, as well as numerous local, regional, and special-purpose bodies, binational cooperation is essential. Thus, the Agreement encourages cooperation, in the form of public consultations of the IJC with citizens, private organizations, and industrial and government representatives, as an essential component of the transboundary decision-making process for the sustainable use of the Great Lakes Basin Ecosystem.

Based on annual reports of the IJC over the past two decades, the water and living resources of the Great Lakes Basin Ecosystem have improved since the Agreement went into effect. Accordingly, the Great Lakes Water Quality Agreement, implemented within the structure of a transboundary organization such as the IJC, provides a model for others to emulate in addressing similar problems. The experience in the Great Lakes Basin illustrates that its drainage basin inhabitants and its ecosystems have benefited from this approach. Successful transfer of the IJC model and experience to other international water resources, however, will require concerted and cooperative efforts involving governments, the public, and the media, as well as adequate technical and financial resources.

As a closing observation, increasing population growth, industrialization, and urbanization, and increasing competition for limited natural resources (including freshwater) are major causative factors for environmental degradation and increasing poverty, particularly in the developing world. Escalating costs, lack of investment funds, increasing technical complexities, and lack of understanding of fundamental water issues, also impede development and implementation of necessary remedial programs and projects for addressing the issue of sustainable supplies of clean, safe freshwater resources for human uses and for maintaining essential ecosystems. Nevertheless, human recognition that water is precious, finite, and irreplaceable, and that we have *no* substitutes for it, will hopefully provide humanity locally, regionally, and globally, with the impetus for a proactive approach to the integrated management of freshwater for sustainable use, both within and between countries. The only consolation, if it can be described as such, is that in the absence of proactive human actions to address such problems, we can be assured that nature will ultimately take care of the problem for us. Unfortunately, however, we must also recognize that nature can be a cruel taskmaster when left to its own devices, and we may not necessarily like its solutions to our problems.

Note: The opinions expressed in this report are those of the author, and do not necessarily represent the views or policy of UNEP, the United Nations System, the IJC, or of any governments identified herein.

References

Costanza, R., R. d'Arge, R. de Groot, S. Farber, M. Grasso, B. Hannon, K. Limburg, S. Naeem, R. V. O'Neill, J. Paruelo, R. G. Raskin, P. Sutton, and M. van den Belt. 1997. The value of the world's ecosystem services and natural capital. *Nature* 387:253–260.

IJC (International Joint Commission). 1994. *Revised Great Lakes Water Quality Agreement of 1978*. Washington, D.C.: International Joint Commission.

———. 1998. *The International Joint Commission and the Boundary Waters Treaty of 1909*. Washington, D.C.: International Joint Commission.

Laszlo, J. D., G. N. Golubev, and M. Nakayama. 1988. The environmental management of large international basins. The EMINWA Programme of UNEP. *Water Resources Development* 4:103–107.

PLUARG (Pollution from Land Use Activities Reference Group). 1978. *Environmental management strategy for the Great Lakes system*. Final Report of the International Reference Group on Great Lakes Pollution from Land Use Activities, International Joint Commission, Washington, D.C.

Rast, W. 1996. International cooperation for global water problems. Pp. 221–233 in *International forum on technology for water management in the 21st century, Nov. 25–27, 1996*. International Environmental Technology Centre, United Nations Environment Programme, Shiga, Japan.

———. 1999. Overview of the status of implementation of the freshwater objectives of Agenda 21 on a regional basis. *Sustainable Development International* 1:53–57.

Shiklomanov, I. A. 1997. Assessment of water resources and water availability in the world. World Meteorological Organization, Comprehensive Assessment of the Freshwater Resources of the World, Geneva, Switzerland.

UNEP (United Nations Environment Programme). 1997. *Global environment outlook*. Oxford, U.K.: Oxford University Press.

———. 1999. *Global environment outlook 2000*. London, U.K.: Earthscan.

United Nations. 1992. Agenda 21. *The United Nations Programme of Action from Rio*. Development and Human Rights Section, United Nations, New York.

WMO (World Meteorological Organization). 1992. The Dublin statement and report of the conference. *International Conference on Water and the Environment: Development Issues for the Twenty-first Century, Jan. 26–31.* Dublin, Ireland.

————. 1997. *Comprehensive assessment of the freshwater resources of the world.* World Meteorological Organization, Geneva, Switzerland.

PART I

FRESHWATER SYSTEMS FROM PAST TO PRESENT

The demands placed by humans on freshwater resources are intense, and they continue to grow, often to the detriment of wetlands and other species that depend upon them. As scientific knowledge about wetlands increases, policy decisions should reflect this growing store of knowledge and act to preserve aquatic resources for all living things. The chapters in this section focus on the direct relationship between humankind and the freshwater systems of the world. We are shown the linkage between environmental policy and its effects, the inescapable connection between water quality and human health, and the toxic effects of human pollution in aquatic ecosystems. With examples from around the globe of misguided environmental policies and insults to the environment resulting from ignorance and outright disregard for environmental consequences, these are the saddest chapters of the book. However, there is heuristic value in examining such cases, and from them we can gain perspective on our historical—and often poor—relationship with the environment.

The future of wetlands, we believe, is directly tied to the effective development and enforcement of environmental laws. Chapter 2, an overview of the history of American wetland law, retraces the steps of our past attitudes toward wetlands and argues for the need for cooperation between private citizens and local, state, and federal governments in order to preserve the natural water systems.

Wetlands history in the United States dates back to the nineteenth century when the federal government encouraged the draining and filling of swamps. Not until the late 1960s did the federal government acknowledge the ecological benefits of wetlands. By 2001, thirty-four states had wetland laws and between 4,000 and 5,000 local governments had adopted wetland protection ordinances.

U.S. policies attempt to combine national interests with stewardship programs at the state and local levels, primarily by using incentive programs to ensure adherence to regulatory programs. Proper wetland management will help the United States accomplish its national goal of zero net loss.

Ineffective management of our aquatic systems can result in catastrophic consequences, as shown in Chapter 3. In this chapter, the authors show how directly human lives are affected by freshwater contaminants. This chapter should emphasize the inherent interconnection between ecological health and human health with examples that discuss mercury levels in Minimata Bay, disposed chemicals in the Love Canal, and pollution in the Rhine River.

The complex interaction between contaminants and hydrology in ecological systems is demonstrated with examples in Chapter 4. Hydrological changes resulting from anthropogenic activities like irrigation and surface-water impoundments have exacerbated pollution problems throughout the world. There are major emerging patterns in water ecosystem integrity loss. Wetlands are experiencing impacts resulting from reduced freshwater inflows, toxins, and subsurface irrigation drainage. There are severe impacts on fish, wildlife, and agriculture. Estuarine and coastal ecosystems are negatively impacted by hydrological modifications and nutrient loading that specifically target fish and wildlife.

The chapters in this section illustrate the complex and far-reaching problems concerning water quality that have surfaced within the last two decades. These issues have not yet been properly addressed by scientists and policy-makers. Improved screening methods, ecological action plans, and chemical awareness are essential elements in preserving our freshwater ecosystems. These elements must be part of a holistic approach that addresses the interconnections among the ecological and human systems. It is not only the health of freshwater systems that is in peril, but in fact the health of our waterways directly impacts human health.

Chapter 2

Wetlands Laws and Policies: How We Got Where We Are Today

Kristen M. Fletcher

United States domestic law is far from adequately addressing the needs of wetland ecosystems, those of the public that depend on wetland functions, or those of nearby landowners. The shortcomings of U.S. law result, in part, from the limited authority issued in statutes that were created for purposes other than protecting wetlands and from the labyrinth of code and regulations that emerged when these statutes were expanded to address wetlands. Given the intricate cooperation among federal, state, local, and private players necessary to preserve a dwindling reserve of these natural filtering systems, it is easy to see the hurdles the nation faces in making sense of wetlands law but difficult to see solutions. This chapter presents a brief history of U.S. laws that have been employed to regulate activities in wetlands, from statutes instituted to drain wetlands to federal agency "guidance" intended to extend jurisdiction to unprotected isolated wetland areas. The chapter presents some of the policy dilemmas the regulation of wetlands has created and concludes with some examples of the modern, and often controversial, approaches that serve in addition to and as alternatives to regulation.

The future of wetlands and water resources is intricately tied to the laws, regulations, and policies that local, state, and federal governments employ. Rarely does a conversation about development near or in wetlands occur without debate about the necessity of permits. While individuals that consider themselves wetlands stewards recognize a need to preserve wetland ecosystems and the natural services they provide, they are met by the reality that landowners, developers, and political leaders do not always understand the necessity of wetlands and may support imprudent development in wetland areas. This conflict between the conservation and development communities may ultimately move the nation from the regulatory-based system now employed to a system of privately held lands chosen for significant ecosystem benefits and withdrawn from the pool of lands available for alterations.

Dating back to the political origins of the United States of America, the national perception of wetlands has evolved from the notion that wetlands were nothing more than nuisances to the realization that wetlands are a useful and vital part of ecosystem management. As described in greater detail below, the 1972 Federal Water Pollution Control Act (Clean Water Act) is the primary federal statute that provides the statutory authority and the regulatory framework, putting responsibility for regulation in the United States Army Corps of Engineers and the United States Environmental Protection Agency (U.S. EPA). Although this statute was by no means the first authority extending to wetlands, the Act is now combined with other federal statutes and state programs designed for individual state needs and landscapes to form the present structure of wetlands regulation. However, this statutory and regulatory arrangement is failing to meet the objectives of the national policy of "no net loss" of wetlands.

As a result, public and private parties interested in reducing the loss of wetlands are increasingly turning to alternative regulatory and nonregulatory approaches such as conservation and preservation methods. Although some of these remain controversial, such as wetland mitigation banking and government-based acquisition programs, the movement toward wetland stewardship partnerships is emerging nationally. Among the challenges these approaches face is the private property rights movement. For example, governments that attempt to halt development (usually by requiring significant mitigation in exchange for the right to develop or by requiring that the developer set aside and maintain a wetland preserve area), must confront the possible impairment of landowners' property rights. Judicial interpretations of landowners' challenges to the denial of a permit to develop in wetlands indicate that governments at all levels are vulnerable to these contests and, as a result, many are working harder to balance the environmental needs of wetland areas with the legitimate concerns of property owners.

Because wetlands law and policy is so complex, this chapter serves only to introduce and explain wetlands law and regulation by comparing the traditional regulatory regime to modern examples of conservation and preservation. However, numerous papers and books provide in-depth analysis of laws and policies at each level of government; several that might be particularly useful are provided in the Suggested Resources section at the end of this chapter.

The Evolution of Wetlands Law and Regulation

The U.S. Army Corps of Engineers (the Corps) defines wetlands as "those areas that are inundated or saturated by surface or ground water at a frequency and duration sufficient to support, and that under normal circumstances do support, a prevalence of vegetation typically adapted for life in saturated soil conditions. Wetlands generally include swamps, marshes, bogs, and similar areas" (33 Code of Federal Regulation section 328.3).

During the eighteenth century, 221 million acres of wetlands existed in the United States. By 1995, less than 101 million acres remained. Because wetlands were considered a nuisance, believed to inhibit navigation and breed mosquitoes and disease, throughout the nineteenth century the federal government encouraged draining and filling of wetlands. For instance, under the Swamp Lands Acts, the federal government granted fifteen states almost 65 million acres for "swamp reclamation," making drainage and filling wetlands a national policy (Swamp Lands Act of 1850; Swamp Lands Act of 1860; Swamp Lands Act of 1874).

By the late 1960s, the federal government took greater notice of the ecological benefits of wetlands. It began regulating the filling and dredging of wetlands under the authority of the Rivers and Harbors Act of 1899, which made it unlawful to excavate from or fill "any navigable water of the United States" without authorization from the secretary of the army (Rivers and Harbors Act). The original purpose of the Act was to prevent obstacles to navigation and to protect fishing and commerce activities in U.S. waters. As early as 1968, the Corps used this authority in concert with its responsibility to review effects of filling wetlands on fish and wildlife under the Fish and Wildlife Coordination Act. Using these two statutes as authority, the Corps included an ecological analysis as part of its public interest review when considering a wetlands permit application. This review assessed not only historically recognized navigational effects but also ecological effects of wetlands filling.

Initially, taking ecological impacts into account was challenged. But federal courts upheld the agency's authority holding that the Corps "was entitled, if not required, to consider ecological factors and, being persuaded by them, to deny that which might have been granted routinely five, ten, or fifteen years ago before man's explosive increase made all, including Congress, aware of civilization's potential destruction from breathing its own polluted air and drinking its own infected water and the immeasurable loss from a silent-spring-like disturbance of nature's economy" (*Zabel v. Tabb*, 430 F.2d 199, 201 [5th Cir. 1970], cert. denied, 401 U.S. 910 [1971]). This opened the door for the Corps to consider the ecological benefits of wetlands and to incorporate more protective methods regarding discharge permits.

This challenge to the Corps' authority was followed closely by the Clean Water Act, which Congress enacted to "restore and maintain the chemical, physical, and biological integrity of the Nation's waters" (Federal Water Pollution Control Act 1972). The Act set forth a national goal to eliminate the discharge of pollutants into the "waters of the United States" by 1985; the term "waters of the United States" has come to include wetlands (33 CFR sec. 328.3). Pursuant to this goal, section 404 of the Clean Water Act prohibits the discharges of dredge or fill material into waters of the United States without a permit from the Corps based on guidelines promulgated by the EPA (Federal Water Pollution Control Act sec. 404).

Section 404 is the primary federal regulatory tool providing protection for the nation's remaining wetlands. When the Corps receives an application to discharge dredged or fill material into a wetland, the agency must provide public notice and an opportunity for the public to comment. The Corps then evaluates the application, in light of comments, to determine its effects on conservation, economics, aesthetics, fish and wildlife values, flood protection, general public welfare, historic values, recreation, land use, water supply, water quality, and navigation (33 CFR sec. 320.4[q]). An application for an individual permit must meet the requirements of the Corps' public interest review and its analysis of compliance with the EPA guidelines (40 CFR sec. 230). The Corps also considers elements of compensatory mitigation for those resources that will be adversely affected or lost as a result of a permitted activity. The EPA guidelines appear to require a rigorous examination of the availability of practicable alternatives and prohibit the authorization of any project that would result in significant adverse impacts. In reality, the Corps denies less than 10 percent of individual permit applications (see U.S. Army Corps of Engineers 1998).

The Clean Water Act also authorizes general permits on a state, regional, or national basis. Rather than applying for an individual permit, a person may qualify to discharge dredged or fill material for projects with small impacts. General permits decrease the administrative burden for the federal and state regulatory agencies but are criticized because of the potential to greatly contribute to overall loss of wetlands. In fact, much of the nation's wetlands loss is a result of activities under general permits.

After adoption of section 404, the Corps gradually expanded the range of wetlands in which it required a permit and the types of activities whose results were deemed to be the filling of wetlands. This perceived overexpansion of the Corps' authority was challenged during the 1990s in two significant ways.

First, confusion existed over what constituted discharge with regard to sediment-disturbing actions associated with mechanized land clearing, ditching, draining, and stream channelization. When a minimal amount of sediment taken from a wetland during a development activity falls back into the same wetland (known as "incidental fallback"), is it considered fill for the purposes of section 404? In 1993, the EPA and the Corps finalized regulations defining the "discharge of dredged material" to include the incidental fallback of dredged materials that usually accompanies dredging. The rule, known as the "Tulloch Rule," required a 404 permit for the discharge or fallback of any excavated materials that occur during dredging operations. In 1998, a federal court overruled the Tulloch Rule and enjoined the Corps from enforcing it, ruling that the Corps had exceeded its authority in regulating the incidental fallback associated with dredging (*National Mining Association, et al. v. U.S. Army Corps of Engineers*, 145 F.3d 1399 [D.C. Cir. 1998]. As a result of confusion over what activities required a permit, it is estimated that more than 20,000 acres of wetlands were destroyed and 150 miles of streams drained and channelized during the two years after the 1998 decision (66 Federal Register 4550).

In January of 2001, the Corps and the EPA issued a final regulation to strengthen wetlands protection (66 Fed. Reg. 4550). The new regulation indicates that the Corps and the EPA will regard land clearing, ditching, channelization, instream mining, and other mechanized earth-moving activities as resulting in a discharge of dredged materials unless evidence from each project shows the discharge to be only incidental fallback. The new rule defines incidental fallback consistent with the 1998 court decision and specifically outlines the types of activities likely to result in discharge of dredged materials requiring a 404 permit.

The second significant challenge to Corps authority came in the form of a jurisdictional challenge to the Corps' "migratory bird rule." The Corps issued interpretive guidelines in 1986 that claimed section 404 jurisdiction over intrastate waters that are or could be inhabited by migratory birds (51 Fed. Reg. 41206). The Corps based this authority on the Commerce Clause: because Congress can consider the aggregate effect an activity has on interstate commerce, certain practices that do not appear to involve interstate commerce may be subject to regulation (*Wickard v. Filburn*, 317 U.S. 111 [1942] [holding that Congress can regulate activities that have a substantial economic effect on interstate commerce]). The presence of migratory birds, along with large amounts of money spent by citizens to view or hunt these birds, was seen to constitute interstate commerce and the necessary constitutional connection.

The Solid Waste Agency of Northern Cook County (SWANCC), a group of twenty-three Chicago-area municipalities, purchased an abandoned sand and gravel pit in order to construct a nonhazardous-waste landfill. Before construction could commence, SWANCC had to dredge and fill several excavation trenches that had become the home to migratory birds during the site's abandonment. When SWANCC initially inquired about the need for a permit, the Corps disclaimed authority over the site because it did not contain any wetlands directly connected to navigable waters of the United States. After a third party informed the Corps of the presence of several species of migratory birds around the quarry, the Corps claimed jurisdiction under the migratory bird rule.

In order to secure the section 404 permit, SWANCC submitted numerous plans to mitigate the removal of the migratory birds. The group also agreed to keep a great blue heron nesting site on the property intact. Although the Illinois Environmental Protection Agency approved SWANCC's water quality certification, the Corps denied the permit application because the group failed to demonstrate it adopted the most environmentally safe disposal method. According to the Corps, SWANCC's proposal would subject the public's drinking water to an unacceptable risk because the group did not have enough money reserved to repair possible leaks. Due to its unique character, the Corps concluded that the migratory birds' habitat could not be mitigated because it would be impossible to recreate it in another area.

When the Corps denied the permit application, the SWANCC challenged its jurisdictional authority over isolated water bodies claimed merely because of the presence of migratory birds. One of the challenges to the Corps' authority stemmed from the fact that the migratory bird rule was merely a guide and that the Corps had not undergone proper public review and comment procedures for the guidance to be instituted as a rule. In spite of the Corps' failure to follow rule-making procedures, the agency's authority was upheld at both the federal district court and federal appeals court levels. When it reached the Supreme Court, the SWANCC argued that section 404 reveals that Congress sought to include only navigable waters, their tributaries, and wetlands that surround navigable waters within the Clean Water Act's scope.

The Supreme Court agreed with the SWANCC and held that the Corps exceeded its authority under the Clean Water Act when it asserted jurisdiction over the landfill pursuant to the migratory bird rule. Although the Court recognized that section 404 was intended to include some nonnavigable waters, Congress failed to specify what type of waters should be incorporated. The Court found that the text of the Clean Water Act does not support such a broad view that allows the Corps to obtain jurisdiction over isolated, intrastate, nonnavigable waters merely because of the presence of migratory birds.

The reality of recent federal court decisions is that the jurisdiction of the Corps is being limited and may continue to be challenged following the 2001 Supreme Court decision. Prior to these decisions, a state's regulation of activities in wetlands was seen as secondary to the Corps' authority; skeptics of the regulatory program speculate that many states have relied upon the Corps to deny controversial permit applications so that the state agency could avoid potential political backlash. Without the Corps' authority over isolated wetlands and certain mechanized clearing activities, the responsibility for regulating these activities falls to the states. State governments find themselves reviewing their state wetland statutes to determine if the state can claim the jurisdiction of which the Corps was stripped. State statutes, regulatory programs, and stewardship activities have become increasingly important with the change in jurisdictional authority at the federal level.

Interaction of Federal and State Wetlands Laws

At a time when many federal regulatory programs are criticized as too expansive and permit denials are challenged in court, efforts to protect wetlands are increasingly occurring at the state level. Many states regulate wetland filling in areas where the Corps does not claim jurisdiction and engage in activities to acquire ecologically critical wetland areas as state public lands. Considering the recent limitations on the Corps' authority and express invitations from the Congress and the executive branch, for better or worse, state legislatures continue to consider methods of increasing control over state wetlands and the signs indicate that the momentum behind the state initiatives will continue.

During the last two decades, the executive branch has consistently encouraged reducing federal involvement and replacing federal wetlands regulators with those at the state level. Specifically, the George Herbert Walker Bush administration preferred a minimum level of federal involvement, citing federal regulatory programs as burdensome (U.S. Department of the Interior 1994). The Clinton administration called for greater state action in its Wetlands Policy of 1993 (White House 1993). Two of its five principles directly related to increasing state responsibilities: avoidance of duplication between regulatory agencies and expansion of partnerships with state and local governments. Although the George W. Bush administration has not issued a specific wetlands policy during its first year (2001–2002), its push for reduced federal regulation will likely be translated into a push for greater state responsibility of wetlands.

State Legislation

Since the passage of the Clean Water Act in 1972, states have been encouraged to establish their own conservation and permitting programs and to work as partners with the federal Army Corps of Engineers in order to manage wetland areas. Some state programs predated the federal protections of wetlands, such as the Massachusetts Wetland Protection Statute (2000), which began to take shape in 1965. In addition, many states took action in favor of their coastal wetlands before extending protection to nontidal freshwater wetlands. In 1972, Congress adopted the Coastal Zone Management Act, including a grant program for states. From 1968 through 1975, most coastal states adopted coastal wetland regulation statutes or included wetland protection as part of broader coastal zone or shoreland zoning statutes. By 2001, thirty-four states had wetlands laws, based on either coastal wetlands or freshwater wetlands, and an estimated 4,000–5,000 local governments had adopted wetland protection ordinances. (The states are Alabama, Alaska, California, Connecticut, Delaware, Florida, Georgia, Hawaii, Idaho, Iowa, Louisiana, Maine, Maryland, Massachusetts, Michigan, Minnesota, Mississippi, Nebraska, New Hampshire, New Jersey, New York, North Carolina, North Dakota, Ohio, Oregon, Pennsylvania, Rhode Island, South Carolina, Texas, Vermont, Virginia, Washington, Wisconsin, and Wyoming [Want 2001].)

Other states joined programs sponsored by the federal government that combine federal, state, local, and private efforts at restoring and preserving wetlands.

Partners for Wildlife, a stewardship program administered by the U.S. Fish and Wildlife Service arranges federal, state, and private cost sharing of wetlands restoration projects. An excellent example of state participation is Louisiana's contribution under the Coastal Wetlands Planning, Protection, and Restoration Act, which authorizes federal cost sharing and oversight of the development and implementation of a coastal wetlands conservation plan by Louisiana. The U.S. Department of Agriculture, Natural Resources Conservation Service (NRCS) Wetlands Reserve Program (WRP) is a similar cost-sharing approach that purchases easements from private landowners to protect wetlands. Finally, the North American Waterfowl Management Plan includes efforts by the United States, Canada, Mexico, state and local governments on a regional basis through "joint ventures" of public and private organizations, conservation groups, and local, state, regional, and federal agencies.

State Regulation: The State Programmatic General Permit

The state programmatic general permit (SPGP) is one type of general permit issued by the U.S. Army Corps of Engineers and is an opening for a state to increase its role in regulating activities in wetlands. Today, the Corps uses general permits to authorize 80 percent of the regulated activities. The secretary of the Army issues general permits on a programmatic, regional, or nationwide basis. To qualify for a general permit, the project must meet the following requirements under the Clean Water Act: (1) the activities authorized under the general permit must be "similar in nature"; (2) the activities may cause only minimal adverse environmental effects when performed separately; (3) the activities may have only minimal cumulative adverse effect on the environment; (4) the permit must be based on EPA guidelines; (5) the permit must be limited to a five-year life span; and (6) the secretary can revoke or modify the permit if the authorized activities have an adverse impact on the environment or such activities are more appropriately authorized by individual permits.

The administration of the general programmatic permit is based upon the goal that state and federal regulatory programs should not duplicate one another. Corps regulations define programmatic permits as "a type of general permit founded on an existing state, local, or other federal agency program and designed to avoid duplication with that program" (33 CFR sec. 325.5[c][3]). Under an SPGP, the Corps delegates to a state the primary responsibility under section 404 for permit review of the activities meeting the requirements of the SPGP. As a general permit, the SPGP must comply with the congressionally mandated requirements set forth in section 404.

Before authorizing an SPGP, the Corps must analyze the state program upon which it is based. Often, because of the limited scope of some state programs, an SPGP will not necessarily cover the entire state in question. For example, a state that has a statute that only applies to coastal wetlands does not have the requisite authority to manage an SPGP over freshwater wetlands. Instead, the Corps refers to any general permit program based on a state program to assure the protection of wetlands as an SPGP.

States with SPGPs cite greater control over wetlands as a reason to take on this authority. Through an SPGP, the state can control the permitting of those actions with minimal impacts, does not have to rely on the Corps, and avoids duplication for these permit applications. Finally, the SPGP gives states an alternative to the 404 permitting process, which can often be more arduous.

The SPGP can be a win-win for the Corps as well. By giving the state the authority to review and issue or deny these permits, the Corps can reduce duplication between state and federal regulatory programs and reduce the Corps' regulatory workload without compromising, at least from the Corps' perspective, the overall effectiveness of section 404 and section 10 permit reviews in protecting wetlands. In addition, most SPGPs specifically exclude activities affecting sensitive areas, such as endangered species habitat or historic properties, and provide for permit applications addressing these types of activities to be automatically "kicked back" to the Corps for review.

State Regulation: Assumption

The second option for states is "state assumption" of the Corps' permitting authority: the state becomes the primary wetlands regulator. Many states perceive that SPGPs provide adequate control of state wetlands without assuming the responsibility offered under state assumption while others view SPGPs as merely a stepping stone to assumption, which can offer a state more regulatory authority than a general permit.

Unlike SPGPs, the Clean Water Act and accompanying regulations specify the requirements for assuming section 404 authority. The U.S. Environmental Protection Agency must approve a state's application to assume the 404 permitting program. The statute requires the governor of the applicant state to submit a description of the program to the EPA, along with a statement from the state attorney general that the laws of the state "provide adequate authority to carry out the described program" (Federal Water Pollution Control Act, 33 USC sec. 1344[g][1]). A state must submit to the EPA regional administrator the following six items: (1) a letter from the governor of the state requesting approval of the state program; (2) a complete program description; (3) an attorney general's statement confirming that the laws of the state provide adequate authority to carry out the described program; (4) a Memorandum of Agreement (MOA) with the EPA regional administrator; (5) a MOA with the secretary of the Army; and (6) copies of applicable state statutes and regulations, including those governing applicable state administrative procedures.

In order to assume, the state will enter MOAs with both the EPA and the Corps. The MOA with the EPA must set out state and federal responsibilities for program administration and enforcement, including provisions specifying classes and categories of permit applications for which EPA will waive federal review authority and provisions addressing EPA and state roles and coordination with respect to compliance monitoring and enforcement activities. The MOA with the secretary of the Army must include a description of the waters within the state over which the secretary retains jurisdiction and an identification of all general permits issued by the secretary, the terms and conditions of which the state intends to administer and enforce upon receiving approval of its program, and a plan for transferring responsibility for these general permits to the state.

The EPA retains oversight authority and receives copies of all permit applications. The state must notify the EPA of any action that it takes with respect to such applications. The EPA administrator provides copies of the application to the Corps, and other federal agencies, including the Department of Interior, the Fish and Wildlife Service, and the National Marine Fisheries Service, and must notify the state within thirty days if the administrator intends to comment on the state's handling of the application. The state must then await comment before it may issue the permit. If the EPA objects to the application, the state cannot issue the proposed permit but may request a hearing before the EPA or alter the permit to accommodate the EPA objections. If the state does not request a hearing, the EPA transfers authority to issue the permit to the Corps. Once in the Corps' hands, jurisdiction remains there. The EPA also maintains the authority to withdraw approval of the program. If the administration of the state program does not meet EPA guidelines, the EPA may take corrective action and may, within a reasonable time, withdraw approval of the program and redirect authority to the Corps.

Challenges for State Regulation

Improving the efficiency of the permitting process is a high priority for those states considering regulation. The Corps is often criticized for slow responses on permits, taking an "average of 373 days from the time the Corps decided on the application or the application was withdrawn" (Albrecht and Goode 1996). States can impose a strict time limit on their permitting agencies, as Michigan has done by requiring turnaround by its Department of Natural Resources in ninety days and potentially provide a larger workforce than the Corps. With more field offices, decision makers can be more readily available to applicants and can be closer to the wetlands actually under their jurisdiction.

An element of improving efficiency of the 404 program is to reduce the ever-present regulatory duplication. Under a state assumed program, paperwork for the applicant is reduced and the state agency becomes directly responsible for the application. A state can also consolidate several different wetland statutes to reduce the burden on the regulated public and streamline the process.

Finally, advocates of state assumption argue that wetlands will receive better protection under an assumed program for three reasons. First, the state is in a better position to address regional and local concerns about the conservation and use of wetlands resources. Assumption supporters claim that state agency regulators are more familiar with the treatment and use of the regulated lands. Second, because the state assumes permitting authority over a smaller square acreage of wetlands than the Corps had been responsible for, a state can potentially provide closer examination of cumulative impacts. Third, assumption advocates claim that a state regulator will be more aggressive than its Corps predecessor and a state can avoid the inconsistency problems that often plague Corps regulators.

There are, of course, weaknesses in state regulation of wetlands. State regulatory programs can be vulnerable to applications for state-sponsored activities such as Department of Transportation road or bridge projects. In addition, political pressures are especially detectable at the state level; local and state officials are easily affected by development pressures and economic priorities set without consideration for the ramification on wetlands. State agencies are at risk of losing funding if they make unpopular decisions regarding permitting and often do not have the necessary resources to manage an entire wetlands regulatory program without federal assistance. These factors, along with the challenges to wetlands regulation by property owners, as discussed in the next section, are leading private parties and governments to turn to nonregulatory options to protect wetlands.

Property Rights as a Hurdle to Traditional Regulation

The right of property owners to be paid for property that the government "takes" is not new. In 1215, the Magna Carta expressed the notion that a person has the right to compensation when a government takes away that person's property. The Fifth Amendment of the U.S. Constitution recognizes that private property shall not be taken for public use without just compensation. This guarantee extends beyond the physical appropriation of property to include governmental regulations that effectively accomplish the same result by restricting a property's use. As the U.S. population moves toward coastal areas and waterbodies, wetlands regulations are often the subject of contentious property rights battles.

The foundation for regulatory takings began in Justice Holmes' opinion in *Pennsylvania Coal Co. v. Mahon* (260 U.S. 393, 415 [1922]), warning that "while property may be regulated to a certain extent, if regulation goes too far, it will be recognized as a taking." Prior to this opinion, courts generally treated property as taken for Fifth Amendment purposes only when it had been directly appropriated by the government or when the owner had been effectively stripped of physical possession. Physical invasion remains an easy question for courts, but there is still a struggle to determine when a regulation overburdens property to the level of a taking.

The Court neglected to establish such a per se rule for regulatory takings for many years. In the last two decades, however, the Supreme Court has reviewed a number of such cases, often touching on wetlands and water-related lands. However, the reviews have provided only cloudy analysis to determine when a governmental regulation goes "too far" as suggested by Justice Holmes in 1922 and is so burdensome that it takes property without compensating the owner, prohibited by the Fifth Amendment. In the 1992 case *Lucas v. South Carolina Coastal Council* (505 U.S. 1003 [1992]), the Court decided that when a regulation denies all economically beneficial or productive use of land, a taking has occurred. Developer David Lucas sued South Carolina for denying him the right to build residential homes on two waterfront lots on a South Carolina barrier island, the Isle of Palms. The Court found that a taking had occurred since the legislature's actions deprived the land of all of its economic viability. South Carolina bought the land from Lucas for over $1.5 million.

For those cases that fall in between a physical invasion and a total loss of property value, a state must show a legitimate state purpose for the governmental regulation. Without such a legitimate purpose, the state must generally provide compensation for the taking of part of their property. The challenge in wetlands law is how to determine this legitimate state interest when a state is attempting to conserve wetlands while not reducing a property owner's economic interest in the property.

In the spring of 2001, the latest in a series of "regulatory takings" cases that can affect both state and federal regulation of wetlands made its way to the U.S. Supreme Court. A Rhode Island property owner, Mr. Anthony Palazzolo, was the sole shareholder in a corporation that invested in a coastal property with salt marshes that were later designated as protected coastal wetlands. Palazzolo took title to the wetland property in 1978 and later challenged the state's refusal to allow him to build houses and a beach club when he applied for a permit. He alleged that the state's denial of his application to fill 18 acres of coastal wetlands constituted a taking of his property for which he was entitled to compensation pursuant to the U.S. and Rhode Island Constitutions. The Rhode Island Supreme Court found that the denial of Palazzolo's application was not a taking for which compensation was owed. One reason was that "until the plaintiff had explored, and sought permission for, development options less grandiose than filling 18 acres of salt marsh, he could not maintain a claim that the defendant had deprived him of all beneficial use of the property" (*Palazzolo v. State of Rhode Island*, 746 A.2d 707, 714 [2000]). The U.S. Supreme Court reversed this decision, holding that the landowner obtained a final decision from the council determining the permitted use for the land and that the fact that the landowner acquired title after the wetlands regulations took effect did not bar him from seeking compensation (*Palazzolo v. Rhode Island*, 121 S.Ct. 2448 [2001]).

As the Supreme Court continues to build on its takings jurisprudence, state legislatures have taken action to provide landowners greater protection from regulatory takings. By the early 1990s, state legislatures were seriously considering and passing takings statutes; by 1997, four of the five states bordering the Gulf of Mexico had adopted statutes (save Alabama) with the Florida and Texas statutes serving as models for states across the country (Florida Private Property Rights Protection Act, Texas Private Real Property Rights Preservation Act). The Supreme Court's decisions defining the scope of the Fifth Amendment in regulatory takings terms has played a key role in establishing the breadth of these laws, as legislatures take action to grant their citizens rights that are above and beyond those granted under the Fifth Amendment. In January of 2002, the U.S. Supreme Court heard arguments in the dispute between landowners near Lake Tahoe and a regional planning commission that regulates land use around the lake. The question, whether a temporary (three-year) moratorium on development that prevented some landowners from building on their land, was decided in the spring of 2002. The court found that a temporary moratorium such as the one used in Lake Tahoe was not an automatic taking though a moratorium longer than three years may constitute a taking (*Tahoe-Sierra Preservation Council v. Tahoe Regional Planning Agency*, 121 S.Ct. 1495 [2002]).

Wetland Mitigation and Mitigation Banking: Benefit or Detriment for Wetlands?

As mentioned above, the Corps considers mitigation elements when issuing permits. A growing share of compensatory mitigation is being provided by commercial mitigation banks and similar mitigation programs (Zedler and Shabman 2001). Federal regulations define mitigation banking as wetland restoration, creation, enhancement, and preservation undertaken expressly for the purpose of compensating for unavoidable wetland losses in advance of development actions when such compensation cannot be achieved at the development site or would not be as environmentally beneficial. Under the federal Clean Water Act, a developer whose project will alter or destroy wetlands must apply for a permit from the Corps. Corps regulations require that the developer avoid adverse impacts on wetlands. If impacts are unavoidable, the applicant must take steps necessary to minimize the impact on the wetlands through restoration or rehabilitation of wetlands. As a last resort, the developer can compensate for the destruction of wetlands by creating new wetlands. Corps regulations favor that the applicant create the new wetlands on the same site in order to provide similar characteristics and functions. If impossible, the developer may apply to a mitigation bank to buy "credits" to compensate for the wetland losses. These banks are often managed by private entities.

The Corps' compensatory mitigation program was reviewed in 2001 and found by the National Research Council to be insufficient. While many critics of section 404 regulation and advocates of private property rights champion the use of wetland mitigation banking as a method to balance development interests with wetlands protection, opponents of banking argue that this effort is not restoring the structure and function of wetlands lost through development. In response to the National Research Council's critique of and recommendations for the Corps' compensatory mitigation element, the Corps issued the Corps of Engineers Compensatory Mitigation Guidance on October 31, 2001 (U.S. Army Corps of Engineers 2002). This guidance has been criticized because it was adopted without public comment and provides that replacement for destroyed wetlands could be provided by preservation or enhancement of existing wetlands, small buffer strips along streams, upland areas, ponds and other waters, or simply deepening an existing wetland for swimming or fishing. However, the Corps still looks to mitigation banking as an option.

One bank was created in November 1996. At that time, the Mississippi chapter of The Nature Conservancy acquired over 1,700 acres in Jackson County, Mississippi, to establish the Old Fort Bayou Mitigation Bank, the state's first coastal wetland mitigation bank located 6 miles (9.7 kilometers) inland from the Gulf of Mexico. The proceeds from the sale of credits are used by The Nature Conservancy to restore and maintain the area in its historical wet savanna habitat. Like other mitigation bank managers, The Nature Conservancy has discretionary authority to sell credits to developers. These credits represent actual wetland acreage inside the bank area that compensates for those unavoidable impacts to wetlands at the project area.

The applicant may qualify for credits by meeting a number of requirements. First, the altered habitat type must occur within the mitigation bank area. Second, the quality of the wetland destroyed must meet the quality of that habitat created in the bank. Third, the functions of the destroyed wetlands must be replaceable by the new wetland. These requirements ensure that the replacement wetlands conform to the destroyed ones and that the bank does not create new wetlands but replaces lost wetland functions. The managing entity will determine the value of the wetland that is lost. If this wetland is particularly valuable to an ecosystem or a species, then the developer may have to buy additional acreage in the mitigation bank to compensate.

Mitigation banks have been proposed by developers as a method by which their compensatory mitigation requirements may be met. Despite the growing use and popularity of mitigation banks, no express federal statutory requirements exist and only scarce regulatory guidance is provided through a

Memorandum of Agreement between the EPA and the Corps. States may be tempted to respond to this void and enact a mitigation statute, but this raises the risk that states will relax their mitigation requirements as they compete for business development investment (Le Desma 1995).

The lack of requirements for mitigations banks can be perilous for wetland ecosystems. Banks often form as "creatures of informal negotiations" that occur before permit approval is obtained rather than as the result of a well-considered design plan and strict requirements on location and trading systems. In addition, while other market-based environmental trading schemes can easily be based on a one-on-one trading system, great differences exist among wetlands, and their functional value is often difficult to quantify.

In choosing a bank site, several factors must be considered, including diversity of habitat, contribution of wetland functions, and ease of restoration and management. The Old Fort Bayou Wetland Mitigation Bank site offered the same coastal ecological unit and contained similar wetland and aquatic habitats to those found in the four eligible Mississippi coastal counties. The habitat types located within the Old Fort Bayou site include the pine-dominated forested wetland, hardwood-dominated forested wetland, pitcher plant emergent wetland, and emergent marsh; to be eligible for credit purchase, the impacted area must match one of these habitat types.

Location is also important for reducing the amount of temporal loss, for providing access for monitoring purposes and for connecting important isolated ecosystems. For example, Old Fort Bayou provides a habitat corridor for the endangered Mississippi sandhill crane. The site adjoins two portions of the Mississippi Sandhill Crane Wildlife Refuge managed by the U.S. Fish and Wildlife Service to preserve habitat for the Mississippi sandhill crane. The lands represent critical habitat for the crane, which was listed as an endangered species in 1973. Historically, these birds nested in small colonies along the Gulf coastal plain in Louisiana, Mississippi, and Florida, but the refuge now harbors the only breeding population of the Mississippi sandhill crane. The bank site makes the refuge easier to manage, since the lands are no longer disconnected, and it potentially allows The Nature Conservancy and the U.S. Fish and Wildlife Service to combine restoration and monitoring efforts.

Management of mitigation banks can be controversial. Ideally, each bank will establish a long-term management plan providing for land acquisition, site assessment, inventories, restoration, and conservation plans. Restoration usually includes removing roads, filling ditches and canals, monitoring, and acquiring and protecting important habitats outside of the bank area in order to address cumulative impacts associated with rapid growth and development.

Because mitigation banks present a web of complex issues, critics of mitigation banking seek additional government research and the authority to require bank sponsors to meet increasingly higher standards of performance (Le Desma

1995). Developed in the early 1980s as a mechanism to compensate for unavoidable adverse impacts associated with future development activities, wetland mitigation banks represent a method of off-site creation, restoration, and enhancement of wetlands. Supporters herald the banking concept as a means of expediting the permitting process for development that alters or destroys wetlands and preserving property rights. Critics respond that by allowing filling in one area for preservation in another, the result is still a net loss of U.S. wetlands.

Techniques to Modernize Wetlands Protection

Both state programmatic general permits and state assumption rely upon state participation in and, in some instances, almost total assumption of the regulatory arm of wetlands protection. Dependence on the regulatory side, however, diminishes the significance state actions can have on the nation's overall wetland preservation and conservation programs because regulatory programs tend to be limited in their scope. Increased regulation may also be impossible in an age of private property rights and successful regulatory takings claims. However, an ecosystem management approach for wetlands protection rather than the targeted and reactive responses to private activities that are currently employed may prove more effective (Flourney 1996).

States have several other options to implement their own wetland conservation strategies that may be, in some cases, more effective than a state accepting federal regulatory responsibility. In the alternative, these "stewardship" options should at least be combined with the regulatory capabilities of the states to create a more comprehensive program and avoid overreliance on regulatory programs as a primary tool.

These nonregulatory tools include incentive and disincentive programs, acquisition and legal restriction, restoration, educational efforts, policy statements, and inventories. Stewardship programs recognize that because the majority of wetlands are privately owned, partnerships between the federal government, state and local governments, and the private sector may best conserve those wetlands out of public control. Most of these programs focus on acquiring or restoring wetlands. Three key programs worth analyzing are the state wetland conservation plans, the acquisition of wetlands or creation of trusts, and conservation easement programs.

State Wetland Conservation Plans

State wetland conservation plans require states to develop broad conservation and preservation goals that identify methods to assess the condition of wetlands, threats to their well-being, and current protection efforts. Some wetland conservation plans include strategies for action, funding, and monitoring and evaluation. Critics of the regulatory program argue that the use of conservation plans can supplement and bring continuity to the regulatory program.

Wetland Conservation Plans are gaining support as methods to fill the gaps left by the permitting program. The National Wetland Forum in 1988 recommended delegating primary responsibility of the regulatory program to those states with adequate wetland conservation plans and by providing financial and technical assistance to ensure the efficacy of those programs. The Clinton administration endorsed these plans in 1993 by stating that "Congress should endorse the development of State/Tribal comprehensive wetland plans, with the goal of supporting State and Tribal efforts to protect and manage their wetlands resources" (White House 1993).

Oregon has sanctioned wetland conservation plans to supplement its regulatory program. It defines a wetland conservation plan as a written plan providing for wetland management that contains a detailed and comprehensive statement of policies, standards, and criteria to guide public and private uses and protection of wetlands, waters, and related adjacent uplands; that has specific measures for implementation; and that apply to designated geographic areas of the state of Oregon (Oregon Wetlands and Rivers Statute 2000). It specifically states that dredging or filling of a wetland in a manner contrary to conditions set out in a permit *or* set out in an order approving a wetlands conservation plan is illegal under the statute. Thus, even if a permit is not required, the filling of a wetland may still be considered illegal or a nuisance under the terms of the wetland conservation plan. The state agency is given authority to approve and enforce the conditions of the wetland conservation plan.

Texas and Louisiana are both developing plans to apply to their coastal wetlands. Texas' plan provides numerous tolls not available in a regulatory scheme. It includes a policy framework for achieving a goal of no overall net loss of state-owned coastal wetlands, including monitoring and enforcement, an inventory, guidelines for mitigation, dredging, disposal, and reduction of nonpoint source pollution. It specifically calls for interaction through a networking strategy for better coordination between state and federal agencies, and through a public education program (Texas Parks and Wildlife Code). Finally, it includes a plan to acquire coastal wetlands. Louisiana is developing a similar coastal wetlands conservation plan under the guidance of the Coastal Wetlands Planning, Protection and Restoration Act. The act provides that if Louisiana develops such a plan under a state agency, with state, federal, and public input that avoids the net loss of wetlands, then the EPA may contribute grants of up to 75 percent of the cost of the plan.

Acquisition of Wetlands

A second key stewardship program a state can use to supplement regulatory wetlands programs is acquisition of lands. The government can readily control uses of wetlands by purchasing full fee title to environmentally significant lands or by acquiring such lands via a land exchange.

The first method of acquisition is outright purchase. Most states recognize the effectiveness of acquisition to further long-term conservation or preservation of wetland resources but often lack the requisite funds to operate effective state acquisition programs. Federal funding may be available to assist states in acquiring private lands. In 1997, the Department of the Interior granted $25 million to a Florida state matching fund for the acquisition of 31,000 acres of Florida land previously privately held. The funds helped the Florida Department of Environmental Protection obtain high-priority lands to preserve the pristine area near the Everglades National Park.

A second method of acquiring privately held wetlands is a land exchange. Although rarely used, land swaps are becoming more popular as a creative way to acquire ecologically valuable sites. One example is the acquisition of 4,225 acres of undisturbed wetland and upland habitat on the Mississippi Gulf Coast in return for 6.73 acres of partially filled tidelands (Duff and Fletcher 1998). With the Mississippi chapter of The Nature Conservancy acting as a go-between, the developer transferred title of the wetlands, which then became part of the state's public trust lands. Without expending state funds, Mississippi acquired title over pristine wetlands in the three coastal counties. With title, Mississippi gained management authority without increasing regulation over private wetlands.

Conservation Easements

A third stewardship program is the conservation easement. Because outright acquisition can be an expensive means of achieving conservation or preservation goals, some states have shifted their focus to acquiring less costly conservation easements from private landowners (Korngold 1984). A conservation easement is a restriction on the use of property usually created between a landowner and a government agency whereby the landowner gives up certain rights in the land and gives the agency the right to perpetually enforce the restriction. Because the easements are purchased from landowners who voluntarily agree to such restrictions, the government can influence land use without directly regulating it.

In its basic form, a conservation easement will protect a conservation attribute to real property, such as habitat or wetlands, while prohibiting most potential commercial uses. Easements have been highly praised by conservation and environmental interest groups as an ideal device to achieve conservation and preservation goals. Landowners may retain some limited rights for residential or recreational uses, but the land is generally set aside and protected from development. Because of the public benefit provided by conservation easements, federal, state, and local income tax incentives are available for the landowner granting the easement (Poston 1998).

The trend toward conserving or preserving diverse land resources through easements is evidenced by the high number of recently established federal conservation programs that include conservation easement provisions. The Wetlands Reserve Program, described earlier, which is administered by the USDA Natural Resources Conservation Service and was created as part of the 1985 Farm Bill to "assist owners of eligible lands in restoring and protecting wetlands" authorizes the U.S. Department of Agriculture to purchase conservation easements. Eligible lands include farmed wetlands, wetlands converted prior to 1985, and lands adjacent to wetlands. Once the landowner has granted the easement and implemented a wetland conservation plan, the government provides compensation based on the difference in fair market value of the land before and after the easement is recorded. Landowner acceptance of the easement acquisition program was obvious as 2,730 landowners indicated a willingness to enroll 466,000 acres in the program (Grier 1991). It offers a unique opportunity for the landowner to use the conserved acres as a buffer for the farmed land and to retain title of the land.

The benefits of creating a conservation easement program are many. First, the state may preserve wetlands at a lower cost than acquiring the property outright. Second, the incentive to create easements such as tax advantages or reimbursement for fair market value makes landowners more aware of their ability to preserve the state's wetlands. Third, the state becomes a partner *with* the private landowner rather than the regulator *over* the landowner. Finally, with the federal program and other state programs as blueprints, the cost to create a program at the state level will be minimal.

Conclusion

Together, scientists, policy-makers, and the public are learning more each year about the value of wetlands to overall quality of life, water quality, and ecosystem health in the United States. However, at best, the country struggles to balance property rights, the economic need for development, environmental values, and ecosystem needs. Recognizing that U.S. policies have indeed progressed from the days of filling wetlands as national policy, governments, private entities, and the public must recognize the need for a national wetlands regime that encourages the supplementation of regulatory programs with stewardship programs, combines federal and regional ideas into state initiatives, and provides realistic opportunities for states and local initiatives to implement these initiatives.

Given the high stakes in wetland management, these alternatives to a failing regulatory scheme will need to prove immediate results if, as a nation, we are to reach our "no net loss" goal.

References

Albrecht, V. S., and B. N. Goode. 1996. All is not well with section 404. *National Wetlands Newsletter*, Mar.–Apr.

Duff, J. A., and K. M. Fletcher. 1998. Augmenting the public trust. *Mississippi Law Journal* 67:1.

Flourney, A. C. 1996. Beyond the balance of nature: Environmental law faces the new ecology: Preserving dynamic systems: Wetlands, ecology and law, *Duke Environmental Law and Policy Forum* 7:105, 108.

Grier, T. 1991. Conservation easements: Michigan's land preservation tool of the 1990s. *University of Detroit Law Review* 69:193, 197–198, n. 47.

Korngold, G. 1984. Privately held conservation servitudes: A policy analysis in the context of in gross real covenants and easements. *Texas Law Review* 63:433, 443–446.

Le Desma, M. G. 1995. A sound of thunder: Problems and prospects in wetlands mitigation banking. *Columbia Journal of Environmental Law* 19:497.

National Biological Survey. 1993. Louisiana coastal wetlands restoration plan, main report and environmental impact statement executive summary 1. Baton Rouge, Louisiana.

Poston, C. W., Jr. 1998. Conservation easements: Now more attractive by addition of IRC sec. 2031(c). *South Carolina Lawyer* 9:5.

U.S. Army Corps of Engineers. 2001. *Compensatory mitigation guidance.* Online: www.usace.army.mil/inet/functions/cw/hot_topics/regmitigation.htm. Accessed site Feb. 12, 2002.

————. 1998. USACE Regulatory Program: Section 404 of the Clean Water Act. Online: www.hq.usace.army.mil/cepa/pubs/wetland.htm. Accessed site Feb. 12, 2002.

U.S. Department of the Interior. March 1994. *The impact of federal programs on wetlands.* Volume II. 4–5. A Report to Congress by the Secretary of Interior, Washington, D.C. Available from National Technical Information Service, Springfield, VA.

Want, W. L. 2001. *Law of wetlands regulation.* West Publishing Company.

White House. 1993. *Protecting America's wetlands: A fair, flexible, and effective approach.* White House Office on Environmental Policy, Washington, D.C.

Zedler, J., and L. Shabman. 2001. Compensatory mitigation needs improvement, panel says. *National Wetlands Newsletter* 1:23–24.

Statutes and Regulations

33 CFR sec. 320.4(q) (2001).
33 CFR sec. 325.5(c)(3) (2001).
33 CFR sec. 328.3 (2001).

33 USC sec. 1344(g)(1) (2001).
Swamp Lands Act of 1850, 9 Stat. 520 (1850).
Swamp Lands Act of 1860, 12 Stat. 3 (1860).
Swamp Lands Act of 1874, 18 Stat. 16 (1874).
Florida Private Property Rights Protection Act, Fla. Stat. sec. 70.001 et seq. (2001).
Massachusetts Wetland Protection Statute, Massachusetts Annotated Laws ch. 131, sec. 40 (2000).
Oregon Wetlands and Rivers Statute, Oregon Revised Statutes sec. 196.800 (2000).
Texas Private Real Property Rights Preservation Act, Tex. Government Code Ann. sec. 2007.001 (2001).

Suggested Resources

Yandle, B., ed. 1995. *Land rights: The 1990s' Property Rights Rebellion.* Lanham, Maryland: Rowman and Littlefield.
Kusler, J., and T. Opheim. 1996. *Our National Wetland Heritage: A Protection Guide.* 2d ed.
Environmental Law Institute. *National Wetlands Newsletter.*

Chapter 3

Aquatic Resources and Human Health

K. Erica Marsh, Kristine L. Willett,
Christy M. Foran, and Bryan W. Brooks

In 1990, the United States Environmental Protection Agency (U.S. EPA) Science Advisory Board ranked the greatest risks facing ecological resources. These risks included habitat destruction, pesticides, toxics, nutrients, groundwater pollution, radionucleotides, airborne toxics, and loss of biological diversity. Nine years later in a National Institute of Environmental Health Sciences town hall meeting, many of the same ecological risks cited by the EPA Science Advisory Board were listed as human health concerns. Issues such as pesticide use, endocrine disruption, lawn chemicals, clean water, air pollution, and dredging topped the list of concerns. The notion that human and ecological health concerns are separate and noninteracting is slowly fading. In fact, as history will show, ecological and human health are often interlinked. Stimuli that affect ecological health may also adversely affect human health. The link can be ambiguous but over the past five decades has become increasingly apparent. The intent of this chapter is to present historical as well as present and future perspectives on the implications of aquatic resource and human health interactions.

Historical Perspectives

Human activities have profoundly altered aquatic ecosystems and resource availability. Historical evidence showcases our mistakes as a society, highlighting the fact that economic gain was sometimes favored over ecological health interests. Investigating the impacts of anthropogenic sources on aquatic systems is an environmental issue of global concern, and is necessary to understand past and present dynamics, and to promote sustainable aquatic environments in hopes of preserving their integrity and productivity.

Mercury and Minamata Bay

One of the first incidents highlighting the intrinsic links between ecological resources and human health occurred in the Minamata Bay region of Japan five decades ago. In this region, Chisso Corporation discharged sludge containing 2,010 micrograms per kilogram of mercury. The effects of mercury on human health were well known at the time, because mercury was an early treatment for syphilis and was the basis for the neurological condition known as "Mad Hatters Syndrome." However, what was not realized at the time was that aquatic organisms in the region had the ability to accumulate high levels of mercury in their tissues. Subsistence fishing predominated in the area, and therefore residents were harvesting and consuming seafood contaminated with mercury. In 1956, Minamata Bay disease was officially named (Ui 1992; Harada 1995). Residents suffered from sensory and gait disturbances, ataxia, and tremors. Prior to the naming of the disease, there were reports of fishes swimming in circles and birds falling from midair (Harada 1995). These extraordinary behaviors in wildlife were probably an indicator of what was to happen to human health. While it is easy to critique the actions of officials at the time, one can only wonder what would have happened had officials adopted a more holistic approach and acted on the strange behavior of the fishes and birds by banning seafood consumption. Would the number of residents impacted by Minamata Bay disease have decreased?

The events at Minamata Bay have spurred decades of mercury research, which is continuing today. The EPA continually makes mercury a research priority. Over the years, it has become evident that the mercury cycle is a combination of atmospheric, sedimentary, and biological processes. Mercury is a common earth element, but it is introduced anthropogenically into the atmosphere mainly through coal-fired power plants (Zillioux et al. 1993; Expert Panel on Mercury Atmospheric Processes 1994). Once in the atmosphere, mercury can be deposited in aquatic or terrestrial catchments. Once in aquatic systems, inorganic mercury can be converted into methylmercury (MeHg), which is considered the most bioaccumulative and toxic form of mercury. Plants and microorganisms play an important role in this transformation. Researchers in the Experimental Lakes Area of Canada observed that wetlands have the ability to transform inorganic mercury into MeHg (St. Louis et al. 1994, 1996). Once accumulated by fishes, it may induce MeHg resistance, but developmental and reproductive impacts need to be better elucidated (Weis and Weis 1989). Although more work is needed to understand the global mercury cycle, it is clear that mercury placed into the environment by humans cycles through the atmosphere and different biotic compartments only to eventually impact humans through seafood consumption.

Environmentally sound paths of action against the mercury problem are being addressed by a network of researchers and policy-makers. Elucidation of the mechanism of action of mercury has brought two major questions into play: (1) Does MeHg itself cause the neurological alterations, or does MeHg become demethylated in the brain so that inorganic mercury is causing the alterations; and (2) Is the MeHg-induced oxidative stress, mitochondrial changes, or disruption of microtubules in the cytoskeleton the exact mechanism, or is it a combination of all mechanisms (NRC 2000)? While research scientists wrestle with these questions, policy-makers are trying to determine the appropriate reference dose, which is the highest dose causing no toxic effects. This is an important issue, because the reference dose is a main determinant in fish and seafood consumption advisories. With mercury being found in areas that several years ago did not have high levels (e.g., the state of Mississippi), the issues of both source and reference doses are very important (Huggett et al. 2001). Looking at the rate of mercury accumulation in the southeastern United States, one can only wonder if any freshwater fish will be considered safe for human consumption fifty years from now.

Hooker Chemical Company and Love Canal

One of the greatest environmental disasters to impact human health occurred at Love Canal in the state of New York. Originally designed in the 1890s by William T. Love as a hydropower conduit between Lake Ontario and Lake Erie, the Love Canal was begun but never completed. In 1942, the nearby Hooker Electrochemical Company, which manufactured pesticides and petrochemicals in its Niagara Falls plant, took over the half-mile-long "ditch," which was being used at the time by local residents as a swimming hole and seasonal ice-skating rink. The canal was surmised to be ideal for the disposal of chemicals because, by design, it was built to retain water and had relatively impermeable clay walls. From 1942 to 1953, the company disposed of 21,800 tons of chemical wastes by dumping them into the canal, sometimes in metal drums, sometimes as liquid or sludge (Wildavsky 1995). The city of Niagara Falls also used the site for disposal of municipal wastes until 1953 (Mazur 1998). In April of 1953, Love Canal was filled in and sold to the Niagara Falls School District for $1. An elementary school and many homes were built on the filled canal. In addition, parts of the city's storm sewer system ran next to the canal.

In the 1970s, chemical leakage was detected after six years of abnormally heavy rains and flooding. Chemical barrels were deteriorating, leaving sink holes on playgrounds and baseball fields, and thick, black material was found in sump pumps and on basement walls. In 1977, a Niagara Falls city employee wrote to his local congressman about concern over "dangerous chemicals" (Levine 1982). In response to residents' complaints and media attention, the New York State Environmental Conservation Department began testing air, surface water, and samples from sump pumps in basements near the Love Canal site. Some eighty industrial chemicals were detected, including many carcinogens (Wildavsky 1995). At that time, Niagara County and Hooker Chemical began a remediation project with tiles and wells designed to lower the water table, and also began to look at treating the leachates (Wildavsky 1995).

In July of 1978, residents were supplied with lists of airborne chemicals detected in homes. These lists included benzene, toluene, lindane, methylene chloride, carbon tetrachloride, and chloroform. A media blitz contributed to the scare, reporting on the chemicals that had been detected, emphasizing the hazards of mercury, dioxins, and furans and pointing out the higher incidence of birth defects, miscarriages, cancer, and respiratory disorders observed in and around Love Canal (Levine 1982). By August, the health commissioner declared Love Canal a health emergency, and recommended that pregnant women and their families, and families with children under two years old, move from their homes in the "inner rings" of the area, meaning those that were directly abutting the canal. He also urged people not to go into their basements or eat food from their gardens (Mazur 1998). By 1980, Biogenics Corporation began chromosome testing on Love Canal area residents on behalf of the EPA. The *New York Times* reported that eleven of the thirty-six test subjects had "exhibited rare chromosomal aberrations" (Mazur 1998). On May 21, President Jimmy Carter declared an emergency to permit state and federal governments to temporarily relocate approximately seven hundred families, with a permanent buyout following in October. In the end, more than $20 million in settlement damages was paid to a group of former residents by the city of Niagara Falls and Hooker Chemical (now part of Occidental Chemical Corporation) (Wildavsky 1995).

The Love Canal story itself is alarming, characterized by intense activity and media coverage at the time, providing a profusion of information which frustrates those interested in a realistic account of events. Much work has been required and huge sums have been spent on research and litigation. Love Canal is a reminder of "the social and human costs of toxic waste disposal" (Levine 1982). Interestingly, much like at Minamata Bay, aquatic species were the first to be impacted. In 1976, a warning that Lake Ontario fishes were unsafe for consumption was issued by the New York State health commissioner due to the detection of traces of an insecticide called Mirex in water samples (Levine 1982). One source of this appeared to be a dump site adjacent to Love Canal, also used by Hooker Chemical, among others (Levine 1982). Leaching and drainage into the Niagara River was a problem affecting wildlife and aquatic species, which in turn presented a health problem for humans in the surrounding areas.

Rhine River: Pollution Abatement and Restoration

Human activities in the Rhine River basin in western Europe date back to Roman times with dyking and canalization of the Rhine reported from the Middle Ages (Van Dijk et al. 1995). During the 1800s, the upper Rhine was channelized to reduce annual flooding. Uncoupling the main river channel from its floodplain resulted in decreased groundwater levels, erosion, and increased risk of downstream flooding (Wieriks and Schulte-Wulwer-Leidig 1997). Early this century, a dramatic decrease in Rhine River water quality resulted from increased population, industrialization, and agriculture (Wieriks and Schulte-Wulwer-Leidig 1997). Currently, about 20 percent of its average flow is diverted for human consumption or industrial purposes (Malle 1996) and over 50 percent of the Rhine drainage area is dominated by agriculture (Anderberg and Stigliani 1994).

Historical sources of pollution in the Rhine River are municipal and industrial effluents, as well as agricultural runoff, which introduced metals, organics, and pesticides (Stigliani et al. 1993). Few municipal sewage treatment plants were located along the Rhine in the 1940s, and consequently raw wastes were diverted to the river (Cals et al. 1998). Whereas the Rhine comprises approximately 0.2 percent of total world river flow, 10 percent of chemical industries belonging to the Organization for Economic and Cooperative Development are located within the Rhine River basin (Stigliani et al. 1993). Located downstream from other countries in the Rhine basin, The Netherlands was subjected to severe pollution, including decreased drinking-water quality, lake eutrophication, deposition of contaminated sediments, and aquatic habitat degradation (de Jong 1990). Again, one of the first links between the environmental and potential human effects was reflected in Rhine fish communities. Impacts of effluents were first noted when salmon catches declined from over 200,000 per year in the late 1800s to almost zero in 1950 (Van Dijk et al. 1995). By the 1960s, the Rhine was known as the sewer of Europe; peak pollution led to the lowest observed fish diversity in the early 1970s (Van Dijk et al. 1995). In addition, benthic macroinvertebrate species in the upper, middle, and lower Rhine decreased almost 50 percent by the late 1970s (de Jong 1990).

Steps toward improving water quality of the Rhine River began in 1976 when the European Commission joined the International Commission for the Protection of the Rhine (ICPR) and set new standards for contaminants (ICPR 1999). Over the past twenty years, improved treatment of wastewater and industrial effluents, better waste management and recycling, and technological advances have led to decreased metal and organic contaminants (Malle 1996). Present day instream concentrations of mercury, cadmium, copper, lead, nickel, chromium, and zinc have declined by 90 percent since the 1970s (Malle 1996). Recent increases in Rhine River fish species diversity are attributed to such reductions of metal and organic contaminants coupled with increased dissolved oxygen concentrations (Van Dijk et al. 1995).

Progress toward water resources improvement stalled in 1986 when an industrial warehouse near Basel, Switzerland, caught fire (Halfon and Bruggemann 1989). Approximately 30 tons of pesticides and other chemicals spilled into the Rhine, resulting in fish kills (estimated to be 500,000) and closings of water systems in France, West Germany, and The Netherlands (Capel et al. 1988). In 1987, prompted by this accident, and in order to promote action through effective networks, the ICPR created the Rhine Action Program that set four goals to be reached by the year 2000. These included (1) improvement of North Sea ecology, (2) reduction of sediment contamination, (3) protection of drinking water, and (4) improvement of aquatic habitats to promote the return of higher species (e.g., salmon) to the Rhine River (Benoist and Broseliske 1994).

Although levels of metal and organic contaminants have dramatically decreased over the past two decades, agricultural inputs have concurrently increased relative to point source pollution (Malle 1996). Large algal blooms observed in the North Sea in 1988 may be attributed to increased nitrate levels in the Rhine of which 75 percent is due to agricultural fertilizers (Malle 1996). These blooms are quite similar to algal blooms and subsequent anoxic zones observed in the Gulf of Mexico; agricultural fertilizers and channelization are likely responsible for increased nitrate inputs to Mississippi River and Gulf of Mexico hypoxic zones (Rabalais et al. 2001). To reduce agricultural impacts on Rhine River water quality and aquatic habitats, The Netherlands adopted a river management policy to reconnect floodplains with the main stream channel. One goal of this program includes restoration of 5,000 hectares of aquatic floodplain and wetland habitats over the next twenty-five years (Van Dijk et al. 1995). Other programs intend to convert large agricultural areas into forestlands (Stigliani et al. 1993). Forestation and wetland issues are further discussed in Chapter 9.

Current Perspectives

Recent advances in our understanding of the relationships between environmental toxicants and biological mechanisms of toxicity have been crucial additions to the development and application of bio-indicators capable of assessing ecological conditions. Establishing these bio-indicators aids in the movement towards more sustainable practices for effective management of present and future ecological challenges.

Endocrine Disruption

In the wave of media attention that followed the publication of *Our Stolen Future*, by Colburn, Dumanoski, and Myers (1996), endocrine disruption has become one of the leading environmental and public health concerns. This focus on endocrine function is resulting in several changes in policy for testing new chemicals and has added a new perspective to traditional environmental toxicology. For generations, toxicology has focused on the dose, the mechanisms of chemical exposure, and any resulting impacts on an organism's health. The processes involved have generally been grouped into necrosis, apoptosis, and genotoxicity. In contrast, endocrine disruption generally involves xenobiotic chemicals that act as signals in normal physiological processes. These inappropriate signals can disrupt physiology in a way that alters tissue function and developmental processes. One well-described example of endocrine disruption is the case of diethylstilbestrol (DES) (Colburn et al. 1996; Rogers and Kavlock 1996). DES is a pharmaceutical that was taken by approximately 5 million women during the 1950s and 1960s. DES was used predominantly to prevent miscarriages, although it was also prescribed for several other problems. DES maintained pregnancies by acting to increase placental estrogen availability. Unfortunately, in the years following DES use, the children of mothers who took DES exhibited a suite of unusually rare cancers, malformations of the reproductive track, and infertility. The saga of DES-exposed children provides an important lesson into the potential for synthetic estrogens to influence development.

Studies of wildlife from contaminated sites also indicate the potential for significant impacts of endocrine disruptors on development and reproductive capacity. The studies of alligators in Lake Apopka have demonstrated the potential for organochlorine pesticides to alter male development, endocrine function, and fertility (Guillette et al. 1994). Numerous other studies have noted the effect on fishes, birds, and other animals that developed in areas near sites with significant contamination, particularly around the Great Lakes (Rolland et al. 1995). Though it is generally agreed that the evidence for endocrine disruption in contaminated sites is strong, it has not been determined that these studies are predictors of human health effects. The links between human and natural systems are still being delineated.

Temporal trends in breast cancer rates and declining semen quality in humans have received considerable media attention. While the trends reported in studies have not been supported in subsequent epidemiological work, what is clear from collections of epidemiological studies is that living and working in an environment highly contaminated with toxicants can impact health, development, and fertility (Schettler et al. 1999). In addition, there are clearly specific environments and professions that increase the risk of exposure to endocrine disruptors and other toxic contaminants. The missing variable in our understanding of the risk of endocrine disruption is the susceptibility of people with an average or routine exposure to low and infrequent concentrations of endocrine disruptors.

Reviews of the literature indicate that endocrine-disrupting chemicals can be detected in low concentration in rivers and streams that receive effluent from municipal wastewater or industrial plants (Desbrow et al. 1998; Ternes et al. 1999a,b). In some cases, exposure to wastewater has been shown to mimic the actions of estrogen on gene expression and even gonadal development in resident fish populations (Rolland et al. 1997). The collection of environmental data on the occurrence of endocrine disruptors has justified the concern of widespread exposure to these contaminants. However, as yet there have been few reports of contamination of sources of drinking water, such as well water or municipal water delivery systems. We cannot at this time completely evaluate the concern regarding waterborne exposure to endocrine disruptors. Therefore, the risk of exposure of average populations cannot currently be estimated.

Yet another issue is what, if any, effects of endocrine disruption would result from "average" exposure to endocrine disruptors. The media have emphasized the role of xenoestrogens in the development of cancer and the decline in sperm counts in some areas of the United States. Animal studies with realistic intrauterine exposure to weak estrogens have seen subtle developmental, behavioral, and reproductive changes (Palanza et al. 1999). A concern is that human epidemiologists focused on specific outcomes might miss less-apparent changes associated with developmental exposure to endocrine disruptors. Research and policy decisions to deal with the issue of endocrine disruption and its consequences are still being developed.

Carcinogenesis

Previous examples in this chapter highlighted the effect of acute toxicities from environmental exposures on wildlife; many of these instances have been predictive of human symptoms. Similar examples exist for cancer. In wildlife, exposure to carcinogens and subsequent death as a result, might be considered less significant for the species than acute toxicants such as mercury or developmental toxicants. This is because cancer typically develops after organisms have reproduced. However, cancer in humans has a significant impact in both children and adults. In fact, cancer is the second leading cause of death in Americans (one in four deaths). For 2000, the U.S. National Institutes of Health estimate overall annual costs for cancer at $180.2 billion: $60 billion for direct medical costs (total of all health expenditures), $15 billion for indirect morbidity costs (cost of lost productivity due to illness), and $105.2 billion for indirect mortality costs (cost of lost productivity due to premature death) (American Cancer Society 2001).

In many cases, the contaminants that cause cancer in fishes are the same as those known or reasonably expected to be human carcinogens (Bailey et al. 1996; EHIS 2000). In fact, a significant amount of research both in the laboratory and the field has used fishes as models to study environmental carcinogenesis. Advantages of using fishes in cancer studies include a relatively short life span and reproductive cycle, which facilitate lifetime monitoring; low cost and portability permitting in situ biomonitoring; and evolutionary similarities in biochemical and physiological processes (Bailey et al. 1996). For example, fishes form the same critical benzo(a)pyrene DNA adduct as mammals. Likewise, fishes have similar cytochrome P450 genes and cellular oncogenes. A disadvantage of using fishes as a human model is the lack of identical physiology and organ homology between species.

Some of the tumors that have been reported in freshwater fishes in the United States include oral papillomas, dermal melanomas, lymphosarcomas, and hepatocellular/cholangiocellular carcinomas (Black and Baumann 1991). In some geographical locations extraordinarily high prevalences of lesions in fishes are detected. For example, in the Elizabeth River in Virginia, adjacent to a creosote-contaminated Superfund site, Vogelbein et al. (1990) found 93 percent of the mummichog (*Fundulus heteroclitus*) had hepatic lesions and 33 percent of these fishes had hepatocellular carcinomas. Brown bullhead catfish (*Ameiurus nebulosus*) appears to be a very sensitive species with respect to cancer formation, and hence it has been used as a sentinel species in several U.S. waterways. A steel complex released polynuclear aromatic hydrocarbons (PAHs) into the Black River in Ohio until the complex was closed in 1983. Tumors in bullhead populations have been monitored since the early 1980s in this waterway. In 1987, the tumor incidence in fishes was reported as 10 percent, reduced by one-third as compared to a reported 32 percent in a 1982 survey. This decline in tumor formation was mirrored by a decrease in sediment PAHs (Baumann and Harshbarger 1995). Following dredging of the Black River sediments in 1990, the tumor incidence increased to 48 percent, higher than when the plant was in operation (Baumann and Harshbarger 1998). The increase in cancer following the "clean-up" operation clearly shows that there can be profound implications of secondary exposure during remediation efforts. Tumors in brown bullhead have also corresponded with Chesapeake Bay Regions of Concern. Up to 60 percent of the bullhead population had liver tumors in the Anacostia River, where sediment is contaminated with PAHs, polychlorinated biphenyls, and pesticides (Pinkney et al. 2000). While brown bullhead may be one of the most commonly reported fishes with tumors, other examples are also found in the literature. Other affected species include winter flounder from Boston Harbor, English sole and rock sole from the Puget Sound in Washington (Malins et al. 1985), white suckers from Lake Ontario (Stalker et al. 1991), and walleye from the Great Lakes (Baumann et al. 1991).

Although PAHs and creosote contamination corresponded with tumor formation in most of the fish examples described above, these compounds were also some of the first human carcinogenic mixtures identified. Creosote is made up of PAHs, phenolic compounds, and heterocyclic compounds. In 1775, Sir Percival Pott discovered the relationship between scrotal cancer and chimney cleaning (Gallo 1996). Chimney sweeps were occupationally exposed to PAHs in soot, creosote, and coal tar. Whereas occupational exposure to carcinogens has greatly decreased in the United States today due to strict regulations, humans still are exposed to high levels of PAHs from tobacco smoking. In the United States, increasing trends of "combustion PAHs" in environmental samples track closely with increases in automobile use (van Metre et al. 2000; Dickhut et al. 2000). For this reason, PAHs will likely be an environmental problem for some time and appropriate methods of bioassaying exposure to PAHs for both wildlife and humans must be characterized. Even though it has been established that environmental contaminants such as PAHs and creosote are carcinogens in wildlife and probably humans, we still do not have a good understanding of the concentrations necessary to initiate cancer (or protect from it) or the reasons for species and individual differences in susceptibility to tumor formation.

Biological Toxicants

Historical anthropogenic eutrophication of aquatic systems and subsequent impacts upon water resources is well documented. Recent eutrophication of Atlantic U.S. coast estuaries has resulted in harmful dinoflagellate blooms from Delaware to Florida (Hudnell et al. 2001; Mallin et al. 2000). First identified in the Chesapeake Bay, *Pfiesteria* spp. release toxins in the presence of fishes (El-Nabawi et al. 2000). Whereas *Pfiesteria* may indirectly affect aquatic health by reducing zooplankton grazing (Stoecker et al. 2000), widespread fish kills and river closures to fishing and swimming have received considerable attention (Mallin et al. 2000). In addition, "persistent" impacts of *Pfiesteria* toxin on human health, known as an estuary-associated syndrome, include memory loss, learning disabilities, and visual system impairment (Levin et al. 1997; Hudnell et al. 2001). A recent study found that *Pfiesteria* toxin's inhibition of N-methyl-D-aspartate neurotransmitter receptor function may be a mechanism of action for such effects on human neurological processes (El-Nabawi et al. 2000).

Recent estuary closures are not limited to eutrophication and *Pfiesteria* blooms. Numerous fishery and recreational area advisories are linked to water-borne pathogens (U.S. EPA 1999a). Although permitted water quality standards exist for point source pathogen discharges, pathogens enter aquatic systems from accidental spills of wastewater effluents, and nonpoint sources often associated with rainfall events (U.S. EPA 1999b). Current EPA monitoring guidelines include *Escherichia coli* and enterococci as indicator organisms for waterborne pathogens (U.S. EPA 1999a). Numerous human diseases result from exposure to waterborne pathogens following direct contact (i.e., swimming) or ingestion of contaminated food or water (Miyagi et al. 2001; Guyon et al. 2000). In addition to adverse effects on human health and fishing industries, economic impacts on recreational activities are evidenced by a steady increase of annual beach closings due to pathogens since 1988. For example, Dorfman (2001) found that beach closings and advisories for 2000 increased 83 percent from 1999.

The Environmental Protection Agency initiated the Beach Environmental, Assessment, Closure, and Health (BEACH) Program in 1997. This network was formed to address public health waterborne pathogen concerns and to improve monitoring programs (U.S. EPA 1999a). Less than a year later, a Clean Water Action Plan was developed to implement the BEACH monitoring and public notification programs (U.S. EPA 1999b). In October 2000, the BEACH Act was signed into law. The Act amended the Clean Water Act and required EPA to publish performance criteria for monitoring and notification of coastal recreation waters by April 2002. At the time of publication, a public comment period was open for EPA's National Beach Guidance and Grant Performance Criteria for Recreational Waters.

Pharmaceutical Contaminants

In addition to biological contaminants, pharmaceutical and personal care products are an emerging environmental issue. The use of antibiotics has been described as rampant and indiscriminant, and their ultimate destination is release into the environment (Daughton and Ternes 1999). Antibiotics are commonly used to fight infection, prevent the spread of disease among animals, and accelerate the growth of fishes and poultry that are farmed in close conditions. The prevalence of resistant microbial strains has lead to a debate on the contribution of environmental antibiotics to the development of resistance and the need for new regulations on antibiotic use (Witte 1998; Williams and Heymann 1998). Infections with resistant microbial agents have the potential to be more virulent, leading to more severe adverse health effects. The environmental occurrence and concentration of several classes of antibiotics was recently described by European researchers (Hirsch et al. 1999). One such example was the antibiotic fluoroquinolone, which was found in a study of hospital wastewater by Hartmann et al. (1998). They described the potential release of fluoroquinolone antibiotics based on a model excluding the effects of metabolism or degradation. They observed this model to be a reasonable approximation for ciprofloxacin, a fluoroquinolone antibiotic reported to be excreted 70 percent unmetabolized. The percentage of the prescribed dose (100–3,000 milligrams) that is excreted unchanged for many of the commonly prescribed antibiotics, including amoxicillin and tetracycline, is greater than 60 percent (Hirsch et al. 1999).

In addition to antibiotics, data are now becoming available indicating that a wide range of personal care products and pharmaceuticals (cardiovascular agents, chemotherapeutic agents, lipid regulators, etc.) are present in municipal wastewater effluent and surface waters (Daughton and Ternes 1999; Huggett et al. 2001; Kolpin et al. 2002). The impact of these compounds on aquatic resources is largely unknown, but the physiochemical properties of several compound classes indicate the potential for accumulation in aquatic biota. Humans may be ingesting fishes and shellfish that contain biologically active pharmaceuticals. Although this is only speculation, the topic merits future investigation. Further discussion of pharmaceutical contaminants in the environment is found in the Recommendations section of this chapter, and elsewhere (Daughton and Jones-Lepp 2001; Kummerer 2001).

Constructed wetlands are often used to mitigate pollution associated with nutrient, metal, petrochemical, and pesticide-laden effluents (Hawkins et al. 1997; Huddleson et al. 2000; Hemming et al. 2002). More recent research has found constructed wetlands valuable for tertiary treatment of municipal effluents containing pharmaceutical compounds (Hemming et al. 2001; Huggett and Brooks unpublished data). However, paramount to any treatment wetland or restoration process is an appropriate design based on functional objectives. If designed properly, riparian buffer zones and constructed wetlands provide current and future means to transform a milieu of contaminants often associated with nonpoint- and point-source effluents, as discussed in Chapters 8 and 10.

Interestingly, design flaws are highlighted in a recent study that suggests that beach closures in Huntington Beach, California, were due to waterborne enterococci from biota in restored coastal wetlands (Grant et al. 2001). Wetlands may effectively remove pathogens when flow velocities are slow; however, the residence time of Talbert Marsh, California, was less than one hour and effective treatment was compromised (Grant et al. 2001).

Recommendations

Ideally, scientists would like to predict and prevent future environmental and human health problems. Endocrine disruption, carcinogenesis, and biological toxicants are relatively new research areas that will remain important. Researchers face challenges concerning the aquatic and human interface on numerous fronts, including (1) assessment of nonpoint source watershed contaminants; (2) nontarget pesticide effects (see Hayes et al. 2002); (3) sublethal, long-term exposure to chemical mixtures; and (4) mechanisms for incorporating precautionary action in the risk assessment paradigm (see O'Brien 2000; Riley 2001). As discussed above, pharmaceutical and personal care products are increasingly found in surface waters. Information on the impact of these compounds on aquatic and human health is lacking (Huggett et al. 2002). Further, the magnitude, frequency, and duration of exposure to such compounds is largely unknown (Kolpin et al. 2002).

Presently, water quality and drinking water criteria do not exist for pharmaceuticals and personal care products. Examples of personal care products include synthetic musk compounds, sunscreen, and caffeine (Daughton and Ternes 1999; Snyder et al. 2001). The U.S. Food and Drug Administration (FDA) requires an environmental assessment for pharmaceuticals if predicted environmental introduction concentrations (EIC) exceed 1 part per billion (FDA-CDER 1998). An inadequacy of this approach is evidenced by widespread estrogenicity in municipal and contained-animal feeding-operation effluents. Whereas steroid pharmaceuticals are present in municipal effluents at low part per trillion levels, vitellogenin, an egg yolk precursor protein, is routinely induced in male fishes exposed to such discharges (Harries et al. 1997; Nichols et al. 1999; Hemming et al. 2001). The FDA's approach is also criticized because it does not address interaction effects of compounds with similar or different mechanisms of toxicological action, and it relies on traditional ecotoxicological endpoints such as survival, growth, and reproduction to assess risk (Daughton and Ternes 1999). In addition, a default dilution factor of 10 is applied to EICs to estimate realistic environmental exposure. Although such a procedure is acceptable for many waterbodies, it is not appropriate in regions where municipal effluent discharges do not receive instream dilution. Greater than 90 percent of the Trinity River stream flow below the Dallas-Fort Worth, Texas, metroplex is often reclaimed water from municipal treatment plants (Dickson et al. 1989). Environmental pharmaceutical exposure in these waterbodies may impact water quality and result in a "worse-case scenario" risk to aquatic life. Understanding the sublethal effects of pharmaceutical and personal care product contaminants on aquatic and human health should command intensive study in the near future.

Conclusions

From case histories of Minamata Bay, Love Canal, and the Rhine River, it is evident that humans discharge contaminants into waterbodies and that some of these compounds may eventually find their way back to human populations. In the past, human and ecological health interests had often been set aside for economic gain. Short-term economic benefits may be achieved by anthropocentric decision making, but workers' compensation, litigation, clean-up expenses, and external market costs resulting from adverse effects on human health and ecosystem functions may counterbalance such gains. In addition, these costs do not include economic losses experienced by commercial fishermen when fisheries bans occur. Sustainable practices are decidedly critical to obtaining a balance between environmental and economic costs and benefits.

The linkage between aquatic resources and human health is clearly cyclical. Effects on one component of the cycle may ultimately influence another, positively or negatively. Research interests inevitably experience temporal change when effective networks of researchers, policy-makers, and industry representatives come together to address environmental issues. When events like Love Canal and Minamata Bay heightened public awareness of the relationship between aquatic resources and human health, few could have predicted that endocrine disruptors, biological toxicants, carcinogens, and pharmaceuticals in surface waters would be at the forefront of contemporary environmental research.

Acknowledgements

The authors would like to acknowledge Duane B. Huggett, Ph.D., who originally presented these ideas at the May 2000 Conference on Sustainability of Wetlands and Water Resources. We appreciate his contributions to the preparation of this chapter.

References

American Cancer Society. 2001. *Cancer facts and figures, 2001.* American Cancer Society, New York.

Anderberg, S., and W. M. Stigliani. 1994. An integrated approach for identifying sources of pollution: The example of cadmium pollution in the Rhine River basin. *Water Science and Technology* 29:61–69.

Bailey, G. S., D. E. Williams, and J. D. Hendricks. 1996. Fish models for environmental carcinogenesis: The rainbow trout. *Environmental Health Perspectives* 104 (Supplement 1):5–21.

Baumann, P. C., and J. C. Harshbarger. 1995. Decline in liver neoplasms in wild brown bullhead catfish after coking plant closes and environmental PAHs plummet. *Environmental Health Perspectives* 103:168–170.

———. 1998. Long term trends in liver neoplasm epizootics of brown bullhead in the Black River, Ohio. *Environmental Monitoring and Assessment* 53:213–223.

Baumann, P. C., M. J. Mac, S. B. Smith, and J. C. Harshbarger. 1991. Tumor frequencies in walleye (*Stizostedion vitreum*) and brown bullhead (*Ictalurus nebulosus*) and sediment contaminants in tributaries of the Laurentian Great Lakes. *Canadian Journal of Fisheries and Aquatic Sciences* 48:1804–1810.

Benoist, A. P., and G. H. Broseliske. 1994. Water quality prognosis and cost analysis of pollution abatement measures in the Rhine basin (the River Rhine Project: EVER). *Water Science and Technology* 29:95–106.

Black, J. J., and P. C. Baumann. 1991. Carcinogens and cancers in freshwater fishes. *Environmental Health Perspectives* 90:27–33.

Cals, M. J. R., R. Postma, A. D. Buijse, and E. C. L. Marthun. 1998. Habitat restoration along the Rhine River in The Netherlands: Putting ideas into practice. *Aquatic Conservation: Marine and Freshwater Ecosystems* 8:61–70.

Capel, P. D., W. Giger, P. Reichert, and O. Wanner. 1988. Accidental input of pesticides into the Rhine River. *Environmental Science and Technology* 22:992–997.

Colburn, T., D. Dumanoski, and J. P. Myers. 1996. *Our stolen future.* New York: Penguin Books.

Daughton, C. G., and T. L. Jones-Lepp. 2001. Pharmaceutical and personal care products in the environment: Scientific and regulatory issues. *ACS Symposium Series 791,* American Chemical Society, Washington, D.C.

Daughton, C. G., and T. A. Ternes. 1999. Pharmaceuticals and personal care products in the environment: Agents of subtle change? *Environmental Health Perspectives* 107 (Supplement 6):907–938.

de Jong, J. 1990. Management of the river Rhine. *Water and Environmental Technology* 2:44–51.

Desbrow, C., E. J. Routledge, G. C. Brighty, J. P. Sumpter, and M. Waldock. 1998. Identification of estrogenic chemicals in STW effluent. 1. Chemical fractionation and in vitro biological screening. *Environmental Science and Technology* 32:1549–1558.

Dickhut, R. M., E. A. Canuel, K. E. Gustafson, K. Liu, K. M. Arzayus, S. E. Walker, G. Edgecombe, M. O. Gaylor, and E. H. MacDonald. 2000. Automotive sources of carcinogenic polycyclic aromatic hydrocarbons associated with particulate matter in the Chesapeake Bay region. *Environmental Science and Technology* 34:4635–4640.

Dickson, K. L., W. T. Waller, J. H. Kennedy, W. R. Arnold, W. P. Desmond, S. D. Dyer, J. F. Hall, J. T. Knight Jr., D. Malas, M. L. Martinez, and S. L. Matzner. 1989. *A water quality and ecological survey of the Trinity River.* Vols. 1 and 2. City of Dallas, Texas: Dallas Water Utilities.

Dorfman, M. 2001. *Testing the waters 2001: A guide to water quality at vacation beaches.* New York: Natural Resources Defense Council.

El-Nabawi, A., M. Quesenberry, K. Saito, E. Silbergeld, G. Vasta, and A. Eldefrawi. 2000. The N-methyl-D-aspartate neurotransmitter receptor is a mammalian brain target from the dinoflagellate *Pfiesteria piscicida* toxin. *Toxicology and Applied Pharmacology* 169:84–93.

EHIS (Environmental Health Information Service). 2000. *Ninth report on carcinogens.* U.S. Department of Health and Human Services, Public Health Service, National Toxicology Program. ehis.niehs.nih.gov/roc/toc9.html. Accessed 12/15/02.

Expert Panel on Mercury Atmospheric Processes. 1994. *Mercury atmospheric processes: A synthesis report.* Electric Power Research Institute Report No. TR-104214. Electric Power Research Institute, Palo Alto, California.

FDA-CDER. 1998. Guidance for industry—environmental assessment of human drugs and biologics applications, Rev. 1. FDA Center for Drug Evaluation and Research, Rockville, Maryland. www.fda.gov/cder/guidance/1730fnl.pdf. Accessed 3/15/02.

Gallo, M. A. 1996. History and scope of toxicology. Pp. 3–10 in *Casarett and Doull's toxicology: The basic science of poisons,* 5th ed., edited by C. D. Klaassen. New York: McGraw-Hill.

Grant, S. B., B. F. Sanders, A. B. Boehm, J. A. Redman, J. H. Kim, R. D. Mre, A. K. Chu, M. Gouldin, C. D. McGee, N. A. Gardiner, B. H. Jones, J. Svejkovsky, G. V. Leipzig, and A. Brown. 2001. Generation of enterococci bacteria in a coastal saltwater marsh and its impact on surf zone water quality. *Environmental Science and Technology* 35:2407–2416.

Guillette, L. J., T. S. Gross, G. R. Mason, J. M. Matter, H. F. Percival, and A. R. Woodward. 1994. Developmental abnormalities of the gonad and abnormal sex hormone concentrations in juvenile alligators from contaminated and control lakes in Florida. *Environmental Health Perspectives* 102:680–688.

Guyon, R., F. Dorey, J. Collobert, J. Foret, C. Goubert, V. Mariau, and J. Malas. 2000. Detection of Shiga toxin-producing *Escherichia coli* O157 in shellfish (*Crassostrea gigas*). *Sciences des Aliments* 20:457–466.

Halfon, E., and R. Bruggemann. 1989. Environmental hazard of eight chemicals present in the Rhine River. *Water Science and Technology* 21:815–820.

Harada, M. 1995. Minamata disease: Methylmercury poisoning in Japan caused by environmental pollution. *Critical Review in Toxicology* 25:1–24.

Harries, J., D. Sheahan, S. Jobling, P. Matthiessen, P. Neall, J. Sumpter, T. Tylor, and N. Zaman. 1997. Estrogenic activity in five United Kingdom rivers detected by measurement of vitellogenesis in caged male trout. *Environmental Toxicology and Chemistry* 16:534–542.

Hartmann, A., A. C. Alder, T. Koller, and R. M. Widmer. 1998. Identification of fluoroquinolone antibiotics as the main source of umuC genotoxicity in native hospital wastewater. *Environmental Toxicology and Chemistry* 17:377–382.

Hawkins, W. B., J. H. Rodgers, W. B. Gillespie, A. W. Dunn, P. B. Dorn, and M. L. Cano. 1997. Design and construction of wetlands for aqueous transfers and transformations of selected metals. *Ecotoxicology and Environmental Safety* 36:238–248.

Hayes, T. B., A. Collins, M. Lee, M. Mendoza, N. Noriega, A. A. Stuart, and A. Vonk. 2002. Hermaphroditic, demasculinized frogs after exposure to the herbicide atrazine at low ecologically relevant doses. *Proceedings of the National Academy of Sciences* 99:5476–5480.

Hemming, J. M., P. K. Turner, B. W. Brooks, W. T. Waller, and T. W. La Point. 2002. Assessment of toxicity reduction in wastewater effluent flowing through a treatment wetland using *Pimephales promelas, Ceriodapnia dubia*, and *Vibrio fischeri*. *Archives of Environmental Contamination and Toxicology* 42:9–16.

Hemming, J. M., W. T. Waller, M. C. Chow, N. D. Denslow, and B. Venables. 2001. Assessment of the estrogenicity and toxicity of a domestic wastewater effluent flowing through a constructed wetland system using biomarkers in male fathead minnow (*Pimephales promelas* Rafinesque, 1820). *Environmental Toxicology and Chemistry* 20:2268–2275.

Hirsch, R., T. Ternes, K. Haberer, and K.-L. Katz. 1999. Occurrence of antibiotics in the aquatic environment. *The Science of the Total Environment* 225 (1,2):109–118.

Huddleson, G. M., W. B. Gillespie, and J. H. Rodgers. 2000. Using constructed wetlands to treat biochemical oxygen demand and ammonia associated with a refinery effluent. *Ecotoxicology and Environmental Safety* 45:188–193.

Hudnell, H. K., D. House, J. Schmid, D. Koltai, W. Stopford, J. Wilkins, D. A. Savitz, M. Swinker, and S. Music. 2001. Human visual function in the North Carolina clinical study on possible estuary-associated syndrome. *Journal of Toxicology and Environmental Health*, Part A 62:575–594.

Huggett, D. B., B. W. Brooks, B. Peterson, C. M. Foran, and D. Schlenk. 2002. Toxicity of select beta-adrenergic receptor blocking pharmaceuticals (beta-blockers) on aquatic organisms. *Archives of Environmental Contamination and Toxicology* 42:229–235.

Huggett, D. B., J. A. Steevens, J. C. Allgood, C. B. Lutken, C. A. Grace, and W. H. Benson. 2001. Mercury in sediment and fish from north Mississippi lakes. *Chemosphere* 8:923–929.

ICPR (International Commission for the Protection of the Rhine). 2002. www.iksr.org/icpr. Accessed 12/15/02.

Kolpin, D. W., E. T. Furlong, M. T. Meyer, E. M. Thurman, S. D. Zaugg, L. B. Barber, and H. T. Buxton. 2002. Pharmaceuticals, hormones, and other organic wastewater contaminants in U.S. streams, 1999–2000: A national reconnaissance. *Environmental Science and Technology* 36:1202–1211.

Kummerer, K. 2001. *Pharmaceuticals in the environment: Sources, fate, effects, and risks.* Berlin: Springer-Verlag.

Levin, E. D., D. E. Schmechel, J. M. Burkholder, H. B. Glasgow, N. J . Deamer-Melia, V. C. Moser, and G. J. Harry. 1997. Persisting learning deficits in rats after exposure to *Pfiesteria piscicida. Environmental Health Perspectives* 105:1320–1325.

Levine, A. G. 1982. *Love Canal: Science, politics, and people.* Lexington, Mass.: Lexington Books.

Malins, D. C., M. M. Krahn, M. S. Myers, L. D. Rhodes, D. W. Brown, C. A. Krone, B. B. McCain, and S. L. Chan. 1985. Toxic chemicals in sediments and biota from a creosote-polluted harbor: Relationships with hepatic neoplasms and other hepatic lesions in English sole (*Parophrys vetulus*). *Carcinogenesis* 6:1463–1469.

Malle, K. 1996. Cleaning up the river Rhine. *Scientific American* 274:70–75.

Mallin, M. A., J. M. Burkholder, L. B. Cahoon, and M. H. Posey. 2000. North and South Carolina coasts. *Marine Pollution Bulletin* 41:56–75.

Mazur, A. 1998. *A hazardous inquiry: The Rashomon Effect at Love Canal.* Cambridge, Mass.: Harvard University Press.

Miyagi, K., K. Omura, A. Ogawa, M. Hanafusa, Y. Nakanao, S. Morimatsu, and K. Sano. 2001. Survival of Shiga toxin-producing *Escherichia coli* O157 in marine water and frequent detection of the Shiga toxin gene in marine water samples from an estuary port. *Epidemiology and Infections* 126:129–133.

Nichols, K., E. Snyder, S. Miles-Richardson, S. Pierens, S. Snyder, and J. P. Giesy. 1999. Effects of municipal wastewater exposure in situ on the reproductive physiology of the fathead minnow (*Pimephales promelas*). *Environmental Toxicology and Chemistry* 18:2001–2012.

NRC (National Research Council). 2000. *Toxicological effects of methylmercury.* Washington, D.C.: National Academy Press.

O'Brien, M. 2000. *Making better environmental decisions: An alternative to risk assessment.* Cambridge, Mass.: MIT Press.

Palanza, P., F. Morellini, S. Parmigiana, and F. S. vom Saal. 1999. Prenatal exposure to endocrine disrupting chemicals: Effects on behavioral development. *Neuroscience and Biobehavior Reviews* 23:1011–1027.

Pinkney, A. E., J. C. Harshbarger, E. B. May, and M. J. Melancon. 2000. Tumor prevalence and biomarkers of exposure and response in brown bullheads (*Ameiurus nebulosus*) from the tidal Potomac River watershed. CBFO-C99-04. U.S. Fish and Wildlife Service. Annapolis, Maryland.

Rabalais, N. N., R. E. Turner, and W. J. Wiseman. 2001. Hypoxia in the Gulf of Mexico. *Journal of Environmental Quality* 30:320–328.

Riley, T. 2001. Redressing the silent interim: Precautionary action and short-term tests in toxicological risk assessment. *Risk: Health, Safety, and Environment* 12:281–297.

Rogers, J. M., and R. J. Kavlock. 1996. Developmental toxicity. Pp. 301–331 in *Casarett and Doull's toxicology: The basic science of poisons*. 5th ed. Edited by C. D. Klaassen. New York: McGraw-Hill.

Rolland, R., M. Gilbertson, and T. Colborn. 1995. Environmentally induced alterations in development: A focus on wildlife. *Environmental Health Perspectives* 103 (Supplement):4.

Rolland, R., M. Gilbertson, and R. E. Peterson. 1997. *Chemically induced alterations in functional development and reproduction of fishes: Proceedings from a session at the Wingspread Conference Center, Jul. 21–23 1995, Racine, Wisconsin*. Pensacola, Fla.: Society of Environmental Toxicology and Chemistry (SETAC) Press.

Schettler, T., G. Soloman, M. Valenti, and A. Huddle. 1999. *Generations at risk*. Cambridge, Mass.: MIT Press.

Snyder, S. A., K. L. Kelly, A. H. Grange, G. W. Sovocool, E. M. Snyder, and J. P. Giesy. 2001. Pharmaceuticals and personal care products in the waters of Lake Mead, Nevada. Pp. 116–139 in *Pharmaceutical and personal care products in the environment: Scientific and regulatory issues*, edited by C. G. Daughton and T. L. Jones-Lepp. ACS Symposium Series 791, American Chemical Society, Washington, D.C.

St. Louis, V., J. Rudd, C. Kelly, and K. Beaty. 1994. Importance of wetlands as sources of methylmercury to boreal forest ecosystems. *Canadian Journal of Fisheries and Aquatic Sciences* 51:1065–1071.

St. Louis, V., J. Rudd, C. Kelly, K. Beaty, R. Flett, and N. Roulet. 1996. Production and loss of methylmercury and loss of total mercury from boreal forest catchments containing different types of wetlands. *Environmental Science and Technology* 30:2719–2730.

Stalker, M. J., G. M. Kirby, T. E. Kocal, I. R. Smith, and M. A. Hayes. 1991. Loss of glutathione S-transferases in pollution-associated liver neoplasms in white suckers (*Catostomus commersoni*) from Lake Ontario. *Carcinogenesis* 12:2221–2226.

Stigliani, W. M., P. R. Jaffe, and S. Anderberg. 1993. Heavy metal pollution in the Rhine basin. *Environmental Science and Technology* 27:786–793.

Stoecker, D. K., K. Stevens, and D. E. Gustafson Jr. 2000. Grazing on *Pfiesteria piscicida* by microzooplankton. *Aquatic Microbial Ecology* 22:261–270.

Ternes, T. A., P. Kreckel, and J. Mueller. 1999a. Behavior and occurrence of estrogens in municipal sewage treatment plants- 2. Aerobic batch experiments with activated sludge. *The Science of the Total Environment* 225:91–99.

Ternes, T. A., M. Sumpf, J. Mueller, K. Haberer, R.-D. Wilken, and M. Servos. 1999b. Behavior and occurrence of estrogens in municipal sewage treatment plants- 1. Investigations in Germany, Canada, and Brazil. *The Science of the Total Environment* 225: 91–99.

Ui, J. 1992. *Industrial pollution in Japan*. Tokyo: United Nations University Press.

U.S. EPA (United States Environmental Protection Agency). 1999a. *Action plan for beaches and recreational waters.* EPA 600-R-98-079. Office of Research and Development, Office of Water, Washington, D.C.

U.S. EPA (United States Environmental Protection Agency). 1999b. *Review of potential modeling tools and approaches to support the BEACH program.* EPA 823-R-99-002. Office of Science and Technology, Washington, D.C.

Van Dijk, G. M., E. C. L. Marteihn, and A. Schulte-Wulwer-Leidig. 1995. Ecological rehabilitation of the river Rhine: Plans, progress, and perspectives. *Regulated Rivers: Research and Management* 11:377–388.

van Metre, P. C., B. J. Mahler, and E. T. Furlong. 2000. Urban sprawl leaves its PAH signature. *Environmental Science and Technology* 34:4064–4070.

Vogelbein, W. K., J. W. Fournie, P. A. Van Veld, and R. J. Huggett. 1990. Hepatic neoplasms in the mummichog *Fundulus heteroclitus* from a creosote-contaminated site. *Cancer Research* 50:5978–5986.

Weis, J., and P. Weis. 1989. Tolerance and stress in a polluted environment. *Bioscience* 39:89–95.

Wieriks, K., and A. Schulte-Wulwer-Leidig. 1997. Integrated water management for the Rhine River basin, from pollution prevention to ecosystem improvement. *Natural Resources Forum* 21:147–156.

Wildavsky, A. 1995. *But is it true? A citizen's guide to environmental health and safety issues.* Cambridge, Mass.: Harvard University Press.

Williams, R. J., and D. L. Heymann. 1998. Containment of antibiotic resistance. *Science* 279:1153–1154.

Witte, W. 1998. Medical consequences of antibiotic use in agriculture. *Science* 279:996–997.

Zillioux, E., D. Porcella, and J. Benoit. 1993. Mercury cycling and effects in freshwater wetland ecosystems. *Environmental Toxicology and Chemistry* 12:2245–2264.

Chapter 4

Interacting Effects of Altered Hydrology and Contaminant Transport: Emerging Ecological Patterns of Global Concern

Catherine M. Pringle

We can no longer ignore the interactive and cumulative effects of hydrologic change and contaminant transport, which threaten the sustainability of freshwater ecosystems. The negative interaction between hydrologic change and pollution is not well understood by scientists, managers, or the general public. Yet hydrologic alterations, such as dams and water diversions, are interacting with nutrient runoff and toxic releases on landscape scales—threatening the ecological integrity of ecosystems and resulting in emerging patterns in wildlife of global concern. Ecological integrity is defined as an ecosystem's undiminished ability to continue its natural path of evolution, its normal transition over time, and its successional recovery from perturbations (Westra et al. 2000). In some instances, ecological effects are obvious, as in rivers where so much water is extracted for human use that there is insufficient water to dilute pollutants, which become harmful to wildlife and humans alike. In other instances, cumulative and interacting effects of hydrologic change and pollution are more complex, such as when irrigation and the creation of dams and reservoirs result in changes in biogeochemical cycling of both natural elements and synthetic compounds leading to toxic effects in wildlife.

Humans have appropriated one-half of the accessible global freshwater runoff—usage that could climb to 70 percent by the year 2025 (Postel et al. 1996). Four out of every ten persons currently live in river basins that are experiencing water scarcity, and by 2025, at least 50 percent of the world's population will face water scarcity. In addition, twenty-nine of the world's river basins, with a projected population of 10 million each by 2025, will experience further scarcity (WRI 2000). Correspondingly, freshwater habitats and native biota have faced regional and global declines. Negative ecological trends include fragmentation of river channels (e.g., Benke 1990; Dynesius and Nilsson 1994; Arthington and Welcomme 1995; Pringle et al. 2000; Rosenberg et al. 2000); deterioration of lower watersheds, deltas, and receiving coastal waters (e.g., McCully 1996; Hinrichsen 1998); deterioration and loss of riverine floodplains, connecting wetlands, and riparian ecosystems (e.g., DeCamps et al. 1988; Welcomme 1995; Sparks et al. 1998); deterioration of irrigated lands and connecting surface waters (e.g., Zaletaev 1997; Postel 1999; Lemly et al. 2000); and isolation of upper watersheds (e.g., Pringle 1997). As a result of such extensive habitat destruction, animal populations have declined or have been lost entirely. A recent comprehensive assessment of the world's freshwater ecosystems issued by the World Resources Institute (WRI 2000) states that more than 20 percent of the world's freshwater fish species have become extinct or have been designated as threatened or endangered in recent decades. The loss of functional hydrologic landscapes has effects well beyond the boundaries of aquatic ecosystems themselves, affecting everything from migratory waterfowl to terrestrial mammals.

It is ironic that, just as we begin to understand direct human effects on local scales, freshwater ecosystems are affected increasingly by *cumulative* local effects operating via broad feedback loops on regional and global scales (e.g., Young et al. 1994; Chao 1995; Rosenberg et al. 1997; Vorosmarty et al. 1997a,b; Lundqvist 1998; Postel 1999; Pringle and Triska 1999; Naqvi et al. 2000; Rosenberg et al. 2000; Vorosmarty and Sahagian 2000; Driscoll et al. 2001). We are now just becoming aware that the magnitude and extent of hydrologic change and pollutant loading are resulting in emergent patterns in wildlife which are of global concern. In many instances, the causes behind such patterns are extremely complex and our understanding is often confounded by time lags. In some cases, technological advances have been necessary before we could even measure minute concentrations of harmful substances transported in water and accumulated in biota. This is particularly true with respect to assessing effects of low levels of endocrine-disrupting chemicals that have nonlinear effects and are adversely affecting wildlife throughout the world (e.g., Colburn et al. 1998; NRC 1999; Colburn and Thayer 2000; Vos et al. 2000).

In this chapter, I focus on three emerging patterns in the loss of ecological integrity of aquatic ecosystems: (1) regional declines in migratory waterfowl and other wildlife resulting from contaminated irrigation drainage and the loss of natural wetlands; (2) fish and wildlife response to methylmercury (MeHg) in newly created reservoirs; and (3) deterioration of estuarine and coastal ecosystems that receive the discharge (and nutrient loading) of highly regulated (e.g., dammed and channelized) rivers. Scientific, technical, and societal solutions are necessary to address these problems in order to achieve sustainability of both freshwater and terrestrial ecosystems.

Effects of Contaminated Irrigation Drainage and Wetlands Loss on Wildlife

The area of irrigated land in the world (estimated at 274 million hectares at the end of the twentieth century) is expanding. The resultant drainage of wetlands and rivers has made migratory waterfowl and other wildlife even more dependent on remaining surface water supplies. This is particularly true in arid regions that have been intensively developed for agricultural production (through irrigation) and where only a small portion of historic wetlands remain. Increasingly, these remaining wetlands are contaminated with subsurface irrigation drainage (Lemly et al. 1993; Lemly 1994; Presser 1994; Presser et al. 1994), pesticides (e.g., Forsyth 1995; Donald et al. 1999), or both, creating *population sinks* (areas that may appear to benefit wildlife, but in reality do not) (Pulliam 1988) for wildlife.

Subsurface irrigation drainage emerged as a major threat to wetlands and wildlife in the western United States in the early 1980s. Before 1980, regulation of irrigation return flow from agricultural projects focused mainly on management of salts, nutrients, and pesticide residues (Seiler et al. 1999). This changed when mortality (and in some cases deformities) of migratory waterfowl and fishes was linked to application of irrigation water to soils naturally rich in elements such as selenium (Ohlendorf et al. 1986). Later studies indicated that selenium was not the only culprit. Environmental problems also were associated with irrigation-related arsenic and boron and atypical ratios of calcium, chloride, magnesium, sodium, and sulfate (Camardese et al. 1990; Whitworth et al. 1991; Hoffman et al. 1992; Saiki et al. 1992). Elements such as selenium, arsenic, and boron become mobilized in saturated soils and eventually enter the food chain (Presser and Ohlendorf 1987), causing toxic effects in wildlife. Although agricultural reductions in natural water supplies have caused the demise of wetlands for centuries, more recent threats are just now being identified (Lemly et al. 2000), such as the complexity of interactions between pesticides and naturally occurring trace metals, both of which reach abnormally high levels in irrigation drainage. The Kesterson National Wildlife Refuge disaster is a highly publicized example of the problems associated with irrigation drainage (Presser 1994).

Located in California's San Joaquin Valley, the Kesterson Refuge was created at the terminus of an artificial drainage system originally intended to divert subsurface agricultural drainage to San Francisco Bay. Five years of progressively higher proportions of drainage water entering the artificial ponds resulted in extremely high levels of selenium and the subsequent embryonic deformities and death in birds. Snakes and frogs also were found to contain significantly higher selenium concentrations than those from reference sites. Concentrations were sufficiently high to warrant concern about potential adverse effects in these animals and their predators (Ohlendorf et al. 1988). In the mid-1980s, 15,000 adult birds died each year at Kesterson, which ultimately led to its removal from the national refuge system and its classification as a toxic waste dump in 1987. The Kesterson area has since been drained and partly buried and it is now managed as a contaminated landfill (Presser 1994).

The Kesterson disaster raised questions about the extent of irrigation drainage contamination in other areas. A federal multi-agency program, established by the Department of the Interior and headed by the U.S. Geological Survey, investigated irrigation-related drainage water problems throughout the western United States, with emphasis on areas receiving water from large-scale federal irrigation projects (Hoffman 1994). Twenty areas in thirteen states, including twenty national wildlife refuges, were screened for contaminants. Eleven sites in the western United States were contaminated with selenium at concentrations exceeding toxicity thresholds for fish and wildlife (Presser et al. 1993). Two examples from these sites are discussed below: the Salton Sea (located in southern California's Imperial Valley) and the Stillwater National Wildlife Refuge (in western Nevada).

Like the Kesterson Reservoir—the Salton Sea is an artificial water body, in this case created by accident, when engineers attempted to open a new intake from the Colorado River to the Imperial Valley. The Colorado River broke through a dike, changed its course, and filled the ancient Cauhilla Basin, now known as the Salton Sea. Following intensive farming in the 1920s, *maquiladora* factories and inadequate sewage systems served as the source for the New River, which was considered the most polluted river in the United States by the 1990s. Ironically, the Salton Sea is now the largest body of water in the state of California. It is also one of the most polluted, with consequent deleterious effects on wildlife. Because 95 percent of interior wetlands in California have been lost (primarily to irrigated agriculture), over 60 percent of the Pacific migratory flyway waterfowl population are channeled into available wetlands (Frayer et al. 1989) such as the Sonny Bono Salton Sea National Wildlife Refuge, one of the few wetlands in southern California. The Salton Sea lures more than 380 species of migratory birds to its contaminated habitats. Irrigation drainage from massive farming operations in the Imperial Valley results in an influx of pesticides, fertilizers, and salts into the Salton Sea, contributing to wildlife mortality and disease. With no outlet and a high evaporation rate, incoming contaminants are effectively trapped and accumulated. During the past decade, bird and fish die-offs were fueled by increased salinity, phosphate, and nitrate inputs from the New River. As just one example, over 14,000 birds (representing sixty-six species) perished in 1997 as a result of an outbreak of avian botulism—including over 1,400 endangered brown pelicans. Bird mortality is so high that the U.S. Fish and Wildlife Service operates an incinerator to dispose of dead birds. The National Audubon Society uses the Salton Sea

National Wildlife Refuge as one of ten examples that illustrate the state of crisis of wildlife refuges in the United States. A journalist makes the observation at the confluence of the New River and Salton Sea: "The stench of rotting fish grew overwhelming. Thousands of dead tilapia, the Salton Sea's most ubiquitous fish, lay in rows under a skim of mud in the shallows and all across the mudflats" (Graham 1998).

As another example, the Stillwater National Wildlife Refuge in Nevada is a Western Hemisphere Shorebird Reserve because of its importance to migratory shorebirds and waterfowl. These wetlands also are critical to Pacific Flyway waterfowl and support breeding populations of shorebirds, ducks, grebes, and colonial nesting birds. This desert marsh is located at the terminus of the Carson River, which is extensively tapped for agricultural uses prior to entering the refuge. Like the Salton Sea, Stillwater is an aquatic system with no outflow and is therefore particularly susceptible to water withdrawal and quality degradation from irrigation return flow. These factors contributed to the massive mortality of fishes (approximately 7 million) and birds (approximately 1,500) near the mouth of the Carson River in late 1986 and early 1987 (Rowe and Hoffman 1987). Toxicity of drain water varied with location. Some samples caused no effects, while others caused high mortality even after almost 90 percent dilution (Finger et al. 1989). Field and laboratory studies at the refuge revealed what is now acknowledged as a classic pattern of toxicity associated with irrigation drainage: raw drain water is a complex effluent whose chemical profile and toxic potential vary spatially and temporally within a given irrigation area (Lemly et al. 1993).

The wetland ecosystem (70,000 hectares) that once existed in the Carson Desert of western Nevada has been reduced by 84 percent and the remaining marshland (e.g., Stillwater National Wildlife Refuge) receives water that contains up to 100 times the historic concentrations of dissolved solids, including toxic trace elements (Hoffman et al. 1990). Effects on wildlife include reduced fish and bird populations; extirpation of the Lahontan cutthroat trout (*Oncorhynchus clarki henshawi*, a federally listed endangered species); loss of largemouth bass (*Micropterus salmoides*, an introduced species that once supported a recreational fishery); precipitous declines in the American curlew (*Numenius americanus*); and extirpation of river otter (*Lutra canadensis*) and mink (*Mustela vison*). Only remnant populations of muskrats (*Ondatra zibethicus*), freshwater clams and aquatic snails remain. Pollution-tolerant fishes such as common carp (*Cyprinus carpio*) and mosquito fish (*Gambusia affinis*) are still present in the wetlands (Hallock and Hallock 1993; Lemly et al. 2000). The number of nesting birds and the percentage of successfully fledged waterfowl and shorebirds have declined steadily; only about 25 percent of nests succeed in producing even one chick and the birds that fledge contain elevated concentrations of mercury and selenium (Lemly et al. 2000). There are also human health concerns, since tissue residues of selenium in waterfowl are four times the safe level for human consumption (Hallock and Hallock 1993).

Wildlife refuges represent just a small portion of historical wetlands in arid regions and are especially valuable as wintering grounds for migratory waterfowl and shorebirds (along both the Pacific and Central Flyways) and as refuges for resident wildlife populations. Consequently, there is a danger that the cumulative and long-term effects of trace metal bioaccumulation in fishes and migratory waterfowl could result in regional losses in biodiversity. In a recent review, Lemly et al. (2000) concluded that major wetlands in the world (including those of California and Nevada in North America, the Macquarie Marshes in Australia, and the Aral Sea in Central Asia) have lost most of their historic supplies of water, have become contaminated with pesticides and irrigation drainage, and are now "mere shadows of what they once were in terms of biodiversity and wildlife production." The authors go on to conclude that "many of the so-called *wetlands of international importance* are no longer the key conservation strongholds that they were in the past" and "that a ripple effect has impacted migratory birds worldwide."

In summary, reduced freshwater inflows, pesticides, and contaminated subsurface irrigation drainage have compromised the ecological integrity of wetlands throughout many arid regions of the world. Resultant impacts on fish and wildlife are severe, particularly given that many of these wetlands comprise only a small portion of historic wetlands and are important to wildlife on regional scales (e.g., as stopovers for migratory waterfowl). Similar problems also can be expected to occur in wetter regions of the world as water demands and pollutant inputs increase. The role of irrigated agriculture, as a landscape impact on hydrogeochemistry and wildlife, merits much future investigation given that nutrient and pesticide applications continue to increase, as do hydrologic modifications via irrigation. As illustrated by this discussion, most detailed studies of the effects of contaminated irrigation drainage on wildlife were conducted in the western United States, and the problem probably received the attention it did because of the deterioration of wildlife on federally managed public lands (see Pringle 2000). Substantial regional effects of subsurface drainage on wildlife in other regions of the world seem quite likely (Lemly 1994).

Seeking Solutions to the Effects of Contaminated Irrigation Drainage and Wetlands Loss on Wildlife

A scientifically based screening method has been developed recently to identify areas vulnerable to contamination from irrigation drainage in the western United States and it may serve as an effective model for development of similar tools for other regions of the world. This screening method predicts the susceptibility of irrigated lands to contamination from irrigation drainage (Seiler 1995; Seiler et al. 1999) and is based on geologic and climatic features that are characteristic of already-known selenium problem areas (Fig. 4.1).

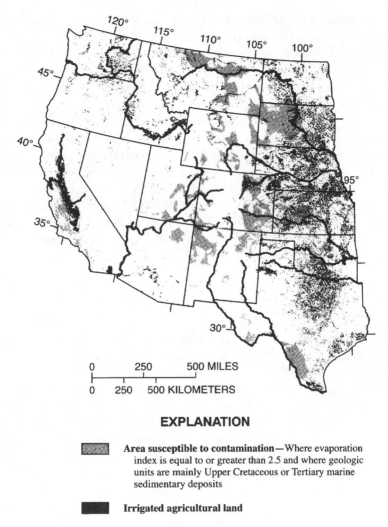

EXPLANATION

Area susceptible to contamination—Where evaporation index is equal to or greater than 2.5 and where geologic units are mainly Upper Cretaceous or Tertiary marine sedimentary deposits

Irrigated agricultural land

Figure 4.1. Spatial relationship between irrigated areas and areas susceptible to irrigation-induced selenium contamination in the western United States (modified from Seiler et al. 1999)

Contamination risks in broad geographic regions of the western United States can now be evaluated without the need to gather new information (Seiler et al. 1999). Screening methods developed for other regions of the world may help to avoid harmful agricultural development practices in vulnerable areas. The potential of this predictive tool aside, however, we need to move beyond predicting where environmental problems with irrigation drainage might occur.

As a society, we need to proactively reevaluate fundamentally unsustainable agricultural practices. Even in the western United States, where the issue of contaminated irrigation drainage has received much attention, there is no coordinated effort to address the problem (Postel 1999). For example, while the cessation of flow of contaminated irrigation drainage to Kesterson Reservoir was achieved in 1985 by a federal order, the consequence of this was the creation of numerous toxic evaporation ponds throughout the San Joaquin Valley. Selenium-laced ponds in the southern part of the valley represent part of the only breeding habitat available for migratory waterfowl (Postel 1999). A joint federal-state management plan was issued in 1990, which identified the need to construct clean waterfowl habitats (to mitigate effects of toxic evaporation ponds) and to retire 30,000 hectares of toxic and degraded valley farmland over the next fifty years. However, as pointed out by Postel (1999), "mitigation merely buys time and does not address the fundamental unsustainability of current agricultural practices."

Reservoirs and the Toxic Effects of Methylmercury

All water bodies in the northern hemisphere are contaminated with mercury as a result of long-range transport and deposition from anthropogenic sources (Wiener and Spry 1994). Mercury also occurs naturally in the landscape in rocks and soils (U.S. EPA 1999). Inorganic mercury derived from anthropogenic sources is transported in the atmosphere and deposited in freshwater ecosystems via wet and dry deposition. Solid waste incineration and fossil-fuel combustion account for about 87 percent of the emissions of mercury in the United States. It is estimated that over 90 percent of the inorganic mercury derived from anthropogenic sources and released to the atmosphere in the last one hundred years is bound up in the terrestrial environment (Nater and Grigal 1992; Mason et al. 1994) where it is released slowly to streams and rivers.

Hydrological alterations can affect the biogeochemical cycling of mercury, resulting in mobilization. The creation of new reservoirs and wetland disturbance serve to increase the mobility of organic matter, contributing to the mobilization of both natural and anthropogenic sources of mercury that become available to fishes (U.S. EPA 1999). Conditions often exist in reservoirs that stimulate the transformation of inorganic mercury into toxic methylmercury (MeHg). Where oxygen is absent and sulfate is present (e.g., the hypolimnion of many stratified reservoirs), sulfate-reducing bacteria take up inorganic mercury and transform it into MeHg. Similar to the trace elements (e.g., selenium) discussed previously, MeHg in water is absorbed readily into living tissue via bioaccumulation much faster than it is released, resulting in the buildup of concentrations in large fishes to levels millions of times higher than the surrounding water.

MeHg effects were first reported from South Carolina (Abernathy and

Cumbie 1977). Elevated levels were reported subsequently in many northern reservoirs of Canada (Waite et al. 1980; Bodaly et al. 1984; Boucher et al. 1985) and Finland (e.g., Lodenius et al. 1983). More recently, mercury contamination was documented in temperate zones throughout the United States, where it has now become a national concern (U.S. EPA 1999).

The spatial and temporal extent of mercury contamination associated with a given reservoir depends on many factors. The amount of MeHg in fish is related initially to the degree of flooding of terrestrial areas (Bodaly et al. 1984; Johnston et al. 1991), and the presence of organic materials stimulates MeHg bioaccumulation by fishes (e.g., Hecky et al. 1991). Greatly enhanced rates of conversion of inorganic mercury to MeHg occurred in newly flooded sediments of reservoirs compared with natural lake sediments (Hecky et al. 1991). Natural boreal wetlands are also sites of MeHg production, and flooding of such wetlands to form reservoirs can result in very high MeHg production from flooded vegetation and peat (Kelly et al. 1997). Other environmental factors affecting mercury levels in fish tissue include regional and climatic trends; type of water body; trophic structure of water body; volume and depth; and pH, calcium, and nutrient levels (U.S. EPA 1999).

Elevated MeHg occurs in fish downstream of reservoirs because of the transport of MeHg in water and invertebrates (e.g., Johnston et al. 1991; Bodaly et al. 1997) and downstream piscivorous fish feed on fish that are injured passing through turbines (Brouard et al. 1994). A recent study (Schetagne et al. 2000) indicated that the dissolved fraction and suspended particulate matter were the major components by which MeHg is transferred downstream of reservoirs. Further, it showed that zooplankton were the major component by which MeHg was transferred directly to nonpiscivorous fish downstream. Mercury levels in predatory fishes can remain elevated for decades after reservoir creation. For example, fish mercury levels in reservoirs of northern Manitoba remained elevated for ten to twenty years following impoundment (Strange et al. 1991; Bodaly et al. 1997).

Since fish consumption dominates the pathway for human exposure to mercury (e.g., Fitzgerald and Clarkson 1991; Clarkson 1992), studies have focused primarily on the bioaccumulation of mercury in fishes and humans who eat fishes (e.g., Wiener and Spry 1994). Studied *categories* of fish-eating humans include both recreational and subsistence-level fisherpeople who routinely consume large amounts of locally caught fishes, and subsistence hunters who regularly consume fishes and the tissues of fish-eating marine mammals. MeHg can affect the immune system, brain, liver, and kidney of animals and humans. It also can have adverse effects on egg and fetus development in exposed mothers (U.S. EPA 1999).

The magnitude of the problem is indicated by the number of fish consumption advisories that inform the public when mercury concentrations in local fish are at levels of public health concern (Fig. 4.2). As of July 1999, forty states in the United States had issued 1,931 fish advisories for mercury. With the exception of North Carolina, the ten states that have statewide advisories for mercury in fresh waters are located in the Midwest and East (i.e., Connecticut, Indiana, Maine, Massachusetts, Michigan, New Hampshire, New Jersey, North Carolina, Ohio, and Vermont). However, fish advisories also can be numerous in other regions of the United States, including three southeastern states (e.g., Florida [97], Georgia [80], South Carolina [24]); one state in the southwest (New Mexico [26]) and one northwest state ([Montana [22]). In addition, five states have statewide advisories for mercury in their coastal waters (Alabama, Florida, Louisiana, Massachusetts, and Texas). States with no advisories primarily occur in the central United States (i.e., Utah, Wyoming, South Dakota, Kansas, Iowa, and Missouri; Fig. 4.2). Since pregnant women, nursing mothers, and young children are extremely sensitive to methylmercury, some states have issued *no consumption* advisories or *restricted consumption* advisories.

Although fish-consumption advisories (and advice about reducing fish-consumption risks, for instance through food preparation; see U.S. EPA 2001) may help limit the consumption of harmful levels of MeHg in human populations, wildlife obviously does not benefit from such advisories. Relatively few studies have examined mercury bioaccumulation—resulting from reservoir creation—in organisms outside of fishes and humans. However, organisms exposed to

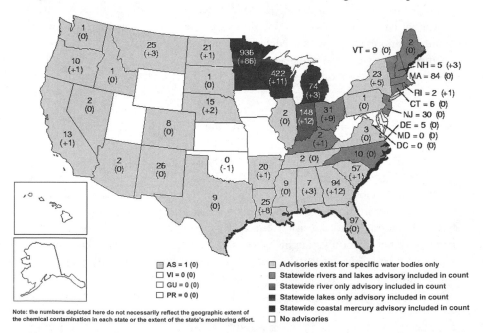

Figure 4.2. Mercury advisories in the United States (modified from U.S. EPA 1999)

higher-than-average levels of MeHg in an experimentally flooded wetland included mussels (*Pyganodon grandis*; Malley et al. 1996), predatory shoreline insects, and tree swallows (*Tachycineta bicolor*; Gerrard and St. Louis 2001).

Although mercury bioaccumulation is associated with health problems in top predators in the Florida Everglades (Frederick and Spalding 1994; Roelke et al. 1991), hydrological alterations are just one of the many factors that affect the methylation of mercury (Atkeson and Parks 2001). High mercury emissions, combined with many other factors such as levels of sulfate and phosphorus, resulted in high variability and patchiness in mercury bioaccumulation, with the southern Everglades being the most strongly affected. The emphasis for action on the mercury issue in the Everglades initially focused on human health issues. This changed in 1989 when a Florida panther (*Felis concolor coryi*) was found dead in the southern Everglades with relatively high levels of mercury in its liver. Since populations of the Florida panther are estimated at less than thirty individuals in the wild, mercury bioaccumulation in wildlife became a major concern (Loftus and Bass 1992). Alligators (*Alligator mississippiensis*) have since been found to exhibit elevated mercury levels and hunting of alligators is now restricted (Loftus and Bass 1992). Mercury bioaccumulation has also been associated with declines in wading bird populations and toxicity to raccoons (*Procyon lotor varius*) (Loftus and Bass 1992; Stober et al. 1995; Bouton et al. 1999; Frederick et al. 1999). A recent study (Duvall and Baron 2000) applied a screening-level probabilistic risk assessment to piscivorous wildlife in the Everglades. The assessment identified alligators (*Alligator mississippiensis*) and great egrets (*Ardea alba*), feeding in the south-central region of the Everglades, at high risk from consumption of mercury-contaminated prey. Risks were substantially lower in the northern Everglades. Mercury risks were lowest for raccoons because of their limited consumption of the largest and most contaminated fishes; however, raccoons may serve as a key pathway of mercury exposure to Florida panthers. Panthers that consumed more raccoons and alligators exhibited higher blood levels of mercury and had lower reproductive success than panthers that primarily consumed deer (Roelke et al.1991).

In summary, many factors affect the biogeochemical cycling of mercury in the environment—but hydrological modifications such as wetland disturbance and reservoir creation can lead to MeHg bioaccumulation by fish and the consequent toxic effects on fish-eating wildlife and humans. Although mercury contamination poses a serious global environmental problem, our understanding is constrained by lack of data on concentrations in the environment (e.g., in fish and wildlife tissue), mercury sources, and interactions of hydrological alterations and the biogeochemical cycling of mercury on a regional and global basis.

Seeking Solutions to the Toxic Effects of Methylmercury Exacerbated by Hydrological Change

Progress has been made in mapping mercury concentrations in fish tissue for each state in the United States and a national mercury database has been recently created (U.S. EPA 1999). This database is an ideal tool with which to examine trends in mercury concentrations across ecoregions and could serve as the foundation for development of a predictive tool to examine MeHg bioaccumulation and wildlife effects and to begin to elucidate the extent to which hydrological alterations (e.g., reservoirs, wetland disturbance) exacerbate the problem. As with other issues discussed in this chapter, it is a challenge to seek solutions to such a recently identified problem. It is imperative that society understands the relatively subtle, yet harmful, environmental consequences of hydrological modifications and related effects on the bioaccumulation of methylmercury in both aquatic and terrestrial food chains. Such environmental effects must be carefully considered by managers and policy-makers when making land-use decisions.

Effects of Hydrological Modifications and Nutrient Loading on Ecosystems

The combined and interacting effects of nutrient loading within river basins, water withdrawals, and the retention of sediments behind dams can have dramatic negative impacts on ecological processes and associated fish and wildlife in estuaries and coastal zones. While fluxes of mineral nutrients (e.g., phosphorus and nitrogen) to the oceans have increased dramatically (Howarth et al. 1996), dams along rivers impede the transport of sediments and associated elements such as silica. Silicate in algal diatom frustules is deposited and retained in sediments behind dams and is also used by planktonic diatoms experiencing enhanced growth in reservoirs (i.e., relative to attached diatoms in riverine conditions). Although nitrogen and phosphorus also get trapped behind dams, human activities downstream more than make up for what is retained in reservoirs (Ittekkot et al. 2000). Recent evidence indicates that shortages of silicon (relative to nitrate and phosphate) can translate into shifts in nutrient stoichiometry in coastal regions. This shift discourages silicate-using diatoms and favors nuisance algae (Justic et al. 1995a,b) that negatively affect the ecological integrity of estuaries and coastal food webs (e.g., Turner et al. 1998; Humborg et al. 2000).

Accelerated algal growth and deterioration of water quality due to oxygen depletion has occurred increasingly in coastal areas worldwide that are receiving riverine inputs (Turner and Rabalais 1994; Justic 1995b; Diaz and Rosenberg 1995). The oxygen budgets of most major estuarine and coastal ecosystems are adversely affected by eutrophication and related hydrological modifications; oxygen-starved "dead zones" have tripled in number worldwide in the last thirty years (Fig. 4.3). To date, no large system has recovered after development of persistent hypoxia or anoxia (Diaz and Rosenberg 1995). Ecological effects of marine benthic hypoxia are profound and include structural changes in benthic communities and disruptions in benthic-pelagic coupling (Diaz and Rosenberg 1995).

The Gulf of Mexico "dead zone" has received much recent attention (e.g., Malakoff 1998; Rabalais et al. 2002). The zone covered 9,000 square kilometers in 1989 but doubled in size after the 1993 Mississippi River flood (Rabalais et al. 1998). By 1997, it receded slightly to 16,000 square kilometers. This chronic seasonal hypoxia has led to reductions in species diversity, mortality of benthic communities, and stresses in fisheries resources. Mobile animals such as fishes and shrimps can flee the anoxic zone; however, less mobile animals (e.g., snails, crabs, clams, marine worms, etc.) often suffer mortality.

Most studies focusing on coastal eutrophication have concentrated on the major nutrients, nitrogen, and phosphorus. The contribution of biogenic silica (carried in suspension by rivers) to the world's ocean silica budget wasn't recognized until recently (Conley 1997). Rivers supply more than 80 percent of the

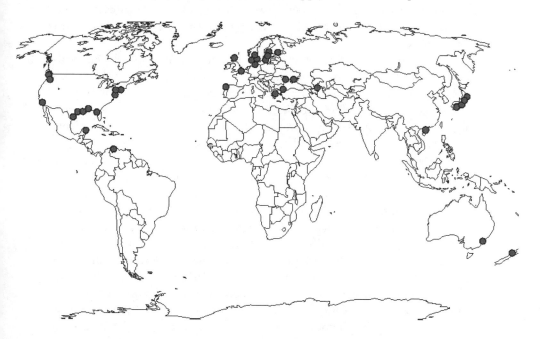

Figure 4.3. Oxygen-starved coastal "dead zones" throughout the world (redrawn from Malakoff 1998)

total input of silicate to the oceans (Treguer et al. 1995), which stimulates the production of diatoms that, in turn, fuel food webs and play a critical role in CO_2 uptake (Smetacek 1998). Researchers report decreased levels of dissolved silicate in many coastal areas of the world (e.g., Conley et al. 1993), which is attributed to the increased growth of diatoms and the removal of silica via sedimentation (Billen et al. 1991; Rahm et al. 1996). Changes in ratios of silica, nitrogen, and phosphorus have been associated recently with changes in phytoplankton numbers and relative species abundance and deep-water oxygen declines (e.g., Jickels 1998) in coastal areas of restricted water exchange. This is major cause for concern given that half of the world population now lives within 60 kilometers of the coast and coastal ecosystems and adjacent upwellings provide most of the world's fish catch.

Increasing evidence links construction of dams to decreased transport of silicate and alterations in coastal food web structure. For example, Conley et al. (2000) reported that concentrations of dissolved silicate decreased as the percentage of area occupied by lakes and reservoirs increased along rivers in Sweden and Finland. River discharge and nutrient data from sixty-one sites in Sweden and thirty sites in Finland indicated that lakes and reservoirs act to reduce dissolved silicate concentrations: rivers with greater than 10 percent lake and reservoir area in their watersheds had lower silicate levels (46 micro-molar) than those with less than 2 percent lake and reservoir area (164 micro-molar).

A recently reported link between patterns of silicate uptake and iron availability suggested that the effects of changing river inputs as a result of hydrological modifications may have far-reaching effects beyond the coastal ecosystem (Hutchins and Bruland 1998). Reduction of riverine inputs of iron (as a result of hydrological alterations) might affect the uptake of silicate in areas of nutrient-rich upwelling far from the coast (Ittekkot et al. 2000).

The Danube River–Black Sea connection provides a well-documented example of the complex effects of dams on the biogeochemistry of river inputs and the deterioration of water quality and food webs in receiving waters. The Danube contributes about 70 percent of riverine inputs to the Black Sea. Both the Danube Delta and the Black Sea are highly eutrophic, with severe negative effects on fisheries and wildlife (e.g., Pringle et al. 1993). Damming of the Danube in the early 1970s resulted in a two-thirds reduction of dissolved silicate loads (from 800×10^3 tons to 230–320×10^3 tons SiH_4O_4; Humborg et al. 1997). Dissolved silicate concentrations decreased by more than 60 percent in surface waters of the central Black Sea. Humborg et al. (1997) attributed the dramatic shifts in phytoplankton species composition in the Black Sea (i.e., from diatoms to coccolithophores [a unicellular photosynthetic organism that possesses calcareous plates] and flagellates) to corresponding changes in silicon to nitrogen ratios that reflect the decreased silicate load—not just increasing nitrogen inputs. The occurrence of potentially toxic flagellate (a flagellate is a unicellular microorganism which is motile in its adult stage, swimming by means of a flagella) blooms may become more frequent as a result of these changes in geochemistry. Furthermore, the spreading of the deoxygenated zone toward the surface and the increase in nitrate concentrations above the pycnocline (zone in the oceans where water density increases rapidly with depth in response to changes in temperature and salinity) may also be related to alterations of silicate input from the Danube (Humborg et al. 1997).

In summary, further declines in the delivery of sediments, dissolved silicate, and other elements to estuaries and coastal oceans can be expected as new dams are constructed on rivers, with consequent effects on coastal food webs and wildlife. It is critical that the scientific community develops a better understanding of biogeochemical cycling and how elements, such as silica and iron, interact with major nutrients such as nitrate and phosphate.

Seeking Solutions to the Effects of Hydrological Modifications and Nutrient Loading on Coastal Ecosystems

Of immediate concern is the development and implementation of detailed water resource management plans for individual basins to reduce, mitigate, and, control coastal hypoxia. Although this is a daunting challenge for large developed basins such as the Mississippi, an action plan addressing the hypoxia situation in the northern Gulf of Mexico was recently presented to Congress (Mississippi River/Gulf of Mexico Watershed Nutrient Task Force 2001). The plan was developed through intensive dialogue among managers, scientists, and the public. A quantitative environmental goal was decided upon that represented a compromise among environmental, agricultural, economic, and scientific interests: reduction of the five-year running average of the areal extent of Gulf hypoxia to less than 5,000 square kilometers by 2015 (Rabalais et al. 2002). Moreover, the action plan recognizes that a 30 percent nitrogen load reduction is probably needed to reach that goal and that implementation should be based on voluntary, incentive-based sub-basin strategies (Rabalais et al. 2002). A major challenge to the implementation of such strategies (e.g., agricultural best management practices, wetlands restoration and creation, riparian buffer strips, and stormwater and wastewater nutrient removal) is the increasing demand for agricultural products and energy within the Mississippi Basin. Public education will be imperative in communicating management successes and progress to stakeholders throughout the process. Time lags between management actions and marine responses also necessitate that the action plan be based on a long-term adaptive management strategy that will link management actions with monitoring, modeling, research, and reassessment of conditions at five-year intervals (Rabalais et al. 2002). To date, this action plan can be considered to be effective in terms of the openness of the process of building consensus among stakeholders and the strength of the science. It merits close evaluation as a model for other similar basinwide plans (Rabalais et al. 2002).

Conclusions

Cumulative and interactive effects of hydrologic change and pollutant loading are threatening the ecological integrity of ecosystems worldwide. Scientists are just becoming aware that the magnitude and extent of these two processes are resulting in emerging patterns in wildlife of global concern. The three emergent patterns discussed in this chapter focus on wildlife but they also are related to human health issues: (1) regional declines in migratory waterfowl and wildlife in arid regions of the world as a result of contaminated irrigation drainage and the loss of wetlands, (2) fish and wildlife response to MeHg in newly created reservoirs and other hydrologically disturbed areas, and (3) deterioration of estuarine and coastal ecosystems receiving the discharge of highly regulated rivers. All three of these patterns surfaced within the last two decades and are not receiving the attention that they deserve by scientists, land managers, policy-makers, and the general public. They illustrate the complexity of interactions between hydrologic change and pollutant loading and the confounding effects of time lags between cause and environmental consequence. They also indicate the degree to which our ability to identify negative environmental impacts of technological change lag behind the application of those advances. Moreover, they suggest that the current extent and magnitude of global hydrologic alterations and pollutant loading will result in new environmental problems. This chapter illustrates the necessity of understanding harmful interactions between hydrologic alterations and contaminant transport and of proactively addressing resultant environmental problems on a scientific, technological, and societal level to achieve ecosystem sustainability.

Acknowledgements

I gratefully acknowledge Garth Redfield for his many helpful suggestions on the manuscript. I also thank two anonymous reviewers for their excellent editorial advice. Special thanks to Marge Holland, Elizabeth Blood, and Lawrence R. Shaffer for their dedicated efforts in putting this volume together.

References

Abernathy, A. R., and P. M. Cumbie. 1977. Mercury accumulation by largemouth bass (*Micropterus salmoides*) in recently impounded reservoirs. *Bulletin of Environmental Contamination and Toxicology* 17:595–602.

Arthington, A. H., and R. L. Welcomme. 1995. The condition of large river systems of the world. Pp. 44–75 in *Condition of the world's aquatic habitats: Proceedings of the World Fisheries Congress Theme 1*, by N. B. Armantrout. Lebanon, N.H.: Science Publishers.

Atkeson, T., and P. Parks. 2001. The Everglades mercury problem. Chap. 7 in *The Everglades consolidated report*. Joint Report of the South Florida Water Management District and the Florida Department of Environmental Protection. Accessed 12/03/02: glacier.sfwmd.gov/org/ema/everglades/consolidated_01/chapter%2007/ch07.pdf.

Benke, A. C. 1990. A perspective on America's vanishing streams. *Journal of the North American Benthological Society* 9:77–88.

Billen, G., C. Lancelot, and M. Meybeck. 1991. N, P, and Si retention along aquatic continuum from land to ocean. Pp. 19–44 in *Ocean margin processes in global change*, edited by R. F. C. Mantoura, J. M. Martin, and R. Wollast. Chichester, U.K.: John Wiley and Sons.

Bodaly, R. A., R. E. Hecky, and R. J. P. Fudge. 1984. Increases in fish mercury levels in lakes flooded by the Churchill River diversion, northern Manitoba. *Canadian Journal of Fisheries and Aquatic Sciences* 41:682–691.

Bodaly, R. A., V. L. St. Louis, M. J. Paterson, R. J. P. Fudge, B. D. Hall, D. M. Rosenberg, and J. W. M. Rudd.1997. Bioaccumulation of mercury in the aquatic food chain in newly flooded areas. Pp. 259–287 in *Mercury and its effects on environment and biology*, edited by H. Sigel and A. Sigel. New York: Marcel Dekker.

Boucher, R., R. Schetagne, and E. Magnin. 1985. Teneur en mercure des poissons des reservoirs la Grande 2 et Opinaca (Quebec, Canada) avant et apres la mise en eau. *Revue française des sciences de l'eau* 4:193–206.

Bouton, S. N., P. C. Frederick, M. G. Spaulding, and H. McGill. 1999. Effects of chronic, low concentrations of dietary methylmercury on the behaviour of juvenile great egrets. *Environmental Toxicology and Chemistry* 18:1934–1939.

Brouard, D., J. F. Doyon, and R. Schetagne. 1994. Amplification of mercury concentrations in lake whitefish (*Coregonus clupeaformis*) downstream from the La Grande 2 Reservoir, James Bay, Quebec. Pp. 369–379 in *Mercury pollution: Integration and synthesis*, edited by C. J. Watras and J. W. Huckabee. Boca Raton, Fl.: Lewis Publishers.

Camardese, M. B., D. J. Hoffman, L. J. LeCaptain, and G. W. Pendleton. 1990. Effects of arsenate on growth and physiology in mallard ducklings. *Environmental Toxicology and Chemistry* 9:785–795.

Chao, B. F. 1995. Anthropogenic impact on global geodynamics due to reservoir impoundment. *Geophysical Research Letters* 22:3529–3532.

Clarkson, T. W. 1992. Mercury: Major issues in environmental health. *Environmental Health Perspectives* 100:31–38.

Colburn, T., and K. Thayer. 2000. Aquatic ecosystems: Harbingers of endocrine disruption. *Ecological Applications* 10:949–957.

Colburn, T., F. Von Saal, and P. Short. 1998. Environmental endocrine-disrupting chemicals: Neural, endocrine, and behavioral effects. Princeton, N.J.: Princeton Scientific Publishing.

Conley, D. J. 1997. Riverine contribution of biogenic silica to the oceanic silica budget. *Limnology and Oceanography* 42:774–777.

Conley, D. J., C. L. Schelske, and E. F. Stoermer. 1993. Modification of the biogeo-chemical cycle of silica with eutrophication. *Marine Ecology Progress Series* 101:179–192.

Conley, D. J., P. Stalnacke, H. Pitkanen, and A. Wilander. 2000. The transport and retention of dissolved silicate by rivers in Sweden and Finland. *Limnology and Oceanography* 45:1850–1853.

DeCamps, H., M. Fortune, F. Gazelle, and G. Patou. 1988. Historical influence of man on the riparian dynamics of a fluvial landscape. *Landscape Ecology* 1:163–173.

Diaz, R. J., and R. Rosenberg. 1995. Marine benthic hypoxia: A review of its ecological effects and the behavioural responses of benthic macrofauna. *Oceanography and Marine Biology* (Annual Review) 33:245–303.

Donald, D. B., J. Syrgiannis, F. Hunter, and G. Weiss. 1999. Agricultural pesticides threaten the ecological integrity of northern prairie wetlands. *The Science of the Total Environment* 231:173–181.

Driscoll, C. T., G. B. Lawrence, A. J. Bulger, T. J. Butler, C. S. Cronan, C. Eagar, K. F. Lambert, G. E. Likens, J. L. Stoddard, and K. C. Weathers. 2001. Acidic deposition in the northeastern United States: Sources and inputs, ecosystem effects, and man-agement strategies. *BioScience* 51:180–198.

Duvall, S. E., and M. G. Baron. 2000. A screening level probabilistic risk assessment of mercury in Florida Everglades food webs. *Ecotoxicology and Environmental Safety* 47:298–305.

Dynesius, M., and C. Nilsson. 1994. Fragmentation and flow regulation of river systems in the northern third of the world. *Science* 266:753–762.

Finger, S. E., S. J. Olson, and A. C. Livingston. 1989. *On-site toxicity of irrigation drain-water from Stillwater National Wildlife Refuge to aquatic organisms.* United States Fish and Wildlife Service, Columbia, Mo.

Fitzgerald, W., and T. Clarkson. 1991. Mercury and monomethylmercury: Present and future concerns. *Environmental Health Perspectives* 96:159–166.

Forsyth, D. J., 1995. Potential effects of herbicides on wildlife in prairie Canada. Pp.107–115 in *Proceedings of the Fourth Prairie Conservation and Endangered Species Workshop*, edited by W. D. Williams and J. F. Dormaar. Natural History Paper No. 23. Provincial Museum of Alberta, Canada.

Frayer, W. E., D. D. Peters, and H. R. Pywell. 1989. *Wetlands of the California Central Valley: Status and trends: 1939 to the mid-1980s.* U.S. Fish and Wildlife Service Report. Portland, Ore.

Frederick, P. C., and M. G. Spalding. 1994. Factors affecting reproductive success of wading birds (*Ciconiiformes*) in the Everglades ecosystem. Pp. 659–691 in *Everglades: The ecosystem and its restoration*, edited by S. M. Davis and J. C. Ogden. Delray Beach, Fla.: St. Lucie Press.

Frederick, P. C., M. G. Spalding, M. S. Sepulveda, G. E. Williams, L. Nico, and R. Robins. 1999. Exposure of great egret (*Ardea albus*) nestlings to mercury through diet in the Everglades ecosystem. *Environmental Toxicology and Chemistry* 18:1940–1947.

Gerrard, P. M., and V. L. St. Louis. 2001. The effects of experimental reservoir creation on the bioaccumulation of methylmercury and reproductive success of tree swallows (*Tachycineta bicolor*). *Environmental Science and Technology* 35:1329–1338.

Graham, F., Jr. 1998. Midnight at the oasis. *Audubon* (May) 100:82–89.

Hallock, R. J., and L. L. Hallock. 1993. *Detailed study of irrigation drainage in and near wildlife management areas, west-central Nevada, 1987–90. Part B. Effect on biota in Stillwater and Fernley Wildlife Management Areas and other nearby wetlands.* Water Resources Investigations Report 92-4024B. United States Geological Survey, Carson City, Nev.

Hecky, R. E., D. J. Ramsey, R. A. Bodaly, and N. E. Strange. 1991. Increased methylmercury contamination in fish in newly formed freshwater reservoirs. Pp. 33–52 in *Advances in mercury toxicology*, edited by T. Suzuki, N. Imura, and T. W. Clarkson. New York: Plenum Press.

Hinrichsen, D. 1998. *Coastal waters of the world: Trends, threats, and strategies.* Washington, D.C.: Island Press.

Hoffman, R. J. 1994. *Detailed study of irrigation drainage in and near wildlife management areas, west-central Nevada 1987–1990. Part C. Summary of irrigation-drainage effects on water quality, bottom sediment, and biota.* Water Resources Investigations Report 92-4024C. United States Geological Survey, Denver, Colo.

Hoffman, R. J., R. J. Hallock, T. G. Rowe, M. S. Lico, H. L. Burge, and S. P. Thompson. 1990. *Reconnaissance investigation of water quality, bottom sediment, and biota associated with irrigation drainage in and near Stillwater Wildlife Management Area, Churchill County, Nevada, 1986–87.* Water Resources Investigations Report 89-4105. United States Geological Survey, Carson City, Nev.

Hoffman, R. J., C. J. Sanderson, L. J. LeCaptain, E. Cromartie, and G. W. Pendleton. 1992. Interactive effects of arsenate, selenium, and dietary protein on survival growth and physiology in mallard ducklings. *Archive of Environmental Contaminants and Toxicology* 22:55–62.

Howarth, R. W., G. Billen, D. Swaney, A. Townsend, N. Jaworski, K. Lajtha, J. A. Downing, R. Elmgren, N. Caraco, T. Jordan, F. Berendse, J. Freney, V. Kudeyarov, P. Murdoch, and L. Zhu-Zhao. 1996. Regional nitrogen budgets and riverine N and P fluxes for the drainages to the North Atlantic Ocean: Natural and human influences. *Biogeochemistry* 35:75–79.

Humborg, C. D., J. Conley, L. Rahm, F. Wulff, A. Cociasu, and V. Ittekkot. 2000. Silicate retention in river basins: Far-reaching effects on biogeochemistry and aquatic food webs. *Ambio* 29:45–50.

Humborg, C., V. Ittekkot, A. Cociasu, B. Bodungen. 1997. Effect of Danube River dam on Black Sea biogeochemistry and ecosystem structure. *Nature* 386:385–388.

Hutchins, D. A., and K. W. Bruland. 1998. Iron-limited diatom growth and Si: N uptake ratios in a coastal upwelling. *Nature* 393:561–564.

Ittekkot, V., C. Humborg, and P. Schäfer. 2000. Hydrological alterations and marine biogeochemistry: A silicate issue? *BioScience* 9:776–782.

Jickels, T. D. 1998. Nutrient biogeochemistry of the coastal zone. *Science* 281:217–222.

Johnston, T. A., R. A. Bodaly, and J. A. Mathias. 1991. Predicting fish mercury levels from physical characteristics of boreal reservoirs. *Canadian Journal of Fisheries and Aquatic Sciences* 48:1468–1475.

Justic, D., N. N. Rabelais, and R. E. Turner. 1995a. Stoichiometric nutrient balance and origin of coastal eutrophication. *Marine Pollution Bulletin* 30:41–46.

Justic, D., N. N. Rabelais, R. E. Turner, and Q. Dortch. 1995b. Changes in nutrient structure of river-dominated coastal waters: Stoichiometric nutrient balance and its consequences. *Estuarine Coastal Shelf Science* 40:339–356.

Kelly, C. A., J. W. M. Rudd, R. A. Bodaly, N. T. Roulet, V. L. St. Louis, A. Heyes, T. R. Moore, S. Schiff, R. Aravena, K. J. Scott, B. Dyck, R. Harris, B. Warner, and G. Edwards. 1997. Increases in fluxes of greenhouse gases and methyl mercury following flooding of an experimental reservoir. *Environmental Science and Technology* 31:1334–1344.

Lemly, A. D. 1994. Agriculture and wildlife: Ecological implications of subsurface drainage. *Journal of Arid Environments* 28:85–94.

Lemly, A. D., S. E. Finger, and M. K. Nelson. 1993. Annual Review: Sources and impacts of irrigation drainwater contaminants in arid wetlands. *Environmental Toxicology and Chemistry* 12:2265–2279.

Lemly, A. D., R. T. Kingsford, and J. R. Thompson. 2000. Irrigated agriculture and wildlife conservation: Conflict on a global scale. *Environmental Management* 25:485–512.

Lodenius, M., A. Seppanen, and M. Herranen. 1983. Accumulation of mercury in fish and man from reservoirs in northern Finland. *Water, Air, and Soil Pollution* 19:237–246.

Loftus, W., and O. Bass Jr. 1992. Mercury threatens wildlife resources. *Park Science* 12:18–20.

Lundqvist, J. 1998. Avert looming hydrocide. *Ambio* 27:428–433.

Malakoff, D. 1998. Death by suffocation in the Gulf of Mexico. *Science* 281:190–192.

Malley, D. F., A. Stewart, and B. D. Hall. 1996. Uptake of methylmercury by the floater mussel, *Pyganodon grandis* (Bivalvia, Unionidae), caged in a flooded wetland. *Environmental Toxicology and Chemistry* 15:928–936.

Mason, R. P., W. F. Fitzgerald, and F. M. M. Morel. 1994. The biogeochemical cycling of elemental mercury: Anthropogenic influences. *Geochim Cosmochim Acta* 58:3191–3198.

McCully, P. 1996. *Silenced rivers: The ecology and politics of large dams.* London: Zed Books.

Mississippi River/Gulf of Mexico Watershed Nutrient Task Force. 2001. Action plan for reducing, mitigating and controlling hypoxia in the northern Gulf of Mexico. Washington, D.C.: Office of Wetlands, Oceans, and Watersheds. U.S. Environmental Protection Agency.

Naqvi, S. W. A., D. A. Jayakumar, P. V. Narvekar, H. Nalk, V. F. S. S. Sarma, W. D'Souza, S. Joseph, and M. D. George. 2000. Increased marine production of N_2O due to intensifying anoxia on the Indian continental shelf. *Nature* 408:348–349.

Nater, E. A., and D. F. Grigal. 1992. Regional trends in mercury distribution across the Great Lakes states, north central USA. *Nature* 358:139–141.

NRC (National Research Council). 1999. *Hormonally active agents in the environment.* Washington, D.C.: National Academy Press.

Ohlendorf, H. M., D. J. Hoffman, M. K. Saiki, and T. W. Aldrich. 1986. Embryonic mortality and abnormalities of aquatic birds: Apparent impact of selenium from irrigation drainwater. *The Science of the Total Environment* 52:49–63.

Ohlendorf, H. M., R. L. Hothem, and T. W. Aldrich. 1988. Bioaccumulation of selenium by snakes and frogs in the San Joaquin Valley, California. *Copeia* 3:704–710.

Postel, S. L. 1999. *Pillar of Sand: Can the irrigation miracle last?* New York: W.W. Norton.

Postel, S. L., G. C. Daily, and P. R. Ehrlich. 1996. Human appropriation of renewable freshwater. *Science* 271:785–788.

Presser, T. S. 1994. The Kesterson effect. *Environmental Management* 18:437–454.

Presser, T. S., and H. M. Ohlendorf. 1987. Biogeochemical cycling of selenium in the San Joaquin Valley, California, USA. *Environmental Management* 11:805–821.

Presser, T. S., M. A. Sylvester, and W. H. Low. 1993. Bioaccumulation of selenium from natural geologic sources in the western states and its potential consequences. *Environmental Management* 18:423–436.

Pringle, C. M. 1997. Exploring how disturbance is transmitted upstream: Going against the flow. *Journal of the North American Benthological Society* 16:425–438.

————. 2000. Threats to U.S. public lands from cumulative hydrologic alterations outside of their boundaries. *Ecological Applications* 10:971–989.

Pringle, C. M., M. C. Freeman, and B. J. Freeman. 2000. Regional effects of hydrologic alterations on riverine macrobiota in the New World: Tropical-temperate comparisons. *BioScience* 50:807–823.

Pringle, C. M., and F. J. Triska. 1999. Emergent biological patterns in streams resulting from surface-subsurface water interactions at landscape scales. Pp. 167–193 in *Surface-subsurface interactions in stream ecosystems*, edited by J. B. Jones and P. J. Mulholland. New York: Academic Press.

Pringle, C. M., G. Vellidis, F. Heliotis, D. Bandacu, and S. Cristofor. 1993. Environmental problems of the Danube Delta. *American Scientist* 81:348–361.

Pulliam, R. H. 1988. Sources, sinks, and population regulation. *American Naturalist* 132:652–661.

Rabalais, N. N., R. E. Turner, and D. Scavia. 2002. Beyond science into policy; Gulf of Mexico hypoxia and the Mississippi River. *Bioscience* 52:129–142.

Rabalais, N. N., R. E. Turner, W. J. Wiseman Jr., and Q. Dortch. 1998. Consequences of the 1993 Mississippi River flood in the Gulf of Mexico. *Regulated Rivers: Research and Management* 14:161–177.

Rahm, L., D. Conley, P. Sanden, F. Wulff, and P. Stalnacke. 1996. Time series analysis of nutrient inputs to the Baltic Sea and changing DSi: DIN ratios. *Marine Ecology Progress Series* 130:221–228.

Roelke, M. E., D. P. Schultz, C. F. Facemire, and S. F. Sundlof. 1991. Mercury contamination in the free-ranging endangered Florida panther (*Felis concolor coryi*). Pp. 277–287 in *Proceedings of the American Association of Zoo Veterinarians*. Hills Division, Riviana Foods, Topeka, Kans.

Rosenberg, D. M., F. Berkes, R. A. Bodaly, R. E. Hecky, C. A. Kelly, and J. W. M. Rudd. 1997. Large-scale impacts of hydroelectric development. *Environmental Review* 5:27–54.

Rosenberg, D. M., P. McCully, and C. M. Pringle. 2000. Global-scale environmental effects of hydrological alterations: Introduction. *BioScience* 9:746–751.

Rowe, T. G., and R. J. Hoffman. 1987. Wildlife kills in the Carson Sink, western Nevada, winter 1986–87. Pp. 37–49 in *National Water Summary 1987—Water supply and use: Selected events*. Water Supply Paper 2350, United States Geological Survey, Denver, Colo.

Saiki, M. K., M. R. Jennings, and R. H. Wiedmeyer. 1992. Toxicity of agricultural sub-surface drainwater from the San Joaquin Valley, California, to juvenile chinook salmon and striped bass. *Transactions of the American Fisheries Society* 121:78–93.

Schetagne, R., J. F. Doyno, and J. J. Fournier. 2000. Export of mercury downstream from reservoirs. *The Science of the Total Environment* 260:135–145.

Seiler, R. L. 1995. Prediction of areas where irrigation drainage may induce selenium contamination of water. *Journal of Environmental Quality* 24:973–979.

Seiler, R. L., J. P. Skorupa, and L. A. Peltz. 1999. *Methods to identify areas susceptible to irrigation-induced selenium contamination in the western U.S.* United States Geological Survey, Circular 1180, Denver, Colo.

Smetacek, V. 1998. Diatoms and the silicate factor. *Nature* 391:224–225.

Sparks, R. E., J. C. Nelson, and Y. Yin. 1998. Naturalization of the flood regime in reg-ulated rivers. *BioScience* 48:706–720.

Stober, Q. J., R. D. Jones, and D. J. Scheidt. 1995. Ultra trace level mercury in the Everglades ecosystem, a multi media canal pilot study. *Water, Air, Soil Pollution* 80:991–1001.

Strange, N. E., R. A. Bodaly, and R. J. P. Fudge. 1991. Mercury concentrations in fish in Southern Indian Lake and Issett Lake, Manitoba, 1975–88: The effect of lake impoundment and Churchill River diversion. *Canadian Technical Report on Fisheries and Aquatic Sciences* 1824:1–36.

Treguer, P., D. M. Nelson, A. J. van Bennekom, D. J. DeMaster, A. Leynart, and B. Queguiner. 1995. The silica balance in the world ocean: A reestimate. *Science* 268:375–379.

Turner, R. E., N. Qureshi, N. N. Rabelais, Q. Dortch, D. Justic, R. F. Shaw, and J. Cope. 1998. Fluctuating silicate: nitrate ratios and coastal plankton food webs. *Proceedings of the National Academy of Sciences* 95:13048–13051.

Turner, R. E., and N. N. Rabalais. 1994. Coastal eutrophication near the Mississippi River delta. *Nature* 368:619–621.

U.S. EPA. (United States Environmental Protection Agency). 1999. Database: National survey of mercury concentrations in fish (1990–1995). Accessed 12/2/02: www.epa.gov/ost/fish/mercurydata.html.

———. 2001. Consumption advice fact sheet. No. EPA-823-F-01-004. Office of Water. Accessed 12/6/02: www.epa.gov/waterscience/fishadvice/factsheet.html.

Vitousek, P. M., J. D. Aber, W. Howarth, G. E. Likens, P. A. Matson, D. W. Schindler, W. H. Schlesinger, and D. G. Tilman. 1997. Human alteration of the global nitro-gen cycle: Sources and consequences. *Ecological Applications (Issues in Ecology)* 7:737–750.

Vorosmarty, C. J., M. Meybeck, B. Fekete, and K. Sharma. 1997a. The potential impact of neo-Castorization on sediment transport by the global network of rivers. Pp. 261–272 in *Human impact on erosion and sedimentation*, edited by D. Walling and J. L. Probst. Wallingford, U.K.: International Association of Hydrological Sciences Press.

Vorosmarty, C. J., and D. Sahagian. 2000. Anthropogenic disturbance of the terrestrial water cycle. *BioScience* 50:753–765.

Vorosmarty, C. J., K. P. Sharma, B. M. Fekete, A. H. Copeland, J. Holden, J. Marble, and J. A. Lough. 1997b. The storage and aging of continental runoff in large reservoir systems of the world. *Ambio* 26:210–219.

Vos, J. G., E. Dybing, H. A. Greim, O. Ladefoged, C. Lambre, J. V. Tarazona, I. Brandt, and D. Vethaak. 2000. Health effects of endocrine disrupting chemicals on wildlife, with special reference to the European situation. *Critical Reviews in Toxicology* 30:71–133.

Waite, D. T., G. W. Dunn, and R. J. Stedwell. 1980. *Mercury in Cookson Reservoir (East Poplar River)*. WPC-23. Saskatchewan Environment, Regina, Saskatchewan.

Welcomme, R. L. 1995. Relationships between fisheries and the integrity of river systems. *Regulated Rivers: Research and Management* 11:121–136.

Westra, L., P. Miller, J. R. Karr, W. E. Rees, and R. E. Ulanowicz. 2000. Ecological integrity and the aims of the global integrity project. Pp. 19–44 in *Ecological integrity: Integrating environment, conservation, and health,* edited by D. Pimentel, L. Westra, and R. F. Noss. Washington, D.C.: Island Press.

Whitworth, M. R., G. W. Pendleton, D. J. Hoffman, M. B. Camardese. 1991. Effects of dietary boron and arsenic on the behavior of mallard ducklings. *Environmental Toxicology and Chemistry* 10:911–916.

Wiener, J. G., and D. J. Spry. 1996. Toxicological significance of mercury in freshwater fish. Pp. 297–339 in *Environmental Contaminants in Wildlife: Interpreting Tissue Concentrations.* W. N. Beyer, G. H. Heinz, and A. W. Redmon-Norwood (eds). Boca Raton, Fla..: Lewis Publishers.

WRI (World Resources Institute). 2000. Pilot analysis of global ecosystems: Freshwater systems. Special Report of the World Resources Institute. Accessed 12/08/02: www.wri.org/wri/wr2000.

Young, G. J., J. C. I. Dooge, and C. Rodda. 1994. *Global water resource issues.* New York: Cambridge University Press.

Zaletaev, V. S. 1997. Ecotones and problems of their management in irrigation regions. Pp. 185–193 in *Groundwater/surface water ecotones: Biological and hydrological interaction and management options,* edited by J. Gibert, J. Mathieu, and F. Fournier. New York: Cambridge University Press.

PART II

RECENT SCIENTIFIC PERSPECTIVES IN WATER AND WETLANDS

Even the best examples of adaptive management, ecosystem management, or holistic management focus primarily on major structural or functional aspects of the freshwater system (e.g., hydrology, plant structure, presence or absence of specific animals) and do not consider what is taking place at the molecular or biochemical levels. But scientists have recently recognized that the factors possibly having the greatest effect on maintaining the health of the freshwater system are occurring at molecular or biochemical scales. Naturally occurring organic compounds exuded from plants, resulting from the breakdown of leaves, hormones, and toxins released by organisms, and organic films formed by microbes, are critically important in controlling biological, chemical, geological, and physical processes in freshwater systems. Important ecological services (e.g., filtering and trapping nutrients and toxics) result from these complex and poorly understood pathways. We are coming to understand that maintaining the tremendous diversity of life that occurs in freshwater systems will become increasingly important in maintaining human health, and, through new discoveries in natural products and biotechnology, even provide new economic opportunities. Part II discusses the importance of water and wetlands to human health, freshwater system physiology, and functional metabolism, and argues reasons for maintaining wetland biodiversity.

Chapter 5 begins by discussing the interaction between human health and water quality. Water quality is linked to microbes that mediate the cycling of natural and anthropogenic substances. It is essential to understand how aquatic ecosystems are affected by humans. Humankind's survival relies on fresh water, and more effort needs to be put into studying biological responses in order to safeguard this resource. To understand why freshwater ecosystems act the way they do, scientists need to conduct controlled manipulations of parts or whole ecosystems. Chapter 5 concludes with the observation that understanding interactions between humans and freshwater ecosystems can help us to better protect and preserve sustainable freshwater ecosystems.

Chapter 6, the most technically oriented chapter, broadens the discussion to include other processes within wetlands and the role of wetlands in moderating human actions. It describes biogeochemical processes that occur in wetlands—processes that govern nutrient availability, plant growth and productivity, and nutrient dynamics, which in turn are responsible for many recognized functions of wetlands, such as serving as a nutrient sink. Wetlands play a major role as a sink and transformer for many nutrients and ions that affect water quality. Understanding biogeochemical processes is therefore important in sustaining freshwater resources. Hydrology is critical to maintaining the structure and function of wetlands. In water-saturated wetland soils, the diffusion of oxygen is very slow, and therefore microbes must rely on anaerobic metabolism, which means that nitrification-denitrification, sulfate reactions, and methanogenesis are crucial processes in the proper functioning of wetlands. This chapter also addresses hydrological conditions and wetland processes representative of a range of wetland types, demonstrating the importance of understanding biogeochemical processes as well as wetland functions to the management of freshwater ecosystems.

Chapter 7 argues that heightened interest in preserving wetlands is due not only to an increased awareness of the detrimental ecological impacts of human activity on wetlands but also because of the role wetlands play in maintaining biodiversity and because of their possible economic importance. This chapter examines ongoing research projects from relatively diverse scientific fields, including chemistry, biology, and ecology, which seek to understand the complex interactions between chemicals produced by wetland species and the environment in which these organisms exist. Such research suggests that wetlands may contain unique and potentially valuable natural products that may cure diseases and control agricultural pests. The chapter concludes that wetlands are a potentially untapped resource for biotechnology markets.

These chapters provide insights into the importance of good science and how that science can lead to better management. If we are to understand the links among freshwater and human systems and manage these systems sustainably, we must also develop mechanisms for incorporating scientific knowledge and emerging scientific frontiers into policy and management decisions.

Chapter 5

Freshwater and Wetland Ecology: Challenges and Future Frontiers

Robert G. Wetzel

Freshwater ecosystems are biological systems. Water quality of fresh waters is inextricably coupled to biological, largely microbial metabolism, which influences and mediates the cycling and retention of natural and anthropogenic substances. Gaining an understanding of regulatory mechanisms governing biological metabolism and growth is essential if we are to understand what is likely to happen as aquatic ecosystems are variously disturbed by human activities.

Accrual of needed information must be greatly accelerated in order to understand how these ecosystems function as they are altered by human activities. As has been demonstrated so well in the human medical profession, there is not an alternative to devoting a greater percentage of our intellectual and financial resources to understanding biotic regulation, in this case of freshwater quality. Allocations to this critical resource, the foremost resource of human survival, have thus far been token. We have passed the point at which we can continue to take unabatedly without casting back some comprehensive understanding and wise use in return.

Nature is remarkably resilient to human insults. Yet, humans must learn the dynamic capacities of nature, because excessive violation without harmony will only unleash her intolerable vengeance. The very survival of humankind depends on our understanding and wise use of our finite freshwater resources. Where are we in that quest for understanding? How effectively can our present understanding be applied to effective management of surface water resources? How can we improve our understanding and predictive capacities to best utilize these finite resources over the long term?

Approaches to Gaining Understanding

Freshwater ecology has been an integrative science since its inception. Although inquiry into organization and functions of inland waters can be traced to medieval times, serious inquires and understanding began somewhat over a century ago. Initial investigations were descriptive of both biota and their environments. A long period of comparative analyses ensued for some four decades. During this time, complex classification schemes organized fresh waters into groups on the basis of different physical, chemical, and biological properties. The comparative analyses were important because the heterogeneity of freshwater ecosystems was delineated and analyzed.

These analyses, and much of the work that followed from the 1940s to the 1960s, were strongly influenced by the evolving trophic dynamic concepts initiated by Hutchinson and his protégé Lindeman (cf. Wetzel 1995, 2001). Feeding and predation relationships among organisms were a predominant emphasis, which persist in modified form to the present day. In a gradual further conceptual evolution, population and community structural analyses were combined with evaluations of energy and material fluxes. Gradually expanded directions are emerging toward the essential functional integration of all ecosystems components.

Approaches for acquiring understanding varied and evolved as the discipline matured. Hypotheses can be generated from descriptive observations of patterns of biological processes and communities in relation to dynamic patterns of environmental properties: that is, generation of a conceptual predictive "model" of relationships among observed patterns. These relationships may be compared statistically with correlations of the strength of co-occurrence of two or multiple variables. Such regressional correlations are only an extension of descriptions and indicate relationships within a certain statistical probability. Thus, the correlations generate a hypothesis but do not show the accuracy of relationships. Even though the probability of relationship of patterns may be high, they do not provide any direct evidence of causality. Similarly, comparative correlations can suggest relationships and pattern, but they cannot evaluate or test general patterns of cause and effect. And positive correlations can narrow the search for controlling factors of observed patterns, but spurious and erroneous positive correlations can obfuscate the analyses.

Our understanding of why freshwater ecosystems operate as they do has emanated from experimentally controlled disturbances and manipulations of parts of or whole ecosystems. These experimental approaches, emerging largely in the 1960s and subsequently, integrate physiological and biochemical understanding with observed population and community responses to experimentally and naturally induced changes. In spite of the natural variability of ecosystem properties, quantification is essential to understanding interactive regulating processes. Clearly, these manipulative studies have demonstrated that great insight into the control of parameters can be gained from experimental manipulation or from imposing known, controlled disturbances of specific environmental or community parameters on specific components of the community or ecosystem. Quantitative responses include changes in growth, productivity, reproduction, competition, metabolic adaptations, and other processes of populations and communities as ecosystem components are manipulated and compared with components not exposed to this treatment.

It also should be noted that unplanned disturbances may provide much insight into ecosystem functions and biotic responses to alterations. For instance, episodic events (e.g., fires, floods, hurricanes) and unusual events (species invasions) can perturb an ecosystem and reveal previously unrecognized connections among components and control points on processes. Although these adventitious disturbances may not be as powerful statistically or as useful as carefully executed experiments of existing hypotheses, their effects have often been quite incisive in relation to regulating properties.

Application of quantitative predictive models based on experimentally *established*, not random, governing variables allow expansion of experimentally understood quantitative relationships. One can insert hypothetical data of various parameters and theoretically estimate system responses to those variables. Models cannot predict anything not built into them from the beginning (Lehman 1986). Even "counterintuitive results" are simply unrecognized consequences of initial assumptions. Models are a tool. Most models greatly overestimate understanding and falsely and naïvely generate confidence but can be enormously instructive in application to these complex, heterogeneous ecosystems.

The Search for Common Ground

Throughout the development of our understanding of freshwater and wetland ecology, we have emphasized the differences among various habitats, particularly physical and chemical characteristics among different waters of various geomorphologic regions, and the diversity of different biota and their growth characteristics. That differentiation among lakes, rivers, and estuaries and their physical, chemical, and biological properties was the impetus underlying the half century of comparative studies. Attempts to demonstrate functional relationships among different groups of lakes and organisms were frustrated because of the inherent limitations of correlation analyses. Progress has now extended to examination of physiological, biochemical, and molecular variations among biota, commonly with the coupling of these differences to variations in the environmental habitats in which the organisms reside. Some of this continued differentiation of species at the molecular level is most important from evolutionary, biogeographic, and systematic viewpoints, particularly in relation to biodiversity and losses of biodiversity.

Biotic and habitat variability is enormous and often difficult to fathom because of the dynamic properties of metabolism, growth, and reproductive capacities of organisms as they respond to the bewildering array of dynamic environmental factors influencing growth and development. Although reductionism is essential to provide information on properties involved, regulatory generality prevails across the individual species and diversity of processes (Wetzel 2001). Regulation of quantitative process rates of metabolism, energy fluxes, and material fluxes is where commonality emerges among highly disparate and complex interacting parameters within ecosystems. That understanding is essential from both theoretical relationships, particularly in regard to thermodynamic energetic fluxes, and in the management of controlling the effects of human-induced disturbances to the ecosystems.

The Need for an Altered Perspective

Fresh waters and wetlands are biological systems, and biogeochemical processes control the water quality within and moving through them. We have a reasonable understanding of the "anatomy" or structure of these ecosystems. The thrust now is to achieve an understanding of the "physiology," or functional metabolism, of these ecosystems and controlling factors regulating biotic physiology, growth, and reproduction. Such understanding is essential for effective management and addressing practical problems of water quality and how water quality is influenced by human-induced changes. Good management of wetlands can be founded only in good science. Regardless of the structural and functional heterogeneity of wetlands, order does prevail at the functional level (physiological and chemical).

It is essential to evaluate entire ecosystems, not just a small portion of those of potential interest to human culture, for effective management and utilization of the whole ecosystem. That integrative perspective must include an emphasis on rates of metabolism and regulation of rates of biogeochemical cycling by that metabolism, because it is essential to understand how species interactions alter rates of energetic flows and storage and of biogeochemical cycling, rather than the prevailing focus on how feeding relationships influence individual population or community growth and reproduction. The processes are certainly related and coupled, but the present imbalances of understanding are conspicuous.

In addition, microbial metabolism and its regulation of nutrient and carbon cycling must be understood for efficient and effective management and utilization of aquatic ecosystems, since material and energy flows and cycling are regulated largely at the biochemical and microbial levels, and microbial metabolism totally dominates at the ecosystem level.

Paradigm Change and the Functional Importance of Wetlands

Efficiencies of energy transfers among trophic levels have dominated aquatic ecology for decades, particularly in relation to the effects of trophic structure and complexity on transfer rates (Lindeman 1942; Hutchinson 1959; Wetzel 1995). These relationships were focused almost totally on the open-water pelagic trophic structure and energy fluxes of particulate organic carbon (i.e., ingestion of particulate organic matter [POM]). Flows of energy and control mechanisms regulating those flows within trophic structures addressed predation (i.e., ingestion of POM). Gains in understanding have been excellent regarding the size of ingested POM, morphological aspects of ingestion (e.g., filtration, mouth gape) and avoidance of ingestion (e.g., transparency/visibility, interference by cellular or body projections), behavioral capabilities of organisms for movements within the pelagic zone in relation to refuges or escape from predators, nutritional differences in particulate food, and others. Although many organisms ingest variable amounts of particulate detritus (i.e., nonliving POM), and this particulate detritus commonly dominates over living POM of the plankton (e.g., Saunders 1971, 1972), practically nothing is known of rates of consumption, assimilation of it and associated microbes, and egestion of it *under natural conditions*.

As the metabolism of community components was analyzed with increasing accuracy, flux pathways and rates of transfer of organic carbon demonstrated many complexities and inconsistencies that could not be explained by the conventional food-web paradigms. Assimilation efficiencies of ingested particles are modest, usually less than 50 percent, under natural conditions and much of the ingested organic matter is released as soluble and particulate detrital organic matter. Predation by ingestion of living POM is not the prevailing cause of mortality under most situations. Most organisms reach physiological and biochemical senescence and simply die or shift to a dormant stage.

More recent findings complicate these dogmatic paradigms even further. Massive amounts of organic matter that are produced within the drainage basin of the aquatic ecosystem and that are allochthonously (originating or formed within the drainage basin and brought to the lake or stream in various forms) imported to the ecosystems from terrestrial and wetland sources are metabolized within the lakes and streams but are never consumed by particulate-ingesting metazoans. This altered perspective, which has been only gradually accepted in recent times, indicates that up to 99 percent of the ecosystem organic carbon budget, particularly in rivers, can be detrital based and imported to lakes and rivers per se (e.g., Benke and Meyer 1988; reviews in Wetzel 2001). In spite of that recognition, predation-based paradigms continue to be tenaciously retained as primary constructs (e.g., Hairston and Hairston 1993) despite their minor roles in total ecosystem metabolism. In no manner do these statements diminish the importance of predation-based relationships and their importance to food-web structure and metabolic couplings among higher trophic levels. But, rather, management of aquatic ecosystems requires understanding of the dominating microbial mediators of biogeochemical cycling and energy fluxes via detrital pathways.

Aquatic Microbial Heterotrophy

The observed heterotrophic biotic productivity of most lakes and rivers, as estimated in detailed organic carbon budgets, could not possibly be supported by the autochthonous (originated or formed in the lake or stream where found) organic carbon generated by phytoplankton within these waters. Among the earliest detailed quantitative budgets that included both dissolved and particulate organic carbon from autochthonous, allochthonous, and littoral sources and compartments of utilization and losses, were those of Lawrence Lake (Wetzel et al. 1972) and of Mirror Lake (reviewed in Likens 1985 and Wetzel 1983, 2001). External allochthonous organic matter imported from terrestrial, wetland, and littoral regions supplements heterotrophic productivity within a lake or stream. Considering the lake or river per se, bounded by the shoreline water demarcation, the lake or river is a heterotrophic ecosystem that decomposes much more organic matter than is produced within those boundaries. Essentially all inland water ecosystems are heterotrophic ecosystems.

A large portion, usually more than 90–95 percent, of the organic matter imported to these aquatic ecosystems is predominantly in dissolved or colloidal (extremely small particles that do not settle from water by gravity) form. Although a small portion of the dissolved organic compounds may aggregate and form particles that settle from the water, most of the imported dissolved organic matter (DOM) is dispersed within the water, is moved about with the hydrodynamics of the water, and becomes available for utilization downgradient over varying time scales.

Much of that DOM originates from lignin and cellulose and related structural precursor compounds of higher plants. The productivity of the terrestrial vegetation and aquatic plants associated with the land-water interface region is manifold, usually several orders of magnitude greater than that of algae. These imported organic compounds are abundant, chemically complex, and relatively recalcitrant to rapid biological degradation. During oxidative and anaerobic degradation, these compounds are modified by microbial activities in detrital masses, including standing dead tissues of forests and wetlands that can remain in oxidative aerial environments for months or years. This microbial modification continues during partial decomposition in soils and during transport through the microbial sieves of wetlands and littoral areas before final movement into the receiving lake body or river channel per se (Wetzel 1990).

Because of the bonding structure and limited accessibility of large portions of these commonly acidic macromolecules to enzymatic hydrolysis, slow degradation rates result in long turnover times. These compounds have relatively long environmental residence times. Recent studies demonstrate that humic substances (naturally occurring organic substances of biological, largely plant, origins that are generally dark-colored, moderately resistant to microbial degradation, and high in molecular weight), particularly relatively recalcitrant fulvic acids (a group of relatively soluble low molecular weight humic substances that have a high proportion of oxygen-containing functional groups), are generated by algae and contribute to the multitude of diverse compounds within the DOM pool derived primarily from higher plants. This source is particularly important in littoral wetland areas, where productivity of attached and sessile algae is often many orders of magnitude greater than that of phytoplankton per unit area of habitat (e.g., Wetzel 1996). Because of the recalcitrance of these dominating dissolved organic compounds, often largely from wetland and littoral areas, the DOM can reside *within* lakes and rivers for long periods of time, often for months or years.

Organic carbon budgetary evidence in early lake studies indicated that the DOM did not accumulate or precipitate and that large quantities of carbon dioxide (CO_2) evaded to the atmosphere (e.g., Otsuki and Wetzel 1974; Kling et al. 1992; globally reviewed in Cole et al. 1994). This quantity of evading CO_2 was greatly in excess of autochthonous photosynthetic organic carbon production by phytoplankton. In spite of this evidence, for decades in aquatic ecology the apparent chemical recalcitrance of dissolved humic substances that dominate the instantaneous bulk-dissolved organic carbon of standing and running waters led to the belief that these compounds were poorly used by microbiota. Loss rates were slow but consistently in the range of 0.5 to 2 percent or greater per day under many different environmental conditions.

These dissolved organic macromolecules of the structural tissues of terrestrial and wetland higher plants can be modified by photochemical alterations by the ultraviolet radiation portion of the electromagnetic spectrum UV-B (280–320 nanometers), and UV-A (320–400 nanometers), as well as photosynthetically active radiation (400–700 nanometers). The photochemical alterations can change biological availability of portions of these complex heterogeneous dissolved organic compounds. Processes include (1) alterations of enzymatic accessibility of the macromolecules; (2) partial photolysis of macromolecules, particularly with the generation of volatile fatty acids and related simple compounds that serve as excellent substrates for bacterial degradation (Wetzel et al. 1995; Moran and Zepp 1997); (3) degradation of dissolved organic nitrogen and phosphorus compounds to release inorganic nutrient compounds; and (4) complete photolysis of humic substances of wetland higher-plant origins to carbon monoxide and carbon dioxide. Although ultraviolet radiation, particularly UV-A, can contribute to more than half of photochemical mineralization, photosynthetically active radiation also is a major photolytic agent (Vähätalo et al. 2000, 2002; Wetzel 2000b).

Continued studies of natural dissolved organic substances of terrestrial and wetland origins in aquatic ecosystems show diverse ways in which these compounds, particularly humic compounds, interact metabolically. For example, dissolved organic compounds can

- combine with inorganic compounds and elements, and alter solubility and bioavailability.
- interact with other organic compounds, such as peptides, and alter biological susceptibility to enzymatic hydrolysis, thereby affecting membrane characteristics and nutrient transport mechanisms. Humic substances of wetland plant origins can bond chemically with proteins, particularly enzymes, and result in noncompetitive inhibition. Some enzymes can be stored in this complexed chemical form for long periods (days, weeks) in an inactive state, be redistributed in the ecosystem with water movements, and be reactivated by partial photolytic cleavage by ultraviolet irradiance (Wetzel 1991, 1995, 2000b; Boavida and Wetzel 1998).
- alter redox and water acidity, and under anaerobic conditions can serve as electron donors for microbial reduction reactions.
- change physical properties, such as selective modifications of light penetration that can alter photosynthesis, photodegradation of organic compounds, hormonal activities of plants, and migratory and reproductive behavior of planktonic organisms.

Most of the detrital organic pool, both in particulate and dissolved phases, of inland aquatic ecosystems consists of residual organic compounds of plant structural tissues. The more labile organic constituents of complex DOM and POM are hydrolyzed and metabolized more rapidly than the more recalcitrant organic compounds that are less accessible enzymatically. The result is a general increase in concentration of the more recalcitrant compounds with slower rates of metabolism and turnover. These recalcitrant compounds, however, are metabolized at slow rates regulated in large part by their molecular complexity and modifications by photolysis. Such organic recalcitrance to degradation provides a thermodynamic stability to metabolism within lake, reservoir, wetland-littoral land-water interface, and river ecosystems. The chemical recalcitrance is truly a "brake" on ecosystem metabolism, is critical for maintenance of stability, and provides a commonality that transcends numerous structural and functional differences in the systems.

Assessing our Future Direction

Obviously, as the discussion above has shown, we have a responsibility to understand causality—the controlling regulatory parameters that result in quantitative regulation of physical and biological states of surface waters, including wetland-littoral regions of these ecosystems. Managing these areas effectively requires that we first understand how dynamic states interactively control water quality. Importantly, water quality is biologically mediated (or "regulated" or "controlled"). Four areas are particularly important and offer exceptional promise to influence effective water resource management on a sustainable basis: (1) microbial aquatic ecology, (2) biochemical processes, (3) genetic and molecular regulation, and (4) land-water interface regions.

Microbial Aquatic Ecology

No other area of aquatic ecology is more important, more poorly understood, and more likely to produce greater insight into the functional operation of aquatic ecosystems than is the physiological ecology of microbes. Over 90 percent of the metabolic utilization and degradation of organic matter in lake and river ecosystems is by viruses, bacteria, fungi, and protists of a size less than 100 micrometers(μm). However, less than 10 percent of our research efforts and understanding has been devoted to the physiological ecology of these organisms. The utilization of organic matter and biogeochemical couplings of freshwater ecosystems are almost totally controlled by the metabolism of microbes, especially bacterial metabolism of DOM and fungal decay of larger POM.

The interactively coupled metabolic mutualism among microorganisms must be known in order to properly evaluate the rate controls of nutrient regeneration and recycling. These rates are critical to understanding the regulation of productivity of higher trophic levels. Modern methods, such as biochemical and molecular probes, genetic markers, and similar methods allow evaluation of factors controlling rate functions at a level unattainable a few years ago. Just as the most effective human health management is coincident with physiological and biochemical understanding, effective management of water quality cannot be achieved without understanding the control mechanisms of these metabolic and chemical cycling rates under natural and disturbed conditions.

Biochemical Processes

We are often preoccupied with the biological productivity of aquatic ecosystems and their apparent regulation by macronutrients such as phosphorus and nitrogen or toxic substances. But true composite metabolism and growth is regulated by myriad dynamic parameters affecting the bioavailability and recycling of nutrients and energy. Despite the complexity of variable regulatory parameters, usually a few (three to five) dominate under natural conditions (Hutchinson 1978), which makes analyses more tractable. The response and capabilities of the organisms to these regulatory parameters can be effectively evaluated at the biochemical level.

The metabolism, growth, productivity, and behavior of biota of aquatic ecosystems are integrated and regulated by many organic compounds in addition to traditionally emphasized macronutrients. Many membrane-associated compounds, such as enzymes, allelochemical compounds, extracellular enzymes, metabolic regulators (e.g., cyclic AMP), and immunological substances permit elaborate chemical reactions and communication among organisms (Wetzel 1991). The reactivity of these substances can be modified or inactivated by bonding to organic and inorganic particles and surfaces. Although it is difficult to study these functionally important biochemical reactions under natural conditions, techniques allowing us to do so are evolving rapidly, because we must evaluate such regulatory mechanisms to understand how ecosystems integrate and compensate for changes, including human-induced disturbances. Specifically, we must break from the prevailing dogma that organic matter from phytoplankton is the primary or only significant driver of metabolism in most freshwater ecosystems and take a "bottom up" rather than a "top down" approach. Terrestrial and especially wetland and littoral sources of organic matter are fundamental if not dominant sources in most freshwater aquatic ecosystems. Our greatest advances in understanding, therefore, will likely concern the base of the trophic system, at the decomposition level.

Genetic and Molecular Regulation

Molecular genetic differentiation among species has allowed, and will continue to allow, unprecedented interpretations and understanding of biogeographic origins and connections, as well as evolutionary and systematic relationships among biota. The biodiversity of most microbial, plant, and animal groups of stream, lake, and wetland ecosystems is poorly known. However, biodiversity within inland aquatic ecosystems is very large (nearly half of the total), particularly in wetland and littoral regions, in spite of the very small proportion (only a few percent) of the biosphere occupied by inland waters (Wetzel 1999).

Artificially modified microbial hybrids hold great potential for evaluating characteristics of bacterial development on, and the metabolism of, both natural and toxic organic compounds. Artificially modified microbial hybrids can be used to decompose certain toxic compounds of human origin and become an important tool in pollution control and remediation. Transfer and rearrangement of recombinant DNA molecules in microorganisms are being used for microbial detoxification of specific pollutants. These approaches hold great potential for attacking complex organic pollution problems but also for our understanding of controls of natural microbial metabolism and community growth.

Ecosystem Couplings: Land–Water Interface Regions

One cannot understand the structure and processes within lakes and streams without understanding the quantitative coupling of those processes to the drainage basin. The wetland-littoral regions between land and water vary greatly in size and in metabolic activity. Most of these interface regions of wetlands, littoral areas, and floodplains are sedimentary zones where water moves slowly relative to elsewhere in the ecosystem, and deposits of organic matter and associated nutrients from the drainage basin tend to accumulate. Plant productivity tends to be exceptionally high in these interface regions. The prolific numbers of living plants and abundant particulate organic detritus provide a very large surface area for colonization and extremely high productivity of attached photosynthetic and heterotrophic microorganisms. This three-dimensional myriad of highly productive and metabolically active mutualistic microbes and higher plants provides a metabolic sieve that efficiently recycles and conservatively retains resources, especially nutrients, in these interface areas (e.g., Wetzel 1990, 1993).

Whether in natural or constructed wetlands, it must be recognized that the organisms are integrated and interdependent. The macrophytes provide physical structure and support, in the form of organic matter, for the microbes, while they in turn depend on the attached microflora for nutrient regeneration and availability from organic detrital and soil sources. Wetlands export large quantities of relatively recalcitrant organic matter in dissolved form. That organic export is utilized within the receiving waters as a subsidy of autochthonous organic matter from phytoplankton, as was discussed earlier, which functions to slow and stabilize overall ecosystem metabolism. That stability is coupled back to the structural tissues and high production associated with the littoral and wetland components of the ecosystem. Any alterations to the sources or the use of the organic matter production will alter the stability of the aquatic ecosystem.

Recommendations

Freshwater ecology has always been an integrative science. As one examines the progression of developments of the discipline over the past century, a clear evolution of transitions emerges through descriptive, comparative, and correlative analyses. These approaches continue at present, particularly in sophisticated modeling of hypothetical ecosystem functioning. Comprehension of why freshwater ecosystems operate as they do emanates best from experimentally controlled disturbances and manipulations of parts of or whole ecosystems. Adventitious disturbances, such as from fire or floods, can also help researchers recognize couplings among ecosystem components and regulatory mechanisms.

Interactive metabolism among biota must be quantified on several spatial and temporal scales in order to evaluate and manage the composite effects of natural or human-induced disturbances to natural ecosystems. General interactions are prevalent across individual species and throughout ecosystem processes, and we must seek these generalities, rather than the differences, among communities in order to manage fresh waters effectively and efficiently.

Fresh waters are biogeochemical systems that require understanding of the *entire* ecosystem. Wetland-littoral land-water interface regions are enormously effective in controlling both loadings to, and influencing metabolism and biotic development within, receiving waters. Particular emphasis is needed on understanding how material and energy flows are regulated and modified by the metabolism of the land-water interface communities. Understanding must occur at the biochemical and microbial levels where most (more than 90 percent) of the material and energy fluxes are occurring and being regulated. Examination of the couplings among biochemical, microbial, and genetic and molecular experimental approaches to address common questions are essential for quantifying functional interactions and regulation in freshwater ecosystems. Organic matter from terrestrial and wetland sources subsidizes metabolism of lakes and streams. Because that imported DOM consists largely of compounds derived from structural tissues of higher plants and is relatively recalcitrant to biological degradation, this subsidy is degraded slowly and provides an inherent metabolic stability to the ecosystems. Factors or human activities that alter loading or degradation rates of this organic matter alter the stability of freshwater ecosystems.

References

Benke, A. C., and J. L. Meyer. 1988. Structure and function of a blackwater river in the southeastern USA. *Verhandlungen der Internationale Vereinigung für Theoretische und Angewandte Limnologie* 23:1209–1218.

Boavida, M. J., and R. G. Wetzel. 1998. Inhibition of phosphatase activity by dissolved humic substances and hydrolytic reactivation by natural UV. *Freshwater Biology* 40:285–293.

Cole, J. J., N. F. Caraco, G. W. Kling, and T. K. Kratz. 1994. Carbon dioxide supersaturation in the surface waters of lakes. *Science* 265:1568–1570.

Hairston, N. G., Jr., and N. G. Hairston Sr. 1993. Cause-effect relationships in energy flow, trophic structure, and interspecific interactions. *American Naturalist* 142:379–411.

Hutchinson, G. E. 1959. Homage to Santa Rosalia, or why are there so many kinds of animals? *American Naturalist* 93:145–159.

———. 1978. *An introduction to population ecology.* New Haven, Conn.: Yale University Press.

Kling, G. W., G. W. Kipphut, M. C. Miller. 1992. The flux of CO_2 and CH_4 from lakes and rivers in arctic Alaska. *Hydrobiologia* 240:23–36.

Lehman, J. T. 1986. The goal of understanding in limnology. *Limnology and Oceanography* 31:1160–1166.

Likens, G. E., ed. 1985. *An ecosystem approach to aquatic ecology: Mirror Lake and its environment.* New York: Springer-Verlag.

Lindeman, R. L. 1942. The trophic-dynamic aspect of ecology. *Ecology* 23:399–417.

Moran, M. A., and R. G. Zepp. 1997. Role of photoreactions in the formation of biologically labile compounds from dissolved organic matter. *Limnology and Oceanography* 42:1307–1316.

Otsuki, A., and R. G. Wetzel. 1974. Calcium and total alkalinity budgets and calcium carbonate precipitation of a small hard-water lake. *Archiv für Hydrobiologie* 73:14–30.

Saunders, G. W. 1971. Carbon flow in the aquatic system. Pp. 31–45 in *The structure and function of fresh-water microbial communities*, edited by J. Cairns Jr. Research Division Monograph 3, Virginia Polytechnic Institute, Blacksburg.

———. 1972. The transformations of artificial detritus in lake water. *Memorie di Istituto Italiano Idrobiologia* 29 (Supplement):261–288.

Vähätalo, A. V., M. Salkinoja-Salonen, P. Taalas, and K. Salonen. 2000. Spectrum of the quantum yield for photochemical mineralization of dissolved organic carbon in a humic lake. *Limnology and Oceanography* 45: 664–676.

Vähätalo, A. V., K. Salonen, U. Münster, M. Järvinen, and R. G. Wetzel. 2002. Photochemical transformation of allochthonous organic matter provides bioavailable nutrients in a humic lake. *Archiv für Hydrobiologie* (In press).

Wetzel, R. G. 1983. *Limnology.* 2d ed. Philadelphia: Saunders College Publishing.

———. 1990. Land-water interfaces: Metabolic and limnological regulators. *Verhandlungen der Internationale Vereinigung für Theoretische und Angewandte Limnologie* 24:6–24.

———. 1991. Extracellular enzymatic interactions in aquatic ecosystems: Storage, redistribution, and interspecific communication. Pp. 6–28 in *Microbial enzymes in aquatic environments*, edited by R. J. Chróst. New York: Springer-Verlag.

———. 1993. Microcommunities and microgradients: Linking nutrient regeneration and high sustained aquatic primary production. *Netherlands Journal of Aquatic Ecology* 25:122–128.

———. 1995. Death, detritus, and energy flow in aquatic ecosystems. *Freshwater Biology* 33:83–89.

———. 1996. Benthic algae and nutrient cycling in standing freshwater ecosystems. Pp. 641–667 in *Algal ecology: Benthic algae in freshwater ecosystems,* edited by R. J. Stevenson, M. Bothwell, and R. Lowe. New York: Academic Press.

———. 1999. Biodiversity and shifting energetic stability within freshwater ecosystems. *Archives of Hydrobiology Special Issue: Advances in Limnology* 54:19–32.

———. 2000a. Freshwater ecology: Changes, requirements, and future demands. *Limnology* 1:3–11.

———. 2000b. Natural photodegradation by UV-B of dissolved organic matter of different decomposing plant sources to readily degradable fatty acids. *Verhandlungen der Internationale Vereinigung für Theoretische und Angewandte Limnologie* 27:2036–2043.

———. 2001. *Limnology: Lake and river ecosystems.* San Diego: Academic Press.

Wetzel, R. G., P. G. Hatcher, T. S. Bianchi. 1995. Natural photolysis by ultraviolet irradiance of recalcitrant dissolved organic matter to simple substrates for rapid bacterial metabolism. *Limnology and Oceanography* 40:1369–1380.

Wetzel, R. G., P. H. Rich, M. C. Miller, and H. L. Allen. 1972. Metabolism of dissolved and particulate detrital carbon in a temperate hard-water lake. *Memorie di Istituto Italiano Idrobiologie* 29 (Supplement):185–243.

Chapter 6

Wetland Biogeochemistry

*S. Reza Pezeshki, Ronald D. DeLaune, John A. Nyman,
W. James Catallo, Clifford A. Ochs, Scott A. Milburn,
John M. Melack, Leal Mertes, Laura Hess, and
Bruce Forsberg*

The biogeochemical processes occurring in wetlands govern nutrient availability, plant growth and productivity, nutrient dynamics, and, thus, the many recognized functions of wetlands, including serving as nutrient sinks (Mitsch and Gosselink 1993). In fact, wetlands play a great role as sink, stabilizer, and transformer for many ions and nutrients and as such contribute significantly to water quality (e.g., Walbridge and Lockaby 1994; Moustafa 1999) and the overall quality of freshwater systems. Understanding biogeochemical processes, therefore, is important to any long-term plans to effectively manage sustainability of water and wetland resources. For instance, a lack of information on nutrient storage rates in wetlands underlies public and professional controversy regarding the benefits of certain water-quality regulations, wetland restoration efforts, and assessment of the success of such efforts. Relationships among nutrient sources, nutrient sinks, and nutrient dynamics in wetlands should be better quantified. Wetlands, normally found at the interface of terrestrial and open-water aquatic ecosystems, have unique properties that are primarily governed by hydrology. Wetland processes also exist outside of traditional wetland ecosystems. Many of the biogeochemical processes associated with wetlands are also important in agriculture and forestry, wastewater treatment, and constructed wetlands. Hydrology is critical to maintaining structure and functions of wetlands. Seasonal patterns of water-level change (*hydroperiod*) affect many factors, including soil oxygen availability and elemental cycling, which in turn govern plant species composition and productivity (Mitsch and Gosselink 1993).

Water-saturated soils or sediments limit soil oxygen availability, lowering soil redox conditions and creating anoxic conditions, which in turn govern biogeochemical transformations and nutrient fluxes. Excess water can exist for either short periods or for extended periods depending on the location of the ecosystem and time of year.

Microbial processes differ in anoxic soils as compared to well-drained, oxygenated soils (Fenchel and Finlay 1995). Diffusion of oxygen into water-saturated wetland soils is up to 10,000 times slower than diffusion into porous or well-drained soils. The lack of oxygen leads to anoxic conditions, which force bacterial populations to rely on electron acceptors other than oxygen, including nitrate, iron, manganese and sulfate, and influence processes of elemental cycling. Nitrification-denitrification reactions, sulfate reduction, and methanogenesis are important processes in wetlands.

As a result of lack of oxygen and limited quantities of alternate electron acceptors, degradation of organic matter by microorganisms in wetland soils is less rapid and complete as compared to upland or aerated soils. Wetland soils, due to the slow rate of organic matter degradation, may serve as carbon (C) sinks (Mitsch and Gosselink 1993).

The reducing or anoxic conditions in soil or sediment prevent plants from carrying out aerobic root respiration. Plants native to wetland soils have developed specific adaptations for growing in such environments. These adaptations include anatomical, morphological, and metabolic features. One example of such a feature is the development of aerenchyma tissue that allows oxygen diffusion from the aerial portions of the plant (leaves and stems) deep into the root system.

The topics in this chapter address hydrological conditions and wetland processes representative of a range of wetland types and environments. The topics covered also demonstrate the geographical extent, the spatial and temporal concerns, and the number of disciplines involved in the field of wetland biogeochemistry, including agriculture, hydrology, soil chemistry, plant physiology, and ecology. Representative data of selected wetland biogeochemical processes occurring in natural wetlands and flooded agricultural soils are presented. The wetland soil environment impacting growth and function of wetland plants, including physiological responses of plants to the intensity and capacity of soil reduction, is addressed. The significance of hourly and daily shifts in soil redox conditions as related to biogeochemical processes is discussed. Processes governing nutrient storage in rapidly accreting marsh soils in a subsiding estuary environment are detailed. The importance of denitrification and nitrate-reducing bacteria in a constructed wetland designed to treat daily runoff is also addressed. Nutrient transformation resulting from winter flooding of agricultural soils in the Mississippi Delta is also documented. Methods for estimating carbon storage, including inputs and outputs for wetland habitats in a large floodplain ecosystem, the Amazon Basin floodplain, are presented. Using this background information along with examples from various wetlands from the United States and abroad, we hope readers appreciate the importance of understanding various critical biogeochemical processes as well as the relationship between wetland functions and long-term planning to successfully manage for sustainable wetland resources and freshwater ecosystems.

Effects of Soil Oxidation-Reduction Conditions on Wetland Plant Functioning

In a typical flooded wetland soil, plants primarily respond to soil physicochemical changes (Pezeshki 1994; DeLaune et al. 1998b). Wetland plants are adapted to endure soil oxygen deficiency; however, various species may differ in their ability to withstand certain levels of intense soil-reducing conditions. These responses may lead to a wide range of plant stress symptoms. Although various plant responses to flooded soil conditions have been addressed in numerous publications (Kozlowski 1984a,b, 1997; Jackson et al. 1991; Armstrong et al. 1994; Pezeshki 1994; Drew 1997; Vartapetian and Jackson 1997), little information can be found on the relationship between wetland plant functions and the two aspects of soil redox potential, the intensity and the capacity of reduction (DeLaune and Pezeshki 2001).

The reduction of the inorganic redox systems in a flooded soil may be characterized in intensity or capacity terms. The intensity factor determines the relative ease of reduction, usually represented by the free energy of reduction or by the equivalent electromotive force of the reaction (oxidation-reduction potential, or redox potential). The capacity factor refers to the amount of electrons accepted by the soil oxidants in support of microbial respiration (e.g., oxygen consumption at root interface) (DeLaune and Pezeshki 1991, 2001). From a plant physiological-ecology standpoint, there are many uses of interpretations of redox processes in soils; one example is that soil redox potential is an indication of the oxidation-reduction status of various soil compounds. For example, a redox potential of 0 mV (zero millivolt) indicates that oxygen and nitrate are not likely to be present and that the bioreducible iron and manganese compounds are in a reduced state. At this same potential, however, sulfate is stable in the soil with no sulfide, which is toxic to plants, being formed. A redox potential of +400 millivolts indicates that oxygen may be present even though there may be excess water in the soil (DeLaune and Pezeshki 1991). Thus, in the following section the significance of the intensity and capacity of reduction in soils to wetland plant functioning will be examined. Emphasis will be placed on the relationships between soil flooding, reduced soil conditions (low soil redox potential), the components of the soil oxidation-reduction system (namely the intensity and the capacity of reduction) and their influence on plant internal oxygen transport, rhizosphere oxygenation, growth, and survival of wetland species.

Soil Oxidation-Reduction Potential

Soil flooding initiates a chain of reactions leading to reduced soil conditions (low soil oxidation-reduction potential [Eh]). These reactions include physical, chemical, and biological processes that have significant implications for wetland plant functioning, survival, and productivity (see Ponnamperuma 1984; Gambrell et al. 1991). Physical processes include restriction of soil-atmospheric gas exchange and depletion of soil oxygen needed for root respiration. Once flooded, the limited supply of oxygen in floodwater is rapidly depleted by roots, soil microorganisms, and soil reductants (Ponnamperuma 1972). The depletion of oxygen results in a series of chemical changes in soil, including accumulation of CO_2, CH_4, N_2 and H_2 (Ponnamperuma 1984). In a typical series of reduction, NO_3^{-1} is reduced to NO_2^{-1} and N_2 (denitrification), followed by reductions of Mn^{4+} to Mn^{2+}, Fe^{3+} to Fe^{2+}, SO_4^{2-} to S^{2-} (Fig. 6.1) and accumulations of acetic and butyric acids produced by fermentative microbial metabolism (Ponnamperuma 1984). Thus, soil redox potential decreases (becomes more negative) in response to flooding (Patrick and DeLaune 1977; Gambrell and Patrick 1978; Ponnamperuma 1984). Aerated soils have characteristic redox

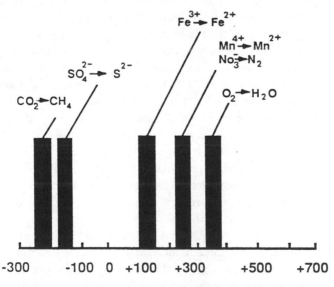

Figure 6.1. Redox potential at which various inorganic substrates in wetland soils are reduced (redrawn from DeLaune et al. 1998b)

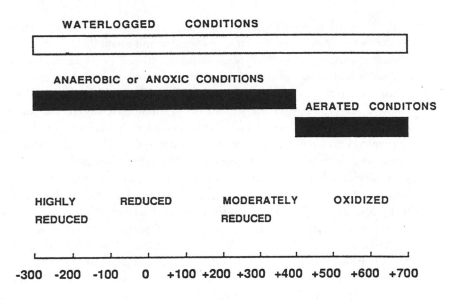

Figure 6.2. Redox range in soils compared to oxidation-reduction status (redrawn from DeLaune et al. 1998b)

potentials in the range of +400 to +700 millivolts whereas waterlogged soils may exhibit redox potentials as low as –300 millivolts (Fig. 6.2).

In wetland soils, plants are faced with not only the lack of oxygen but also a substantial demand for oxygen in the root medium (DeLaune et al. 1990; van Wijck et al. 1992). Such conditions create the potential for root oxygen loss to soil by diffusion, thus, additional root stress (DeLaune et al. 1990; Kludze and DeLaune 1995a,b; Brix and Sorrell 1996).

Intensity and Capacity of Reduction

As mentioned earlier, the reduction of the inorganic redox systems, including oxygen in hydric soils following flooding, can be described in terms of intensity and capacity. In natural systems, such as soils where there is biological activity and where many redox couples exist (Fe^{3+}/Fe^{2+}), the oxidation-reduction or redox potential is ordinarily used to denote the intensity of reduction. The capacity factor of a redox system is best described in terms of its oxygen equivalent—a comparison of various soil electron acceptors (e.g., NO_3, MnO_2, FeOOH, SO_4) or redox couples, to soil oxygen and ability to serve as electron acceptor (Reddy et al. 1980; Patrick et al. 1986; Kludze and DeLaune 1995a,b). The capacity factor of the various redox systems can vary from one soil to another.

Proper evaluation of wetland plant responses to soil flooding requires the evaluation of both intensity and capacity of soil reduction, since these two components influence oxygen consumption (Kludze and DeLaune 1995a,b). DeLaune et al. (1990) were the first to demonstrate that oxygen demand or consumption (capacity of reduction) in conjunction with intensity of reduction (as determined from soil Eh measurements) in the root medium were important for predicting wetland plant functioning. Furthermore, they noted that using solutions depleted in oxygen that are created by the introduction of nitrogen gas did not represent a high-oxygen-demand root environment such as those under reducing conditions. Thus, these solutions are poor analogues for wetland soils. Using titanium citrate solution to create a high-oxygen-demand root environment, DeLaune et al. (1990), Kludze et al. (1993), and Sorrell et al. (1993) reported that root oxygen transport and release of a number of wetland species were affected by oxygen demand in soil. However such a solution, while a significant improvement over deoxygenated solutions, at best mimics wet soil conditions (Kludze and DeLaune 1995a,b) but does not represent other important characteristics of wet soils. These characteristics include the soil's capacity for phytotoxin production (e.g., H_2S production) under strongly reducing conditions, which has significant effects on most wetland species.

Plant Responses to Reducing Soil Conditions

In wetland plants, aerenchyma tissue facilitates oxygen diffusion from aerial plant parts to the roots. Such a system may exist in roots, stems, and leaves but is found primarily in roots (Armstrong et al. 1994). This system allows a plant to transport the needed oxygen to the roots for maintaining aerobic respiration and to oxidize reducing compounds in the rhizosphere. In addition, the internal system of large gas spaces also reduces internal volume of respiring tissues and oxygen consumption, and thus enhances the potential for oxygen to reach the distant underground portions of the plant (Armstrong et al. 1994, 1996). The oxygen transport system is considered to be a major mechanism critical to a plant's ability to cope with soil oxygen deficiency (Armstrong et al. 1994, 1996; Pezeshki 1994; Drew 1997; Kozlowski 1997).

There is a limited body of data on the relationship between functional aspects of gas transport within plants and soil oxidation-reduction conditions. In a few studies that evaluated the relationship between plant responses and the intensity of soil reduction, it became evident that intense soil reduction (low soil Eh) promoted oxygen loss from the root to the rhizosphere (Kludze 1994). For instance, in some wetland species, high correlation (r = 0.96) was found between radial oxygen loss (ROL) from roots and soil Eh intensity. In other words, there was an increasingly higher oxygen loss rate as soil Eh became more reduced (Kludze and DeLaune 1995a). In addition, low soil Eh led to decreased leaf carbon assimilation (Pezeshki et al. 1993; Kludze 1994; Pezeshki 1994) and substantial inhibition of root elongation (Pezeshki and DeLaune 1990). Root porosity (percent root air space) in *Spartina patens*, a dominant U.S. Gulf coastal marsh species, increased as soil Eh decreased, resulting in root porosity of 22 percent in plants grown at +200 millivolts while porosity was 45 percent in plants grown at −300 millivolts. Also ROL was significantly greater for plants in −300-millivolts Eh treatment as compared to the +200-millivolt Eh treatment (Kludze and DeLaune 1994). Other studies have shown similar responses for the root porosity-soil Eh intensity relationship in other wetland plants, including swamp and bottomland woody species (Kludze et al. 1994; Pezeshki and Anderson 1997). In a study conducted on a swamp species, *Taxodium distichum* (baldcypress), a significant increase in root porosity and ROL was noted at an Eh intensity of −240 to −260 millivolts in root medium (Kludze et al. 1994). ROL increased from 12.7 in the control (aerated) to 42.3 mmol O_2 g^{-1} day^{-1} (millimol oxygen per gram per day) at −250 millivolts. Similarly, root air space increased from 13.3 to 41.4 percent in response to the intensity of reduction. In *Oryza sativa* (rice), ROL increased in response to a drop in soil Eh, concomitant with root porosity that increased from 26.8 to 35 percent when Eh dropped from +200 to −300 millivolts (Kludze et al. 1993).

Despite the reported increase in aerenchyma tissue formation in many wetland species and, thus, the increase in porosity in response to reducing soil conditions, such increase may not be sufficient to satisfy the root respiratory needs for oxygen, perhaps due to the greater ROL in response to high intensity of reduction. Pezeshki et al. (1991, 1993) concluded that despite a substantial enhancement of aerenchyma tissue formation in *Spartina patens*, alcohol dehydrogenase activity continued to be higher in flooded than control plants, indicating continued oxygen stress in the roots of flooded plants. In addition, the increase in ROL reported under negative soil Eh may explain the reported reductions in root growth of several wetland species in anoxic soils. For instance, in *S. patens* root and shoot dry weights decreased by 40 percent and 25 percent, respectively, as soil Eh dropped from +200 millivolts to −300 millivolts. Results clearly indicated the influence of soil Eh intensity on the growth of this marsh species (Fig. 6.3). Roots were more sensitive to Eh intensity than shoots were (Kludze and DeLaune 1994). Pezeshki and DeLaune (1990) reported cessation of root growth in *S. patens* at soil Eh below −100 millivolts. In addition, Pezeshki et al. (1991) noted a smaller root system in *S. patens* under reducing conditions and concluded that such reduction in root mass may in part, be responsible for a negative feedback inhibition of photosynthesis thus reducing the productivity of this species. DeLaune et al. (1990) studied plant responses to the intensity of soil reduction using titanium-citrate solution. They demon-

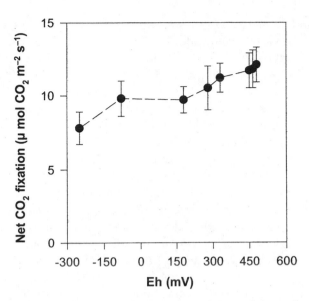

Figure 6.3. Influence of intensity of reduction on photosynthetic carbon fixation of *Spartina patens* along the anaerobic portion of the redox scale (redrawn from Kludze and DeLaune 1995b)

strated that the intensity of the reduction in growth medium—and therefore the demand for oxygen in the root zone—exerted significant influence on plant physiological functioning.

The soil redox capacity factor is also important although much less is known about its effects on wetland plants than is known about the effects of the intensity factor. In fact, two different soils with the same level of intensity of reduction may differ substantially in the capacity for reduction. Soil reduction capacity can be determined using measurements of soil respiration and calculating oxygen equivalent by stoichiometry (Kludze and DeLaune 1995b). Levels of soil redox capacity may be created and manipulated by providing extra carbon and an energy source (organic matter) to the soil while maintaining the same redox intensity level. In an experimental setup, reduction capacity may be controlled by adding different amounts of granular D-glucose to the root medium, which is also maintained under preset reducing conditions (such as when Eh is less than +350 millivolts, Kludze 1994).

Differences in Eh capacity among wetland soils may influence many plant functions, including oxygen transport, rhizosphere oxygenation, and photosynthetic rates (Fig. 6.4) (Kludze and DeLaune 1995b). Kludze and DeLaune (1995b) demonstrated that increased Eh capacity under a constant Eh intensity of –200 millivolts did not have a significant effect on root porosity in *S. patens*, but oxygen release was increased in response to the increasing Eh capacity.

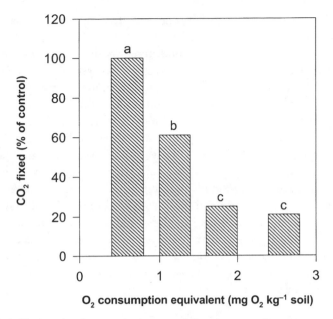

Figure 6.4. Changes in photosynthetic rates of *Spartina patens* in response to the increasing soil redox capacity. Redox capacity was manipulated by adding an energy source to the root medium. Soil was maintained at the same redox intensity (–250 mV) but oxygen consumption (capacity) was increased from 0.6 to 2.6 mg O_2kg^{-1} soil. (Redrawn from Kludze and DeLaune 1995b)

However, the authors reported that there was a threshold of Eh capacity beyond which oxygen release remained constant and/or decreased in this species. The response was attributed to the potential effects of several factors, such as soil phytotoxins, as well as plant physiological responses, including stomatal closure. However, the reasons for such a response remain unknown. Plant carbon fixation, root, and shoot growth were significantly inhibited in *S. patens* under increasing soil reduction capacity. Root and shoot dry weights decreased by 70 and 37 percent in high reduction capacity conditions compared to control plants, respectively (Kludze and DeLaune 1995b).

In addition to affecting plant growth, the intensity and capacity of reduction may govern nutrient uptake in wetland plants. In a study of seedlings of two bottomland woody species grown in soil suspension maintained at three Eh levels, +560, +340, and +175 millivolts, fertilizer [15]nitrogen (N) uptake decreased with decreasing soil redox potential, a response to the intensity of reduction (DeLaune et al. 1998a,b). Phosphorus uptake by *Typha domingensis* (southern cattail) was inhibited in response to decreases in soil redox potential (intensity of reduction) in the rooting medium. Increasing capacity of reduction (using titanium citrate solution) resulted in a further decrease in phosphorus uptake

(DeLaune et al. 1999) further confirming the effects of reduction capacity on nutrient uptake.

Based on the literature discussed, both intensity and capacity of reduction appear to influence plant functioning in wetland ecosystems. In wetland soils, plants are faced with a substantial demand for oxygen in the rhizosphere and the potential for loss of oxygen to soil and thus must deal with additional root stress. As soil reduction continues and intensifies, there is a progressively greater demand imposed upon roots for oxygen and a corresponding greater potential for loss of oxygen to the rhizosphere. The severity of oxygen loss and the effects of reduction intensity and capacity on plant functioning appear to be broad across wetland species. The need for additional data on various aspects of plant functioning and growth in wetland ecosystems in response to soil phytotoxins and redox conditions, especially of capacity of reduction, is clear. For example, under strongly reducing conditions, hydrogen sulfide, which is toxic to plants, is produced. Under some reducing soil conditions (high reduction capacity) plant roots may not be able to create an oxidized rhizosphere, which helps neutralize the sulfide produced.

Variations in Biogeochemical Processes in Tidal Wetlands

The distribution, productivity, and ecological functioning of plants in many types of wetlands are influenced by hydrological and other cycles operating over a wide temporal range (Mitsch and Gosselink 1993). While seasonal and other long-term changes in some ecological processes are well established, quantitative studies of more rapid variations (e.g., hourly or daily) in these processes are limited. Recent work evaluated rapid changes in sediment biogeochemical process variables, such as Eh, pH, microbial activity, trace gas evolution, pore water chemistry, carbon and pollutant mobilization and transformation, and plant root zone processes, in sediment-plant systems exposed to diurnal tides versus more static drained or flooded conditions.

These studies were conducted using specially designed hydrodynamic micro- and mesocosm systems equipped with automated data acquisition for numerous biogeochemical process outputs in laboratory and field settings. This work has shown that numerous important biogeochemical variables can change rapidly (within hours) in response to periodic tidal and other forcing functions in natural and artificial settings. These included Eh, pH, pore water chemistry, and trace gas exchanges, which were significantly influenced by water-level variations. For example, when sampled with high temporal resolution (e.g., 1–55 per hour), Eh values in sediment-plant systems oscillated in response to the diurnal flood-drain cycle for extended periods (3–104 days), with typical amplitudes of the Eh oscillations on the order of 40–300 millivolts. No such pattern was observed under any static hydrological condition, even though diurnal (and longer-period) light and heat cycles were present. Results indicated that fast biogeochemical process dynamics need to be encompassed in models and designs of experiments on tidal wetlands.

The research was conducted to understand the time structuring of diurnal and hourly biogeochemical process variations in wetlands using microcosms. Results indicated that hydrodynamic mesocosms (1,200 to more than 4,000 liters) can be constructed and used efficiently with a high degree of reproducibility (Catallo 1999). Thus, long- and short-term studies in hydrology, chemical ecology, wetland restoration, pollutant wastewater treatment wetlands, and environmental toxicology can be conducted in these systems economically.

In addition to the large spatial heterogeneities in wetlands, many biogeochemical processes display temporal dynamics over a broad range. In tidal wetlands, biogeochemical process outputs were found to be significant on the order of hours, and driven primarily by diurnal tidal variations. Tidal pulsing promoted sediment Eh and pH variations, which followed the tide. Lack of pulsing (flooding or draining for extended periods) gave rise to relatively static and well-poised conditions. Over the long term (e.g., months to years) hydrological condition (flooded, drained, tidal) can influence slower processes such as plant growth, production, and organic chemical transformation. Clearly, environmental restoration, remediation, and mitigation attempts also must address these issues over the long term, particularly because critical ecological endpoints can be influenced by these rapid process variations.

Nutrient Storage Rates in a Natural Marsh System Receiving Wastewater

Artificial wetlands are now commonly used to improve water quality; long-term operational information exists for many full-scale projects (Kadlec and Knight 1996). Despite a growing body of data relating artificial wetlands and wastewater, there have been few studies of the effects of natural wetlands on wastewater (see Kadlec and Knight 1996 for a historical perspective). Those studies generally focused on denitrification, which converts nitrate to nitrogen gas or nitrous oxide, rather than on burial, because in most regions burial is too slow to remove significant quantities of nutrients. In subsiding environments, however, burial might permanently store significant amounts of nutrients. Nutrient burial rates have been studied in natural wetlands in the Florida Everglades, in North Carolina estuarine marshes, and in southwestern Louisiana (Craft and Richardson 1993; Craft et al. 1993; Foret 1997). Nutrient storage rates in soil have rarely been studied in natural wetlands receiving wastewater.

A lack of information on nutrient storage rates in wetlands underlies the public and professional controversies regarding the benefits of water-quality regulations, wetland protection, and restoration activities, and the benefits of introducing nutrient-rich water to estuarine marshes. Relationships among nutrient sources and rates, and nutrient sinks and rates, need to be better understood in wetland nutrient dynamics as the following case study demonstrates.

Nutrient Storage Rates in a Natural Marsh System: A Case Study

A recent study tested the hypothesis that a natural wetland at the mouth of a freshwater stream emptying into a lake (Lake Pontchartrain is located in coastal Louisiana) does not affect nutrient inputs into the lake. The study was conducted on the northern shore of Lake Pontchartrain in a naturally occurring marsh that predates the earliest aerial photographs.

Lake Pontchartrain is a large (approximately 60 kilometers in diameter) estuary in southeastern Louisiana that receives freshwater from numerous rivers and streams on its northern shore and seawater from a tidal pass at its eastern end. The marsh studied was classified as a brackish and intermediate marsh (Chabreck and Linscombe 1978) and lies on a tributary (Salt Bayou) to Lake Pontchartrain. The construction of railways and highways across Salt Bayou reduced freshwater input from the Pearl River into the marsh in the mid-1950s. That reduction in freshwater inflow is believed to have contributed to subsequent conversion of the marsh to shallow open water. Since 1956, 1,035 hectares of marsh have converted to shallow, open water; 1,432 hectares of marsh remained in 1990 (Natural Resources Conservation Service 1997). A canal adjacent to Fritchie Marsh carries urban runoff and tertiary treated domestic sewage from the community of Slidell to Lake Pontchartrain. Most water in the canal discharges directly into Lake Pontchartrain, but some leaves the canal and flows through the Fritchie Marsh before rejoining the canal and subsequently discharging into the lake.

One data set was collected to quantify long-term nutrient storage rates in Fritchie Marsh. Nutrient storage rates were determined from the accretion rate of soil and the nutrient content of soil in the marsh. Soil cores were collected and vertical accretion since 1963 was determined with the ^{137}cesium (Cs) dating technique (DeLaune et al. 1978). Vertical accretion rates were compared to regional estimates of subsidence to determine if there was a vertical accretion deficit. Vertical accretion deficits are often the mechanism by which sediment starvation and rapid subsidence (Fig. 6.5) cause wetland loss in coastal Louisiana (Nyman et al. 1993).

The gross material accumulation rate, meaning the accumulation of mineral sediments as well as organic matter, was calculated for each core from the bulk density of soil samples overlying the 1963 marsh surface. The accumulation rate of mineral sediments and organic matter was similarly calculated from the bulk density and ash content of each section overlying the 1963 marsh surface. The

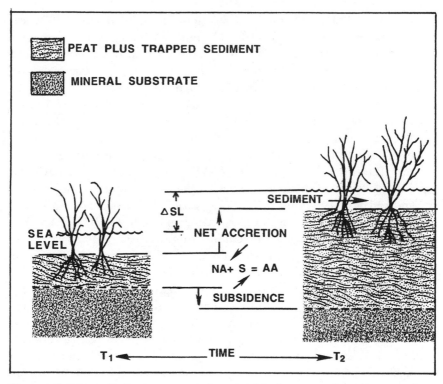

Figure 6.5. Schematic diagram representing a model of processes that govern marsh accretion (ΔSL=change in sea level, NA=Net Accretion, S=Subsidence, and AA=Absolute Accretion)

accumulation rate of nitrogen (N), carbon (C), and phosphorus (P) was similarly calculated from the bulk density and the nutrient content of soil overlying the 1963 marsh surface. Carbon and nitrogen content were determined by ignition in a Carlo-Erba Elemental Analyzer equipped with a thermoconductivity detector. Phosphorus content was determined following acid digestion using Parson's colorimetric analysis (Parsons 1984). A second data set was collected to compare changes in nutrient concentration in waters that empty directly into the lake to changes in nutrient concentration in waters that flow through the Fritchie Marsh before emptying into the lake. Salinity and conductivity were measured simultaneously with the collection of each water sample. Nutrient concentrations were determined on the unfiltered water samples. Total nitrogen and phosphorus content were determined using Parson's colorimetric analysis (Parsons 1984). Changes in nutrient concentration resulting from dilution with lake water were differentiated from nutrient uptake with mixing diagrams, or, in other words, ionic ratios (Day et al. 1989).

Results indicated that accretion in Fritchie Marsh was slightly less than the average for brackish marshes in the Mississippi River Deltaic Plain (0.72 centimeters per year; Nyman et al. 1990). The more rapid average accretion in the entire Mississippi River Deltaic Plain than in the study site results from the more rapid subsidence rate elsewhere in the Mississippi River Deltaic Plain (approximately 1.0 centimeter per year; Penland and Ramsey 1990).

Accretion rates within sites were almost identical but the two sites differed. Accretion at the northern site was 40 percent slower than at the southern site. Accretion at the northern site was similar to estimates of subsidence on the northern shore of Lake Pontchartrain, which is estimated at 0.45 centimeters per year (Penland and Ramsey 1990). However, it is difficult to reconcile the rapid accretion at the southern site with the slow subsidence reported by Penland and Ramsey (1990). It is also unusual for accretion rates to vary so much within such a small area (e.g., Nyman et al. 1990, 1993). The large difference between northern and southern sites suggests that a shallow, active fault runs through Fritchie Marsh. Such faults are common in coastal Louisiana in general and in and around Lake Pontchartrain. Lopez (1991) examined seismic data and reinterpreted the location of Baton Rouge/Denham Springs fault system, and concluded that the fault lay farther south than previously believed and was positioned such that it would bisect the Fritchie Marsh. Our findings support Lopez's (1991) conclusions regarding the position of that fault system. Lopez (1991) also concluded that the fault system was active and responsible for a 6-inch offset on State Highway Bridge 11 crossing eastern Lake Pontchartrain. The substantial difference in accretion rates between the northern and southern sites that we observed support Lopez's (1991) conclusion that the fault system is active, although different faults within the fault system would be required to produce the offset in accretion in the Fritchie Marsh and the offset in the highway bridge. While this active fault may contribute to wetland loss in the Fritchie Marsh, it also increases the potential for burial of nutrients in the marsh.

Gross material accumulation was 20 percent slower at the northern site than at the southern site. The faster accumulation rate at the southern site results from the more rapid vertical accretion induced at the southern site by the fault. Extrapolated to the entire area, it appears that the 433-hectare Fritchie Marsh restoration site stores slightly over 13,660 metric tons of material annually. Some of this material is organic carbon that is produced in the marsh, but the associated nutrients and sediments would otherwise be discharged into Lake Pontchartrain. The material being stored in wetland soil at the Fritchie Marsh includes mineral sediments, organic matter, and the ecologically important elements carbon, nitrogen, and phosphorus. Significant amounts of nutrients nitrogen and phosphorus were being stored in the marsh soils, but the amount stored has decreased 48 percent since the 1950s because of the conversion of wetlands to shallow open water areas. These open water areas are assumed to be stable rather than accreting.

The nitrogen to phosphorus ratio (N: P ratio) of soil at the northern site was slightly higher than at the southern site. Higher ratios indicate a greater potential for phosphorus availability to limit plant growth at the northern site, but the small difference between the sites may not be ecologically meaningful. These ratios appeared typical; they were similar to those reported for an unmanaged, *S. patens*-dominated marsh at Rockefeller Refuge (Foret 1997).

Nutrients were more concentrated in water in the canal than in Lake Pontchartrain water. This situation is typical of estuaries in general (Liss 1976). For example, total nitrogen concentrations in the Mississippi River generally average 3 parts per million but drop rapidly to approximately 1.0 parts per million soon after entering estuarine marshes (Lane et al. 1999). Total phosphorus in the Mississippi River also drops rapidly soon after entering estuarine marshes: from approximately 0.4 parts per million phosphorus in the river to approximately 0.2 parts per million phosphorus after entering estuarine marshes. Nutrient concentrations in the W-14 Canal were less than those reported for the Mississippi River (Antweiler et al. 1995; Lane et al. 1999) and did not exceed 1.5 parts per million nitrogen (108 μmole nitrogen per liter) or 0.5 parts per million phosphorus (16 μmole phosphorus per liter).

A simple comparison of nutrient concentrations between water in the canal and the marsh incorrectly suggests that the marsh was removing nutrients when the water samples were collected. In fact, proper evaluation of the water-quality data indicates that the low nutrient water in the marsh was actually low-nutrient, high-salinity water introduced from Lake Pontchartrain at an earlier date and subsequently stored in the marsh. Thus, the low-nutrient, high-salinity water in the marsh interior indicates at least periodic hydrologic isolation of the marsh interior. The isolation apparently results from a lack of inflow from the canal at the northern (upstream) end of the marsh and possibly from high water levels in the canal that inhibit drainage of the marsh at the southern (downstream) end of the marsh. A restoration project by the Coastal Wetland Planning, Protection, Restoration Act (CWPPRA) Task Force is intended to increase the flow of water from the W-14 Canal into the northern part of the wetland. The increased flow is intended to reduce salinity stress on emergent vegetation but should also reduce the hydrologic isolation that the marsh currently experiences. It could not be determined if the failure to detect nutrient uptake with the water-quality data resulted from a true lack of uptake or from an inability of the technique to detect real differences.

In conclusion, data indicated that the study marsh stored significant amounts of nitrogen and phosphorus each year. Collectively, the marshes remove 240 metric tons of nitrogen and 10.9 metric tons of phosphorus from the Lake Pontchartrain estuary each year. While significant, these rates are only 42 percent of the removal rates that existed before extensive wetland loss that has occurred since 1956. Nutrient storage in wetland soils was faster at the southern end of the marshes compared to the northern end. More rapid soil formation at the southern end of the marshes appears to result from an active fault system previously reported in the area. Water-quality data indicated limited water exchange between the marsh interior and the adjacent water channels. Water-quality data failed to indicate nutrient uptake when mixing diagrams were used, but N: P ratios in water samples indicated that algae production in the marsh interior was phosphorus-limited when samples were collected. Hydrologic modification made during the spring of 2001 as part of the CWPPRA Task Force wetland restoration project should increase nutrient storage rates in marsh soil. Those modifications also may increase production of recalcitrant as well as organic forms of phosphorus that can be stored in bottom sediments of shallow open-water areas common in the marsh interior. The restoration project should also reduce the hydrologic isolation of the marsh interior and may thereby reduce plant stress, increase plant production, and increase nutrient burial in soil.

Biogeochemistry of Carbon in a Large Floodplain: A Case Study

The development of methods for estimating carbon storage, including inputs and outputs for wetland habitats in a large floodplain such as the Amazon Basin in South America, are increasingly needed because floodplains are important components of the biogeochemistry of such regions. Although the proportional coverage of various wetlands habitats (flooded forests, open water, and floating macrophytes) varies spatially and temporally, recent analyses of Landsat thematic mapper imagery and synthetic aperture radar images provide estimates of the phenology and spatial variations in coverage as the following case study in the central Amazon demonstrates. Landsat thematic mapper imagery refers to data expressed as images derived from a satellite-borne sensor with detectors in the visible and near infrared regions. The satellite carrying the thematic mapper is called Landsat. Synthetic aperture radar data are measurements made by generating a series of radar pulses on an aircraft or satellite and recording the radar signals returned to the airborne system after the signals have interacted with the Earth's surface.

Floodplains and associated lakes are important components of the biogeochemistry, ecology, and hydrology of the Amazon Basin. Amazon floodplains contain thousands of lakes and associated wetlands linked to each other and to the many rivers of this immense basin; the floodplains are a mosaic of flooded forests, open water, and floating macrophytes. Floodplain lakes and their associated wetland habitats play an important role in the organic carbon balance of the Amazon River system. They are the sites of aquatic plant production, the principal source of organic carbon for aquatic food chains, and a major source of methane and other biogenic gases to the troposphere. The purpose of this analysis is to summarize primary productivity and methane emission in Amazon lakes and associated wetlands located in the central Amazon Basin; the material is derived from Melack and Forsberg (2001).

A fringing floodplain along the 2,800-kilometer reach of the Amazon River from 52.5° west to 70.5° west contains about 6,500 lakes that vary considerably in shape and size (Sippel et al. 1992). Seasonal changes in river stage along this 2,800 kilometer reach resulted in variations in inundated area from 19,000 to 81,000 square kilometers during the period from 1979 to 1987, based on passive microwave measurements (Sippel et al. 1998).

Apportioning the areas of floodplain occupied by the three major aquatic habitats—open water, herbaceous macrophytes, and flooded forests—and determining their temporal changes remains a challenge. Because approximations are required for calculations of the organic carbon balance of the floodplain, results from recent remote sensing studies of the Amazon Basin were utilized. Sippel et al. (1992) estimated the open-water area of lakes to be 10,370 square kilometers. Partition of vegetated habitats was based on the analyses of Landsat thematic mapper imagery (Mertes et al. 1995; Mertes and Novo personal communication), synthetic aperture radar data (Hess et al. 1995), and aerial videography and ground-based surveys. Based on an average maximum inundated area of 67,900 square kilometers, it was estimated that the average maximum area occupied seasonally by herbaceous macrophytes is 29,300 square kilometers and that the average maximum area occupied seasonally by flooded forest is 28,200 square kilometers. Further basinwide analyses with new remote sensing data will surely modify and improve these estimates and permit additional refinements in floodplain classification.

Four main groups of plants contribute significantly to primary production in floodplain lakes: phytoplankton, herbaceous macrophytes, flooded forest trees, and periphytic algae. The distribution and production dynamics of each of these plant groups varies within and between lakes in response to spatial and temporal variations in lake morphology, biogeochemistry, and flooding patterns.

Phytoplankton communities are limited generally to the open waters of lakes where underwater light availability is sufficient. Forsberg (unpublished) has investigated primary production in thirty-six lakes associated with the Amazon River and its major tributaries in the central Amazon floodplain. Daily integral gross production, averaged over all lakes, was 0.82 g C m^{-2} d^{-1} (grams Carbon per m^2 per day), which corresponds to an annual production rate of about 300 g C m^{-2} y^{-1} (grams Carbon per m^2 per year). Based on Sippel et al.'s (1992) calculation of lake area, it was estimated that the total gross production of phytoplankton on the central Amazon floodplain was 3 Tg C y^{-1}, and net production was about 2 Tg C y^{-1}.

Large expanses of floating macrophytes develop and decay each year on the floodplain of the central Amazon Basin (Junk 1997). Herbaceous macrophytes are especially abundant in lakes associated with white-water rivers, where nutrient-rich sediments and waters stimulate their development. The complex structure and seasonal dynamics of herbaceous macrophyte communities make it difficult to estimate their total annual contribution to floodplain lake production. Junk and Piedade (1993) estimated the cumulative biomass increase of three successive macrophyte communities (terrestrial, semi-aquatic, and aquatic) growing under ideal conditions on the central Amazon floodplain to be 3,000 t dry wt. $km^{-2} y^{-1}$. Assuming a monthly biomass loss of 10–25 percent during the growing season, they estimated net annual primary production to be 5,000 t dry wt $km^{-2} y^{-1}$. Assuming a dry weight carbon content of 50 percent, this represents a net annual production of 2,500 t C $km^{-2} y^{-1}$. Using 29,300 square kilometers as the area of floodplain potentially covered by herbaceous macrophytes, we estimate the total contribution of herbaceous macrophyte communities to floodplain net production along the central Amazon to be about 73 Tg C y^{-1}.

Floodplain forests often occupy a significant portion of the littoral region of Amazon floodplain lakes. Based on Worbes (1997), average net production rate of 1,150 t C $km^{-2} y^{-1}$ for well-developed floodplain forest is projected. Applying this value to a maximum high-water flooded forest area of 28,200 square kilometers, the total contribution of flooded forests to production along the central Amazon floodplain is estimated to be about 32 Tg y^{-1}. To the extent that some floodplain forests are of lower density and stature than well-developed forests growing in nutrient-rich environments, this estimate is high.

Periphytic algae require solid substrata and adequate light levels for growth. They are generally found near the water surface in the littoral regions of lakes attached to the submerged portions of emergent macrophytes and flooded forest trees. The contribution of periphytic algal communities associated with herbaceous macrophytes and floodplain forests to lacustrine production along the central Amazon floodplain was determined by multiplying the maximum area of each habitat (28,000 and 29,300 square kilometers for floodplain forest and herbaceous macrophytes, respectively) by the corresponding daily areal production rate and the average estimated inundation period. Since most lakes along the central Amazon floodplain are associated with the main or side channels of the Amazon River, the area production values of Doyle (1991) for macrophyte habitat (1.2 t C $km^{-2}d^{-1}$) and Putz (1997) for floodplain forest (0.76 t C $km^{-2}d^{-1}$) were considered appropriate. Assuming an average inundation period of 135 days, the annual areal and total regional net production of periphyton communities associated with floodplain forests were estimated to be 100 t C $km^{-2}y^{-1}$ and about 3 Tg C y^{-1}, respectively.

Assuming an average inundation period of half a year, the annual areal and total regional gross production of periphyton associated with herbaceous macrophytes were estimated at 220 t C km^{-2} y^{-1} and about 6 Tg C y^{-1}, respectively; total regional net production of periphyton associated with herbaceous macrophytes is about 3 Tg C y^{-1}. Hence, the regional net production of periphytic algae in both habitats was estimated to be about 6 Tg C y^{-1}. For the entire floodplain, herbaceous macrophytes accounted for the largest share of total primary production, 65 percent, followed by floodplain forests, periphyton, and phytoplankton, which accounted for 28 percent, 5 percent and 2 percent, respectively.

Our study also focused on methane emission. Methane is produced predominantly in anoxic environments associated with flooded habitats. Methane emission rates have been estimated in a variety of habitats and sites along the central Amazon floodplain (Bartlett et al. 1988; Wassmann et al. 1992; Devol et al. 1994). The average emission rates encountered in aquatic macrophyte beds, flooded forest, and open water, including data from both seasonal and regional studies, were 0.23, 0.10, and 0.05 t C km^{-2} d^{-1}, respectively. Using these values, together with average flooding periods of 182.5, 135, and 365 days, and maximum flooded areas of 29,300, 28,200, and 10,370 square kilometers, the total methane emissions from aquatic macrophyte beds, flooded forests, and open-water areas in lakes were estimated to be 1.3, 0.4, and 0.2 Tg C y^{-1}, respectively, and total regional methane emission to be about 1.8 Tg C y^{-1}.

The total organic carbon balance for lakes on the central Amazon floodplain can be examined by comparing total inputs due to primary production and external loading with total losses (Melack and Forsberg 2001). The combined input of organic carbon due to primary production, river import, and local runoff was estimated at 117 Tg C y^{-1}. Combined losses due to biogenic gas emission and permanent burial were estimated to be 28 Tg C y^{-1}. The residual loss term of 90 Tg C y^{-1} is high, but the majority of the residual probably corresponds to organic carbon export to the Amazon River.

Richey et al. (1990) used flow-weighted estimates of organic carbon flux and microbial respiration measurements to evaluate the organic carbon balance along 1,800 kilometers of the Amazon River. Organic carbon inputs estimated from tributaries were half those required to support in situ oxidation. They hypothesized that the residual oxidation was sustained by diffuse inputs of labile organic carbon from floodplains with a total flux at least as large as the final total organic carbon flux of the mainstem, 36 Tg C y^{-1}. The large organic carbon residual calculated suggests that the flux from the floodplain may be significantly greater.

In conclusion, floodplains are important components of the biogeochemistry of the Amazon Basin. Based on recently published results and ongoing research, carbon inputs and outputs for the floodplain of the Amazon were estimated. Although proportional coverage of various wetlands habitats (flooded forests, open water, and floating macrophytes) varies spatially and temporally, recent analyses of Landsat and synthetic aperture radar images provide estimates of the phenology and spatial variations in coverage. The metabolism of the organic carbon in transit down the rivers will lead to emission of carbon dioxide to the atmosphere. To properly evaluate the overall carbon balance of the entire Amazon Basin, it will be necessary to include carbon emissions from the rivers and wetlands throughout the basin.

Wintertime Flooding of Agricultural Fields

Wetlands are valued for a number of reasons, including their capacity to absorb runoff of sediments and chemicals from the land. Widespread removal of both freshwater and coastal wetlands in the last century allows an increasing amount of materials to be translocated from land into water, with occasional detrimental consequences for aquatic ecosystems (Environmental Protection Agency, EPA OPA-87-016; U.S. EPA 1988). Excessive loading of sediments and chemicals to streams, lakes, and coastal environments can lead to eutrophication, exposure of organisms to agricultural poisons, smothering of fish spawning beds and benthic invertebrate communities, and a reduced life of both natural systems and reservoirs. By obstructing movements of sediments and by absorption of chemicals in surface runoff, wetlands are important in protecting the integrity of open-water aquatic ecosystems.

Much of the erosion of chemicals and sediments in the United States is from croplands. Although the exact degree of erosion from agricultural fields is unclear, estimates of annual losses range from 2 to 6.8 billion tons of soil (Trimble and Crosson 2000). For instance, intensively farmed land has contributed to a doubling of nutrients entering the Mississippi River since the first half of the century (Turner and Rabalais 1994). In the southeastern United States, much of the loss by erosion from agricultural soils occurs during the non-growing season, when precipitation is high and the fields are without a plant cover to break the direct impact of precipitation (Palis et al. 1997). In Mississippi, where agriculture is intense, the problem of soil erosion is a serious concern (Cooper 1993).

Various approaches have been utilized to reduce erosion losses from croplands, including conservation tillage (e.g., Lal and Kimble 1997) and the use of cover crops (Edwards 1998). A novel approach currently being evaluated in the Mississippi Delta agricultural region is to intentionally allow fields to flood during the nongrowing season, between late fall (November–December) and early spring (March). Managed flooding of fields is accomplished by installation of a barrier, such as a slotted-board riser, at a place in the field where precipitation runoff would normally exit the field. The barrier acts to sustain a specific water level on the field, in essence producing a "wet blanket" that protects the underlying soils from disturbance by precipitation. Prior to preparation of the soils for planting in the spring, the field is slowly drained. Secondary benefits associated with this practice include temporary creation of aquatic habitat for migrating waterfowl (Maul and Cooper 1998) and possible suppression of soil pathogens.

Oxygen diffusion rates are drastically lowered in flooded soils, and with the onset of flooding, an anoxic (reduced) soil layer may form under the already established oxidized zone (Mitsch and Gosselink 1993). Seasonal development of an anoxic soil layer in flooded agricultural soils lasting up to several months could have important consequences for soil biogeochemical processes and microbial community structure. Where oxygen is present, soil organic matter is decomposed primarily by aerobic, heterotrophic bacteria and fungi. Where oxygen is depleted, microbial communities switch to alternative sources of electron acceptors to sustain respiratory activity (Hedin et al. 1998). Redox reactions involving these alternative electron acceptors can transform and alter the mobility of materials, as occurs for example in ferric iron reduction, denitrification, or methanogenesis. In addition, less free energy is yielded when using electron acceptors other than oxygen, less ATP is produced, and per capita rates of organic matter decomposition may decline (Gambrell et al. 1991).

Nitrogen is a major limiting nutrient for microbial and plant production in both agricultural and wetland soils (Mitsch and Gosselink 1993). In the anoxic environment typical of wetland sediments, ammonium from decomposed organic matter may accumulate in the soil environment, largely bound to soil particles (Reddy and Patrick 1986). Where ammonium diffuses into the oxic sediment layer or water column, it may be oxidized by nitrifying bacteria to nitrate (Gambrell et al. 1991). Unlike ammonium, nitrate is highly mobile in water and may accumulate in an overlying water column. Alternatively, nitrate diffusing into a hypoxic or anoxic region can be reduced by denitrifying bacteria, forming nitric oxide (Fig. 6.6), nitrous oxide, and dinitrogen gas (Reddy and Patrick 1986; DeLaune et al. 1996). In some wetlands, denitrification is an important vector for nitrogen export from the system (Davidson 1992; Groffman 1994). If either nitrate accumulation or denitrification rates are significant in seasonally flooded agricultural soils, there could be serious losses from the field of this critical soil nutrient.

Phosphorus cycling may also be influenced by the development of anoxic conditions in flooded soils. Where there is free oxygen, inorganic phosphorus compounds occur predominately in a particulate form, as for example ferric phosphate (Mitsch and Gosselink 1993). As oxygen is depleted, phosphorus is released in a soluble form, principally as orthophosphate (PO_4^{3-}) (Wetzel 1983). In this manner, although phosphorus does not have a gaseous phase, flooding

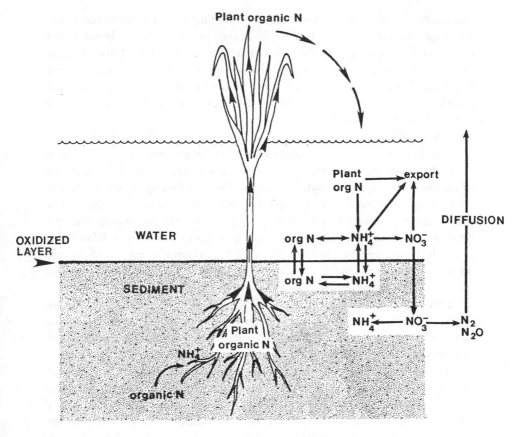

Figure 6.6. Schematic diagram representing nitrogen cycle in vegetated zones

potentially could reduce soil phosphorus concentrations by leaching of soil phosphorus into the overlying water column followed by surface runoff.

Wintertime Flooding of Agricultural Fields: A Case Study

A series of field and laboratory experiments were conducted to evaluate the effect of managed temporary flooding during the nongrowing season on the chemistry and microbial properties of agricultural fields in the Mississippi Delta (the floodplain of the Yazoo and Mississippi Rivers) (Milburn 1999; Ochs et al. 1999; Ochs and Milburn 2003).

Experiments varied in scale, from laboratory microcosm experiments using only 2.6 kilograms (DW) of soil per replicate, to field mesocosm experiments using 45 kilograms of soil per replicate, to a field-scale experiment in which an entire field was flooded. In the microcosm and mesocosm experiments, the soils were contained in either 4-liter or 52-liter containers, respectively. Only in the field experiment were the soils uncontained. The basic experimental protocol was that agricultural soils were flooded for a period of two to three months during winter and their chemistry and microbial properties compared to nonflooded control soils before flooding, during flooding, and, in three experiments, from seven to thirty-five days following drainage of the flooded soils. Soils used in all experiments came from cotton and soybean fields in the Mississippi Delta agricultural region. Depending on the experiment, the effects of flooding on soil concentrations of nitrate, ammonium, total nitrogen, organic carbon, and total phosphorus were examined. Microbial community characteristics examined included microbial biomass, densities of cultivable heterotrophic bacteria, denitrifying bacteria abundance, and rates of denitrification (N_2O flux) and soil respiration (CO_2 flux).

The results of all experiments were similar, regardless of the spatial scale used. During the period of flooding there were higher (up to 3.5 times) concentrations of ammonium and lower (up to 10 times) concentrations of nitrate in flooded compared to nonflooded soils. There were no other significant observed effects on soil chemistry during flooding, and even these differences in inorganic nitrogen concentrations disappeared after drainage of the flooded soils (see below). A relatively high concentration of ammonium in the flooded soils is presumably due to ammonification in the absence of oxygen and is an expected property of flooded wetland sediments. A higher concentration of nitrate in nonflooded soils, in contrast, is presumably the result of ammonium oxidation by nitrosifying and nitrifying bacteria, which require oxygen as an electron acceptor. Considering the generally cold, wintertime temperatures at which these experiments were conducted (4–20 °C), the microbial influence on nutrient transformations would be expected to be low in both flooded and nonflooded conditions. Besides low temperatures, low concentrations of organic matter in these highly eroded agricultural soils also may have limited microbial activity.

Only in the field experiment, where soils were uncontained, was there a significant difference in soil chemistry between soils before flooding and after drainage. In that case, one week after drainage the concentration of nitrate in previously flooded soils was about 5 times higher than in the same soils prior to flooding. Furthermore, after drainage there was a higher (approximately 3.5 times) concentration of nitrate in previously flooded soils compared to previously nonflooded soils. These results appear to be in contrast to the results for patterns in the nitrate concentration described above for experiments using soils placed into containers, and they require explanation. Under field conditions, nitrate produced in nonflooded soils would be continually removed with surface runoff. Additionally, although nitrate would not be expected to be produced in flooded soils (see above), nitrification in the week between drainage and sample collection may have added nitrate to previously flooded soils, a phenomenon observed in experiments using enclosed soils following drainage. These factors, taken together, may explain the discrepancy in results of this field experiment compared to the other studies described in this section. Unfortunately, in this experiment additional samples were not taken at longer time intervals following drainage to determine the temporal pattern of these results.

Denitrification and microbial respiration were measured in only one experiment, in which both cotton and soybean soils were used (Ochs and Milburn 2003). Denitrification was unaffected by flooding in soils from both types of fields during the period of flooding. In post-flooded soils, however, denitrification rates were much higher in previously flooded cotton soils compared to previously nonflooded soils, although still minor compared to the soil pool of nitrogen (less than 0.003 percent per day of the total nitrogen concentration in the top 10 centimeters of soil). In contrast, no differences in denitrification rates in post-treatment soybean soils were observed. During flooding, soil respiration rates were negatively affected by the presence of overlying water, but following drainage no difference between flooded and nonflooded soils was detected (Ochs and Milburn 2003).

Flooding did not have an effect on soil microbial biomass in either of the two experiments in which it was measured, but there were differences in other microbial community properties due to flooding. In the one experiment in which heterotrophic colony-forming units were examined, counts were significantly higher in previously flooded soils seven days following drainage, although not after thirty-five days. Denitrifying bacteria were also more abundant in previously flooded soils, with most probable number (MPN) population estimates up to four times greater in flooded soils even fourteen days after drainage. Reproduction of denitrifying bacteria in previously flooded soils may have been favored by anoxia (Patrick and Tusneem 1972; Groffman and Hanson 1997) and may partly account for an enhanced denitrification rate in these soils following drainage.

These studies and the supporting literature indicate that wintertime flooded agricultural soils exhibit positive properties of natural wetlands in at least three ways: (1) Nitrification rates are reduced in flooded soils, which should reduce rates of nitrogen loss in surface runoff, (2) wintertime-flooded agricultural fields provide waterfowl habitat (Maul and Cooper 1998), and (3) flooded fields trap particulate materials and nutrients that would otherwise erode into adjacent streams (Green 1997, 1998).

There was no evidence of any adverse effects of flooding on soil properties. Furthermore, the low amounts of nitrogen and phosphorus that leached into overlying water from flooded soils (Ochs et al. 1999) are unlikely to promote downstream eutrophication problems, especially in comparison to unprotected soils.

We concluded that wintertime flooding of agricultural fields can serve as an effective management practice to reduce soil erosion without causing detrimental changes to either agricultural soil properties or downstream ecosystems; however, multiyear studies should be conducted to examine the long-term effects of wintertime inundation of these soils. Future studies should also consider the impact of flooding of agricultural soils on methylmercury formation, which is enhanced in anoxic environments (Atlas and Bartha 1998).

Recommendations

Biogeochemical processes occurring in natural wetlands, constructed wetlands, and flooded agricultural soils addressed in this chapter are closely related to the issues of water and water resource conservation and, therefore, important to any long-term plans to effectively manage sustainability of freshwater and wetland resources. The wetland soil environment and the impacts of variations in intensity and capacity of soil reduction on growth and functioning of wetland plants were demonstrated. In addition, the potential differences in the response of various wetland species to soil redox conditions are apparent and deserve further study.

There were significant effects associated with short-term (hourly to daily) shifts in soil redox conditions as related to biogeochemical processes (Catallo 1999). Many biogeochemical processes display temporal dynamics over a broad range. For instance, in tidal wetlands, biogeochemical process outputs were found to be significant on the order of hours, and driven primarily by diurnal tidal variations. Tidal pulsing promoted sediment Eh and pH variations that followed the tide. Lack of pulsing gave rise to relatively static and well-poised conditions. Over the long term (months to years), hydrological condition can influence slower processes such as plant productivity, community structure, and organic chemical transformation. Thus, environmental mitigation attempts must address these issues over the long term because critical ecological endpoints can be influenced by rapid variations in these processes.

As has been previously demonstrated, the role of wetlands in nutrient storage is significant. Data from Louisiana presented in this chapter indicated that the studied marshes stored significant amounts of nitrogen and phosphorus each year (240 metric tons of nitrogen and 10.9 metric tons of phosphorus). However, further improvement in storage capacity may be achieved through management planning and restoration. The wetland restoration project discussed in the case study should increase nutrient storage rates in marsh soil and may increase the production of recalcitrant, organic forms of phosphorus that can be stored in bottom sediments of shallow, open water areas common in the marsh interior. The restoration project should also reduce the hydrologic isolation of the marsh interior and may thereby reduce plant stress, increase plant production, and increase nutrient burial in soil.

Methods for estimating carbon storage, including inputs and outputs for wetland habitats in a large floodplain in the Amazon Basin, are presented. Clearly, floodplains are important components of the biogeochemistry of such a system. Although the proportional coverage of various wetlands habitats (flooded forests, open water, and floating macrophytes) varies spatially and temporally, recent analyses of Landsat and synthetic aperture radar images provide estimates of the phenology and spatial variations in coverage. The combined input of organic carbon due to primary production, river import and local runoff was estimated at 117 Tg C y^{-1}. Combined losses due to biogenic gas emission and permanent burial were estimated to be 28 Tg C y^{-1}. The residual loss term of 90 Tg C y^{-1} is high, but the majority of the residual probably corresponds to organic carbon export to the Amazon River.

In this chapter, the role of temporary wetlands created for the purpose of improving soil protection has been examined in detail. Creating temporary wetlands to prevent soil erosion in large agricultural regions is an important initiative. For instance, in the southeastern United States, much of the loss by erosion from agricultural soils occurs during the nongrowing season, when precipitation is high and the fields are without a plant cover to break the direct impact of precipitation. An approach currently being evaluated in the Mississippi Delta agricultural region is to intentionally allow fields to flood during the nongrowing season, between late fall (November–December) and early spring (March). Managed flooding of fields sustains a specific water level on the field, producing a wet blanket that protects the underlying soils from disturbance by precipitation. Secondary benefits associated with this practice include temporary creation of aquatic habitat for migrating waterfowl and possible suppression of soil pathogens. Studies conducted indicate that wintertime flooding of agricultural fields can serve as an effective management practice to reduce soil erosion without causing detrimental changes to either agricultural soil properties or downstream ecosystems. However, before this technique is adopted on a large scale, it is critical to conduct multiyear studies to examine the long-term effects of wintertime inundation on agricultural soils and the potential impact on methylmercury formation that is enhanced in anoxic environments.

Summary

Biogeochemical processes occurring in natural wetlands, constructed wetlands, and flooded agricultural soils addressed in this chapter are closely related to the issues of water and water resource conservation and, therefore, important to any long-term plans to effectively manage for sustainability of freshwater and wetland resources. The unique wetland soil environment impacts diversity, growth, and functioning of wetland plants as well as soil microorganisms. Using selected background information, along with examples from various wetlands from the

United States and elsewhere, we demonstrated the importance of understanding biogeochemical processes as well as the relationship between wetland functions and successful management of freshwater ecosystems. Although some background scientific information is available, the relationship between nutrient sources and sinks in various wetlands should be further explored and quantified. It is also recognized that wetland processes exist outside of traditional wetland ecosystems. Many of the biogeochemical processes associated with wetlands are also important in agriculture and forestry, wastewater treatment, and constructed wetlands. The biogeochemical processes occurring in wetlands contribute significantly to water quality and the quality of freshwater ecosystems. Understanding these processes is critical to any long-term plan to manage sustainable freshwater and wetland resources.

References

Antweiler, R. C., D. A. Goolsby, and H. E. Taylor. 1995. Nutrients in the Mississippi River. Pp. 73–86 in *Contaminants in the Mississippi River, 1987–92*, edited by R. H. Meade. United States Geological Survey Circular No. 1133. United States Geological Survey, Denver, Colo.

Armstrong, J., W. Armstrong, and W. H. Van Der Putten. 1996. *Phragmites* die-back: Bud and root death, blockage within the aeration and vascular systems and the possible role of phytotoxins. *New Phytologist* 133:399–414.

Armstrong, W., R. Brandle, M. B. Jackson. 1994. Mechanisms of flood tolerance in plants. *Acta Botanica Neerlandica* 43: 307–358.

Atlas, R. M., and R. Bartha. 1998. *Microbial ecology: Fundamentals and applications.* Menlo Park, Calif.: Benjamin/Cummings.

Bartlett, K. B., P. M. Crill, D. I. Sebacher, R. C. Harris, J. O. Wilson, and J. M. Melack. 1988. Methane flux from the central Amazonian floodplain. *Journal of Geophysical Research* 93:1574–1582.

Brix, H., and B. K. Sorrell. 1996. Oxygen stress in wetland plants: Comparison of de-oxygenated and reducing root environments. *Functional Ecology* 10:521–526.

Catallo, W. J. 1999. *Hourly and daily variations of sediment redox potential in tidal wetland sediments.* Biological Science Report No. USGS/BRD/BSR-1999-0001. United States Geological Survey, Biological Resources Division. National Wetlands Research Center: Lafayette, La.

Chabreck, R. H., and G. Linscombe. 1978. *Vegetative type map of the Louisiana coastal marshes.* Louisiana Department of Wildlife and Fisheries, Baton Rouge.

Cooper, C. M. 1993. Biological effects of agriculturally derived surface water pollutants on aquatic systems. *Journal of Environmental Quality* 22:402–408.

Craft, C. B., and C. J. Richardson. 1993. Peat accumulation and N, P, and organic C accumulation in nutrient-enriched and natural everglades peatlands. *Ecological Applications* 3:446–458.

Craft, C. B., E. D. Seneca, and S. W. Broome. 1993. Vertical accretion in microtidal regularly and irregularly flooded estuarine marshes. *Estuarine, Coastal and Shelf Science* 37:371–386.

Davidson, E. A. 1992. Sources of nitric oxide and nitrous oxide following wetting of dry soil. *Soil Science Society of American Journal* 56:95–102.

Day, J. W., C. A. S. Hall, W. M. Kemp, and A. Yanez-Arancibia. 1989. *Estuarine ecology.* New York: John Wiley and Sons.

DeLaune, R. D., and S. R. Pezeshki. 1991. Role of soil chemistry in vegetative ecology of wetlands. *Trends in Soil Science* 1:101–113.

———. 2001. Plant functions in wetland and aquatic systems: Influence of intensity and capacity of soil reduction. *The Scientific World* 1:636–649.

DeLaune, R. D., A. Jugsujnda, and K. R. Reddy. 1999. Effect of root oxygen stress on phosphorus uptake by cattail. *Journal of Plant Nutrition* 22:459–466.

DeLaune, R. D., W. H. Patrick Jr., and R. J. Buresh. 1978. Sedimentation rates determined by ^{137}Cs dating in a rapidly accreting salt marsh. *Nature* 275:532–533.

DeLaune, R. D., W. H. Patrick Jr., and T. Guo. 1998a. The redox-pH chemistry of chromium in water and sediment. Pp. 241–252 in *Metals in surface waters,* edited by H. E. Allen, A. W. Garrison, and G. W. Luthes. Ann Arbor, Mich.: Ann Arbor Press.

DeLaune, R. D., R. R. Boar, C. W. Lindau, and B. A. Kleiss. 1996. Denitrification in bottomland hardwood wetland soils of the cache river. *Wetlands* 16:309–320.

DeLaune, R. D., S. R. Pezeshki, and C. W. Lindau. 1998b. Influence of soil redox potential on nitrogen uptake and growth of wetland oak seedlings. *Journal of Plant Nutrition* 21:757–768.

DeLaune, R. D., S. R. Pezeshki, and J. H. Pardue. 1990. An oxidation-reduction buffer for evaluating physiological response of plants to root oxygen stress. *Environmental and Experimental Botany* 30:243–247.

Department of Natural Resources. 1996. *Monitoring Plan, Project No. PO-06, Fritchie Marsh.* Louisiana Department of Natural Resources, Coastal Restoration Division. Baton Rouge.

Devol, A. H., J. E. Richey, B. R. Forsberg, and L. A. Martinelli. 1994. Environmental methane in the Amazon River floodplain. Pp. 155–166 in *Global wetlands,* edited by W. J. Mitsch. Amsterdam: Elsevier.

Doyle, R. D. 1991. Primary production and nitrogen cycling within the periphyton community associated with emergent aquatic macrophytes in an Amazon floodplain lake. Ph.D. diss., University of Maryland., College Park, Md.

Drew, M. C. 1997. Oxygen deficiency and root metabolism: Injury and acclimation under hypoxia and anoxia. *Annual Review of Plant Physiology and Plant Molecular Biology* 48:223–250.

Edwards, L. 1998. Comparison of two spring seeding methods to establish forage cover crops in relay with winter cereals. *Soil and Tillage Research* 45:227–235.

Fenchel, T., and B. J. Finlay. 1995. *Ecology and evolution in anoxic worlds.* New York: Oxford University Press.

Foret, J. D. 1997. Accretion, sedimentation, and nutrient accumulation rates as influenced by manipulations in marsh hydrology in the Chenier Plain, Louisiana. M.S. thesis, University of Southwestern Louisiana, Lafayette, La.

Gambrell, R. P., and W. H. Patrick Jr. 1978. Chemical and microbiological properties of anaerobic soils and sediments. Pp. 375–423 in *Plant life in anaerobic environments,* edited by D. D. Hook and R. M. M. Crawford. Ann Arbor, Mich.: Ann Arbor Science Publishers Inc.

Gambrell, R. P., R. D. DeLaune, and W. H. Patrick Jr. 1991. Redox processes in soils following oxygen depletion: Plant life under oxygen deprivation. The Netherlands: SPB Academic Publishing.

Green, B. 1998. *Roebuck lake water quality monitoring project.* Final Report. Mississippi Department of Environmental Quality, Jackson.

Groffman, P. E. 1994. Denitrification in freshwater wetlands. *Current Topics in Wetlands Biogeochemistry* 1:15–35.

Groffman, P. M., and G. C. Hanson. 1997. Wetland denitrification: Influence of site quality and relationships with wetland delineation protocols. *Soil Science Society of America Journal* 61:323–329.

Hedin, L. O, J. C. Von Fischer, N. E. Ostrom, B. P. Kennedy, M. G. Brown, and G. P. Robertson. 1998. Thermodynamic constraints on nitrogen transformations and other biogeochemical processes at soil-stream interfaces. *Ecology* 79:684–703.

Hess, L. L., J. M. Melack, S. Filoso, and Y. Wang. 1995. Delineation of inundated area and vegetation along the Amazon floodplain with the SIR-C synthetic aperture radar. *IEEE Transactions in Geoscience and Remote Sensing* 33:896–904.

Jackson, M. B., D. D. Davies, and H. Lambers. 1991. *Plant life under oxygen deprivation: Ecology, physiology, and biochemistry.* The Hague: SPB Publishing.

Junk, W. J., ed. 1997. *The central Amazon floodplain. Ecological studies.* Berlin: Springer.

Junk, W. J., and M. T. F. Piedade. 1993. Biomass and primary-production of herbaceous plant communities in the Amazon floodplain. *Hydrobiologia* 263:155–162.

Kadlec, R. H., and R. L. Knight. 1996. *Treatment wetlands.* Boca Raton, Fla.: CRC Press.

Kludze, H. K. 1994. Gaseous exchange and wetland plant response to soil redox conditions. Ph.D. diss., Louisiana State University, Baton Rouge.

Kludze, H. K., and R. D. DeLaune. 1994. Methane emission and growth of *Spartina patens* in response to soil redox intensity. *Soil Science Society of America Journal* 58:1838–1845.

———. 1995a. Straw application effects on methane and oxygen exchange and growth in rice. *Soil Science Society of America Journal* 59:824–830.

———. 1995b. Gaseous exchange and wetland plant response to soil redox intensity and capacity. *Soil Science Society of America Journal* 59:939–945.

Kludze, H. K., R. D. DeLaune, and W. H. Patrick Jr. 1993. Aerenchyma formation and methane and oxygen exchange in rice. *Soil Science Society of America Journal* 51:386–391.

Kludze, H. K., S. R. Pezeshki, and R. D. DeLaune. 1994. Evaluation of root oxygenation and growth in bald cypress in response to short-term soil hypoxia. *Canadian Journal of Forest Research* 24:804–809.

Kozlowski, T. T. 1984a. Plant responses to flooding of soil. *Bioscience* 34:162–167.

———. 1984b. *Flooding and plant growth.* New York: Academic Press.

———. 1997. Responses of woody plants to flooding and salinity. *Tree Physiology Monograph* 1:1–29.

Lal, R., and J. Kimble. 1997. Conservation tillage for carbon sequestration. *Nutrient Cycling in Agroecosystems* 49:243–253.

Lane, R. R., J. W. Day Jr., and B. Thibodeaux. 1999. Water quality analyses of a freshwater diversion at Caernarvon, Louisiana. *Estuaries* 22:327–336.

Liss, P. S. 1976. Conservative and non-conservative behaviour of dissolved constituents during estuarine mixing. Pp. 93–130 in *Estuarine chemistry*, edited by J. D. Burton and P. S. Liss. New York: Academic Press.

Lopez, J. A. 1991. Origin of Lake Pontchartrain and the 1987 Irish Bayou earthquake. Pp. 103–110 in *Coastal depositional systems of the Gulf of Mexico: Quaternary framework and environmental issues*. 12th Annual Research Conference Gulf Coast Section Society of Economic Paleontologists and Mineralogists Foundation. Earth Enterprises, Austin, Texas.

Maul, J. D., and C. M. Cooper. 1998. Aspects of seasonal field flooding: Water quality and waterfowl. Pp. 79–85 in *Proceedings of the Twenty-eighth Mississippi Water Resources Conference*, edited by B. J. Daniel. Mississippi Water Resources Research Institute, Mississippi State.

Melack, J. M., and B. Forsberg. 2001. Biogeochemistry of Amazon floodplain lakes and associated wetlands. Pp. 235–274 in *The biogeochemistry of the Amazon Basin and its role in a changing world*, edited by M. E. McClain, R. L. Victoria and J. E. Richey. New York: Oxford University Press.

Mertes, A. K. L., D. L. Daniel, J. M. Melack, B. Nelson, L. A. Martinelli, and B. R. Forsberg. 1995. Spatial patterns of hydrology, geomorphology and vegetation on the floodplain of the Amazon River in Brazil from a remote sensing perspective. *Geomorphology* 13:215–232.

Milburn, S. A. 1999. Chemical and microbial properties of flooded Mississippi Delta agricultural soils. M.S. thesis, University of Mississippi, Oxford, Miss.

Mitsch, W. J., and J. G. Gosselink. 1993. *Wetlands*, 2d ed. New York: Van Nostrand Reinhold.

Moustafa, M. Z. 1999. Nutrient retention dynamics of the Everglades Nutrient Removal Project. *Wetlands* 19:689–704.

Natural Resources Conservation Service. 1997. *Project plan and environmental assessment, Fritchie Marsh hydrologic restoration, PO-6, St. Tammany Parish*. U.S. Department of Agriculture, Natural Resources Conservation Service, Alexandria, La.

Nyman, J. A., R. D. DeLaune, and W. H. Patrick Jr. 1990. Wetland soil formation in the rapidly subsiding Mississippi River Deltaic Plain: Mineral and organic matter relationships. *Estuarine, Coastal and Shelf Science* 31:57–69.

Nyman, J. A., R. D. DeLaune, H. H. Roberts, and W. H. Patrick Jr. 1993. Relationship between vegetation and soil formation in a rapidly submerging coastal marsh. *Marine Ecology Progress Series* 96:269–279.

Ochs, C. A., S. A. Milburn, and K. B. Overstreet Jr. 1999. *Evaluation of managed flooding of Mississippi Delta agricultural fields for control of nonpoint source nutrient pollution*. A report to the Mississippi Department of Environmental Quality. EPA No. C9994866-96-1. Jackson, Miss.

Ochs, C. A., and S. A. Milburn. 2003. Effects of wintertime flooding to control erosion on selected chemical and microbial properties of agricultural soils in the Mississippi Delta. *Journal of the Mississippi Academy of Sciences* 48:102–114.

Palis, R. G., H. Ghandiri, C. W. Rose, and P. G. Saffigna. 1997. Soil erosion and nutrient loss. 3. Changes in the enrichment ratio of total nitrogen and organic carbon under rainfall detachment and entrapment. *Australian Journal of Soil Research* 35:891–905.

Parsons, T. R. 1984. *A manual of chemical and biological methods for seawater analysis*. New York: Pergamon Press.

Patrick, W. H., Jr. and R. D. DeLaune. 1977. Chemical and biological redox systems affecting nutrient availability in the coastal wetlands. *Geoscience and Man* 18:131–137.

Patrick, W. H., Jr., and M. E. Tusneem. 1972. Nitrogen loss from flooded soil. *Ecology* 53:735–737.

Patrick, W. H., Jr., R. P. Gambrell, and S. P. Faulkner. 1986. Redox measurements of soils. Pp. 1255–1273 in *Methods of Soil Analysis: Part 3—Chemical Methods*. Soil Science Society of America Book Series, no. 5. Madison, Wisc.: Soil Science Society of America.

Penland, S., and K. E. Ramsey 1990. Relative sea-level rise in Louisiana and the Gulf of Mexico: 1908–1988. *Journal of Coastal Research* 6:323–342.

Pezeshki, S. R. 1994. Plant responses to flooding. Pp. 289–321 in *Plant-environment interactions*, edited by R. E. Wilkinson. New York: Marcel Dekker.

Pezeshki, S. R., and P. A. Anderson. 1997. Responses of three bottomland woody species with different flood-tolerance capabilities to various flooding regimes. *Wetland Ecology and Management* 4:245–256.

Pezeshki, S. R., and R. D. DeLaune. 1990. Influence of sediment oxidation-reduction potential on root elongation in *Spartina patens*. *Acta Oecologia* 11:377–383.

Pezeshki, S. R., S. W. Matthews, and R. D. DeLaune. 1991. Root cortex structure and metabolic response of *Spartina patens* to soil redox conditions. *Environmental and Experimental Botany* 31:91–97.

Pezeshki, S. R., J. H. Pardue, and R. D. DeLaune. 1996. The influence of oxygen deficiency and redox potential on alcohol dehydrogenase activity, root porosity, ethylene production, and photosynthesis in *Spartina patens*. *Environmental and Experimental Botany* 33:565–573.

Ponnamperuma, F. N. 1972. The chemistry of submerged soil. *Advances in Agronomy* 24:29–96.

———. 1984. Effects of flooding on soils. Pp. 1–44 in *Flooding and plant growth*, edited by T. T. Kozlowski. Orlando, Fla.: Academic Press.

Putz, R. 1997. Periphyton communities in Amazonian black- and whitewater habitats: Community structure, biomass and productivity. *Aquatic Sciences* 59:74–93.

Reddy, K. R., and W. H. Patrick Jr. 1986. Denitrification losses in flooded rice fields. *Fertilizer Research* 9:99–116.

Reddy, K. R., P. S. C. Ras, and W. H. Patrick, Jr. 1980. Factors influencing oxygen consumption rates in flooded soil. *Soil Science Society America Journal* 44:741–744.

Richey, J. E., J. I. Hedges, A. H. Devol, P. D. Quay, R. Victoria, L. Martinelli, and B. R. Forsberg. 1990. Biogeochemistry of carbon in the Amazon River. *Limnology and Oceanography* 35:352–371.

Sippel, S. J., S. K. Hamilton, and J. M. Melack. 1992. Inundation area and morphometry of lakes on the Amazon River floodplain, Brazil. *Archiv für Hydrobiologie* 123:385–400.

Sippel, S. J., S. K. Hamilton, J. M. Melack, and E. M. M. Novo. 1998. Passive microwave observations of inundation area and the area/stage relation in the Amazon River floodplain. *International Journal of Remote Sensing* 19:3055–3074.

Sorrell, B. K., H. Brix, and P. T. Orr. 1993. Oxygen exchange by entire root systems of

Cyperus involucratus and *Eleocharis sphacelata*. *Journal of Aquatic Plant Management* 31:24–28.

Trimble, S. W., and P. Crosson. 2000. U.S. soil erosion rates: Myth and reality. *Science* 289:248–250.

Turner, R. E., and N. N. Rabalais. 1994. Coastal eutrophication near the Mississippi River delta. *Nature* 368:619–621.

U.S. EPA (United States Environment Protection Agency). 1988. *America's wetlands: Our vital link between land and water*. OPA-87-016. Office of Wetlands Protection, Washington, D.C.

van Wijck, C., C. J. de Groot, and P. Grillas. 1992. The effect of anaerobic sediment on the growth of *Potamogeton pectinatus* L.: The role of organic matter, sulphide, and ferrous iron. *Aquatic Botany* 44:31–49.

Vartapetian, B. B., and M. B. Jackson. 1997. Plant adaptations to anaerobic stress. *Annals of Botany* 79 (Supplement A):3–20.

Walbridge, M. R., and B. G. Lockaby. 1994. Effects of forest management on biogeochemical functions in southern forested wetlands. *Wetlands* 14:10–17.

Wassmann, R., U. G. Thein, M. J. Whiticar, H. Rennenberg, W. Seiler, and W. J. Junk. 1992. Methane emissions from the Amazon floodplain: Characterization of production and transport. *Global Biogeochemical Cycles* 6:3–13.

Wetzel, R. G. 1983. Limnology. 2d ed. Philadelphia: Saunders College Publishing.

Worbes, M. 1997. The forest ecosystem of the floodplains. Pp. 223–260 in *The central Amazon floodplain: Ecology of a pulsing system*, edited by W. J. Junk. Berlin: Springer-Verlag.

Chapter 7

Chemical Ecology and Natural Products from Wetlands: Emerging Perspectives

Dale G. Nagle, Marc Slattery, and Alice M. Clark

An increase in published research and recent wetlands-related conferences and symposia suggests that scientific interest in the ecology of wetlands is growing. This heightened interest may be sparked by an increased awareness of the ecological impact of wetlands, not just on water supplies, flood control, and fisheries, but also as an important resource of biodiversity with unrealized economic potential. Significant research is now underway to identify new natural products from the organisms found in wetland habitats and to describe the complex chemically mediated interactions between these species. This chapter is not intended as a review of the natural products produced by aquatic and wetland species, nor as a review of wetland chemical and ecological interactions. Rather, it is intended to draw attention to a few currently ongoing research projects from relatively diverse scientific disciplines that are beginning to help construct a better picture of the complex interactions between the chemicals produced by wetland species and the environment in which these organisms exist. Emerging

This chapter includes abstracted, summarized, and/or otherwise reviewed materials from a panel of natural products chemists, biologists, ecologists, and other wetland scientists who contributed to the special symposium entitled "Chemical Ecology and Natural Products from Wetlands." This symposium was held as part of The Sustainability of Wetlands and Water Resources: Achieving Sustainable Systems in the 21st Century conference at The University of Mississippi (UM) in May of 2000.

scientific research suggests the promise of new economic incentives to preserve wetland biodiversity—a potentially valuable source of unique biologically active natural products that may one day be used to develop new cures for disease and means to control agricultural pests.

Tens of thousands of biologically active low molecular weight organic molecules (natural products) have been isolated and identified from terrestrial plants and invertebrates. Considerable research has focused on the ecological interactions between agriculturally important plant species and plant or insect pests, yet the ecological roles of the majority of natural products remain largely unknown. In some respects the chemical ecology of many marine organisms has received more careful examination than that of many aquatic and wetland species (Paul 1992; Hay 1996; Nagle and Paul 1999). Plants and microorganisms found in wetlands have proved to be valuable sources of chemically unique and biologically active natural products. Biologically complex wetlands represent highly competitive ecosystems and the secondary metabolites produced by aquatic and wetland organisms may function as chemical defenses. Recent research suggests that wetland plant natural products may act as allelochemicals, deter herbivores, prevent infection, and suppress microbial competition. Regionally, wetland ecosystems represent a range of diverse organisms that often live in relatively dissimilar environments. Geographic and climatic differences, regional variations in species composition, and the ecological effect of competitive pressures all impact the biological community structure of wetlands. Recent findings indicate that secondary metabolite production in some species is related to competition and environmental factors, and may directly influence the overall chemical ecology of wetland ecosystems. This chapter highlights some of the ongoing programs that examine the chemical ecology of wetlands.

Biogeochemical Ecology

Heterotrophic metabolism of organic matter in freshwater ecosystems is critical to nutrient cycling (Fig. 7.1). Microbial heterotrophic nutrient recycling regulates production and organic carbon availability. Evidence suggests that much of the organic carbon for heterotrophic metabolism is soluble and derived from external and wetland littoral sources of both lake and river ecosystems. Much of organic matter imported from land-water interface sources is derived from structural compounds of higher plants. The chemical recalcitrance of this organic matter and its oxidative utilization are fundamentally different from many sources within the aquatic ecosystems. Sources of organic matter are compared, particularly in relation to higher plants and microalgae, with their heterotrophic metabolism. Within the lake or river, complex physical interactions occur that can greatly modify rates of utilization and indirectly affect biochemical reactions. Macromolecular complexation and long-term storage of enzymes can

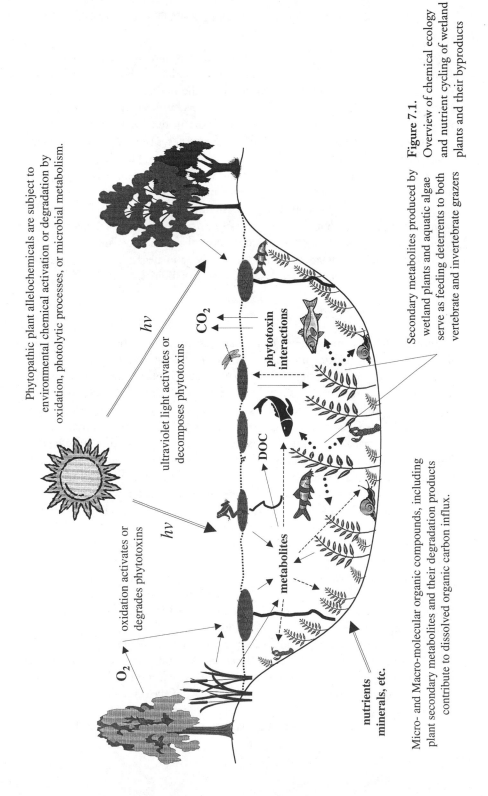

Phytopathic plant allelochemicals are subject to environmental chemical activation or degradation by oxidation, photolytic processes, or microbial metabolism.

hv

ultraviolet light activates or decomposes phytotoxins

CO_2

phytotoxin interactions

oxidation activates or degrades phytotoxins

hv

DOC

O_2

metabolites

nutrients minerals, etc.

Micro- and Macro-molecular organic compounds, including plant secondary metabolites and their degradation products contribute to dissolved organic carbon influx.

Secondary metabolites produced by wetland plants and aquatic algae serve as feeding deterrents to both vertebrate and invertebrate grazers

Figure 7.1.
Overview of chemical ecology and nutrient cycling of wetland plants and their byproducts

suppress hydrolysis of dissolved organic phosphorus and nitrogen compounds. Natural photolysis by photosynthetically active irradiance (PAR), ultraviolet-A (UV-A), and ultraviolet-B (UV-B) can result in the partial degradation of these structural macromolecules, reactivate enzyme activity, and generate simple organic compounds, especially fatty acids, as well as important nutrients (e.g., phosphates and nitrates). A portion of the dissolved organic matter is photolytically degraded completely to carbon dioxide (CO_2) by natural irradiance. The chemical recalcitrance of these allochthonous and especially wetland littoral sources of organic matter (1) are a fundamental, often dominant, subsidy of organic matter that drives metabolism in fresh waters, (2) are essential to maintenance of metabolic stability in aquatic ecosystems, and (3) cause instabilities in metabolism when dominance shifts away from this organic chemical regulation. Climatic changes affect the stability of metabolites in both positive and negative ways. However, climatic changes generally will increase chemical instabilities.

Allelochemical Interactions

In addition to the chemical control of abiotic processes, chemical processes often mediate the biotic interactions of wetland communities. Specifically, natural products produced by wetland cyanobacteria, plants, and invertebrates have been shown to directly influence the distributions, feeding activities, and pathogenicity of relevant competitors, predators, and microbial species. The ecological roles of chemical compounds have received extensive attention in terrestrial and marine systems (Hay and Steinberg 1992). Evidence suggests that natural products produced by plants, algae, and invertebrates play critical roles in species-species interactions, particularly as they relate to predation (or herbivory—a specialized case of predation) and competition.

Recent research has documented the roles of natural products in limiting microbial overgrowth, which effectively reduces the first stage of pathogenicity. Within wetland systems, one can intuitively imagine situations in which any or all of these ecological functions might be requisite. Wetlands are often space-limited or ephemeral habitats where dominance can have significant implications in resource (i.e., light, nutrients, etc.) acquisition. Thus, the production of *allelochemicals* (i.e., those compounds that are released into the environment and influence the behavior or physiology of another species) by resident species can be particularly important in providing a competitive advantage to the producer (Fig. 7.1). Two examples of allelochemical effects on "wetland plants" demonstrate the importance of this chemically mediated interaction. The first example, which occurs in the Florida Scrub system, demonstrates the impact of allelochemicals on community landscape patterns. The second example, which occurs in the Mississippi swamps, provides a view of potential applications of wetland natural products.

Researchers have recently begun working in the Florida Scrub, an ancient natural wetland ecosystem that hosts about 400 plant species including some forty endemics; many of these species are threatened or endangered. In the ongoing debate about the existence or nonexistence of chemical plant-plant interactions (allelopathy), the hypothesis was tested that allelopathic agents released from members of the fire-sensitive Florida Scrub community deter the invasion of fire-prone Sandhill grasses. Combined chemical and biological studies of several dominant species of the Florida Scrub community were performed to learn about the mechanisms of release and action of their potential allelopathic constituents upon selected putative target species of the adjacent Sandhill community (Fischer et al. 1994). Based on preliminary ecological studies, six endemic scrub species, which had previously not been analyzed for their secondary metabolites, were selected for structural studies of their major constituents. Chemical analyses of two mints, *Calamintha ashei* and *Conradina canescens* (Labiatae) and three members of the Asteraceae family, the woody goldenrod (*Chrysoma paucifloculosa*) as well as *Garberia heterophylla* and the federally protected scrub blazing star (*Liatris ohlingerae*), provided a number of biologically active natural products. The dominant white scrub species, the Florida rosemary (*Ceratiola ericoides*, Empetraceae), was used as a model for more detailed allelopathic interactions. The effects of selected isolated compounds on the putative target species of the Sandhill community were investigated. This included studies related to the release mechanism of allelopathic agents from a source plant and their transport to the target species. In several instances, allelopathic oxidative and photochemical activation of nontoxic constituents were observed after release from the source plant into the environment. This work has served to highlight the following series of important considerations, often neglected in the study of plant-plant interactions: First, critical chemical properties of potentially active substances must be directly measured. These include allelochemical storage, water solubility, and the rate of release. Second, the environmental stability of potential allelochemicals must be assessed. Stability studies should address both the chemical degradation of active compounds and the potential for chemical, microbial, or spontaneous activation of inactive plant metabolites into potent phytotoxins. And third, many plants produce complex mixtures of secondary metabolites. It is essential to understand which allelopathic properties observed with crude plant extracts can be directly attributed to individual phytotoxic compounds, as opposed to those properties that are the result of synergistic combinations of active plant metabolites.

Researchers at the University of Southern Mississippi are conducting research on the applications of wetland plant allelochemicals. Although it has been suggested that long-term site-specific aquatic weed control might be possible by replacing undesirable species with desirable ones (Elakovich and

Wooten 1995), research into the nature of aquatic and wetland plant allelopathic interactions lags behind that of terrestrial plants. Of the limited number of aquatic and wetland plants that have been identified as allelopathic, dwarf spikerush (*Eleocharis parvula*) has been examined more extensively than any other plant. Bioassays are crucial to the investigation of all allelopathic interactions, and a range of bioassay methods have been applied by investigators who have reported the allelopathic nature of aquatic and wetland plants. These assays range from germination and growth systems used in laboratory bioassays to a few large-scale field experiments.

Antimicrobial Chemical Defenses

Natural products are also known to influence the distribution of microorganisms in soil, and more recently in aquatic systems. Sometimes this antimicrobial activity serves a competitive role, such as when two microbe species compete for limited environmental resources. Recent evidence suggests that some organisms produce antimicrobial compounds to ward off pathogenic microbes. These antibiotics may be sequestered in surface tissues where pathogens would first contact them, or alternatively they may be released into the surrounding environment (i.e., the water or soil). Interestingly, the ability to produce these compounds can be influenced by local environmental conditions. Presumably, the abundance of nutrients within a site influences the amount of energy available for the production of bioactive metabolites (Herms and Mattson 1992). Thus, the same species in different wetland habitats may be more or less susceptible to pathogenic infections. A series of ephemeral high altitude wetlands in the Rocky Mountains provides a good example of variable antimicrobial resistance in the associated flora.

Researchers at The University of Mississippi are examining the influence of environmental conditions on the antifungal activity of root extracts from wetland plants in the Rocky Mountains (Kuhajek 2001). Specifically, this research is focused on the influence of temporal (ontogenetic), spatial (altitudinal cline), and abiotic (moisture levels) factors on plant bioactivity. Root extracts from twenty-eight common species of herbaceous perennial plants representing fifteen different families that inhabit wet high altitude meadows (Colorado) were evaluated for levels of antifungal activity against several plant pathogens (the aerial pathogen *Colletotrichum* spp., and the root pathogens *Fusarium* sp. and *Phytophora* sp.) and human pathogens (*Candida albicans, Cryptococcus neoformans,* and *Aspergillus flavus*). Samples were collected at early and late stages of the growing season from various sites differing in altitude (i.e., a cline from about 2,800 to 3,300 meters) and soil hydrology (i.e., low moisture is less than 50 percent water representing a water table more than 30 centimeters from the surface; and high moisture is more than 50 percent water representing a water table less than

5 centimeters below the surface). The antifungal activity of root extracts from the different sites were compared by analysis of variance (ANOVA) and, although there were a number of higher-order interactions, the general trends were for increased antifungal activity under high altitude and dry conditions later in the growing season. In addition to this general survey, two species, *Caltha* (marsh marigold) and *Trollius* (globeflower), were transplanted across the altitudinal gradient and between the soil moisture conditions. Both species exhibited phenotypic plasticity of the plant extracts in response to the changing environmental conditions. Specifically, they acquired the chemical profiles of the resident (control) plants at the site where they were relocated. In some cases, this represented a decrease in extract concentrations (i.e., low altitude and wet conditions) while in other cases (i.e., high altitude and dry conditions) it caused an increase in extract concentration. These results support hypotheses relating to costs of metabolite production, and, potentially, induction when requisite. Furthermore, these results suggest that ecological leads may provide insight into the identification of biomedically and agriculturally useful plants.

Herbivore Feeding Deterrents

One of the best-studied ecological roles for natural products is in feeding deterrence of herbivores and predators. Species that lack traditional structural defenses (e.g., shells, spines, etc.) or flight behaviors are particularly susceptible to predation events. Specifically, algae, plants, and sessile invertebrates, which are typically fleshy and nutritious, often produce novel secondary metabolites to prevent grazers or predators from feeding on them (Fig. 7.1). A wealth of examples of chemically defended plants from terrestrial systems and algae and invertebrates from marine systems has been documented. Further research has demonstrated that the deterrent compounds are often localized in the most valuable or apparent regions of the prey species (i.e., intra-organismal chemical variability), and that within populations certain individuals are more or less deterrent than other individuals (i.e., inter-organismal chemical variability). Sometimes the chemical variability is a property of a specific genotype, and the individual is incapable of varying the defensive metabolite levels in response to changing environmental conditions (*constitutive defense*). In other cases, individuals are able to change the expression levels of the defense in response to changes in predation intensity; these *inducible defenses* provide a potentially cost-effective mechanism for dealing with predators when present but allocating valuable resources to other processes (i.e., reproduction and growth) when predators are not present. Predator intensity often follows biogeographic clines such as latitude. Thus, a particular species at two disjunct sites may experience different predation (selective) pressures and express different levels of either a constitutive or an inducible defense.

More than fifty species of aquatic-macrophytes, representing twenty-seven families, from North Carolina, Florida, and Kentucky have been collected by researchers at Georgia Institute of Technology. The hydrophobic and hydrophilic organic extracts of these plants were evaluated as feeding deterrents to the Louisiana red crayfish *Procambarus clarki* (Bolser et al. 1998). Samples were collected from different freshwater habitats (lakes, rivers, streams) with different community structures, yet similar defensive properties were observed within the sixteen bioactive families. In general, the emergent macrophyte tissues were more deterrent than submerged portions of the same species. Studies of macrophyte nutritional quality, including tissue toughness, carbon, nitrogen, protein, and polyphenolic levels, exhibited no obvious patterns. In some cases the least nutritious species were preferred to more nutritious macrophytes that contained deterrent extracts. However, many of the deterrent species were also low-nutrient, and some were moderately protected by tissue toughness. Utilizing bioassay-guided isolation strategies pioneered in marine systems, researchers were able to identify several new metabolites as well as new ecological bioactivities for previously identified metabolites (i.e., lignans). Many of the freshwater macrophytes produced bioactive extracts that were water-soluble (38 percent of the species), but feeding deterrence could not be correlated with phenolic concentrations within these plants. Interestingly, the lipophilic compound habenariol from the orchid *Habenaria repens* doubled in concentration (from 1.1 to 2.0 percent dry mass) when frozen tissues were thawed. These data suggest that habenariol may represent an activated defense strategy, which would allow the plants extremely quick response to grazers. Chemically defended marine algae often contain small mesograzers that gain associational refuge from generalist predators; this was also the case in freshwater systems. When a general survey of marine and freshwater macrophytes was compared, the frequency and magnitude of chemical deterrency from freshwater macrophytes exceeded that from marine systems by almost two to one. Moreover, when the extracts of these surveyed freshwater macrophytes and marine algae were offered to either marine or freshwater herbivores, both groups of grazers consistently rejected more extracts from the freshwater species. The results of these studies indicate that contrary to prior views of herbivory in freshwater systems, the selection pressures for chemical defenses are as high as that of terrestrial or marine habitats.

Research at the Sapello Institute is examining the basic premise that consumer-prey interactions are commonly thought to vary across latitudinal gradients. This biogeographic paradigm has chiefly developed because of studies relating increased rates of predation and herbivory to increased levels of prey defenses in tropical habitats, as contrasted with temperate zones. It is noted that few studies actually compare latitudinal gradients using related plant species. Among the factors that restrict such studies are biogeographic limitations on seasonal temperature tolerances of plant species that often force researchers to search for trends among populations of phylogenetically dissimilar organisms. The relatively wide geographic range of salt-marsh plants found along the Atlantic coast of the United States make them an ideal model for examining this hypothesis. This project directly compared the palatability of ten salt-marsh plants from seven northern (Rhode Island and Maine) and eight southern (Georgia and Florida) coastal salt marshes by flying plant material back and forth and allowing thirteen species of herbivores direct choices between northern and southern conspecific plants. In 127 of 149 assays (85 percent), herbivores showed a significant (P ‹ 0.05, n = 120) or marginally significant (P ‹ 0.06, n = 7) preference for northern plants. In only one assay did herbivores prefer southern plants. These results occurred regardless of the geographic location of the assay, herbivore species, year, or season of plant collection, although there were hints that latitudinal differences became less pronounced for two plant species late in the growing season. These results provide some of the best evidence to date for a latitudinal gradient in plant palatability in any community. Examination of proximate plant traits (toughness, nitrogen content, palatability of extracts) suggests that all these traits may contribute to latitudinal patterns of palatability in some of the plant species examined. The ultimate evolutionary factors responsible for latitudinal patterns in palatability remain to be determined.

New Medicines and Agrochemicals

Wetland plants and aquatic algae are emerging as an exciting yet relatively untapped source of leads for the discovery of new drugs and agrochemicals. Modern spectroscopic methods have greatly enhanced the discovery of chemically novel natural products from wetland plants. The application of two-dimensional nuclear magnetic resonance spectroscopic techniques (2D-NMR), state-of-the-art NMR microprobes to handle minute samples, and pulsed field gradient technologies now facilitate the rapid chemical structure determination of complex natural products from less than a milligram of material. Newly developed high-throughput biological assays are able to rapidly evaluate the ability of thousands of natural products to modulate disease-specific molecular targets (i.e., genes and enzymes) involved in human disease and agriculture. The ability to detect secondary metabolites with previously unknown biological activities that are produced by plants is greatly enhancing the discovery of biologically active natural products from wetland species. These substances show great promise as potential new agents to treat human diseases and control agricultural pests.

Microbial pests continue to represent major problems for the agriculture and aquaculture industries. Fungicide-resistant fungal pathogens threaten crops. Likewise, cyanobacteria (blue-green algae) blooms in aquaculture ponds, and certain species can produce noxious or toxic chemicals that pose a particular problem for fish farmers. New environmentally friendly methods to control microbial pests are urgently needed. Aquatic and marine plants and algae live in fungus-rich environments. These organisms are forced to compete with microalgae for light and nutrients. Therefore, it is hypothesized that natural product constituents of these organisms may afford them protection from microbial infection and that these substances may be potentially useful as antimicrobials to control both human infectious disease and crop pathogens. Using newly developed assay methods that target minor crop-associated fungal pathogens and undesirable cyanobacteria, researchers at The University of Mississippi are examining wetland plants and algae to discover new biologically active natural product leads (Wedge and Nagle 2000).

Molecular biologists and natural products chemists have combined their expertise to develop new biological screening methods that inhibit the formation of blood vessels to tumors and agents that will enhance the immune system as an adjunct to traditional chemotherapies for the treatment of cancer. University of Mississippi researchers have demonstrated that compounds found in aquatic algae and wetland plants can act as potent immunostimulants in a novel transcription-based bioassay for Nuclear Factor kappa B (NF-kappa B) activation in a human macrophage/monocyte cell line, THP-1. The inducible transcription factor NF-kappa B controls gene expression and regulation of many immune and inflammatory responses mediated by macrophages. Wetland plants, cyanobacteria, and marine algae may serve as potential sources for the discovery of immunostimulatory pharmaceuticals. Over one hundred extracts of these organisms have been evaluated from which the most potent extracts have been fractionated. Isolation of pure compounds (both lipophilic and polar) responsible for the observed activity is in progress. Some of these substances have been identified as unusual lipopolysaccharides that mimic the potent immunostimulatory materials found on bacterial cell walls. Characterization of these and other previously unknown molecules may represent potential lead compounds that can be developed into immunostimulant adjuvants for the treatment of cancer and infectious diseases.

Angiogenesis, the formation of new blood vessels from existing vasculature, is a highly complex yet tightly controlled process. It is essential for embryonic development and, in adults, is restricted to tissue remodeling and repair. Pathologic angiogenesis has been implicated in the etiology of a variety of diseases, including solid tumors, ocular diseases, and inflammatory disorders. The growth and metastasis of solid tumors are known to be dependent on the formation of new blood vessels. Angiogenesis is under the concerted control of both angiogenic stimulators and inhibitors. Among the known inducers, vascular endothelial growth factor (VEGF) and basic fibroblast growth factor are the most important for tumor-induced angiogenesis. Blocking the action of VEGF has been shown to be effective in inhibiting the growth and metastasis of solid tumors. University of Mississippi scientists are investigating aquatic and marine plants, cyanobacteria, and algae as potential sources for the discovery of potential angiogenesis inhibitors (Nagle et al. 2000). The objective of their research is to identify inhibitors derived from natural product of angiogenesis that can be used as new treatment options for solid tumors. The molecular target for their drug discovery effort is the inhibition of VEGF gene expression. Using the human heptoma cell line, Hep3B, as an in vitro model, a transcription-based bioassay for detecting inhibitors of VEGF gene expression was developed. It is envisioned that these molecules produced by wetland species represent potential lead compounds that can be developed into new therapeutic options for the treatment of cancer.

Conclusions

Plants and animals that live in wetland ecosystems have been the subject of intense study. However, research to examine the chemical ecology of wetland species lags behind that of terrestrial plants and insects research. In recent years, teams of biologists, ecologists, and chemists have begun to uncover some of the exciting chemically mediated relationships that exist among wetland species. These integrated scientific programs investigate wetlands in order to more clearly understand the nature and impact of biogeochemical interactions, antimicrobial plant defenses, plant-plant allelopathy, and plant-herbivore feeding deterrence in these complex ecosystems. Wetland systems now serve as models to test long-held chemical-ecological tenets. Most recently, the novel natural products chemistry that is represented by wetlands plant, animal, and microorganism biodiversity has become the subject of biomedical prospecting. Using modern approaches that target the molecular mechanisms responsible for specific diseases, natural products researchers are beginning to probe the multitude of unique secondary metabolites produced by aquatic and wetland species in hope of discovering new cures for disease and new products to enhance agriculture.

Wetlands are incredibly important ecosystems that remain relatively underexplored from the standpoints of biodiversity and ecology. It is clear that wetlands provide habitat and resources for (1) endemic, and often threatened, invertebrate species, (2) migratory waterfowl, (3) unique plant life, and (4) other endemic and transient vertebrate species. Recent research in the areas of ecology and biogeochemical cycling has demonstrated the critical relationships between chemistry and ecosystem biodiversity. In addition, the natural products that serve ecological roles within these wetland habitats appear to have great potential for biomedical and agricultural applications. Collaborative teams of chemists, biologists, and ecologists are now working together to begin to clearly address these critical points that require building new bridges between traditional scientific disciplines and applied biotechnology. New insights into potential economic benefits of wetland biodiversity might serve as economic incentives to support wetland preservation.

The economic value of biodiversity has been the subject of heated debate. When the cost of maintaining this biodiversity is discussed, critics note that many species may be redundant, and that saving one species might preclude saving others. Researchers agree, particularly as biodiversity is examined at the landscape/ecosystem scale, that biodiversity may indeed have value in maintaining ecosystem function and providing insurance against future environmental changes (Bengtsson et al. 1997; Loreau et al. 2001). Natural products chemists have long known the value of biodiversity in serving as the evolutionary template for novel chemosynthesis and that these compounds have incredible potential value in biomedical, agrochemical, nutritive, and cosmetic markets. Our survey of the chemical ecology of wetlands suggests that this relatively untapped resource is poised to provide future value to biotechnology markets and that the selective factors that have resulted in the elaboration of wetland natural products should not be disregarded as valueless.

References

Bengtsson, J., H. Jones, H. Setala. 1997. The value of biodiversity. *Trends in Ecology and Evolution* 12:334–336.

Bolser, R. C., M. E. Hay, N. Lindquist, W. Fenical, and D. Wilson. 1998. Chemical defenses of freshwater macrophytes against crayfish herbivory. *Journal of Chemical Ecology* 24:1639–1658.

Elakovich, S. D., and J. W. Wooten. 1995. Allelopathic, herbaceous, vascular hydrophytes. Pp. 58–73 in Allelopathy: Organisms, processes, and applications, edited by Inderjit, K. M. M. Dakshini, and F. A. Einhellig. ACS Symposium Services, 582. Washington, D.C.: American Chemical Society.

Fischer, N. H., G. B. Williamson, J. D. Weidenhamer, and D. R. Richardson. 1994. In search of allelopathy in the Florida Scrub: The role of terpenoids. *Journal of Chemical Ecology* 20:1355–1380.

Hay, M. E. 1996. Marine chemical ecology: What's known and what's next? *Journal of Experimental Marine Biology and Ecology* 200:103–134.

Hay, M. E., and P. D. Steinberg. 1992. The chemical ecology of plant-herbivore interactions in marine versus terrestrial communities. Pp. 371–413 in *Herbivores: Their interactions with secondary plant metabolites*. 2d ed. Vol. 2. *Evolutionary and ecological processes*, edited by G. A. Rosenthal and M. R. Berenbaum. San Diego: Academic Press.

Herms, D. A., and W. J. Mattson. 1992. The dilemma of plants: To grow or defend. *Quarterly Reviews of Biology* 67:283–335.

Kuhajek, J. M. 2001. Temporal and spatial variability in the antifungal chemistry of Rocky Mountain wetland plants, Ph.D. diss., The University of Mississippi, Oxford.

Loreau, M., S. Naeem, P. Inchausti, J. Bengtsson, J. P. Grime, A. Hector, D. U. Hooper, M. A. Huston, D. Raffaelli, B. Schmid, D. Tilman, and D. A. Wardle. 2001.

Biodiversity and ecosystem functioning: Current knowledge and future challenges. *Science* 294:804–808.

Nagle, D. G., and V. J. Paul. 1999. Production of secondary metabolites by filamentous tropical marine cyanobacteria: Ecological functions of the compounds. *Journal of Phycology* 35:1412–1421.

Nagle, D. G., Y. -D. Zhou, P. U. Park, V. J. Paul, I. Rajbhandari, C. J. G. Duncan, and D. S. Pasco. 2000. A new indanone from the marine cyanobacterium *Lyngbya majuscula* that inhibits hypoxia-induced activation of the VEGF promoter in Hep3B cells. *Journal of Natural Products* 63:1431–1433.

Paul, V. J. 1992. *Ecological roles of marine natural products*. New York: Cornell University Press.

Wedge, D. E., and D. G. Nagle. 2000. A new 2D-TLC bioautography method for the discovery of novel antifungal agents to control plant pathogens. *Journal of Natural Products* 63:1050–1054.

PART III

FRESHWATER MANAGEMENT

This section makes the case that because humanity is inherently linked to natural systems such as wetlands through our reliance on them for food and fiber, as well as for nutrient cycling, flood control, and filtration of pollutants, we would do well to view them holistically, recognizing that events harmful to wetlands are also harmful to ourselves.

Chapters 8, 9, and 10 each address the challenges facing the lower Mississippi Alluvial Valley, a unique ecosystem in the southeastern United States which for decades has faced overexploitation. In Chapter 8, Rodrigue and Wright discuss the challenges managers and scientists face in remedying or reversing wetlands damage, and they provide specific suggestions for restoring damaged wetlands and preserving wetland habitats. They argue that sustainability, commonly defined as the ability to meet the needs of the present generation without compromising the ability of future generations to do the same, is an essential component of any plan to restore wetlands, and that our right to make use of the resources derived from these ecosystems also comes with the responsibility to use them sustainably and in such a way that doesn't preclude their use and enjoyment by future generations or by other species. The authors of Chapter 8 also pose some important questions: What are the challenges that arise when attempting to restore something as complex as a hydrology-driven ecosystem? What is the likelihood that such a system can be restored?

In Chapter 9, Stanturf, Gardiner, and Warren examine the role humans have played in deforestation and nonpoint source pollution in bottomland hardwood forests in the lower Mississippi Alluvial Valley. Although discussion about forest afforestation techniques may seem out of place in a volume on freshwater and wetland sustainability, in fact, these bottomland hardwood forests can be classified as wetlands because of (1) the extended periods of saturation and inundation they experience during the growing season, and (2) the morphological and physiological adaptations trees and plants in this system have developed in order to survive such conditions. Although these systems have experienced significant decline since European settlement, immense tracts of bottomland hardwood forests remain. Moreover, they are described as "one of the dominant types of ecosystems in the United States" (Mitsch and Gosselink 1993), making them important to wetland ecology in terms of not only the wood they provide but also for their value in providing habitat and floodwater retention.

Historically, bottomland hardwood forests have been cleared to make room for agricultural uses of the sites they occupy, and in Chapter 10, Cooper and Moore describe the history of the relationship between agriculture and wetlands. Today, wetlands in the lower Mississippi Alluvial Valley are stressed by nonpoint source pollution, most typically from agricultural pollutants including sediments, nutrients, and pesticides, which can accumulate at unhealthy levels in wetlands. The authors examine ways in which current agricultural practices can be altered so as to ease the strain on wetlands and suggest ways in which constructed wetlands (wetlands built to remove specific pollutants) can contribute to a more sustainable agricultural industry.

Chapter 8

Wetland Restoration: Applications on the Land in the Lower Mississippi Alluvial Valley

Paul B. Rodrigue and Keith M. Wright

Wetlands are vital for the existence of life. They filter our water, replenish our aquifers, and retain the rains for use in local ecosystems while reducing the likelihood of floods. Despite their obvious importance, wetlands have suffered anthropogenic impacts in the form of degradation and obliteration from as far back as European immigration. As the twenty-first century begins, humanity is very slowly emerging from an era of intense wetland degradation. A hint of recognition is also emerging, one that recognizes that human and natural systems are inherently linked. Our challenge at this point in history is to reverse the trend of wetland degradation, to learn how to restore those wetlands that have already been degraded, and to restore them successfully. The complexity of this challenge mirrors the complexity of the wetland systems themselves and the society to which they have become inextricably linked. This chapter attempts to answer a number of questions. How have wetlands been degraded over time? What does a relatively intact bottomland hardwood system of wetlands within the Lower Mississippi Alluvial Valley (LMAV) look like? How are practitioners attempting to restore wetlands and wetland functions? Is wetland restoration even feasible? What lessons have we learned from our efforts in this nascent science called wetland restoration? Although this chapter focuses on wetland degradation and restoration attempts in the LMAV, such lessons and challenges are applicable to deltaic regions around the world.

Inasmuch, attention to the LMAV is helpful in that it can contextualize some of the theoretical elements of wetland restoration.

The Lower Mississippi Alluvial Valley: A Representative Wetland Mosaic

The Lower Mississippi Alluvial Valley, situated in the floodplain of the Mississippi River from the tip of southern Illinois to Louisiana (Saucier 1994), is a watershed region of national and international significance. The region provides habitat for myriad migratory birds en route between North and South America, drains approximately one-third of the continental United States, and is home to the highest level of biodiversity found in the country. Like many deltaic regions throughout the world, the LMAV has experienced extremely high rates of land conversion to agriculture. Within this context, efforts to restore wetlands in the LMAV can provide practitioners around the world with ideas and insights as they grapple with their own deltaic restoration projects (King and Keeland 1999).

The Lower Mississippi Alluvial Valley encompasses land on either side of the Mississippi River in Arkansas, Mississippi, Missouri, and Tennessee and consists of level to gently sloping broad floodplains and low terraces, with elevations ranging from sea level in the south to 200 meters in the north (Scott 1998). The LMAV is characterized by the presence of wetlands, defined by the U.S. Army Corps of Engineers (Corps) and the U.S. Environmental Protection Agency as "those areas that are inundated or saturated by surface or ground water at a frequency and duration sufficient to support, and that under normal circumstances do support, a prevalence of vegetation typically adapted for life in saturated soil conditions" (U.S. Army Corps of Engineers 2001). Historically, prior to human-induced hydrological alteration, flooding in the LMAV corresponded to precipitation and season. In years with high precipitation, first bottoms would flood for most of the year, whereas in years of moderate precipitation first bottoms would only flood for several days in the summer, and then only in the event of heavy rainfall. In the winter months first bottoms typically flood from one to three months, often to depths greater than 1.4 meters (Kellison et al. 1998).

Historically, wetlands have been delineated by vegetation type, though it is now recognized that such plant communities are themselves the outcome of a synthesis of hydrologic, biogeochemical, and ecosystem dynamics that characterize a given landscape (Bedford 1996, 1999). For example, hydrologic pathways controlled by geomorphology will influence the cycling of elements, which in turn influences plant distribution. The Corps, the agency responsible for overseeing the nation's wetland systems, evaluates vegetation, soil, and hydrology to assess whether a place is a wetland. Nearly 5,000 plant types and

2,000 soil types may occur in wetlands in the United States. Wetland hydrology refers to water that exists at or above the soil surface for enough time that it significantly influences the plant types and soils that occur in the area. Several observations can be made to detect the presence of water, including standing or flowing water during the growing season, water marks on trees, piles of leaves and debris in tree branches, and marshy soils with spongy decaying matter on top of the soil.

The LMAV was historically characterized by the presence of vast bottomland hardwood forests, which are a type of forested wetland typically found on the alluvial plains of lowland streams and rivers in the eastern and southeastern United States (Mitsch and Gosselink 2000). Bottomland hardwood forests are greatly influenced by the duration of the landscape's hydroperiod; a flood's duration, intensity, and frequency influences abiotic factors such as soil, nutrients, and oxygen concentration. These abiotic factors are in turn responsible for species composition (Winger 1986). In bottomland hardwood forests, hydrology is one of the most important abiotic factors. For example, Hoover and Kilgore (1998) note that the importance of hydrology is commonly emphasized in papers that discuss the structure of freshwater fish communities. Hydrology also affects the dispersal, germination, and establishment of plant species. In addition to influencing soil content, moisture availability, and oxygen levels, hydrology can also affect the distribution of plant species that depend upon hydrochory, the dispersal of seed by water, as their primary dispersal mechanism (King and Allen 1996). The life cycles of many amphibians, reptiles, and other wildlife species are also dependent on variations in the timing, depth, and duration of flooding.

Southeastern forested wetlands provide many functions valuable to humans and other species. They provide for short- and long-term storage of surface water, transform and cycle elements, provide flood abatement, retain and remove dissolved matter from the water, and provide habitat for wildlife as well as food and natural resources for humans (Clewell and Lea 1990; Mitsch and Gosselink 2000).

Bottomland hardwood forests are characterized by high species richness. For example, bottomland hardwood communities can consist of as many as sixty-two species of freshwater fishes (Hoover and Kilgore 1998). Kellison et al. (1998) note that the highly fertile forests produce an abundance of food while providing shelter in an environment with high predation pressure. Prior to intensive agriculture and logging, the LMAV supported panther and the ivory-billed woodpecker. Today, the area still supports white-tailed deer, wild turkey, raccoon, bobcat, black bear, American beaver, squirrel, common muskrat, northern river otter, mink, rabbit, opossum, nutria, short-tailed shrew, and numerous amphibians and reptiles. Smith et al. (1993) further highlight the biodiversity significance of the region by noting that 200 of the 236 landbirds found throughout eastern North America can be found in the Mississippi Alluvial Valley forest (Smith et al. 1993).

Though the Lower Mississippi Alluvial Valley still supports some of the highest biodiversity in the United States, approximately 70 percent of its bottomland hardwood forest wetlands have been altered through land conversion, much of which has been converted to agriculture (Rickets et al. 1999). Human land use has left wildlife populations fragmented throughout the region. The LMAV has experienced such extreme alteration, in fact, that it is considered one of the most endangered ecosystems in the United States (Stanturf et al. 2000). Despite an increase in both awareness of the problem and efforts to remediate it, loss of forested wetlands continues to outpace restored lands by a wide margin. Today 2.8 million hectares of an estimated 10 million hectares of the original bottomland hardwood forest remain (King and Keeland 1999), though much of this land comprises patches less than 100 hectares in size (Mitsch and Gosselink 2000).

The tracts of bottomland hardwood forest that remain in the LMAV have been subjected to alterations besides fragmentation. Regional and local hydrologic cycles have been radically altered by flood-control projects whose consequence has been the separation of the Mississippi River and its tributaries from their corresponding floodplains. These projects further contributed to loss of fish and wildlife habitat, and they decrease the ability of these lands to store floodwater or retain sediments (Stanturf and Gardiner 2000). Natural flooding once periodically covered the floodplain. As the area's hydrology has been altered by flood control, flooding occurs less often, with less intensity, and over less area than before.

The Cache River Basin: A Representative Bottomland Hardwood Forest at the Crossroads

Moving from the Lower Mississippi Alluvial Valley to a specific watershed characterized by bottomland hardwood forested wetlands highlights problems associated with habitat destruction and hydrologic alteration as well as opportunities for protection and restoration. The Cache River Basin is located in northeastern Arkansas and is approximately 229 kilometers long encompassing 288,000 hectares.

The Cache River Watershed is home to the Cache River Wetlands, which were designated as a Wetland of International Importance by the Ramsar Convention in 1996. The Ramsar Convention on Wetlands arose from an international treaty signed in Ramsar, Iran, in 1971. The treaty provides the framework for national action and international cooperation for the conservation and wise use of wetlands and their resources (Ramsar 2001). The 23,000-hectare Cache River Wetlands comprises tupelo gum swamps and bald cypress bottomland hardwood forests that function as habitat for migratory waterfowl, wading birds, neotropical migrant songbirds, rare mammals, and old-growth cypress trees (Smith 1996; Wakely and Roberts 1996). The Cache River Wetlands was chosen for Ramsar designation because of critical waterfowl breeding habitat, wintering and migratory waterfowl, and shorebirds that use the Mississippi Flyway.

The Ramsar designation aside, the Cache River watershed as a whole is significant locally because it represents one of the most unfragmented and undisturbed bottomland hardwood forests in the LMAV (Kleiss 1996a). Nonetheless, the watershed has still experienced significant changes resulting from timber harvest, road construction, and land clearing and drainage for conversion to agriculture. Within the watershed, over 100,000 hectares of forest cover has been eliminated since 1935, meaning forested areas declined from 65 percent to 15 percent of the total land area. Much of the remaining tracts are characterized by increased edge habitat and decreased core habitat due to forest fragmentation (Kress et al. 1996).

One of the most striking features of this landscape is its hydrology. Flooding usually occurs from late February through May, with water depth ranging from a few centimeters up to 2 meters. Despite hydrologic and land-use alterations the region still supports areas of tupelo gum and bald cypress; the lower reaches of the Cache River still support some of the largest unfragmented areas of bottomland hardwood forest. Cache River flooding patterns play a large role in the structuring of wetland fish assemblages by increasing the availability of food and habitat in the floodplain for larval fishes (Kilgore and Baker 1996). In addition to influencing fish populations, hydrology also affects sedimentation rates. Kleiss (1996b) showed that suspended sediments are retained by wetlands systems during high-flow periods when floodwaters are spread over the floodplain and retained for long periods of time. Hydrology is also a factor influencing the diversity and composition of bird communities; Wakely and Roberts (1996) observed that forest zones, which are influenced by flooding regime, affect the distribution of bird species. Wetter zones were inhabited by chimney swifts, prothonotary warblers, and great crested flycatchers, while summer tanagers, red-eyed vireos, and others were skewed toward drier sites.

Hydrology thus plays a major role in determining plant and animal species within the Cache River Basin. Like many other areas within the Lower Mississippi Alluvial Valley, human activities such as stream channelization, levee construction, conversion to cropland, and drainage have radically altered the Cache River Basin's hydrology. The Cache River Basin is used for the production of rice, soybeans, cotton, and wheat. Rice production, which requires flooded fields, increased in the 1970s. Wilber et al. (1996) noticed a correlation at that time between increased rice production and greater frequency in extreme low river flows. In August and September, which are months when water is drained from the fields into drainages that flow into the Cache River, higher flows were observed. It was also observed that annual drawdowns in the alluvial aquifer coincide with increased rice production.

The Cache River study site can be roughly divided into cypress tupelo areas that are permanently flooded and areas dominated by oak that are seasonally flooded. Ecosystem structure and function varied between these sites due to flood regime (Kleiss 1996a). For example, permanently flooded areas show increased tree basal areas, frequent floodwater storage, preference shown by certain species of birds, and higher rates of mineral sediment accretion, while seasonally flooded areas show decreased canopy and tree density, large volume of floodwater storage, highest larval fish abundance, preference shown by different species of birds, and sediment deposition that is proportionately more organic and lower in volume. Results from these multiyear studies contributed to an overarching plan developed by the U.S. Army Engineer Waterways Experiment Station to fill knowledge gaps regarding bottomland hardwood forest functions (Kleiss 1996a). The spatial and hydrologic complexities that these studies high-light underscore an important point—wetlands are complex ecosystems to describe, and wetland functions are difficult to document. Within this context lie interesting ramifications for wetland restoration.

Wetland Restoration: Challenges and Perspectives

Wetland restoration, much like conservation biology (Soule 1985), is a crisis discipline. Demands for restoration come from many segments of society, yet wetland restoration is still a relatively new science. For this reason, practitioners of wetland restoration are scientists who need to employ intuition and art in areas where information is yet unknown. Zedler (2000) highlights some of the information that is yet unknown: how the combination of landscape position within the watershed and degraded water quality affect restoration efforts; how the addition of generic wetland types—ponds—affect biodiversity and func-tions at the landscape scale; and, how hydrologic regime, in terms of frequency and magnitude of high water, as well as duration, timing, and temporal sequence of flooding events, affects biodiversity and wetland function restoration. Wetland restoration is barely able to predict outcomes of wetland restoration efforts, yet around the world demand for restoration increases regularly, corresponding to an increased understanding of the importance of wetland function and ecology and an increased percentage of total wetlands that are degraded.

Despite substantial gaps in scientific understanding of wetland function and ecology, many efforts have been made in the past twenty years in the LMAV to restore wetlands. Much of what has been learned is providing a foundation of lessons that can be applied to deltaic restoration projects worldwide. King and Keeland (1999) have surveyed restorationists from the U.S. Fish and Wildlife Service National Wildlife Refuges, U.S. Natural Resources Conservation Service

(NRCS) State Conservationists, the Corps, and forestry, game, and fish agencies throughout the LMAV in order to determine the amount of land that has been restored (77,698 hectares), the methods that were used for reforestation, and the effects of hydrology. When compared with the amount of forested lands lost during that same period (364,212 hectares), these restoration efforts seem minimal. Projected restoration levels are also expected to be outpaced by projected deforestation, and no legislation or other societal compact is on the drawing board to stave off future degradation of bottomland hardwood forested wetlands.

Within this bleak trend lies reason for both concern and hope. Clearly, there is a need for social and political solutions to the problem of wetland degradation that go beyond the scope of this chapter. Ideally, the need for restoration will one day be greatly reduced because humans will have learned to live harmoniously within their ecosystems. In the meantime, it is important to note that wetland destruction and alteration has been a common practice for centuries. Restoration efforts like the ones documented by King and Keeland (1999) indicate that the literature is expanding and conclusions from earlier studies are being verified. Social and political changes can happen overnight, whereas consensus in scientific understanding, while evolving, takes time.

For example, federal Congressional legislation to remediate the eutrophication of the Gulf of Mexico due to its negative impact on a billion-dollar fishing industry could be passed within a single session. A potential solution to the eutrophication problem would be to restore hydrology within the bottomland hardwood communities. Such legislation aimed at the Gulf would inevitably benefit the LMAV (King and Keeland 1999); numerous studies cite hydrologic restoration as the primary requirement of wetland restoration in the LMAV (King and Keeland 1999; National Research Council 1992). However, due to financial constraints local hydrologic restoration is not widely practiced in the LMAV. The U.S. Natural Resources Conservation Service's Wetlands Reserve Program (WRP), described below, is a notable exception to this generalization. As the relationship between hydrologic restoration and restored wetland function becomes increasingly well documented and understood, the likelihood that it will get the funding and authorization that such a massive project would entail will increase accordingly. The need for understanding the ecological consequences of land- and water-use change through a functional understanding of how such alterations affect ecological processes is one of the key research topics called for in the Ecological Society of America's Sustainable Biosphere Initiative (Lubchenco et al. 1991).

Wetland restoration is a term that has meaning along a wide spectrum of possible definitions. The Society of Wetlands Scientists (SWS) recently defined wetland restoration as "actions taken in a converted or degraded natural wetland that result in the reestablishment of ecological processes, functions, and biotic/abiotic linkages and lead to a persistent, resilient system integrated within its landscape" (Society of Wetlands Scientists 2000). The SWS position paper on wetlands restoration notes that hydrology, geomorphic setting, physical processes such as sediment movement, biological processes, and biogeochemical processes combine to form a wetland. Sediment and water regime restoration can often lead in turn to the restoration of other functions.

An ultimate goal of wetland restoration should be the creation of a persistent and resilient system that is able to respond to disturbances without human intervention, though often wetland systems are so altered that human intervention is required to maintain a restored wetland. To increase the likelihood that hydrology and sediment regimes are restored, Bedford (1999), for example, notes that restoration projects should begin with a clear understanding of what has been lost. Wetlands are linked to the landscape hydrologically, chemically, and biologically, and as such so should a restorationist's view when assessing what is needed for a specific restoration project. Whereas wetlands are linked to their landscapes, a view to the landscape will increase the likelihood that a diversity of wetland types is maintained.

Possible Tools for Assessing Wetland Function

Means for assessing wetlands are necessary for two broad reasons. First, it is often helpful to be aware of the functions of a given wetland in order to clarify the goals of a restoration project. Second, as wetlands are restored, the success of the restoration must be assessed (Keddy 1999). The decision to restore a wetland depends primarily on the site's source of water and the goals for that given site. Sources of water may include direct precipitation, runoff from contributing drainage area, groundwater discharge, or riverine or lake flooding. Pumping, from groundwater or surface water, may also be a water source for the site, but a source that has a significant operation and maintenance component. Pumping can also be used occasionally to provide early season water or water in dry years.

Wetlands are valuable natural resources. They have the ability to provide a multitude of functions, many of which are valuable to us as individuals and to our society. From a plant and wildlife perspective, wetlands are equally valuable in that they provide living space, food, shelter, and other components of habitat for a suite of wetland-dependent species. When wetlands are lost, so are these associated functions and values. When wetlands are restored or enhanced, the potential exists to replace lost functions and values. However, the extent to which the potential replacement of functions and values are realized depends in large part on the effectiveness of monitoring and how well the physical and biological components of the wetland are maintained.

After a restoration project has been undertaken, monitoring methods must be available to assess five-year, ten-year, and sixty-year restoration efforts.

Monitoring is important because it provides a method for assessing a wetland's progression toward its planned objectives while providing documentation on the restoration effort that will prove useful to other restoration practitioners. Monitoring identifies failures or shortcomings that may threaten the project, serves as a feedback mechanism to stimulate maintenance, and provides a means for learning about restoration (Melvin unpublished notes).

Two tools for monitoring the functions of wetlands deserve further attention. The *hydrogeomorphic* (HGM) *approach* provides one possible means of assessing a site's functional characteristics in relation to a reference base (Brinson and Rheinhardt 1996). The HGM approach is a collection of concepts and methods for classifying wetlands based on functional characteristics that can be used to develop indices to assess the capacity of wetlands to perform specific functions. The classification has three components—geomorphic setting, water source, and hydrodynamics, the latter of which refers to the movement of water, with specific reference to sediment and nutrient transport (Brinson 1993). Evaluators who use this method may help to ensure that restoration activities are reaching the desired goals. The method also provides a means for evaluating whether there is a need for modifications to the restoration plan in order to obtain the functions and values desired from the restoration. More applications are needed if the HGM approach is to become widely accepted as a means for assessing wetland function.

Another possible tool for assessing wetland function is the *soil perturbation index*. The soil perturbation index was used in sites in the Lower Mississippi Alluvial Valley to determine how the biogeochemical characteristics of soil organic matter (SOM), total organic carbon (TOC), total Kjeldahl nitrogen (TKN), and total phosphorus (TP) data differed in each wetland from a biogeochemical reference site established in mature wetlands of the same type and ecoregion. Soils from the U.S. Natural Resources Conservation Service Wetlands Reserve Program, the USDA Conservation Reserve Program, and cottonwood sites within Mississippi were analyzed to determine if reforested sites that were previously agricultural exhibit similar biogeochemical trends as forested wetlands previously harvested for timber (Maul and Holland 2002).

In a recent study (Maul and Holland 2002), trends of reforested sites that were previously agricultural exhibited similar biogeochemical trends in forested wetlands previously harvested for timber. The soil perturbation index was used to evaluate the restoration process of created and restored wetlands previously in agriculture. The study was based on the assumption that the agriculturally based sites exhibit similar restoration responses as regenerated wetlands do and therefore indicates that the index is a valid method for evaluating how created and restored sites are developing. It has been shown that the natural regeneration of timbered wetlands exhibits similar trends for soil organic matter, total organic carbon, total Kjeldahl nitrogen, and total phosphorus (Smith 1997). According to the soil perturbation index, biogeochemical conditions decrease after timber harvest, with a low point reached at approximately eight to nine years after alteration. This index predicts that it would take sixteen to seventeen years for SOM, TOC, TKN, and TP to return to pre-harvest conditions (Maul et al. 1999).

The reforested sites (cottonwood) previously in agriculture exhibited similar biogeochemical trends as wetlands allowed to naturally regenerate following timber harvest. Concentrations of soil organic matter, total organic carbon, total Kjeldahl nitrogen, and total phosphorus decrease until the eight-year stage, and then increase toward mature conditions. A similar pattern was exhibited by timber-harvested wetlands (Maul et al. 1999). Several factors promote such a decrease and subsequent rebound of soil nutrient concentrations. Young aggrading stands have higher rates of nutrient uptake than mature systems (Lockaby and Walbridge 1998). The young successional stages produce less foliage and other organic matter than mature systems do. As the sites mature, the vegetation produces more leaf litter that, upon recycling of nutrients, increases the productivity of the wetland (Smith et al. 1996). Changes in the SOM concentrations or in rates of carbon cycling may have important effects on nutrient cycling, vegetative composition, and productivity (Trettin et al. 1996). Thus, time is required in order for the system to reach a dynamic equilibrium.

This study and the Maul et al. (1999) study indicate that wetlands previously altered by human activity (agriculture and timber harvesting) exhibit similar biogeochemical trends following alterations. Further studies should focus on other human alterations as well as on natural disturbances. Wetlands created for mitigation purposes also might be studied to determine if the soil perturbation index is useful as one component in the evaluation of these wetlands. The index can be used to evaluate the biogeochemical trends of created and restored wetlands, such as those found in the Wetlands Reserve and the Conservation Reserve Programs, compared to other wetlands of similar land-use history, type, and ecoregion.

Restoration Success: What Does It Mean?

The challenge in wetlands restoration is knowing when success has been achieved. With regards to wetland restoration success, Craft et al. (1999) raise an interesting point: no long-term studies exist that document the length of time it takes to achieve the complete restoration of wetland functions and values. The idea of success in wetland restoration and creation has been problematic as the discipline has emerged (Mitsch and Wilson 1996); the establishment of a restored forested wetland can take many years before an accurate assessment can be made.

Middleton (1999) notes that the ultimate success of a restored wetland as a functional ecosystem will depend on how well the system can endure natural disturbances. Ehrenfeld (2000) argues that wetland restoration goals should be based on the scope and the reason for each restoration effort. Brinson and Rheinhardt (1996) recommend the use of reference wetlands that can be used for means of comparison. Stanturf et al. (2001) argue against reference stands for bottomland hardwood forests because of the potential for unforeseen changes resulting from the dynamics between plant succession and hydroperiod that are in turn the result of alterations to LMAV hydrology. King and Keeland (1999) note that restoration success in the LMAV is limited by the lack of hydrologic restoration, which is linked to the life history of many plants, animals, and fishes. Instead of reference stands, Stanturf et al. (2001) see restoration in a continuum model, where criteria for success are described in terms of predicted values of wetland functions.

Wetland Restoration in the Lower Mississippi Alluvial Valley: Some Pioneering Attempts

The restoration of wetlands is by definition a human process, so any definition of success must involve a human component. Hey and Philippi (1999) note that successful restoration projects will involve a wide variety of interest groups and institutions. A variety of institutions are involved in efforts to restore wetlands in the Lower Mississippi Alluvial Valley. While there is much still to be learned regarding wetland restoration (Malakoff 1998), much is already known and is being applied to wetland restoration (Hey and Philippi 1999; Keddy 1999).

In light of the fact that the LMAV has lost approximately 70 percent of its bottomland hardwood forest wetlands to land conversion, restoration is clearly needed. The U.S. Natural Resources Conservation Service has made the LMAV a major focus of wetland restoration through the Wetlands Reserve Program (WRP), a voluntary incentive-based wetlands restoration program authorized by the 1990 Farm Bill. Although the Wetlands Reserve Program has sites across the United States, its biggest impact has been in the LMAV, where 121,000 hectares (300,000 acres) have been restored.

The Wetlands Reserve Program provides farmers and other landowners with financial and technical assistance in taking farmed wetlands and prior converted farmlands out of production for the purpose of wetland restoration. The Natural Resources Conservation Service defines "farmed wetlands" as areas that have a 50 percent chance of being flooded or ponded for at least fifteen consecutive days in the growing season (USDA 1996a). Within this arrangement, landowners sell a thirty-year easement to the Department of Agriculture while retaining ownership, hunting and fishing rights, and responsibility for taxes. The Wetlands

Reserve Program has helped family farms by providing opportunities for income diversification through hunting leases (USDA 1996b).

Nearly 324,000 hectares have been enrolled in the Program nationwide; nearly 114,000 hectares are in the LMAV. Innovative techniques and designs have been used in applying wetland restoration to the land. Most Wetland Reserve Programs in the LMAV are planted with species characteristic of bottomland hardwoods, with oak trees being the predominant species. Planting techniques include bare-rooted seedlings, direct seeding (acorns), and natural revegetation. By restoring hydrology and microtopography, practitioners attempt to enhance the diversity of species and wildlife habitat, though owing to the newness of wetland restoration as a science and the LMAV's radically altered hydrology, this challenge is not always achieved. King and Keeland (1999) note that the Wetland Reserve Program appears to be having an important impact on the LMAV and call for policies that provide for additional financial incentives for landowners interested in restoration.

In addition to federal efforts by the National Resources Conservation Service, the U.S. Fish and Wildlife Service, and other agencies, there is also a large effort in wetland restoration by state wildlife and fisheries agencies, industry, and not-for-profit groups such as Ducks Unlimited. Since 1937, the mission of Ducks Unlimited has been to fulfill the annual life cycle needs of North American waterfowl by protecting, restoring, and managing important wetlands and associated uplands. The organization works to compensate for ecological impacts to wetlands caused by human-induced hydrologic alteration by creating or enhancing food webs vital to migratory waterfowl and any species that relies on lands that experience periodic inundation. By engaging in moist soil management, Ducks Unlimited and private landholders are able to mimic an important hydrologic function of altered riparian zones by allowing for the production of warm season grasses whose seed provides food for migratory birds. Ducks Unlimited partners with various state, local, and federal agencies to help achieve this mission. As of February 1999, Ducks Unlimited has conserved almost 9 million acres in the United States, Mexico, and Canada.

Ducks Unlimited has permanent conservation easements on approximately 112,000 acres across the United States. In addition to permanent easements, Ducks Unlimited assists farmers in providing winter-waterfowl habitat in the LMAV by flooding agricultural fields from November to March. In the Delta regions of Arkansas, Missouri, Mississippi, and Louisiana, more than 2 million acres of rice are produced each year. Researchers at the Forest and Wildlife Research Center at Mississippi State University were recently interested in the relationship between the creation of waterfowl habitat and benefits to the farmer.

After the fall harvest, most farms participate in fall disking, a process that assists with the elimination of rice straw, which is followed by letting the fields drain throughout the winter. Researchers found that farmers who allow their fields to flood as the result of water impoundment lose much less soil—33 versus 1,000 pounds per soil acre—than those who do not impound their fields. They also found that flooding performs the rice-straw-degradation function usually performed by fall disking, which can save farmers $14.13 per acre. Flooding also suppresses cool-season grasses and weeds, which could potentially save up to $13 per acre of spring herbicide application (Manley 1999). Great potential exists to further provide habitat for waterfowl habitat creation that lowers production costs; currently only 10 percent of this area is managed to provide waterfowl habitat.

Ducks Unlimited assists with technical design information and in some instances provides water-control structures. Projects are generally surveyed, designed, and built by Ducks Unlimited engineers and technicians with input from organization biologists. Low levees 2.5 to 3.5 feet in height are constructed along field contours to allow for shallow flooding of the units. The units are generally dependent upon rainfall or runoff for water, but occasionally pumps are installed if funding is available. The organization uses the latest satellite technology to provide GPS (global positioning satellite) survey data of the wetland cells for planning and design. Use of this technology allows Ducks Unlimited to plan sites; the water control structure that is used corresponds to the management objective. Ducks Unlimited has been extensively involved with the implementation of the Wetlands Reserve Program. The organization's goal is to replace some of the functions of winter flooding, which has been compromised by the reduction of wetlands and the loss of bottomland hardwoods. Restoring hydrology with moist soil impoundments and planting a variety of bottomland species provides habitat for migratory birds and other wetland-dependent organisms.

The U.S. Fish and Wildlife Service, the Natural Resources Conservation Service, Ducks Unlimited, and respective state wildlife management agencies have been at the vanguard of bottomland hardwood reforestation efforts within Louisiana, Mississippi, and Arkansas. They have planted more than 100,000 hectares of bottomland hardwood forests and are actively pursuing continued restoration activities. A database consisting of the magnitude and distribution, as well as the silvicultural practices employed in the bottomland hardwood reforestation efforts of the LMAV has been compiled. This unique database contains information essential to researchers and managers alike. Moreover, average densities (trees per hectare) of eighty-two randomly sampled fields within the three states were evaluated to determine the effect of planting methods (acorns, seedlings) and planting seasons (spring, winter, fall) on artificially reforested abandoned agricultural fields. A monitoring scheme is being developed resulting from this research, and recommendations for plot size, number of plots per hectare, sampling scheme, and plot location are being refined to improve monitoring effectiveness. A major fact supported by this work is that it can take five years before a meaningful evaluation of woody vegetation success, by any planting means, can be performed (Forest and Wildlife Research Center 2001).

The partnerships between Ducks Unlimited, individual landowners, industry, and government agencies have begun to reverse the historical trend of wetland degradation by restoring some of the vital functions of wetland systems within the LMAV while providing valuable insights into their complexity. As David Brunkhorst, senior vice president of Ducks Unlimited, noted during the dedication of the Cache River Wetlands as a Ramsar site, wetland partnerships are the key to protecting this resource and others like it: "For the past several years, Ducks Unlimited has worked closely with joint venture partners to acquire and subsequently enhance the Cache River Wetlands" (Ramsar 1996). Nearly 75 percent of the land that Ducks Unlimited believes is important wildlife habitat is privately owned (Ducks Unlimited 2001); restoration at the landscape level must involve private landholder cooperation.

Recommendations

Wetlands conservation is a nascent science. Much still has to be learned in both social and scientific arenas if we are to reverse or mitigate the damage that has been caused to wetlands in the past century. While the partnerships and restoration highlighted in this chapter provide examples of how large-scale restoration projects can be successful in restoring some wetland functions, more research is necessary to better understand how these complex systems function.

Additional scientific understanding is vital to the goal of wetland restoration. LMAV hydrology has been completely altered, moving from a riverine system to one driven by precipitation events. In this light, further research is needed to understand how plants and wildlife are responding to the altered hydrology and to determine the best possible utilization of the current hydrology. It is unlikely that the hydrology in the LMAV will be restored; millions of people depend on its altered hydrology for flood prevention. As long as the altered hydrology remains in place, research should focus on the range of possible hydrological configurations that practitioners might mimic in order to arrive at the management scheme that best replaces the strived-for function of the natural hydroperiod.

A second area that deserves further attention is in the area of wetland classification. A more sophisticated scientific basis is needed to evaluate wetland functions and values. The hydrogeomorphic approach, which is a tool for assessing a site's functional characteristics in relation to a reference base, offers one potential method to fulfill this objective. Developing such a system for each individual wetland system, however, will require the commitment of resources to accomplish this labor-intensive task.

While restoring degraded wetlands is necessary, the best strategy is to exit from the historical era of wetland destruction and degradation as quickly as possible. To that end, education, at all levels, regarding the role that wetlands play in the environment is crucial. An educated populace will help to ensure that programs like the Wetlands Reserve Program, the most successful wetland restoration program in the LMAV, will remain politically viable. Success of the program can be attributed to several factors which others interested in conservation on private land would do well to observe. First, the program is voluntary, which avoids the dynamic in which citizens feel that the government is taking away their rights. Second, the program offers an attractive incentive for participation. This is an important component as long as land is viewed as a commodity upon which a return is expected. Without a financial incentive, a program like the Wetlands Reserve Program, in which land is taken out of production, would be much less popular. Third, the program involves a network of stakeholders, including representatives from government, nonprofit organizations, private landholders, and industry, which means that efforts at wetland restoration under the program are a community effort, which is vital to the success of restoration projects on privately owned land. Additionally, the program incorporates the soundest scientific knowledge and technical expertise in its restoration efforts, which ensures that the program will either meet its objectives or provide lessons useful for future efforts; the program complements scientific research efforts by documenting the results of restoration efforts.

Within the LMAV, as much as 1.5 million hectares of marginal farmland could also potentially be restored. At least two prerequisites to restoration of these lands exist: financial support from the federal government and a comprehensive evaluation of the techniques, methods, and species necessary for successful wetland restoration (King and Keeland 1999). A program that reached some conclusions regarding the best scientific methods, followed by an increase in federal funding that would enable farmers to retire marginal farmland, would be the most prudent approach.

Conclusions

Human populations are slowly becoming aware of the importance of wetlands. This awareness is accompanied also by recognition of how wetlands have been degraded over time. Such degradation has grave implications for the countless number of species that depend on wetlands for their survival, not the least of which are humans. For this reason, wetland restoration is critical to biosphere sustainability. Hydrologic cycles determine species composition and wetland function, so any attempt at wetland restoration should seriously consider the extent to which hydrologic restoration is possible. If it is not possible, restoration projects will need to be continuously managed because only a system that has restored hydrology will be self-regulating, which is the ultimate test for sustainability. Pioneering attempts in the LMAV have shown that there is potential for restoring some of the functions and structure of degraded wetlands, but clearly the best strategy would be to eliminate further wetland degradation as part of a long-term strategy. The sustainability of wetlands in the Lower Mississippi Alluvial Valley, like many deltaic regions, depends on the cooperation of private landowners. Increased funding for incentive-based programs that encourage restoration on private lands has proven to be a successful strategy for increasing scientific understanding of the nascent field of wetland restoration. Incentive-based programs have also proved to be an efficient political and economic mechanism to focus the attention of many people and institutions on the challenge of wetland sustainability.

References

Bedford, B. 1996. The need to define hydrologic equivalence at the landscape scale for freshwater wetland mitigation. *Ecological Applications* 6(1):57–68.

———. 1999. Cumulative effects on wetlands landscapes: Links to wetland restoration in the United States and southern Canada. *Wetlands* 19(4):775–788.

Brinson, M. M. 1993. *A hydrogeomorphic classification for wetlands.* Technical Report WRP-DE-4. U.S. Army Engineer Waterways Experiment Station, Vicksburg, Miss.

Brinson, M. M., and R. Rheinhardt. 1996. The role of reference wetlands in functional assessment and mitigation. *Ecological Applications* 6(1):69–76.

Clewell, A. F., and R. Lea. 1990. Creation and restoration of forested wetland vegetation in the southeastern United States, in *Wetland creation and restoration: The status of the science,* edited by J. A. Kusler and M. E. Kentula. Washington, D.C.: Island Press.

Craft, C., J. Reader, J. N. Sacco, and S. W. Broome. 1999. Twenty-five years of ecosystem development of constructed *Spartina alterniflora* (Loisel) marshes. *Ecological Applications* 9(4):1405–1419.

Ducks Unlimited. 2001. RiverCARE. Accessed 7/15/01: http://www.ducks.org/.

Ehrenfeld, J. G. 2000. Defining the limits of restoration: The need for realistic goals. *Restoration Ecology* 8(1):2–9.

Forest and Wildlife Research Center. 2001. Online: www.cfr.msstate.edu/fwrc/fwrc.htm. Accessed 8/01/01.

Hey, D. L., and N. S. Philippi. 1999. *A case for wetland restoration.* New York: John Wiley and Sons.

Hoover, J. J., and K. J. Kilgore. 1998. Fish Communities. Pp. 237–260 in *Southern forested wetlands: Ecology and management,* edited by M. G. Messina and W. H Conner. Boca Raton: CRC Press.

Keddy, P. 1999. Wetland restoration: The potential for assembly rules in the service of conservation. *Wetlands* 19(4):716–732.

Kellison, R. C., M. J. Young, R. B. Braham, and E. J. Jones. 1998. Major alluvial floodplains. Pp. 291–324 in *Southern forested wetlands: Ecology and management,* edited by M. G. Messina and W. H. Conner. Boca Raton: CRC Press.

Kilgore, K. J., and J. A. Baker. 1996. Patterns of larval fish abundance in a bottomland hardwood wetland. *Wetlands* 16(3):288–295.

King, S. L., and James A. Allen. 1996. Plant Succession and greentree reservoir management: Implications for management and restoration of bottomland hardwood wetlands. *Wetlands* 16(4):503–511.

King, S. L., and B. D. Keeland. 1999. Evaluation of reforestation in the Lower Mississippi River Alluvial Valley. *Restoration Ecology* 7(4):348–359.

Kleiss, B. A. 1996a. Foreword. *Wetlands* 16(3):255–257.

———. 1996b. Sediment retention in a bottomland hardwood wetland in eastern Arkansas. *Wetlands* 16(3):321–333.

Kress, M. R., M. R. Graves, and S. G. Bourne. 1996. Loss of bottomland hardwood forests and forested wetlands in the Cache River Basin, Arkansas. *Wetlands* 16(3):258–263.

Lockaby, B. G., and M. R. Walbridge. 1998. Biogeochemistry. Pp. 149–172 in *Southern forested wetlands*, edited by M. G. Messina and W. H. Conne. Boca Raton: CRC Press.

Lubchenco, J., A. M. Olson, L. B. Brubaker, S. R. Carpenter, M. M. Holland, S. P. Hubbell, S. A. Levin, J. A. MacMahon, P. A. Matson, J. A. Melillo, H. A. Mooney, C. H. Peterson, H. R. Pulliam, L. A. Real, P. J. Regal, and P. G. Risser. 1991. The sustainable biosphere initiative: An ecological research agenda. *Ecology* 72 (2):371–412.

Malakoff, D. 1998. Restored wetlands flunk real-world test. *Science* 280:371–372.

Manley, S. W. 1999. Ecological and agricultural values of winter-flooded ricefields in Mississippi. Ph.D. diss., Department of Wildlife and Fisheries, Mississippi State University, Starkville.

Maul, R. S., and M. M. Holland. 2002. Application of the soil perturbation index to evaluate created and restored wetlands. Pp. 126–132 in *Proceedings of a Conference on Sustainability of Wetland and Water Resources*, edited by M. M. Holland, M. L. Warren Jr., and J. A. Stanturf. USDA Forest Service, Southern Research Station, General Technical Report SRS-50.

Maul, R. S., M. M. Holland, A. T. Mikell, and C. M. Cooper. 1999. Resilience of forested wetlands located in the southeastern United States: Demonstration of a soil perturbation index. *Wetlands* 19:288–295.

Melvin, N., III. Unpublished notes. *Why is monitoring important in wetland restoration, enhancement, and monitoring?* United States Department of Agriculture, Natural Resources Conservation Service, Wetland Science Institute, Fort Worth, Texas.

Middleton, B. A. 1999. Wetland restoration: Flood pulsing and disturbance dynamics. New York: John Wiley and Sons.

Mitsch, W. J., and J. G. Gosselink. 2000. *Wetlands*, 3d ed. New York: John Wiley and Sons.

Mitsch, W. J., and R. F. Wilson. 1996. Improving the success of wetland creation and restoration with know-how, time, and self design. *Ecological Applications* 6(1):77–83.

National Research Council. 1992. *Restoration of aquatic ecosystems: Science, technology, and public policy*. Washington, D.C.: National Academy Press.

RAMSAR Convention. 1996. Cache River/Cypress Creek, USA's 15th. Accessed 6/30/01: http://www.ramsar.org/w.n.cypress_creek.html.

———. 2000. http://www.ramsar.org/ Accessed 8/18/01.

Rickets, T. H., E. Dinerstein, D. M. Olson, and C. J. Loucks, eds. 1999. *Terrestrial ecoregions of North America: A conservation assessment*. Washington, D.C.: Island Press.

Saucier, R. T. 1994. *Geomorphology and quaternary geologic history of the lower Mississippi*

Valley. Prepared for the President, Mississippi River Commission, Vol. 2. U.S. Army Engineer Waterways Experiment Station, Vicksburg, Miss.

Scott, H. D., H. M. Selim, and L. B. Ward. 1998. *MLRA 131: Southern Mississippi Valley Alluvium. Southern Cooperative Series Bulletin.* Accessed 6/27/01: http://soilphysics.okstate.edu/S257/book/mlra131/index.html.

Smith, R. D. 1996. Composition, structure, and distribution of woody vegetation on the Cache River floodplain, Arkansas. *Wetlands* 16(3):264–278.

Smith, R. L. 1997. The resilience of bottomland hardwood wetlands soils following timber harvest. M.S. thesis. Department of Biology. The University of Mississippi, University, Miss.

Smith, R. L., M. M. Holland, and C. M. Cooper. 1996. The resilience of bottomland hardwood wetland soils following timber harvest. Pp. 739–745 in *Conference proceedings from the Delta: Connecting points of view for sustainable natural resources.* Memphis, Tenn.

Smith, W. P., P. B. Hamel, and R. P. Ford. 1993. Mississippi Alluvial Valley forest conversion: Implications for eastern North American avifauna. *Annual Conference of the Southeastern Association of Fish and Wildlife Agencies* 47:460–469.

Society of Wetlands Scientists. 2000. *Position paper on the definition of wetland restoration.* Accessed 11/27/02: www.sws.org/wetlandconcerns/restoration.html.

Soule, M. E. 1985. What is conservation biology? *BioScience* 35 (11): 727–734.

Stanturf, J. A., and E. S. Gardiner. 2000. Restoration of bottomland hardwoods in the Lower Mississippi Alluvial Valley. *Sustaining forests: The science of forest management.* Southern Resource Assessment. Accessed 6/14/01: www.srs.fs.fed.us/sustain/conf/.

Stanturf, J. A., E. S. Gardiner, P. H. Hamel, M. S. Devall, T. B. Leininger, and M. E. Warren Jr. 2000. Restoring bottomland hardwood ecosystems in the Lower Mississippi Alluvial Valley. *Journal of Forestry* 98(8):10–16.

Stanturf, J. A., S. H. Schoenholtz, C. J. Schweitzer, and J. P. Shepard. 2001. Achieving restoration success: Myths in bottomland hardwood forests. *Restoration Ecology* 9(2):189–200.

Trettin, C. C., M. Davidian, M. G. Jurgenson, and R. Lea. 1996. Organic decomposition following harvesting and site preparation of a forested wetland. *Soil Science Society of America Journal* 60:1994–2003.

U.S. Army Corps of Engineers. 2001. *Recognizing wetlands: An informational pamphlet.* [Online]: www.usace.army.mil/inet/functions/cw/cecwo/reg/rw-bro.htm. Accessed 08/05/01.

U.S. Department of Agriculture, Natural Resources Conservation Service. 1996a. *National Food Security Act manual.* 3d ed. U.S. Department of Agriculture, Washington, D.C.

———. 1996b. *Farm bill conservation provisions summary.* United States Department of Agriculture, Washington, D.C.

Wakely, J. S., and T. H. Roberts. 1996. Bird distributions and forest zonation in a bottomland hardwood wetland. *Wetlands* 16(3):296–308.

Wilber, D. H., R. E. Tighe, and L. J. O'Neil. 1996. Associations between changes in agriculture and hydrology in the Cache River Basin, Arkansas, USA. *Wetlands* 16(3):366–378.

Winger, P. V. 1986. *Forested wetlands of the Southeast: Review of major characteristics and role in maintaining water quality.* Publication 163, U.S. Department of the Interior, Fish and Wildlife Service, Washington, D.C.

Zedler, J. B. 2000. Progress in wetland restoration ecology. *Trends in Ecology and Evolution* 15 (10):402–407.

Chapter 9

Restoring Forested Wetland Ecosystems

John A. Stanturf, Emile S. Gardiner, and Melvin L. Warren Jr.

Forests as natural systems are intrinsically linked to the sustainability of freshwater systems. Efforts worldwide to restore forest ecosystems seek to counteract centuries of forest conversion to agriculture and other uses. Afforestation, the practice of regenerating forests on land deforested for agriculture or other uses, is occurring at an intense pace in the Lower Mississippi Alluvial Valley (LMAV) of the southern United States. Objectives of this chapter are (1) to place afforestation efforts in the LMAV into a global context of forest restoration by drawing parallels to work in other countries; (2) to summarize available information on afforestation techniques used to restore bottomland hardwood ecosystems; and (3) to document what is known about the effects on ecosystem functions. The dominant goal of all restoration programs in the LMAV, whether on public or private land, has been to create wildlife habitat and improve or protect surface water quality. Complex plantations that retain economic and logistic advantages of simple plantations can best meet some restoration goals. Complex plantations can include various arrangements of multiple species in true mixtures or intercropping mixtures. Potential benefits of mixed-species stands versus single-species stands can include increased pest resistance in the stand, increased productivity or yields if the stand is vertically stratified, increased product diversity, improved quality of crop trees, and increased canopy species diversity. Such healthy, diverse forests are critical to sustaining freshwater ecosystems. Riverine forests such as bottomland hardwoods and depressional swamp forests directly influence freshwater systems, and therefore restoration of these forests is considered essential to improving water quality.

Forests as natural systems are intrinsically linked to the sustainability of freshwater systems. Although commodity production from forests is a well-recognized beneficial use, the value and benefit of ecological linkages between forests, water resources, and humans may not be obvious to the casual observer. Forests play critical roles in moderating extremes in discharge from streams and rivers (e.g., increased flows in drought, decreased flows in floods) and are important in recharge of groundwaters. Forest cover decreases erosion and filters, stores, and moderates nutrient release into streams and rivers. Large wood from forests plays a major ecological role in the functioning of stream, river, and estuarine systems by forming and stabilizing channels, providing fish and aquatic organism habitat, and increasing productivity. Forest cover is often at the heart of the debates about global climate change, and the effect of reduced forest cover on climate has direct implications for the quantity and quality of worldwide freshwater supplies. Reestablishment of forests is a primary component of a holistic approach to worldwide sustainability of freshwater ecosystems.

Efforts worldwide to restore forest ecosystems seek to counteract centuries of forest conversion to agriculture and other uses (Stanturf 2002). Forest restoration in the broad sense is widespread, although there is no agreement on what constitutes restoration. Market forces, changing trade policies, and agricultural incentive programs drive conversion of cleared land back to trees. Afforestation, the practice of regenerating forests on land deforested for agriculture or other uses, is occurring at an intense pace in the LMAV of the southern United States. Objectives of this chapter are to (1) place afforestation efforts in the LMAV into a global context of forest restoration by drawing parallels to work in other countries; (2) summarize available information on afforestation techniques used to restore bottomland hardwood ecosystems; and (3) document what is known about the effects on ecosystem functions.

Forest Restoration Concepts

Restoration generally connotes transition from a degraded state to a former "natural" condition. All restorative activities described (reforestation, rehabilitation, afforestation, and reclamation) have been called forest restoration, but none of these would qualify as true restoration to the purist (Bradshaw 1997; Harrington 1999). In the narrowest interpretation, restoration requires a return to an ideal natural ecosystem with the same species diversity, composition, and structure of a previous ecosystem (Bradshaw 1997) and as such is probably impossible to attain (Cairns 1986). Pragmatically, a broad definition of forest restoration would include situations where forest land use as well as land cover are reestablished (afforestation or reclamation) or where a degraded forest is returned to a more "natural" condition in terms of species composition and stand structure (rehabilitation). This is the approach adopted in this chapter (for a more detailed discussion, see Stanturf and Madsen 2002). Examples of forest restoration abound (Table 9.1) and those in northern

Table 9.1. Examples of forest restoration efforts in various parts of the world

Type of restoration	Region	Former condition	Restored condition
Afforestation	Lower Mississippi Alluvial Valley, United States[1]	Agriculture	Bottomland hardwoods
Afforestation	Nordic countries[2]	Agriculture	Hardwoods, sometimes Norway spruce
Afforestation	Tropical countries[3]	Agriculture	Exotic and native hardwoods
Afforestation	Venezuela	Cerrado	Caribbean pine
Afforestation	Iceland[4]	Eroded grazing land	Birch, lupine/birch
Reclamation	Everywhere	Mined land	Various
Reclamation	Asia[5]	Shrimp ponds	Mangrove
Reclamation	Ireland	Mined peatland	Sitka spruce, various hardwoods
Reclamation	India[6]	Saline and sodic soils	Eucalyptus species, acacia species, other native species
Rehabilitation	Southeastern United States[7]	Loblolly pine Plantations	Longleaf pine Woodlands
Rehabilitation	Interior highlands, southeastern United States	Shortleaf pine/hardwood forests	Shortleaf pine/bluestem grass woodlands
Rehabilitation	Northern Europe[8]	Norway spruce plantations	Oak or beech woodlands
Rehabilitation	England and Scotland	Spruce or pine plantations	Mixed woodlands

[1]Allen 1997; Gardiner et al. 2002; Hamel et al. 2002; Newling 1990; Savage et al. 1989; Schweitzer et al. 1997; Sharitz 1992; Stanturf et al. 1998, 2000, 2001; Twedt and Portwood 1997; Twedt et al. 1999.
[2]Madsen et al. 2002.
[3]Knowles and Parrotta 1995; Lamb and Tomlinson 1994; Parrotta 1992; Parrotta et al. 1997.
[4]Madsen et al. 2002.
[5]Burbridge and Hellin et al. 2002.
[6]Whalley 1988.
[7]Walker and Boyer 1993.
[8]Madsen et al. 2002.

Europe illustrate the diversity of conditions that may occur (Madsen et al. 2002). Nordic forests provide diverse examples of afforestation and rehabilitation. In Iceland, afforestation on barren and degraded land aims to restore birch (*Betula* spp.) woodlands, which covered more than 25 percent of the land area at the time of settlement in the tenth century (Aradottir and Arnalds 2001). In contrast, afforestation in other Nordic and Baltic countries occurs on fertile farmland. Even so, the aims of afforestation differ between these countries. In Finland, Sweden, and Norway, afforestation is limited to replacing small-scale, inefficient agriculture. In Estonia, the post-communist government has returned agricultural property to descendants of the former landowners. Many of these "new" landowners lack knowledge or experience with agronomy. Thus, forestry may provide these landowners with a low-cost land-use alternative. The afforestation program in Denmark emphasizes sustainability, nature conservation, and biodiversity; with provisions to protect groundwater, improve recreational value of the landscape, and reduce agricultural subsidies (Madsen et al. 2002). The Danish government intends to double the nation's forested area within one tree rotation, about 100 years.

Forestry in the Nordic countries traditionally has emphasized conifer management for sawtimber and pulp. Conifers are favored because of their high productivity and low cost of establishment. Concerns for ecological sustainability, nature conservation, and sustainable land use have risen over the past two decades, while prices for softwood timber have fallen. Additionally, some conifer species are prone to windthrow on certain sites. These problems have increased the interest of landowners in managing broadleaf species and natural regeneration practices (Larsen 1995). Broadleaf tree species are being considered for afforestation of former agricultural land and for conversion (rehabilitation) of conifer plantations on better soils in Denmark, southern Sweden, Germany, the United Kingdom, and the Republic of Ireland (Table 9.1).

The Lower Mississippi Alluvial Valley Context

The Lower Mississippi Alluvial Valley has undergone the most widespread loss of bottomland hardwood forests in the United States. Besides the extensive loss of forest cover by clearing for agriculture, regional and local hydrologic cycles were changed drastically by flood-control projects that separated the Mississippi River and its tributaries from their floodplains (Sharitz 1992; Shankman 1999; Stanturf et al. 2000). The LMAV is regarded as one of the most endangered ecosystems in the United States (Noss et al. 1995; Abell et al. 2000). Bottomland systems across the southern United States provide habitats for breeding populations of Neotropical migratory birds as well as staging grounds for these birds during migration. The southern United States is at risk for significant loss of aquatic diversity, particularly native fishes, freshwater mussels, and crayfishes (Williams et al. 1993; Taylor et al. 1996; Warren et al. 2000). The U.S. Environmental Protection Agency (U.S. EPA) has identified the Yazoo-Mississippi basin as an area of significant concern for surface- and groundwater quality (U.S. EPA 1999). In response to concerns for wildlife habitat and water quality protection, the LMAV has been targeted for the most extensive forest restoration effort in the United States.

The Need for Restoration

Before European contact, bottomland hardwood forest occurred on 8.5 to 10.1 million hectares in the LMAV (The Nature Conservancy 1992), although actual forest cover may have been less because of agricultural use by Native Americans (Hamel and Buckner 1998). Fully 96 percent of subsequent deforestation in the LMAV has been by conversion to agriculture (MacDonald et al. 1979; Department of the Interior 1988). About one-half of the original forests were cleared between the early 1800s and 1935 (Fig. 9.1). Flood-control projects straightened and deepened rivers, drained swamps, and encouraged the extension of forest clearing to lower, wetter sites. The most recent surge in deforestation occurred in the 1960s and 1970s when rising world soybean (*Glycine max*)

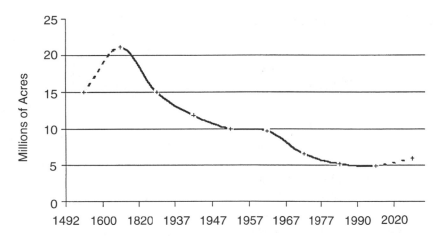

Figure 9.1. Extent of bottomland hardwood forests in the Lower Mississippi Alluvial Valley from pre-European contact (1492) to modern times (1990) with projections to 2020. The estimate of forest cover prior to European contact assumes that Native American agriculture was at least as extensive as early colonial agriculture around 1820. This is probably an underestimate. The prediction of the area to be restored by 2020 is 405,000 hectares, which is roughly double the amount planted through 2005. (Source: Stanturf et al. 2000)

prices made it profitable to convert additional area to agriculture (Sternitzke 1976). However, the passage of "Swampbuster" provisions in the 1985 Farm Bill has minimized further clearing of forested wetlands for agriculture (Shepard et al. 1998).

Restoration Practice

Actions on federal land and federal incentive programs drive restoration in the LMAV, although states also have restoration projects on public land (Savage et al. 1989; Newling 1990). The dominant goal of all restoration programs in the LMAV, whether on public or private land, has been to create wildlife habitat and to improve or protect surface water quality (King and Keeland 1999). In practice, this means afforestation of small areas (usually no more than 120 hectares) within a matrix of active agriculture. Although we know how to afforest many sites (Stanturf et al. 1998), recent experience with the Wetlands Reserve Program (WRP) in Mississippi illustrates the difficulty of applying this knowledge broadly (Stanturf et al. 2001). Currently, restoration on public and private land is planned for 200,000 hectares in the LMAV over the next decade (Table 9.2) but as much as 1 million hectares may be available (Stanturf et al. 2000).

Table 9.2. Forest restoration planned on former agricultural land by federal and state agencies in the Lower Mississippi Alluvial Valley, United States

Program	Agency	Area (ha)[1]		
		1995	Planned to 2005	Total
Wildlife refuges	U.S. Fish and Wildlife Service	5,174	10,004	15,178
Wetland mitigation	U.S. Army Corps of Engineers	2,024	9,704	11,729
State agencies	Mississippi, Louisiana, Arkansas	13,506	40,516	54,022
Wetlands Reserve Program (WRP)	Natural Resources Conservation Service[2]	53,021	47,773	100,795
TOTAL		73,725	107,997	181,724

Source: Adapted from Stanturf et al. 2000.

[1]Estimates furnished by participants at the workshop Artificial Regeneration of Bottomland Hardwoods: Reforestation/Restoration Research Needs, held May 11–12, 1995, in Stoneville, Miss.

[2]Formerly, Soil Conservation Service.

Plantation Forestry as a Restoration Mechanism

It should be self-evident that the first step in restoring a forest is to establish trees, the dominant vegetation. Although this is not full restoration in the sense of Bradshaw (1997), it is a necessary step and far from a trivial accomplishment (Stanturf et al. 1998; Hamel et al. 2002; Stanturf et al. 2001). Nevertheless, many people object to traditional plantations on the grounds of aesthetics or lack of stand and landscape diversity. The correct ecological comparison, however, is between the forest plantation and intensive agriculture rather than between the forest plantation and a mature natural forest (Stanturf et al. 2001). All forest alternatives provide vertical structure, increased plant diversity, wildlife habitat, and environmental benefits. Kanowski (1997) argued for a dichotomy in concepts of plantation forests, between traditional industrial plantations established for fiber production and complex plantation systems established to maximize social benefits other than wood. Perhaps some restoration goals can be met better by developing a concept of complex plantations that retain economic and logistic advantages of simple plantations.

Characteristics of Simple Plantations

Simple plantations are single-purpose, usually even-aged monocultures that can produce up to ten times more wood volume than natural forests (Kanowski 1997). Simple plantations, nevertheless, provide multiple benefits when compared to alternatives such as continuous agriculture. For example, they may satisfy sustainability criteria (e.g., Santiago Declaration 1999) if managed well. Advantages of simple plantations include that they can be established with proven technology, their management is straightforward, and they benefit from economies of scale. Simple plantations may be preferred if financial return is the primary objective of a landowner (Stanturf et al. 2001). However, complex plantations that provide greater social benefit can be established at a reasonable cost. The additional cost may be as little as a 10 percent reduction in timber returns (Kanowski 1997) or at a net financial gain to the landowner (Stanturf and Portwood 1999).

Characteristics of Complex Plantations

Complex plantations diminish concerns associated with how the forest appears (aesthetics) and increase structural and compositional diversity. To optimize these effects, however, requires consideration of surrounding land uses and identification of the best method to establish a mixed-species stand given site conditions, economics, and desired future returns from the stand.

Association with Other Land Uses

Objections to forest plantations are often cast in terms of aesthetics. The "sharp" boundary between a plantation and other land uses is objectionable to some people, as is the uniformity of trees planted in rows. To integrate the plantation with other land uses, sharp edges can be "softened" by fuzzy or curved boundaries. Where plantations are established on small farm holdings, agroforestry systems such as intercropping can blend land uses. Additionally, forested riparian buffers can be established as plantations in agricultural fields. These plantation buffers can protect water quality by filtering sediment, nutrients, and farm chemicals, and they may reduce access by livestock to stream banks. Riparian buffers increase landscape diversity and can serve as corridors between patches of fragmented forests. In floodplain landscapes such as bottomland hardwoods, areas of permanently saturated or inundated soil (respectively, moist soil units and open water areas) are common and diversify the interior of plantations.

The uniformity of plantation rows can be overcome in several ways. Perhaps the simplest technique is to offset rows. Uniform spacing between rows and between seedlings within a row is common, resulting in a square pattern. Such a pattern is necessary only if required for post-planting operations such as disking, or if maximizing stocking is desired. Rows can be offset to produce a parallelogram instead of a square, or rectangular spacing can be used. Alternatively, plantations can be planned with a recreational viewer in mind so that the view from trails and roads is always oblique to the rows, thereby escaping notice. Still, once the canopy reaches sufficient height that ground flora and midstory plants can establish, many plantations take on the appearance of natural stands, at least to the casual observer. This is especially the case following manipulation of structure by thinning.

Species Composition and Vegetation Structure

A more serious objection to plantations is the lack of diversity in terms of species composition and vertical structure. Simple plantations typically are not as diverse as natural stands, at least for many years. Foresters have devised several methods to establish multiple-species stands. For example, planting several blocks of different species in a stand, or even alternate rows of different species, is possible and creates some diversity at the stand level. Distribution, however, remains more clumped than would be typical of a natural stand.

Other methods are available for establishing mixed-species stands. For example, nurse crops of faster-growing native species (Schweitzer et al. 1997) or exotics (Lamb and Tomlinson 1994) may be used to facilitate the establishment of slower-growing species. In this approach, there is no intention of retaining the nurse crop species through the rotation of the slower-growing species (this could also be termed *relay intercropping*). Although the nurse crop method has many advantages, and in the short-term provides species diversity and vertical structure, these characteristics may decline once the nurse crop is removed. The challenge is to develop methods for establishing several species in intimate group mixtures. Such methods must account for species growth patterns, relative shade tolerances, and competitive abilities to avoid excessive mortality during the self-thinning or stem exclusion stage of stand development.

Vertical structure is an important feature of forests for wildlife habitat (Twedt and Portwood 1997; Hamel et al. 2002). Early stages of stand development, whether in natural forests or plantations, are characterized by low light availability in the understory. In most restoration forests, understory and mid-story development does not occur for many years, until overstory crowns differentiate. Annual disturbance while in agriculture depletes buried seed and rootstocks of native plants, and low light levels in the young forest preclude understory development from invaders. Land managers can intervene by planting understory species, but guidance on methods, planting density, or probable success rates is lacking. As indicated above, relay intercropping provides vertical structure for a portion of the rotation. Natural dispersal into gaps may encourage understory development, whether gaps are created by thinning or left during planting (Allen 1997). The critical factor limiting understory development by natural invasion is whether there are seed sources for understory plants within dispersal range (Johnson 1988).

Common Challenges in Restoration

The challenges of forest restoration in different countries are surprisingly similar (Kanowski 1997): overcoming site degradation and limitations, prescribing appropriate species, and applying cost-effective establishment methods. Three steps are key to planning forest restoration: (1) understanding current conditions (the given conditions, a starting point); (2) clarifying objectives and identifying an appropriate goal (the desired future condition); and (3) defining feasible actions that will move toward the desired condition. In most cases, the forester has several options for intervening, as there are multiple silvicultural pathways toward the desired future condition. The choice of intervention affects the financial cost, the nature of intermediate conditions, and the time it takes to achieve the desired condition. It is imperative that silvicultural decisions are made with clear objectives in mind and with an understanding of the probability that a particular intervention will be successful.

Overcoming Site Limitations

Site potential, and whether it has been degraded, sets limits on what can be achieved by intervention. *Site potential* refers to the combination of relatively unchanging physical factors that affect species composition and stand vigor. Soil and landform characteristics determine moisture availability, aeration, and fertility. In wetland forests, hydroperiod characteristics are important (flood frequency, seasonality, duration, and depth). Site potential is not immutable, however, and can be influenced positively or negatively by changes in land cover or land use. Existing forests in need of rehabilitation may have become degraded by past mismanagement such as timber high grading (i.e., removing only the biggest, most merchantable trees), fire suppression, or holding water late into the growing season in greentree reservoirs. In other cases, hydroperiod alterations, hurricanes, severe windstorms, floods, or insect outbreaks may degrade the stands but not usually the site. On the other hand, previous land use may have degraded site conditions, especially for afforestation and reclamation projects. Specific conditions may vary from soil erosion or salinization, in which soil chemistry and physical structure are inhospitable to native trees, to lowered fertility from continuous cropping, which slows or precludes tree growth. In some cases, land becomes available for restoration because the previous land use was unsustainable.

An extreme example of an unsuitable land-use practice leading to site degradation and creating the need for forest restoration can be found in the mangrove (*Rhizophora* spp., *Avicennia* spp., and others) forests of Asia (Burbridge and Hellin 2002). Aquaculture is an important source of income, employment, and exports in many of the world's coastal regions. Extensive aquaculture has been a sustainable part of coastal land and water use for many centuries in Asia. The rapid expansion into mangrove forests of semi-intensive and intensive shrimp aquaculture, often poorly planned and managed, has created significant adverse environmental, economic, and social effects. Unnecessary destruction of coastal wetland forests for nonsustainable aquaculture production has occurred in extensive areas of many of the poorer developing nations such as India, the Philippines, and Indonesia (Burbridge and Hellin 2002). Following abandonment of fishponds, because of acid sulfate potential soils, reclamation projects are necessary to restore mangrove forests (Burbridge and Hellin 2002).

Human-induced disturbances are overlain on the natural disturbance regime in the landscape. Coastal Plain swamp forests of the southern United States, for example, exist with windstorms as normal, episodic events (Conner et al. 1989). Recent hurricanes such as Hugo (in 1989) in the southeastern Atlantic Coastal Plain and Andrew (in 1992) in the northern Gulf of Mexico caused extensive damage to forests in their paths. Such damage may be especially severe to shallow-rooted hardwoods with large crowns that are common on alluvial floodplains. Regeneration in hurricane-damaged areas may be limited if natural hydrological patterns have been altered.

Rehabilitation problems in swamp forests dominated by baldcypress (*Taxodium distichum*) and water tupelo (*Nyssa aquatica*) or Atlantic white-cedar

(*Chamaecyparis thyoides*) illustrate the critical constraint imposed by hydroperiod (Conner and Buford 1998; Conner et al. 2002). Floodplain communities are adapted to a predictable flood pulse, and alteration of the timing, duration, or magnitude of this flooding reduces diversity and productivity (Junk et al. 1989). Human activities have inextricably altered the hydrologic regime of most alluvial floodplains in the United States (Dynesius and Nilsson 1994; Poff et al. 1997; Shankman 1999). Dams reduce the frequency, magnitude, and flashiness of downstream flooding, often extend the length of time the floodplain is inundated, and may change seasonality of peak flows, reduce the rates of erosion and sedimentation (in silt-laden systems). Channelization and canal building, with associated levees or spoil banks, often impound water permanently over large areas of swamplands (Conner et al. 1989). Because many swamp areas are permanently to nearly permanently flooded, natural regeneration is negligible (Conner et al. 1989), and planting is difficult.

Another aspect of flooding that should be considered for coastal swamp forests in the United States is sea-level rise and resulting increases in salinity (Conner and Brody 1989). Although baldcypress and water tupelo can survive extended and even deep flooding (Hook 1984), they seem incapable of enduring sustained flooding by water with salinity levels greater than 8 parts per thousand (McLeod et al. 1996). Atlantic white-cedar is another coastal species that is very intolerant of salinity.

The cause of site or stand degradation should be identified and whether the degradation is still occurring should be noted. For example, alteration of a site by changed hydroperiod poses several questions. Can the hydroperiod be restored or the effects of alteration somehow be mitigated? Should the restoration effort target a vegetation assemblage adapted to present hydroperiod and site conditions? Hydroperiod alterations caused by flood-control projects, dams, or highway construction tend to be irrevocable, at least in the short term. Flooding caused by beaver (*Castor canadensis*) dams, however, can be reduced by removing the dam, but continued management of beaver population levels will be required to avoid recurring problems. The guiding principle for the forester should be to rehabilitate or restore in accordance with existing conditions, unless alteration is feasible, affordable, and within the control of the forester.

Appropriate Species

Most restoration efforts favor the use of native species, although there are situations where exotic species are preferred. In the tropics, population pressures and land scarcity may require that restoration include species that provide early economic returns (Parrotta 1992), and native forest species may be unsuited for degraded sites. Fast-growing exotic species can be used to alter site conditions enough for native species to thrive (Knowles and Parrotta 1995; Parrotta et al. 1997).

The perception of what constitutes "native" species or communities may be contentious. Some fast-growing species may be native but considered undesirable by portions of the public or by agencies. For example, some hold an aversion to planting pine (especially loblolly pine, *Pinus taeda*) rather than broadleaves in the southern United States, and some disapprove of planting eastern cottonwood (*Populus deltoides*) in the LMAV. Furthermore, species on the approved list for afforestation programs may be native to the area but not to the particular site. In the LMAV, for example, extensive hydrologic changes have allowed planting of oak (*Quercus* spp.) in greater proportion than is thought to have been in the forests prior to European settlement (Fig. 9.1). Even documenting the composition of the pre-disturbance forested landscape can be difficult and contentious (Hamel and Buckner 1998; Stanturf et al. 2001).

A wide array of edaphic and hydrologic conditions sculpted by the erosional and depositional processes of rivers provides the foundation for high species richness and spatial diversity of vegetation communities in alluvial floodplains. Site types range from permanently inundated sloughs with very poorly drained, heavy clay soils to rarely inundated ridges of well-drained, sandy loams (Stanturf and Schoenholtz 1998). Associations of tree species with the various site types have been well established since the early 1900s (Putnam et al. 1960; Meadows and Nowacki 1996). Thus, it follows that initial and long-term afforestation success, trajectory of stand development, site productivity, and future management opportunities and costs will be determined largely by the suitability of the species assigned to a given site.

An open question is, to what extent should the manager today consider the possible effects of global climate change in choosing appropriate species to plant. Global Circulation Models used by policy-makers yield very different results for the southern United States at the scale of the forest stand. Nevertheless, managers contemplating long rotations may want to hedge their bets on upland sites by planting species adapted to drier conditions. In bottomlands, the situation is more complicated. Projected rising sea level will not only inundate coastal forests but also cause a rise in the base level of rivers in the region, changing the hydrologic regime of many sites.

Effective Establishment Methods

Choosing species appropriate to the site and management objectives of the landowner is an important first step in restoration. Choice of stock type and proper handling are important as well as adequate site preparation and post-planting practices such as weed control. High survival is needed to ensure adequate stocking (seedling density) and to minimize costs, especially where seedling costs are high (e.g., Scandinavia; Madsen et al. 2002). Survival rates in industrial plantations set the benchmark and are commonly 80 percent to 90 percent. However, it may be unreasonable to expect such high survival in many restoration programs (King and Keeland 1999), because the knowledge base may be insufficient due to limited research, lack of practical experience, or untrained available labor (Gardiner et al. 2002).

Benefits of Restoration

The benefits of restoration usually are identified in terms of agency priorities or social benefits; seldom are the diverse objectives of landowners recognized. In most market economies where rights and obligations of ownership rest with private landowners, what is appropriate for public land may not be the most attractive restoration option for private landowners (Stanturf et al. 2001; Stanturf and Madsen 2002). Nevertheless, there can be considerable overlap in the expected benefits to society and the affected landowner. The array of possible landowner objectives can be illustrated with a limited set of management scenarios from the LMAV (Table 9.3). For simplification, three scenarios are presented: short-rotation management for pulpwood or fuelwood; a longer-rotation typical of management for sawlog production which is suitable for wildlife that requires complex vertical structure, such as certain Neotropical migratory songbirds (Hamel et al. 2002); and an option termed "green vegetation," which is essentially the no-management scenario. In the green vegetation scenario, species composition and stand structure

Table 9.3. Financial, recreational, and environmental benefits expected from three afforestation scenarios common in the Lower Mississippi Alluvial Valley, United States

	Expected benefit level					
	Financial		*Recreational*		*Environmental*	
					Conservation	*Land*
Scenario	*Short-term*	*Long-term*	*Hunting*	*Nonconsumptive*	*practices*	*retirement*
Short rotation (pulpwood, fuelwood)	High	High	High	Medium	Medium	No
Long-rotation (timber, wildlife)	Medium	High	High	High	High	Medium
Green vegetation	Low to no	No	Low	Medium	Medium	High

are secondary concerns to removing land from active agriculture. This option meets the objectives of federal programs such as the WRP (Stanturf et al. 2001). It may also provide habitat conditions for certain wildlife species typical of old fields that otherwise would not occur on the landscape (Hamel et al. 2002).

Benefits comprise financial, recreational, and environmental outcomes. Because cash flow is important to many landowners, and the adjustment from annual to periodic income is often cited as a barrier to afforestation, financial benefits are considered to be both short term and long term. Recreational benefits include hunting (typically for white-tailed deer [*Odocoileus virginianus*], wild turkey [*Meleagris gallopavo*], and waterfowl) and nonconsumptive benefits such as bird watching or hiking. Environmental benefits are separated into conservation practices (such as those installed to control soil erosion, protect water quality, or enhance wildlife habitat) and land retirement, where there is no ongoing management activity.

Financial Benefits

Financial returns from active management are substantial relative to the green vegetation scenario. Sawlog rotations of high-value oak and green ash (*Fraxinus pennsylvanica*) are expected within sixty to eighty years, with the first commercial thinning beginning in twenty to thirty years. Short-term financial returns from growing pulpwood-sized eastern cottonwood in the LMAV are realized within ten years of afforestation (Stanturf and Portwood 1999). Short-term financial returns are low from plantations of other species. Nevertheless, other species can be combined with cottonwood in the nurse-crop technique to produce income for one or two pulpwood rotations, hence the medium rating. The green vegetation scenario, typified by WRP plantings, provides no long-term income because timber management is unlikely, given the understocked stands that will develop (Stanturf et al. 2001). In the short term, there is income from the one-time easement payment made to the landowner (Stanturf et al. 2000).

Some landowners can realize other income from hunting leases and potentially from carbon sequestration payments. In the Mississippi portion of the LMAV, hunting rights are leased for $7.50 to $12.35 per hectare per year. There is also a potential for substantial income to landowners from credits from carbon sequestration (Barker et al. 1996). Although there is considerable uncertainty over accounting for carbon credits in national and international discussions (e.g., the Kyoto Protocol), there seems to be agreement that afforestation will be eligible for offset credit (Schlamadinger and Marland 2000). Current projections in the United States for the value of a carbon credit are on the order of $2.72 to $4.54 per megagram of CO_2 sequestered, but the value is much higher in Europe. Estimates from economic models suggest that a carbon tax of $27 to $109 per megagram of CO_2 would be necessary to stabilize global emissions at the 1990 level (Solberg 1997). Under these conditions, growing biomass for fuel would become an attractive alternative to fossil fuel and landowners in the LMAV may want to optimize carbon sequestration and biofuel benefits by planting black willow (*Salix nigra*) on soils too wet for eastern cottonwood.

Recreational Benefits

The primary recreational benefits assumed in the examples are from creating and enhancing wildlife habitat. Not all wildlife species require the same kind of habitat, so for simplicity the expected benefits can be separated into recreational hunting by the landowner (rather than lease fees) and nonconsumptive wildlife activities, such as bird watching or simply the existence value of wildlife to the landowner. Most species hunted in the LMAV benefit from a range of forest conditions, and expected benefits are high in stands managed for pulpwood or sawlogs. Low expected value is derived from the kind of open stands likely to develop from the green vegetation scenario (Allen 1997; King and Keeland 1999). Neotropical migratory birds and other birds are not uniform in their habitat requirements (Hamel et al. 2002), but some will benefit from the kind of early successional habitat typical of short-rotation stands (Twedt and Portwood 1997) as well as early successional herbaceous fields of the green vegetation scenario. Species of concern are of two kinds: those requiring early successional herbaceous vegetation and those found in the kind of complex vegetation structure found only in older stands, which the sawlog rotation may develop in time (Hamel et al. 2002). Birds that use intermediate conditions of stand development are likely to occur in developing stands for which the intended management purpose is sawtimber production.

Environmental Benefits

Water-quality benefits of afforestation accrue from reducing soil erosion (Joslin and Schoenholtz 1998), and filtering, retaining, and assimilating nutrients and farm chemicals from surface runoff and groundwater (Huang et al. 1990). Among key wetland functions, biogeochemical processes such as filtration have the highest societal value. This function requires flow-through hydrologic regimes typical of riverine forests. However, typical afforestation stands in the LMAV are not subject to the flow-through hydrologic pulse of a riverine system, and their ability to filter nutrients will be limited (Lockaby and Stanturf 2002).

Afforestation of former agricultural areas that are protected from flow-through systems (i.e., flooding) by dikes, ditches, and other barriers cannot be considered restoration in a complete sense unless some semblance of flow-through processes are also restored. Large-scale restoration of natural, riverine flooding regimes is rarely feasible. This limitation of afforestation activities has been recognized previously (Allen 1997; King and Keeland 1999). Suggested remedies have included plugging drainage ditches or building water-control structures on portions of the afforested sites so that controlled flooding can be induced in much the same way that it is applied within greentree reservoirs. On public land such as national wildlife refuges and national forests, relatively large areas have been restored in this fashion as greentree reservoirs, moist soil management units, or permanent water bodies. In addition, it is common for some flooding to occur on lower-lying portions from accumulation of precipitation. Although afforested sites may have water-control structures that produce standing water and appear to function as depressional wetlands, they differ significantly from basin wetlands in their functioning (Lockaby and Stanturf 2002). Because these quasi-depressional afforested systems remain isolated from riverine influences, they contribute little to biogeochemical filtering or to the export of particulate or dissolved organic carbon to aquatic systems.

Improved water quality can be derived from forested riparian buffers. Planted forested buffer strips in an agricultural landscape are uncommon, although several studies have shown that buffer strips are effective in removing soluble nitrogen and phosphorus (up to 99 percent) and sediment (Comerford et al. 1992). The efficiency of pesticide removal by forested buffer strips has been examined in some environmental fate studies, which concluded that buffer strips 15 meters or wider were generally effective in minimizing pesticide contamination of streams from overland flow (Comerford et al. 1992). Recently, forested buffer strips in the LMAV became attractive financially to the landowner by a new incentive program (Continuous Signup/Conservation Reserve Program), which allows landowners to plant fast-growing plantation species, including eastern cottonwood.

The Environmental Protection Agency has identified the Yazoo-Mississippi basin as an area of significant concern for surface and groundwater quality. Although surface water runoff in the LMAV contributes only 20 percent of the nitrate loading implicated in the expansion of the hypoxic zone in the Gulf of Mexico, the EPA is expected to focus significant resources on the LMAV to improve water quality. Policy alternatives under consideration include reducing nitrogen use by 20–40 percent and converting agricultural land to forests in an effort to restore and enhance natural denitrification processes (U.S. EPA 1999). The assumption is made that restoration (afforestation) of bottomland hardwood forests will reduce nutrient export into the Gulf. This will be true to the extent that changing land use from row crop agriculture to forests will reduce a potential source of nutrients (Thornton et al. 1998). However, the restored system will play at most a small role as a nutrient filter unless it is hydrologically linked to a riverine system. Thus a greater benefit, in terms of nutrient filtration, would come from afforestation of the active floodplains of small rivers throughout the basin, and from buffer strips planted along drainage ways (Castelle and Johnson 2000). Nevertheless, the relative effectiveness of forest versus grass buffers in nutrient filtration remains uncertain.

Effects of Restoration on Wildlife and Fish

Afforestation is assumed to benefit "wildlife" (Wesley et al. 1981; Weaver et al. 1990; Cannell 1999b). On the other hand, certain native wildlife and grazing animals can hinder afforestation efforts (e.g., Houston 1991). Recent assessments of afforestation of agricultural lands in the LMAV have stressed the importance of rapidly attaining the physical structure and stature of forests (Schweitzer et al. 1997). Such rapid afforestation implies rapid accumulation on the landscape of the physical structure and stature of forest. Rapid development of vertical forest structure is implicit in the environmental (Joslin and Schoenholtz 1998) and economic (Scholtens 1998) analyses of afforestation. Rapid afforestation is also an essential feature of programs directed toward carbon sequestration benefits (Cannell 1999a).

Afforestation, particularly rapid afforestation, is likely to shorten the early successional period. Herbaceous-dominated plant communities appropriate for wintering birds utilizing early successional habitats consequently will persist for shorter periods if land is afforested rather than allowing natural succession. Rapid afforestation provides winter habitat for a number of species quickly (Wesley et al. 1981; Twedt and Portwood 1997) at the expense of a few high-priority species found in early successional habitats. Less-rapid restoration of forests in the LMAV may provide demonstrable, albeit unintended, benefits to birds that winter within afforested sites in early successional stages. The early successional species that specialize on herbaceous vegetation are of higher-than-average conservation priority among the birds found in afforestation areas (Hamel et al. 2002).

Forested stream buffer zones provide multiple benefits to stream fishes (Angermeier and Karr 1984; Gregory et al. 1991). Indirect benefits include reduction of sediment and nutrient inputs (Lowrance et al. 1984), stabilization of stream banks, and moderation of water temperature extremes (Gregory et al. 1991), all factors that can affect fish productivity, physiology, reproduction, and community composition (Matthews 1987). More directly, organic matter input into streams as leaves and instream wood provides the primary energy source for aquatic macroinvertebrates (Wallace et al. 1997), which form the food base for most stream fishes. In sandy Coastal Plain streams, debris dams and large wood greatly increase macroinvertebrate production (Benke et al. 1984, 1985; Smock et al. 1989), promote channel stability, and increase habitat complexity for fishes (Shields and Smith 1992). Even modest densities of instream wood in channelized or incised, sand-bed streams can shift fish communities from those associated with colonizing stages to those of intermediate or stable stages (Warren et al. 2002).

Many fishes of the southern United States use inundated forests for spawning, nursery, and foraging areas (Finger and Stewart 1987; Baker et al. 1991; Killgore and Baker 1996; O'Connell 2000). As in planting prescriptions for afforestation, hydrology is critical for fishes (Finger and Stewart 1987; Hoover and Killgore 1998). Long-duration flooding in late winter to early spring is especially important for spawning but even short-term flooding of forests can provide fishes with important energy from aquatic and terrestrial invertebrates (O'Connell 2000). Flooded forests provide nursery habitat to both wetland fishes and those of streams and rivers (Killgore and Baker 1996; Hoover and Killgore 1998). In the LMAV, flooded forest habitats support higher larval fish abundance of sport, commercial, and nongame fishes than flooded agricultural fields (recently cropped and fallow) (Hoover and Killgore 1998).

Large-scale afforestation of the LMAV emphasizing flood-prone agricultural areas and stream buffer zones could dramatically affect productivity and diversity of fish and other aquatic communities (Junk et al.1989; Smock 1999). Within the LMAV, seasonally inundated forest habitat is greatly diminished (Hoover and Killgore 1998), most stream and river systems are highly modified (Shankman 1999), and most streams lack forested buffer strips. Nevertheless, southern bottomland hardwood wetland habitats support at least forty-five characteristic fish species (Hoover and Killgore 1998) and in drainages dominated by bottomland forest, most stream and river fishes occur in and actively use inundated forest habitat (Baker et al. 1991). As noted, afforestation in the LMAV now emphasizes small low-lying tracts embedded in a matrix of agriculture. Future emphasis on forested riparian stream buffer strips that connect stream and river systems to afforested tracts is a primary consideration to maintain and enhance fish and aquatic communities (Gore and Shields 1995).

Conclusion

The LMAV is currently experiencing extensive afforestation of former agricultural fields on sites that historically have supported bottomland hardwood forests. The current pace of afforestation may be maintained through the next decade, resulting in the establishment of hundreds of thousands of hectares of bottomland hardwood plantations. Hardwood plantations established on former agricultural fields in the LMAV comprise a diverse suite of plantation types ranging from single-species to mixed-species plantings. Single-species plantations, or monocultures, are often the most efficient plantation type for optimizing production of a single output, for example, fiber production or soil amelioration. In the LMAV, the native "soft" broadleaf species that exhibit indeterminate growth patterns are well suited for culturing in this manner. Eastern cottonwood plantations, which are cultivated for high-quality, printing fiber, are the most extensive example of single-species plantations cultivated in the LMAV. Single-species plantations are not well suited for production of high-quality sawtimber because most valuable species such as the oaks generally develop their highest vigor and quality in stands providing interspecific competition.

Mixed-species plantations can include various arrangements of multiple species in true mixtures or intercropping mixtures. Potential benefits of mixed-species stands versus single-species stands can include increased pest resistance in the stand, increased productivity or yields if the stand is vertically stratified, increased product diversity, improved quality of crop trees, and increased canopy species diversity (Smith 1986). True mixtures generally consist of randomly or systematically assigned species combinations established at the same time. Some mixed plantations are established with species of similar growth rates and developmental patterns, but most successful mixtures require establishment of species that will stratify within the forest canopy (Smith 1986; Clatterbuck et al. 1987). Stand development processes in well-designed species mixtures will track development patterns observed in natural mixed stands (Lockhart et al. 1999). Most current afforestation practices under governmental cost-share programs attempt to establish true species mixtures as a means of providing stand-level species diversity. Unfortunately, many of these plantations are established without consideration for the developmental trajectories and competitive interactions of the individual species comprising the mixed plantation and probably will not meet diversity objectives.

Scientists and land managers working in the LMAV have developed an intercropping scheme using the early successional eastern cottonwood as a nurse species for the slower-growing, disturbance-dependent Nuttall oak (Schweitzer et al. 1997; Twedt and Portwood 1997). Potential benefits of the eastern cottonwood–Nuttall oak (*Q. nuttallii*) intercropping could include rapid rehabilitation of soil quality, rapid development of vertical structure for animal habitat, early financial return on the restoration investment, and development of a favorable understory environment for establishment of oak seedlings and other native woody species. Intercropping systems show great potential for providing multiple ecological and landowner benefits in the LMAV.

Understandably, afforestation efforts have concentrated on establishing the dominant-forest overstory trees, and little is known about the development of understory plants (Stanturf et al. 2000). In addition to vegetative restoration, there may be a need to restore microtopography, especially in areas where the original ridge and swale topography was leveled for agriculture. This is an expensive proposition (King and Keeland 1999) and as yet the actual benefits of these practices are unknown. Nevertheless, such efforts would increase species diversity and result in restoration that is more complete.

Recommendations

Healthy forests are critical to sustaining freshwater ecosystems. Upland forests protect aquatic resources by damping the energy of raindrops and holding soil in place. Riverine forests such as bottomland hardwoods and depressional swamp forests directly influence freshwater systems, and therefore restoration of these forests is considered essential to improving water quality. A successful restoration project should be designed to restore ecological functions as quickly as possible. The following seven criteria provide a guide to successfully restoring bottomland hardwood and swamp forests:

- Restoration objectives should be clearly stated. Not only should the end conditions of restoration success be stated at the outset, but also cost constraints should be recognized, the acceptable time interval identified, and any limitations on intermediate conditions clarified. If objectives are cast in terms of the range of functions that will be restored, then the mechanisms that will produce the successful endpoints should be identified (Stanturf et al. 2001).
- Develop an adequate understanding of present site conditions. At a minimum, this would include current hydroperiod for the previous five years, adjacent land uses that might affect soil limitations and hydroperiod.
- Design a restoration and management plan that will achieve the stated objectives within an acceptable time frame and at an acceptable cost. There is no substitute for expertise and experience in this step, and a bit of art is required as well (Allen et al. 2001; Gardiner et al. 2002; Hamel et al. 2002).
- Invest in high-quality planting material of species appropriate to site conditions (Allen et al. 2001; Gardiner et al. 2002).
- Invest in adequate site preparation for the objectives. If cost is an overriding constraint, then low-intensity methods may be appropriate (disk, plant or direct seed, walk away), although compensating for low survival by planting more seedlings of hardy species such as Nuttall oak may be necessary. If objectives such as high biodiversity are primary and cost is a secondary consideration, then interplanting cottonwood and oaks will meet objectives quicker.
- Supervise planting and check for proper handling and planting (Allen et al. 2001). A good safeguard is to specify in the planting contract what constitutes an adequate seedling ($3/8$-inch root collar diameter and a minimum of three lateral roots seems adequate) and acceptable planting practice. Build in penalties, as well as incentives, based on random inspection of the planting job while in progress.
- Apply post-planting cultural practices in a timely fashion, such as weed control or longer-term stand treatments such as thinning, if they are necessary to achieve objectives.

Much is known about forest restoration, at least in terms of establishing the dominant forest overstory species. Extension of current knowledge or application of conservation principles will be sufficient for many situations. Additional research, focused on improving economic efficiency and more fully restoring ecological functions, will be needed. We see five fundamental areas of vital importance for future research:

- Restoration systems need to be developed that will meet landowner objectives. By systems we mean packages of proven techniques for optimizing benefits at reasonable costs and with low risk of failure.
- In restoration of forested wetlands such as those in the Lower Mississippi Alluvial Valley, guidelines are needed for stock size and qualities that are species specific and well correlated to out-planting performance.
- Protocols are needed for transfer of genetic material. These exist for the commercial conifers but are surprisingly lacking for broadleaves. These will need to be ecotype specific, as well as by latitude and distance.
- New restoration systems are needed that produce an array of benefits quickly and are cost effective. We think the concept of complex plantations needs to be explored more generally.
- What constitutes restoration success should be defined for specific ecosystems, for an array of site conditions and management objectives, within a temporal framework. The essential question is, "What should the landowner expect on a site after a stated time period, given the level of investment in restoration?"

Forest restoration, in the broad sense, is widespread. Similar challenges face foresters attempting large-scale restoration, and there are no easy answers. Simply put, the questions are what to do, how to do it, how to pay for it, and what benefits can we expect? Several fundamental components of afforestation are generally lacking in most regeneration practices currently performed in the LMAV. Developing some of these missing components will require additional research, but others will require only an extension of current knowledge or application of conservation principles. Incorporating silvicultural and ecological principles into public and private restoration activities will provide landowners, natural resource managers, and the general public better methods for evaluating success of these afforestation activities and should improve afforestation efficiency, ecosystem health, and resource sustainability.

References

Abell, R. A., D. M. Olson, E. Dinerstein, P. T. Hurley, J. T. Diggs, W. Eichbaum, S. Walters, W. Wettengel, T. Allnutt, C. J. Loucks, and P. Hedao. 2000. *Freshwater ecoregions of North America: A conservation assessment.* Washington, D.C.: Island Press.
Allen, J. A. 1997. Reforestation of bottomland hardwoods and the issue of woody species diversity. *Restoration Ecology* 5:125–134.

Allen, J. A., B. D. Keeland, J. A. Stanturf, A. F. Clewell, and H. E. Kennedy Jr. 2001. *A guide to bottomland hardwood restoration.* U.S. Geological Survey, Biological Resources Division Information and Technology Report USGS/BRD/ITR-2000-0011, U.S. Department of Agriculture, Forest Service, Southern Research Station, General Technical Report SRS-40, Lafayette, La.

Angermeier, P. L., and J. R. Karr. 1984. Relationship between woody debris and fish habitat in a small warmwater stream. *Transactions of the American Fisheries Society* 113:716–726.

Aradottir, Á. L., and O. Arnalds. 2001. Ecosystem degradation and restoration of birch woodlands in Iceland. Pp. 293–306 in *Nordic mountain birch ecosystems,* edited by F. E. Wielgolaski. Carnforth, U.K.: UNESCO, Paris and Parthenon Publishing.

Baker, J. A., K. J. Killgore, and R. L. Kasul. 1991. Aquatic habitats and fish communities in the Lower Mississippi River. *Aquatic Sciences* 3:313–356.

Barker, J. R., G. A. Baumgardner, D. P. Turner, and J. J. Lee. 1996. Carbon dynamics of the conservation and wetland reserve programs. *Journal of Soil and Water Conservation* 51:340–346.

Benke, A. C., R. L. Henry III, D. M. Gillespie, and R. J. Hunter. 1985. Importance of snag habitat for animal production in southeastern streams. *Fisheries* 10(5):8–13.

Benke, A. C., T. C. Van Arsdall Jr., D. M. Gillespie, and F. K. Parrish. 1984. Invertebrate productivity in a subtropical blackwater river: The importance of snag habitat and life history. *Ecological Monographs* 54:25–63.

Bradshaw, A. D. 1997. What do we mean by restoration? Pp. 8–14 in *Restoration ecology and sustainable development,* edited by K. M. Urbanska, N. R. Webb, and P. J. Edwards. Cambridge: Cambridge University Press.

Burbridge, P. R., and D. C. Hellin. 2002. Rehabilitation of coastal wetland forests degraded through their conversion to shrimp farms. Pp. 20–29 in *Proceedings of a Conference on Sustainability of Wetlands and Water Resources,* edited by M. M. Holland, M. L. Warren Jr., and J. A. Stanturf. USDA Forest Service, General Technical Report SRS-50.

Cairns, J., Jr. 1986. Restoration, reclamation, and regeneration of degraded or destroyed ecosystems. Pp. 465–484 in *Conservation biology,* edited by M. E. Soule. Ann Arbor, Mich.: Sinauer Publishers

Cannell, M. G. R. 1999a. Forests, Kyoto, and climate. *Outlook on Agriculture* 28(3): 171–177.

———. 1999b. Environmental impacts of forest monocultures: Water use, acidification, wildlife conservation, and carbon storage. *New Forests* 17(1/3): 239–262.

Castelle, A. J., and A. W. Johnson. 2000. *Riparian vegetation effectiveness.* Technical Bulletin No. 799, National Council of the Paper Industry for Air and Stream Improvement, Inc., Research Triangle Park, N.C.

Clatterbuck, W. K., C. D. Oliver, and E. C. Burkhardt. 1987. The silvicultural potential of mixed stands of cherrybark oak and American sycamore: Spacing is the key. *Southern Journal of Applied Forestry* 11:158–161.

Comerford, N. B., D. G. Neary, and R. S. Mansell. 1992. *The effectiveness of buffer strips for ameliorating offsite transport of sediment, nutrients, and pesticides from silvicultural operations.* Technical Bulletin No. 631, National Council of the Paper Industry for Air and Stream Improvement Inc., Research Triangle Park, N.C.

Conner, W. H., and M. Brody. 1989. Rising water levels and the future of southeastern Louisiana swamp forests. *Estuaries* 12:318–323.

Conner, W. H., and M. Buford. 1998. Southern deepwater swamps. Pp. 261–287 in *Southern forested wetlands: Ecology and management*, edited by M. G. Messina and W. H. Conner. Boca Raton, Fla.: Lewis Publishers/CRC Press.

Conner, W. H., J. W. Day Jr., R. H. Baumann, and J. Randall. 1989. Influence of hurricanes on coastal ecosystems along the northern Gulf of Mexico. *Wetlands Ecology and Management* 1:45–56.

Conner, W. H., K. W. McLeod, and E. Colodney. 2002. Restoration methods for deepwater swamps. Pp. 39–42 in *Proceedings of a Conference on Sustainability of Wetlands and Water Resources*, edited by M. M. Holland, M. L. Warren Jr., and J. A. Stanturf. USDA Forest Service, General Technical Report SRS-50.

Department of the Interior. 1988. *The impact of federal programs on wetlands*. Vol. 1. *The lower Mississippi alluvial floodplain and the prairie pothole region*. A Report to Congress by the Secretary of the Interior, Washington, D.C.

Dynesius, M., and C. Nilsson. 1994. Fragmentation and flow regulation of river systems in the northern third of the world. *Science* 266:754–762.

Finger, T. R., and E. A. Stewart. 1987. Response of fishes to flooding regime in lowland hardwood wetlands. Pp. 86–92 in *Community and evolutionary ecology of North American stream fishes*, edited by W. J. Matthews and D. C. Heins. Norman: University of Oklahoma Press.

Gardiner, E. S., D. R. Russell, M. Oliver, and L. C. Dorris Jr. 2002. Bottomland hardwood afforestation: State of the art. Pp. 75–86 in *Proceedings of a Conference on Sustainability of Wetlands and Water Resources*, edited by M. M. Holland, M. L. Warren Jr., and J. A. Stanturf. USDA Forest Service, General Technical Report SRS-50.

Gore, J. A., and F. D. Shields Jr. 1995. Can large rivers be restored? *BioScience* 45:142–152.

Gregory, S. V., F. J. Swanson, W. A. McKee, and K. W. Cummins. 1991. An ecosystem perspective of riparian zones. *BioScience* 41:540–551.

Hamel, P. B., and E. R. Buckner. 1998. How far could a squirrel travel in the treetops? A prehistory of the southern forest. Pp. 309–315 in *Transactions of the 63rd North American wildlife and natural resources conference (Mar. 20–24, 1998, Orlando, Florida)*, edited by K. G.Wadsworth. Wildlife Management Institute, Washington, D.C.

Hamel, P. B., T. Nuttle, C. A. Woodson, and F. Broerman. 2002. Forest restoration as ecological succession: Should we speed it up or slow it down? Pp. 98–108 in *Proceedings of a Conference on Sustainability of Wetlands and Water Resources*, edited by M. M. Holland, M. L. Warren Jr., and J. A. Stanturf. USDA Forest Service, General Technical Report SRS-50.

Harrington, C. A. 1999. Forests planted for ecosystem restoration or conservation. *New Forests* 17(1–3):175–190.

Hook, D. D. 1984. Waterlogging tolerance of lowland tree species of the South. *Southern Journal of Applied Forestry* 8:136–149.

Hoover, J. J., and K. J. Killgore. 1998. Fish communities. Pp. 237–260 in *Southern forested wetlands: Ecology and management*, edited by M. G. Messina and W. H. Conner. Boca Raton, Fla.: Lewis Publishers/CRC Press.

Houston, A. E. 1991. Beaver control and reforestation of drained beaver impoundments. Ph.D. diss., University of Tennessee, Knoxville.

Huang, W.-Y., K. Algozin, D. Ervin, and T. Hickenbotham. 1990. Using the Conservation Reserve Program to protect groundwater quality. *Journal of Soil and Water Conservation* 46:251–254.

Johnson, W. C. 1988. Estimating dispersibility of *Acer, Fraxinus,* and *Tilia* in fragmented landscapes from patterns of seedling establishment. *Landscape Ecology* 1:175–187.

Joslin, J. D., and S. H. Schoenholtz. 1998. Measuring the environmental effects of converting cropland to short-rotation woody crops: A research approach. *Biomass and Bioenergy* 15:301–311.

Junk, W. J., P. B. Bayley, and R. E. Sparks. 1989. The flood pulse concept in river-floodplain systems. Pp. 110–127 in *Proceedings of the international large river symposium,* edited by D. P. Dodge. Canadian Special Publication Fisheries and Aquatic Sciences 106. Ottawa, Canada.

Kanowski, P. J. 1997. Afforestation and plantation forestry. In *Proceedings of the 11th World Forestry Congress (Oct. 13–22, 1997, Antalya, Turkey).* Accessed 11/27/02: coombs.anu.edu.au/Depts/RSPAS/RMAP/kanow.htm.

Killgore, K. J., and J. A. Baker. 1996. Patterns of larval fish abundance in a bottomland hardwood wetland. *Wetlands* 16(3):288–295.

King, S. L., and B. D. Keeland. 1999. Evaluation of reforestation in the Lower Mississippi River Alluvial Valley. *Restoration Ecology* 7:348–359.

Knowles, O. H., and J. A. Parrotta. 1995. Amazonian forest restoration: An innovative system for native species selection based on phenological data and field performance indices. *Commonwealth Forestry Review* 74:230–243.

Lamb, D., and M. Tomlinson. 1994. Forest rehabilitation in the Asia-Pacific region: Past lessons and present uncertainties. *Journal Tropical Forest Science* 7:157–170.

Larsen, J. B. 1995. Ecological stability of forests and sustainable silviculture. *Forest Ecology and Management* 73:85–96.

Lockaby, B. G., and J. A. Stanturf. 2002. Potential effects of restoration on biogeochemical functions of bottomland hardwood ecosystems. Pp. 116–119 in *Proceedings of a Conference on Sustainability of Wetlands and Water Resources,* edited by M. M. Holland, M. L. Warren Jr., and J. A. Stanturf. USDA Forest Service, General Technical Report SRS-50.

Lockhart, B. R., A. W. Ezell, J. D. Hodges, and W. K. Clatterbuck. 1999. Development of mixed cherrybark oak-sweetgum plantations planted at different spacings in east-central Mississippi after seventeen years. Pp. 103–106 in *Proceedings of the 10th biennial southern silvicultural research conference (Feb. 16–18, 1999, Shreveport, La.),* edited by J. D. Haywood. USDA Forest Service, General Technical Report SRS-30, Asheville, N.C.

Lowrance, R. R., R. L. Todd, J. Fail Jr., O. Hendrickson, R. Leonard, and L. Asmussen. 1984. Riparian forest as nutrient filters in agricultural watersheds. *BioScience* 34:374–377.

MacDonald, P. O., W. E. Frayer, and J. K. Clauser. 1979. *Documentation, chronology, and future projections of bottomland hardwood habitat losses in the Lower Mississippi Alluvial Plain.* Vols. 1 and 2. U.S. Department of the Interior, Fish and Wildlife Service, Washington, D.C.

Madsen, P., Á. L. Aradóttir, E. Gardiner, P. Gemmel, K. L. Høie, M. Löf, J. Stanturf,

P. Tigerstedt, H. Tullus, S. Valkonen, and V. Uri. 2002. Forest restoration in the Nordic countries. Pp. 120–125 in *Proceedings of a Conference on Sustainability of Wetlands and Water Resources*, edited by M. M. Holland, M. L. Warren Jr., and J. A. Stanturf. USDA Forest Service, General Technical Report SRS-50.

Matthews, W. J. 1987. Physicochemical tolerance and selectivity of stream fishes as related to their geographic ranges and local distributions. Pp. 111–120 in *Community and evolutionary ecology of North American stream fishes*, edited by W. J. Matthews and D. C. Heins. Norman: University of Oklahoma Press.

McLeod, K. W., J. K. McCarron, and W. H. Conner. 1996. Effects of inundation and salinity on photosynthesis and water relations of four southeastern coastal plain forest species. *Wetlands Ecology and Management* 4(1):31–42.

Meadows, J. S., and G. J. Nowacki. 1996. *An old-growth definition for eastern riverfront forests*. USDA Forest Service, General Technical Report SRS-4, Asheville, N.C.

The Nature Conservancy. 1992. *Restoration of the Mississippi River Alluvial Plain as a functional ecosystem*. The Nature Conservancy, Baton Rouge, La.

Newling, C. J. 1990. Restoration of the bottomland hardwood forest in the Lower Mississippi Valley. *Restoration and Management Notes* 8:23–28.

Noss, R. F., E. T. Laroe III, and J. M. Scott. 1995. *Endangered ecosystems of the United States: A preliminary assessment of loss and degradation*. Biological Report 28, U.S. Department of the Interior, National Biological Service, Washington, D.C.

O'Connell, M. T. 2000. The direct exploitation of prey on an inundated floodplain by cherryfin shiners, *Lythrurus roseipinnis*, in a low order, blackwater stream. Ph.D. diss., University of Southern Mississippi, Hattiesburg.

Parrotta, J. A. 1992. The role of plantation forests in rehabilitating tropical ecosystems. *Agriculture, Ecosystems, and Environment* 41:115–133.

Parrotta, J. A., J. W. Turnbull, and N. Jones. 1997. Catalyzing native forest regeneration on degraded tropical lands. *Forest Ecology and Management* 99:1–7.

Poff, N. L., J. D. Allan, M. B. Bain, J. R. Karr, K. L. Prestegaard, B. D. Richter, R. E. Sparks, and J. C. Stromberg. 1997. The natural flow regime. *BioScience* 47:769–784.

Putnam, J. A., G. M. Furnival, and J. S. McKnight. 1960. *Management and inventory of southern hardwoods*. Agriculture Handbook Number 181, USDA Forest Service, Washington, D.C.

Santiago Declaration. 1999. *Statement on criteria and indicators for the conservation and sustainable management of temperate and boreal forests*. 2d ed. Working Group on Criteria and Indicators for the Conservation and Sustainable Management of Temperate and Boreal Forests ("Montreal Process"), Santiago, Chile. Accessed 11/18/02: www.fs.fed.us/global/pub/santiago.htm.

Savage, L., D. W. Pritchett, and C. E. DePoe. 1989. Reforestation of a cleared bottomland hardwood area in northeast Louisiana. *Restoration and Management Notes* 7:88.

Schlamadinger, B., and G. Marland. 2000. *Land use and global climate change—forests, land management, and the Kyoto Protocol*. Pew Center on Global Climate Change, Arlington, Va.

Scholtens, L. J. R. 1998. Environmental, developmental and financial risks of tropical timber plantation investment funds. *Natural Resources Forum* 22(4):271–277.

Schweitzer, C. J., J. A. Stanturf, J. P. Shepard, T. M. Wilkins, C. J. Portwood, and L. C.

Dorris Jr. 1997. Large-scale comparison of reforestation techniques commonly used in the Lower Mississippi River Alluvial Valley. Pp. 313–320 in *Proceedings of the 11th central hardwood forest conference (Mar. 23–26, 1997, Columbia, Mo.)*, edited by S. G. Pallardy, R. A. Cecich, H. G. Garrett, and P. S. Johnson. USDA Forest Service, General Technical Report NC-188.

Shankman, D. 1999. The loss of free-flowing streams in the Gulf Coastal Plain. *Bulletin Alabama Museum of Natural History* 20:1–10.

Sharitz, R. R. 1992. Bottomland hardwood wetland restoration in the Mississippi Drainage. Pp. 496–505 in *National Research Council (U.S.). Restoration of aquatic ecosystems: Science, technology, and public policy*. Report of the Committee on Restoration of Aquatic Ecosystems-Science, Technology, and Public Policy. Washington, D.C.: National Academy Press.

Sharitz, R. R., M. R. Vaitkkus, and A. E. Cook. 1993. Hurricane damage to an old-growth floodplain forest in the southeast. Pp. 203–210 in *Proceedings of the 7th biennial southern silvicultural research conference (Nov. 17–19, 1992, Mobile, Ala.)*, edited by J. C. Brissette. USDA Forest Service, General Technical Report SO-93.

Shepard, J. P., S. J. Brady, N. D. Cost, and C. G. Storrs. 1998. Classification and inventory. Pp. 1–28 in *Southern forested wetlands: Ecology and management*, edited by M. G. Messina and W. H. Conner. Boca Raton, Fla.: CRC/Lewis Press.

Shields, F. D., and R. H. Smith. 1992. Effects of large woody debris removal on physical characteristics of a sand-bed river. *Aquatic Conservation: Marine and Freshwater Ecosystems* 2:145–163.

Smith, D. M. 1986. *The practice of silviculture*. 8th ed. New York: John Wiley and Sons.

Smock, L. A. 1999. Riverine floodplain forests of the southeastern United States. Pp. 137–165 in *Invertebrates in freshwater wetlands of North America: Ecology and management*, edited by D. P. Batzer, R. B. Rader, and S. A. Wissinger. New York: John Wiley and Sons.

Smock, L. A., G. M. Metzler, and J. E. Gladden. 1989. Role of debris dams in the structure and functioning of low-gradient headwater streams. *Ecology* 70:764–765.

Solberg, B. 1997. Forest biomass as carbon sink-economic value and forest management/policy implications. *Critical Reviews in Environmental Science and Technology* 27 (Special):S323–S333.

Stanturf, J. A. 2002. Forest restoration in a global context. Pp. 160–167 in *Proceedings of a Conference on Sustainability of Wetlands and Water Resources*, edited by M. M. Holland, M. L. Warren Jr., and J. A. Stanturf. USDA Forest Service, General Technical Report SRS-50.

Stanturf, J. A., E. S. Gardiner, P. B. Hamel, M. S. Devall, T. D. Leininger, and M. L. Warren Jr. 2000. Restoring bottomland hardwood ecosystems in the Lower Mississippi Alluvial Valley. *Journal of Forestry* 98(8):10–16.

Stanturf, J. A., and P. Madsen. 2002. Restoration concepts for temperate and boreal forests of North America and Western Europe. *Plant Biosystems* 36 (2):143–158.

Stanturf, J. A., and C. J. Portwood. 1999. Economics of afforestation with eastern cottonwood (*Populus deltoides*) on agricultural land in the Lower Mississippi Alluvial Valley. Pp. 66–72 in *Proceedings of the 10th biennial southern silvicultural research conference (Feb. 16–18, 1999, Shreveport, La.)*, edited by J. D. Haywood. USDA Forest Service, General Technical Report SRS-30.

Stanturf, J. A., and S. H. Schoenholtz. 1998. Soils and landforms. Pp. 123–147 in *Southern forested wetlands: Ecology and management,* edited by M. G. Messina and W. H. Conner. Boca Raton, Fla.: CRC/Lewis Press.

Stanturf, J. A., S. H. Schoenholtz, C. J. Schweitzer, and J. P. Shepard. 2001. Achieving restoration success: Myths in bottomland hardwood forests. *Restoration Ecology* 9(2):189–200.

Stanturf, J. A., C. J. Schweitzer, and E. S. Gardiner. 1998. Afforestation of marginal agricultural land in the Lower Mississippi River Alluvial Valley, USA. *Silva Fennica* 32:281–297.

Sternitzke, H. S. 1976. Impact of changing land use on Delta hardwood forests. *Journal of Forestry* 74:25–27.

Taylor, C. A., M. L. Warren Jr., J. F. Fitzpatrick Jr., H. H. Hobbs III, R. F. Jezerinac, W. L. Pflieger, and H. W. Robison. 1996. Conservation status of the crayfishes of the United States and Canada. *Fisheries* 21(4):25–38.

Thornton, F. C., J. D. Joslin, B. R. Bock, A. Houston, T. H. Green, S. Schoenholtz, D. Pettry, and D. D. Tyler. 1998. Environmental effects of growing woody crops on agricultural land: First year effects on erosion, and water quality. *Biomass and Bioenergy* 15:57–69.

Twedt, D. J., and J. Portwood. 1997. Bottomland hardwood reforestation for Neotropical migratory birds: Are we missing the forest for the trees? *Wildlife Society Bulletin* 25:647–652.

Twedt, D. J., R. R. Wilson, J. L. Henne-Kerr, and R. B. Hamilton. 1999. Impact of bottomland hardwood forest management on avian bird densities. *Forest Ecology and Management* 123:261–274.

U.S. EPA (United States Environmental Protection Agency). 1999. *Integrated assessment of hypoxia in the northern Gulf of Mexico.* Draft for public comment. U.S. Environmental Protection Agency, Gulf of Mexico Program, Stennis Space Flight Center, Miss.

Walker, J. L., and W. D. Boyer. 1993. An ecological model and information needs assessment for longleaf pine ecosystem restoration. Pp. 138–147 in *Proceedings of the National Silviculture Workshop on Silviculture: From the cradle of forestry to ecosystem management (Nov. 1–4, 1993, Hendersonville, N.C.),* compiled by L. H. Foley. USDA Forest Service, General Technical Report SE-88.

Wallace, J. B., S. L. Eggert, J. L. Meyer, and J. B. Webster. 1997. Multiple trophic levels of a forest stream linked to terrestrial litter inputs. *Science* 277:102–104.

Warren, M. L., Jr., B. M. Burr, S. J. Walsh, H. L. Bart Jr., R. C. Cashner, D. A. Etnier, B. J. Freeman, B. R. Kuhajda, R. L. Mayden, H. W. Robison, S. T. Ross, and W. C. Starnes. 2000. Diversity, distribution, and conservation status of the native freshwater fishes of the southern United States. *Fisheries* 25(10):7–29.

Warren, M. L., Jr., W. R. Haag, and S. R. Adams. 2002. Fish communities of lowland stream systems: Forest linkages to diversity and abundance. Pp. 168–182 in *Proceedings of a Conference on Sustainability of Wetlands and Water Resources,* edited by M. M. Holland, M. L. Warren Jr., and J. A. Stanturf. USDA Forest Service, General Technical Report SRS-50.

Weaver, K. M., D. K. Tabberer, L. U. Moore Jr., G. A. Chandler, J. C. Posey, and M. R. Pelton. 1990. Bottomland hardwood forest management for black bears in Louisiana.

Proceedings Annual Conference Southeastern Association Fish and Wildlife Agencies 44:342–350.

Wesley, D. E., C. J. Perkins, and A. D. Sullivan. 1981. Wildlife in cottonwood plantations. *Southern Journal of Applied Forestry* 5:37–42.

Whalley, D. N. 1988. Afforestation of salt-affected soils: An international problem. *International Plant Propagator's Society Combined Proceedings* 37:212–221.

Williams, J. D., M. L. Warren Jr., K. S. Cummings, J. L. Harris, and R. J. Neves. 1993. Conservation status of freshwater mussels of the United States and Canada. *Fisheries* 18(9):6–22.

Chapter 10

Wetlands and Agriculture

Charles M. Cooper and Matthew T. Moore

The values of wetlands are commonly known among the general population—waterfowl habitat, sport fisheries, timber, recreation, and so forth. More importantly, ecological wetland functions such as nutrient cycling and mitigation (filtering) of pollutants are becoming more widely recognized, especially in the agricultural community. So then what is the importance of agriculture and wetlands? Although their affiliation may seem antagonistic at first glance, it is more closely related to one of mutualism. Certain agricultural crops thrive in the moist, rich wetland soils, while wetlands near agricultural lands receive nutrient inputs to maintain an ecosystem balance. More importantly, this relationship shows the intricate balance between viable food and fiber production and preservation of natural resources. Wetlands, both natural and constructed, serve as important habitats for a variety of plants and animals. They also serve as natural buffers for rivers, lakes, and streams. By maintaining these wetlands around production agriculture landscapes, significant improvements in water quality may be achieved. This will have a direct effect upon the preservation of our aquatic resources. Therefore it is imperative to not only discuss the historical relationship of agriculture and wetlands, but to also focus on future symbiotic relationships resulting in sustained food and fiber production, while not compromising the ecological integrity of the surrounding watershed. After a brief discussion of the historical relationship between agriculture and wetlands, this chapter will address research results of wetland mitigation of specific agricultural pollutants—sediments, bacteria, pesticides, and nutrients. Further evaluation of the success of riparian wetland habitat will be presented, as well as new discoveries of drainage ditch wetlands for pesticide mitigation. Conclusions and recommendations for future research needs will conclude the chapter.

Background

Agriculture had its beginnings in the fertile floodplains of the large river valleys of the world where fresh silt was deposited annually and seeds were sown in wet soils enriched with new sediment. Today, subsistence cultures still grow plants in the wet areas along wetland fringes, with the most common wetland agriculture being rice paddy cultivation (Hook 1993). Some seasonal marshes and wet floodplains around the world are now human-managed wetlands. The most common example is the rice field; however, freshwater and brackish aquaculture are also common practices.

Until recently, wetlands not directly used for agriculture have been treated by many with contempt as wastelands. This contempt has resulted in the loss of many areas of wetlands over the years. In tropical regions, it is estimated that recent losses of mangroves have been 6 percent in Indonesia, 8 percent in Malaysia, 20 percent in Thailand, and 50 percent in the Philippines (Gosselink and Maltby 1990). In temperate zones, most wetlands have been drained and converted to agricultural systems. It is estimated that over 1.6 million square kilometers of wetlands had been drained prior to 1985 (L'vovich and White 1990), of which three-fourths were in the temperate regions. Williams (1990) and Gosselink and Maltby (1990) have thoroughly discussed wetland drainage for agriculture with detailed examples from the United States, Europe, and Australia. According to the U.S. Department of Agriculture, Natural Resources Conservation Service (USDA NRCS), until the mid-1950s, agriculture was responsible for an estimated 87 percent of wetland conversion. For the period of 1982–1992, only 20 percent of the total wetland losses were attributed to agriculture, while 57 percent were attributed to urban development (USDA NRCS 1999).

Wetland losses generally result in major hydrologic changes and species declines. Impacts from agriculture involve additional complications, including inputs of nutrients (primarily nitrogen and phosphorus), addition of pesticides, and lack of fertility replacement with reduced flooding cycles. At some point, the sustainability of wetland ecosystems becomes intertwined with the sustainability of agro-ecosystems.

Natural wetlands, at the interface of upland or floodplain agriculture, have served as the interface and buffer between agriculture and other ecosystems. However, many natural wetlands are at or beyond their carrying capacity. Constructed wetlands, therefore, are being developed to provide the filtering and processing component of the landscape previously provided by natural wetlands. Constructed wetlands are areas of designed hydrology (water), hydrosoils (soils), and hydrophytes (plants). They may be constructed in former wetland areas or other suitable locations. Thus, constructed wetlands will more and more become partners with agriculture in water-quality improvement and protection.

Nonpoint Source Agricultural Pollutants

Excessive sediments, nutrients, pesticides, and bacteria are the most common potential agricultural contaminants. Fowler and Heady (1981) considered sediments to be the single largest pollutant affecting aquatic systems, and according to the U.S. Environmental Protection Agency (U.S. EPA), sediment is the primary impairment cause listed on individual states' 303(d) lists (U.S. EPA 2001). These lists identify bodies of water targeted for development of total maximum daily loads (TMDLs) for specified pollutants. Sediments were listed as the top cause of impairment, responsible for 6,133 of 37,428 identifiable, reported impairments (16 percent), followed by pathogens (14 percent), and nutrients (13 percent). Pesticides were identified for approximately 4 percent of listed impairments (U.S. EPA 2001).

Nonpoint Source Agricultural Pollutants and Wetlands

With increased concern over water-quality issues across the globe, more emphasis is being placed on best management practices (BMPs) designed to decrease deleterious effects of potential agricultural pollutants to downstream receiving systems. One suggestion involves using constructed wetlands as a buffer between agricultural fields and aquatic receiving systems. This is an approved practice, with standards already put into place by the Natural Resources Conservation Service (USDA NRCS 2000). Mitsch (1993) outlined some preliminary principles regarding ecological engineering of constructed wetlands that minimize nonpoint source pollution. Among his suggestions:

• Constructed wetlands should be designed for minimal maintenance
• Constructed wetlands should mimic natural systems
• Utilization of natural energies should be incorporated in the design
• Wetland systems must be designed with the landscape in mind
• Multiple objectives should be incorporated in the design, with at least one identified major objective and several secondary objectives
• Sufficient time must be allowed for the system to operate properly.

Sediments and Wetlands

Sediments are unique contaminants, since other potential pollutants (such as pesticides, phosphorus, and metals) often piggyback on sediment particles. Therefore, efforts to decrease the amount of sediment entering receiving waterbodies often lead to concomitant decreases in potential pollutants such as phosphorus and pesticides. Several studies have reported on the use of constructed wetlands to reduce sediment outflow into receiving waterbodies. Higgins et al.

(1993) reported on the use of a constructed wetland to control agricultural runoff. Performed on the Long Lake watershed in northern Maine, this study focused on combining several best management practices for optimum nonpoint source runoff mitigation. Utilizing the combination of sedimentation basin, level lip spreader, grass filter strip, constructed wetland, and detention pond, researchers documented that annual removal efficiencies of total suspended solids were 96–97 percent, but that seasonal removal rates were quite variable. Spring outflow of suspended sediment was actually higher than the inflow due to the high groundwater table that surfaced in the system during April and May (Higgins et al. 1993).

In their classic text *Wetlands*, Mitsch and Gosselink (1993) reviewed works reported by Knight (1990) and Mitsch (1992) regarding comparisons of sediment retention by natural, nonpoint source (wetlands receiving nonpoint source effluent) and wastewater constructed wetlands (both surface and subsurface flow wetlands). The only data for a natural wetland indicated approximately 3 percent sediment retention, while nonpoint source wetlands retained between 88 and 98 percent of sediment input. Surface and subsurface flow constructed wastewater wetlands retained between 61 and 98 percent and 49 and 89 percent, respectively.

Elder and Goddard (1996) reported mean suspended sediment retention of 48 percent in the Jackson Creek Wetland. This wetland area is actually a 95-acre shallow prairie marsh housing three sediment retention ponds. The project goals were to decrease the amount of sediment and nutrient inflow into Delavan Lake. Other results indicated that there was consistent sediment retention throughout the year, including periods where retention was up to 80 percent.

Bacteria and Wetlands

Although bacteria are not typically considered agricultural contaminants, with increased poultry, hog, and dairy production, bacteria are becoming more prevalent as nonpoint source pollutants within waterbodies. Much work has been published in the literature regarding the efficiency of constructed wetlands in mitigating potential effects of dairy farm effluent. Going beyond typical reductions in fecal coliforms, most constructed wetland and dairy wastewater research has also examined changes in nutrient concentrations, biochemical oxygen demand (BOD), chemical oxygen demand (COD), and suspended solids.

Cooper and Testa (1997) examined efficiency of three constructed wetland cells located on a dairy farm in northern Mississippi, which housed an average of eighty Holstein cattle (ranging from sixty to one hundred head). The three parallel, non-sloped cells were 6 meters in width and 24 meters in length and were dominated by *Scirpus* (bulrush). Results of nonpoint source pollutant reduction were grouped according to weather patterns—warm and cool—with warm representing spring and summer, and cool representing fall and winter. Warm season results indicated decreases in COD, BOD, and fecal coliforms of 50 percent, 68 percent, and 89 percent, respectively. Cool season results revealed decreases in COD, BOD, and fecal coliforms of 79 percent, 84 percent, and 97 percent, respectively.

Reaves and DuBowy (1997) reported results from constructed wetlands on a similar-sized dairy operation (seventy cows) in Kosciusko County, Indiana. In this system, two wetland cells in series were used, one rectangular-shaped (64.6 × 14 meters) and the other horseshoe-shaped, with the two arms measuring 32.3 × 14 meters each and the upper end measuring 9 × 6.1 meters. Outflow from the second cell indicated an 83–93 percent decrease in COD.

Using a combination of constructed wetland cells, a settling basin, and a vegetative filter strip, Schaafsma et al. (2000) assessed effects of BMPs on dairy wastewater. The system under investigation had been designed to treat waste for 170 cows, basically double that of the above described studies. Several parameters were examined for reduction, including total nitrogen, ammonia, total phosphorus, ortho-phosphate, suspended solids, and BOD. In particular, BOD was decreased by 97 percent following treatment in the settling basin and wetland cell.

Pesticides and Wetlands

Using constructed wetlands to mitigate agricultural pesticide runoff is of increasing research importance. Because of the proximity of agricultural production to aquatic systems such as reservoirs, lakes, rivers, and streams, there is a potential for contamination by a variety of pollutants, especially pesticides (Moore 1999). Rodgers and Dunn (1993) suggested general modeling and design guidelines for using constructed wetlands as buffers between agricultural fields and their receiving aquatic systems (rivers, lakes, streams, etc.). Their model is based on a combination of wetland physical, chemical, and biological characteristics that guide the fate and persistence of pesticides targeted for remediation. To be mitigated, pesticides can only be either transferred or transformed. Transfer of pesticides refers to processes including, but not limited to, volatilization, solubility, flow, retention, sorption, and infiltration. Pesticide transformations refer to, but again are not limited to, photolysis, oxidation, hydrolysis, and biotransformation. In order for the effects of the targeted pesticide to be mitigated, it must be capable of being held within the wetland for a determined amount of time (*pesticide retention time*, or PRT). If pesticides cannot be held within the wetland, then they are not appropriate targets for constructed wetland mitigation. Even though there are several explicit assumptions incorporated in their model, initial efforts by Rodgers and Dunn (1993) have benefited later pesticide studies, discussed below.

Darby (1995) first used the suggested modeling parameters for examining the fate of the organophosphate insecticide chlorpyrifos (sold under the trade names Lorsban and Dursban) in constructed wetlands. She determined that the majority of chlorpyrifos was rapidly bound to the sediment and plant material in the inflow area of the wetland cells. Moore et al. (2000, 2001b, 2002) expanded Darby's original study to also include the herbicides atrazine and metolachlor, and reevaluated chlorpyrifos at worst-case scenario storm runoff concentrations. Targeted inflow chlorpyrifos concentrations were 73 micrograms/L, 147 micrograms/L, and 733 micrograms/L, representing 0.5, 1, and 5 percent estimated chlorpyrifos runoff. Based on water, sediment, and plant data collected weekly for twelve weeks following a simulated storm runoff event, 47–65 percent of the measured chlorpyrifos was located within the first 30–36 meters of wetland mesocosms. Of the measured chlorpyrifos, 55 percent was in sediments and 25 percent was in plant material. Based on models and equations provided by Rodgers and Dunn (1993), wetland travel distances of approximately 184–230 meters would be needed to mitigate chlorpyrifos runoff of the magnitude described above (Moore et al. 2002).

Similar studies were conducted by Moore et al. (2000, 2001b) evaluating the use and efficiency of constructed wetlands in mitigating atrazine and metolachlor. Target concentrations of 73 micrograms/L and 147 micrograms/L atrazine were amended to the wetlands. Mitigation was much less than that observed for chlorpyrifos, with no detectable atrazine measured in either plant or sediment samples collected throughout the five-week exposure period. These results were similar to those obtained by Glotfelty et al. (1984), who reported no detectable atrazine residues in bottom sediments of an estuary from edge-of-field runoff. Between 17 and 42 percent of measured atrazine mass was located within the first 30–36 meters of the wetlands. Based on field data and equations from Rodgers and Dunn (1993), 100–280 meters of wetland travel distances would be needed to mitigate runoff episodes of this magnitude. While this is somewhat lower than distances needed for chlorpyrifos, one must remember that chlorpyrifos is much more potent to nontarget organisms such as fish and aquatic invertebrates than is atrazine (Moore et al. 2000). Identical concentrations of metolachlor were also amended into the constructed wetlands and evaluated for a five-week period. Only 7–25 percent of the measured metolachlor mass was within the first 30–36 meters of the wetlands, and only 10 percent of the total metolachlor was measured in plant material. The range of wetland buffer travel distance needed to mitigate this size event was 100–400 meters (Moore et al. 2001b).

Runes et al. (2001) examined the remediation potential of atrazine in small, 265 liter wetland microcosms. According to their results, less than 12 percent of the applied atrazine was present in the water column after fifty-six days. They also reported that 67 percent of atrazine and hydroxyatrazine residues were detected in the sediments of the wetland microcosms.

Even though the majority of research regarding atrazine and wetlands has been conducted on constructed or artificial systems, some literature exists on use of natural wetland systems. Alvord and Kadlec (1996) reported on atrazine fate and transport within the Des Plaines natural wetlands in northeastern Illinois. Their results indicated that wetlands decreased spikes of atrazine, as well as decreased atrazine concentration, by 26–64 percent from inflow to outflow.

Other studies have examined the effectiveness of small constructed wetlands to buffer against the effects of pesticide runoff and spray drift. Water quality within the Lourens River (South Africa) has been declining over the last few decades because of intensive agriculture, sediment input, and loss of indigenous vegetation (Tharme et al. 1997; Schulz 2002). A study was conducted to determine the capability of a previously constructed wetland (originally designed to decrease sediment input into the Lourens River) to buffer against pesticides associated with particles from runoff, as well as input from spray drift (Schulz 2002). Sediment and nutrient retention, as well as in situ exposures, were examined within the wetland. Little information exists regarding toxicity assessments within constructed wetlands for pesticide or nutrient retention. This information is important, however, since sublethal concentrations of these contaminants may affect growth, reproduction, behavior, and physiology of aquatic organisms (Anderson and Zeeman 1995; Rice et al. 1997). It was determined that 75–84 percent of suspended sediment, orthophosphorus, and nitrate were sequestered within the wetland. Bioassay results indicated decreased *Chironomus* toxicity from wetland inflow to outflow, demonstrating the ability of constructed wetlands in decreasing possible effects from potential agricultural contaminants.

Nutrients and Wetlands

While many other studies combine evaluations of pollutant-trapping efficiencies (e.g., bacteria and nutrients), some have focused primarily on nutrient trapping efficiencies of constructed wetlands. Hey et al. (1994) studied four wetlands at the Des Plaines River Wetlands Demonstration Area in Illinois. Wetlands ranged in size from 2 to 3.5 hectares, and they had trapping efficiencies of 39–99 percent and 52–99 percent for nitrate-nitrogen and total phosphorus, respectively. In another Illinois study, Kovacic et al. (2000) evaluated three wetlands (0.3–0.8 hectares in surface area; 1,200–5,400 cubic meters in volume) for mitigation of nitrate-nitrogen and total phosphorus. Although 37 percent of the total nitrogen inputs were trapped in the wetlands, nitrate-nitrogen concentrations were decreased by 28 percent compared to inflow concentrations. Total phosphorus trapping was only 2 percent for treatment wetlands (Kovacic et al. 2000). Rehabilitated wetlands along the Maryland coastal plain were studied by Whigham et al. (1999). Wetlands ranged in size from 0.4 to 7.3 hectares and were capable of mitigating 50 percent of dissolved phosphate and 70 percent of dissolved nitrate. Likewise, 30–40 percent of dissolved organic nitrogen, phosphorus, and carbon was trapped in the treatment wetlands (Whigham et al. 1999). Smaller-scale (microcosm) wetland studies were conducted by Rogers et al. (1991) and Ingersoll and Kasperek (1998). Plants were responsible for 90 percent of the nitrogen removal in gravel bed wetland microcosms, with total nitrogen removal ranging from 91 to 98 percent (Rogers et al. 1991). Ingersoll and Kasperek (1998) used eighteen flow-through sediment-water wetland microcosms and reported varied nitrate trapping efficiency between 8 and 95 percent. This was believed to be caused by fluctuating hydraulic loading and carbon addition rates.

Riparian and Other Natural Buffers as Wetlands

In some agricultural situations, construction of wetlands may not be a viable option due to constraints such as cost and available land. In such cases, we must look to natural wetland–related buffer systems already in place in the agricultural landscape. In 1997, the U.S. Department of Agriculture established the National Conservation Buffer Initiative, whose goal was to install 3.2 million kilometers of conservation buffers by the year 2002 (USDA NRCS 1998). These buffers are small fringe areas left in permanent vegetation designed to retain potential agricultural contaminants. Buffers may be in many forms, including herbaceous wind barriers, grass filter strips, or the more traditional riparian zone.

Vegetated (grass) filter strips are effective at decreasing concentrations of sediment, as well as nitrogen, phosphorus, and pesticides bound to soil. Research has indicated that a 7.6-meter-wide strip of land with a 6–7 percent slope was capable of decreasing movement of total nitrogen and the herbicides atrazine and alachlor by 70 percent, with total phosphorus being decreased by almost 85 percent (Leeds et al. 1993). Research on fields in Iowa, Virginia, Maryland, and Indiana with slopes of 3–12 percent indicated a decrease in sediment between 56 and 97 percent, depending upon the filter strip width and contributing drainage area (Franti 1997). Trapping efficiencies from vegetated filter strips (4.5–13.7 meters) in Kentucky fields with 9 percent slope ranged from 96 to 99 percent for sediment; 94 to 98 percent for nitrate-nitrogen; and 93 to 99 percent for atrazine (Snyder 1998). Fields in northwest Arkansas (3 percent slope) containing vegetated filter strips exhibited marked reduction in contaminant loss with a 6-meter strip (54 percent decrease in total nitrogen; 70 percent decrease in ammonium-nitrogen; 58 percent decrease in total phosphorus; and 55 percent decrease in orthophosphate-phosphorus). These same studies utilized a 21-meter filter strip, and trapping efficiency rose to 81 percent for total nitrogen, 98 percent for ammonium-nitrogen, 91 percent for total phosphorus, and 90 percent for orthophosphate-phosphorus (Snyder 1998).

The value of riparian zones has been well documented since the early 1980s. According to Henry et al. (1999), riparian corridors and associated wetlands provide flood velocity control and storage, as well as stream-flow maintenance in the dry season. Riparian zones also serve as a source of woody debris within the stream, while helping to maintain a moderate surface water temperature through vegetative shade. Both surface and subsurface water quality are better maintained with a continuously vegetated riparian corridor. Such stable vegetation will also decrease the likelihood of streambank erosion (Henry et al. 1999). As previously stated, there is abundant literature concerning riparian forest and wetland capacity to intercept and remediate nutrient- and sediment-associated waters (Lowrance et al. 1984; Jacobs and Gilliam 1985; Peterjohn and Correll 1986; Pinay and Decamps 1988; Chescheir et al. 1991; Brinson 1993; Haycock and Pinay 1993; Barling and Moore 1994).

Smith et al. (2000) reported on water quality of a forested riparian and wetland area in the Mississippi Delta. As part of the Management Systems Evaluation Area study located in the Mississippi Delta, characterization of water quality in shallow groundwater wells and a pesticide-controlled release experiment were conducted on the Beasley Lake watershed. Evaluation of nutrient analyses from the riparian zone shallow groundwater wells indicated mean concentrations of orthophosphate-phosphorus, ammonium-nitrogen, nitrate-nitrogen, and total organic carbon of 0.02, 0.27, 0.20, and 145 milligrams/L, respectively. Mean concentrations for the entire Beasley Lake watershed (at all sites and shallow groundwater depths) for orthophosphate-phosphorus, ammonium-nitrogen, nitrate-nitrogen, and total organic carbon were 0.16, 1.82, 0.72, and 61 mg/L, respectively. Data from the controlled-release experiment (with two pyrethroid insecticides) indicated rapidly decreasing insecticide concentrations both spatially and temporally with no detection of pyrethroids in the receiving water body, Beasley Lake (Smith et al. 2000).

Agricultural Drainage Ditches—The New Wetlands

Landscape features often overlooked for their contaminant mitigation potential are agricultural drainage ditches. A network of drainage ditches surrounds many agricultural fields for the primary purpose of promoting water removal following rainfall and controlled-release events (Moore et al. 2001a). Originally drainage ditches were constructed to remove water from land destined to serve as agricultural production acreage. Most often, these ditches ran from a wetland or marsh area to an aquatic receiving system. Now, ditches are commonplace, almost to the point of being innocuous, in the agricultural field setting. In today's litigious society, there is a battle over the right to "clean out" a drainage ditch—more specifically, to remove accumulated sediment, plant, and other organic material. Although this debate can better be addressed by legal experts, suffice it to say that drainage ditches are valuable yet controversial ecosystems. Ditches possess many of the same key characteristics that define wetlands: hydroperiod, hydrosoils, and hydrophytes. Many ditches maintain some level of water enabling flooded or waterlogged conditions throughout most, if not all, of the year. This in turn contributes to the presence of hydric soils in ditches. The presence of aquatic vegetation (hydrophytes) is variable depending upon many ditch parameters such as size and water depth—much like that of natural and constructed wetlands. Some of the same aquatic plants one may find in a natural or constructed wetland can also be found in an agricultural drainage ditch. It is for valid reasons then, we consider drainage ditches as a type of wetland ecosystem.

The ditch's ability to mitigate specific agricultural contaminants has been less studied, although Drent and Kersting (1992) briefly reported on the use of experimental ditches in the Netherlands for ecotoxicology research. Other studies in the Netherlands have focused more on ditch maintenance and vegetation (Van Strien et al. 1989, 1991). Little or no information is readily available concerning the ecology or classification of agricultural drainage ditches. Farris et al. (2000) reported initial efforts to categorize soils, water quality, vegetative conditions, and physical dimensions of agricultural drainage ditches in northeast Arkansas. The study also included preliminary information from macroinvertebrate surveys to serve as a possible biotic community index in future drainage ditch classification (Farris et al. 2000). As a result of this preliminary information, a classification of ditch ecosystems is currently under development. By further examining these systems, we can perhaps better define estimates of mitigation capacity. This will provide farmers and other conservationists with specific guidelines on the development, maintenance, and trapping efficiency of drainage ditches. By considering this type of wetland in conjunction with certain other BMPs, perhaps agriculture can better address issues concerning control of nonpoint source pollution.

Recommendations

The most important recommendation derived from this chapter is the need for improved and consistent technology transfer between wetland researchers and the general agricultural community. Historically, researchers interested in wetland functions were misperceived as enemies of agriculture. More participation and understanding on both sides (see Chap. 11) is needed to continue to progress in this area. Wetlands and agriculture, while historically having a less-than-agreeable relationship because of agriculture's past practice of draining wetlands, are intricately bound by commonality. Rice production, for instance, will always be related to wetland systems. As agriculture continues to grow and new production landscape is needed to sustain the world's food and fiber requirements, wetlands will serve an even greater role in water-quality enhancement for aquatic natural resources.

Research needs identified through efforts reported in this chapter include the following:

• Information on plant-specific uptake of agricultural contaminants (pesticides, nutrients, etc.).
• Close collaboration between farmers, resource conservationists, and plant scientists to ensure vegetation used for mitigation will not pose risks to surrounding crops.
• Vegetated drainage ditch research needs validation outside the Mississippi Delta region into other parts of the country, specifically the East and West coasts and the Midwest.
• Better communication between federal agencies responsible for wetlands and farmers. It is imperative that farmers understand their land rights but also have an increased understanding of the benefits of wetlands.
• Encouragement of wetland banking programs, such as those found in the Midwest, as alternatives to farmers.
• Continued practical research on the watershed level, such as reported by Smith et al. (2000) on a riparian zone in the Mississippi Delta.

Conclusions

There is an indelible link between agriculture and water quality. Due to historical conversion of wetlands into agricultural production acreage, nonpoint source pollution from cropland runoff has been identified as a significant source of surface water contamination. To decrease effects of such runoff, the agricultural research community has focused on ways to reduce the quantity and improve the quality of runoff water. These BMPs range from changes in tillage to construction of artificial wetlands. Where wetlands were once intentionally drained, many landowners are now constructing "artificial" wetlands in order to contain and remediate runoff. This chapter has examined the intricate relationship between agricultural pollutants and wetlands. Successful evidence of wetland remediation of sediment-, bacteria-, pesticide-, and nutrient-laden runoff has been documented. Additional consideration was given to riparian and other natural buffer wetland areas with successful remediation results. A final section peered into the future of wetland remediation, focusing on the idea and initial success of vegetated agricultural drainage ditches as small, constructed wetlands. By implementing successful constructed wetland remediation practices, agriculture can continue to decrease the effects of runoff contamination on rivers, streams, lakes, and reservoirs.

Acknowledgments

Authors wish to thank Brij Gopal, Sammie Smith Jr., Ralf Schulz, and Jerry Farris for their gracious contributions to both the May 2000 conference technical session and book chapter. Thanks also to Janet and Jason Greer for their technical assistance during the conference.

References

Alvord, H. H., and R. H. Kadlec. 1996. Atrazine fate and transport in the Des Plaines wetlands. *Ecological Modeling* 90:97–107.

Anderson, D. P., and M. G. Zeeman. 1995. Immunotoxicology in fish. Pp. 371–404 in *Fundamentals of aquatic toxicology: Effects, environmental fate and risk assessment.* 2nd ed. Edited by G. M. Rand. Washington, D.C.: Taylor and Francis Publishers.

Barling, R. D., and I. D. Moore. 1994. Role of buffer strips in management of waterway pollution: A review. *Environmental Management* 18(4):543–558.

Brinson, M. M. 1993. Changes in the functioning of wetlands along environmental gradients. *Wetlands* 13(2):65–74.

Chescheir, G. M., J. W. Gilliam, R. W. Skaggs, and R. G. Broadhead. 1991. Nutrient and sediment removal in forested wetlands receiving pumped agricultural drainage water. *Wetlands* 11:87–103.

Cooper, C. M., and S. Testa III. 1997. A constructed bulrush wetland for treatment of cattle waste. Pp. 14–24 in *Constructed wetlands for animal waste treatment: A manual on performance, design and operation with case histories,* edited by V. Payne. Special Publication of the U.S. EPA Gulf of Mexico Program. Payne Engineering and CH2M Hill. Stennis Space Center, Miss.

Darby, M. A. 1995. Modeling the fate of chlorpyrifos in constructed wetlands. Master's thesis. University of Mississippi, University, Miss.

Drent, J., and K. Kersting. 1992. *Experimental ditches for ecotoxicological experiments and eutrophication research under natural conditions: A technical survey.* DLO Winand Staring Center. Report 65. Wageningen, The Netherlands.

Elder, J. F., and G. L. Goddard. 1996. *Sediment and nutrient trapping efficiency of a constructed wetland near Delavan Lake, Wisconsin, 1993–1995.* U.S. Geological Survey Fact Sheet FS-232-96, Denver, Colo.

Farris, J. L., C. M. Cooper, M. T. Moore, and D. L. Feldman. 2000. Attributes of ditch ecosystems as constricted remnant wetlands. *Abstracts from the Conference on Sustainability of Wetlands and Water Resources.* The University of Mississippi Field Station Publication Number 9. Abbeville, Miss. Abstract No. 19.

Fowler, J. M., and E. O. Heady. 1981. Suspended sediment production potential on undisturbed forest land. *Journal of Soil and Water Conservation* 36:47–49.

Franti, T. G. 1997. *Vegetative filter strips for agriculture.* Nebraska Cooperative Extension Publication NF 97-352, Lincoln, Nebr.

Glotfelty, D. E., A. W. Taylor, A. R. Isensee, J. Jersey, and S. Glenn. 1984. Atrazine and simazine movement to Wye River Estuary. *Journal of Environmental Quality* 13:115–121.

Gosselink, J. G., and E. Maltby. 1990. Wetland losses and gains. Pp. 296–322 in *Wetlands: A threatened landscape*, edited by M. Williams. Oxford, U.K.: Blackwell Publishing.

Haycock, N. E., and G. Pinay. 1993. Groundwater nitrate dynamics in grass poplar vegetated riparian buffer strips during the winter. *Journal of Environmental Quality* 22:273–278.

Henry, A. C., Jr., D. A. Hosack, C. W. Johnson, D. Rol, and G. Bentrup. 1999. Conservation corridors in the United States: Benefits and planning guides. *Journal of Soil and Water Conservation* 54(4): 645–650.

Hey, D. L., A. L. Kenimer, and K. R. Barrett. 1994. Water quality improvement by four experimental wetlands. *Ecological Engineering* 3:381–397.

Higgins, M. J., C. A. Rock, R. Bouchard, and B. Wengrezynek. 1993. Controlling agricultural runoff by use of constructed wetlands. Pp. 357–368 in *Constructed wetlands for water quality improvement*, edited by G. A. Moshiri. Boca Raton, Fla.: Lewis Publishers.

Hook, D. 1993. Wetlands: History, current status, and future. *Environmental Toxicology and Chemistry* 12 (12):2157–2166.

Ingersoll, T. L., and K. Kasperek. 1998. Nitrate removal in wetland microcosms. *Water Research* 32 (3):677–684.

Jacobs, T. J., and J. W. Gilliam. 1985. Riparian losses of nitrate from agricultural drainage waters. *Journal of Environmental Quality* 14:472–478.

Knight, R. L. 1990. Wetland systems. Pp. 211–260 in *Natural systems for wastewater treatment*. Manual of Practice FD-16. Water Pollution Control Federation, Alexandria, Va.

Kovacic, D. A., M. B. David, L. E. Gentry, K. M. Starks, and R. A. Cooke. 2000. Effectiveness of constructed wetlands in reducing nitrogen and phosphorus export from agricultural tile drainage. *Journal of Environmental Quality* 29:1262–1274.

Leeds, R., L. C. Brown, M. R. Sulc, and L. Van Lieshout. 1993. *Vegetative filter strips: Application, installation and maintenance*. Ohio State University Extension, Publication No. AEX-467. Columbus, Ohio.

Lowrance, R., R. Todd, J. Fail Jr., O. Hendrickson Jr., R. Leonard, and L. Asmussen. 1984. Riparian forests as nutrient filters in agricultural watersheds. *BioScience* 34 (4):374–377.

L'vovich, M. I., and G. F. White. 1990. Water. Pp. 235–252 in *The earth as transformed by human action*, edited by B. L. Burner III, W. C. Clark, R. W. Kates, J. Matthews, W. Meyer, and J. R. Richards. New York: Cambridge University Press.

Mitsch, W. J. 1992. Landscape design and the role of created, restored, and natural riparian wetlands in controlling nonpoint source pollution. *Ecological Engineering* 1:27–47.

———. 1993. Landscape design and the role of created, restored, and natural riparian wetlands in controlling non-point source pollution. Pp. 43–70 in *Created and natural wetlands for controlling non-point source pollution*, edited by R. K. Olson. Boca Raton, Fla.: C. K. Smoley Publishing.

Mitsch, W. J., and J. G. Gosselink. 1993. *Wetlands*. 2d ed. New York: Van Nostrand Reinhold.

Moore, M. T. 1999. Fate of chlorpyrifos, atrazine and metolachlor from non-point sources in wetland mesocosms. Ph.D. diss. University of Mississippi, University, Miss.

Moore, M. T., J. H. Rodgers Jr., C. M. Cooper, and S. Smith Jr. 2000. Constructed wetlands for mitigation of atrazine-associated agricultural runoff. *Environmental Pollution* 110 (3):393–399.

Moore, M. T., J. H. Rodgers Jr., S. Smith Jr., and C. M. Cooper. 2001b. Mitigation of metolachlor-associated agricultural runoff using constructed wetlands in Mississippi, USA. *Agriculture, Ecosystems and Environment* 84:169–176.

Moore, M. T., R. Schulz, C. M. Cooper, S. Smith Jr., and J. H. Rodgers Jr. 2002. Mitigation of chlorpyrifos runoff using constructed wetlands. *Chemosphere* 46 (6):827–835.

Moore, M. T., E. R. Bennett, C. M. Cooper, S. Smith Jr., F. D. Shields Jr., C. D. Milam, and J. L. Farris. 2001a. Transport and fate of atrazine and lambda-cyhalothrin in an agricultural drainage ditch in the Mississippi Delta, USA. *Agriculture, Ecosystems and Environment* 87 (3):309–314.

Peterjohn, W. T., and D. L. Correll. 1986. The effect of riparian forest on the volume and chemical composition of baseflow in an agricultural watershed. Pp. 244–262 in *Watershed research perspectives*, edited by D. L. Correll. Washington, D.C.: Smithsonian Institution Press.

Pinay, G., and H. Decamps. 1988. The role of riparian woods in regulating nitrogen fluxes between the alluvial aquifer and surface water: A conceptual model. *Regulated Rivers: Research and Management* 2:507–516.

Reaves, R. P., and P. J. DuBowy. 1997. Tom Brothers' dairy constructed wetland. Pp. 9–13 in *Constructed wetlands for animal waste treatment: A manual on performance, design, and operation with case histories*, edited by V. Payne. Special Publication of the U.S. EPA Gulf of Mexico Program. Payne Engineering and CH2M Hill. Stennis Space Center, Miss.

Rice, P. J., C. D. Drewes, T. M. Klubertanz, S. P. Bradbury, and J. R. Coats. 1997. Acute toxicity and behavioral effects of chlorpyrifos, permethrin, phenol, strychnine and 2,4-dinitrophenol to 30-day-old Japanese medaka (*Oryzias latipes*). *Environmental Toxicology and Chemistry* 16(4):696–704.

Rodgers, J. H., Jr., and A. W. Dunn. 1993. Developing design guidelines for constructed wetlands to remove pesticides from agricultural runoff. *Ecological Engineering* 1:83–95.

Rogers, K. H., P. F. Breen, and A. J. Chick. 1991. Nitrogen removal in experimental wetland treatment systems: Evidence for the role of aquatic plants. *Research Journal of the Water Pollution Control Federation* 63(7):934–941.

Runes, H. B., P. J. Bottomley, R. N. Lerch, and J. J. Jenkins. 2001. Atrazine remediation in wetland microcosms. *Environmental Toxicology and Chemistry* 20 (5):1059–1066.

Schaafsma, J. A., A. H. Baldwin, and C. A. Streb. 2000. An evaluation of a constructed wetland to treat wastewater from a dairy farm in Maryland, USA. *Ecological Engineering* 14:199–206.

Schulz, R. 2002. Use of a constructed wetland to reduce nonpoint-source pesticide contamination of the Lourens River, South Africa. Pp. 154–159 in *Proceedings of a Conference on Sustainability of Wetlands and Water Resources*, edited by M. M. Holland, M. L. Warren Jr., and J. A. Stanturf. USDA Forest Service, General Technical Report SRS-50.

Smith, S., Jr., J. D. Schreiber, C. M. Cooper, S. S. Knight, and P. Rodrigue. 2000. Water quality research in the Beasley Lake forested wetland/riparian area of the Mississippi

Delta MSEA. *Abstracts from the Conference on Sustainability of Wetlands and Water Resources.* The University of Mississippi Field Station. Publication No. 9. Abbeville, Miss. Abstract No. 82.

Snyder, C. S. 1998. Vegetative filter strips reduce runoff losses and help protect water quality. *News and Views.* Potash and Phosphate Institute and the Potash and Phosphate Institute of Canada. Oct.

Tharme, R., G. Ratcliffe, and E. Day. 1997. An assessment of the present ecological condition of the Lourens River, Western Cape, with particular reference to proposals for stormwater management. Cape Town Freshwater Research Unit, University of Cape Town, South Africa.

USDA NRCS (United States Department of Agriculture, Natural Resources Conservation Service). 1998. *Buffer strips: Common sense conservation.* Accessed 12/4/02: www.nrcs.usda.gov.

———. 1999. *State of the land: Wetlands.* Accessed 12/4/02: www.nrcs.usda.gov.

———. 2000. *Conservation practice standard: Constructed wetland.* Code 656. Accessed 12/4/02: www.ms.nrcs.usda.gov/constructedwetland.pdf.

U.S. EPA (United States Environmental Protection Agency). 2001. Total Maximum Daily Load (TMDL) Program. Accessed 12/4/02: www.epa.gov/owow/tmdl/.

Van Strien, A. J., T. Van Der Burg, W. J. Rip, and R. C. W. Strucker. 1991. Effects of mechanical ditch management of the vegetation of ditch banks in Dutch peat areas. *Journal of Applied Ecology* 28:501–513.

Van Strien, A. J., J. Van Der Linden, T. C. P. Melman, and M. A. W. Noordevliet. 1989. Factors affecting the vegetation of ditch banks in peat areas in the western Netherlands. *Journal of Applied Ecology* 26:989–1004.

Whigham, D. F., T. E. Jordan, A. L. Pepin, M. A. Pittek, K. H. Hofmockel, and N. Gerber. 1999. *Nutrient retention and vegetation dynamics in restored freshwater wetlands on the Maryland coastal plain.* Final Report. U.S. Environmental Protection Agency and the USDA Natural Resources Conservation Service, Wetland Science Institute, Laurel, Md..

Williams, M. 1990. *Wetlands: A threatened landscape.* Oxford, U.K.: Blackwell Publishing.

PART IV

CAN WE ACHIEVE SUSTAINABLE FRESHWATER SYSTEMS IN THE FUTURE?

The human dimension is critical to achieving sustainable freshwater resources. The final four chapters of this volume explore ways in which human actions affect the linkages between human and natural systems. These chapters will enable us to take what we have learned in the previous chapters and use that knowledge to shape a future that is beneficial to humans but still sustains freshwater systems.

The authors propose that the philosophy and strategy of economic growth as the means to improve societal well being is often in conflict with the principles of stewardship, conservation, equity, cooperation, and balance needed for long-term sustainability of freshwater resources. Even if all the scientific facts needed to design an environmentally sound management plan were available, the relationship of science to economics, health, and society must be clearly articulated before scientific knowledge can be used for such a purpose. By understanding the structure and function of human behaviors, culture, values, relationships, and institutions, we can gain insight into how to use scientific knowledge to craft effective strategies that will lead to sustainable freshwater systems. By understanding how we function in relation to these ecosystems, we can promote public policy that encourages intergenerational stewardship. Human systems are examined at the individual, group, region, state, country, and cross-boundary scales.

Chapter 11 discusses the ways in which culture influences our ability to achieve sustainability. Increasingly, sustainability is defined within human terms and viewed as the fundamental principle by which freshwater resources can be successfully managed. By understanding concepts of culture, values, and cultural change, we can design meaningful freshwater resource policy that can be embraced, adopted, and implemented.

There are many paths to successful water management. Chapter 12 describes the emergence of comprehensive freshwater management within the state of Georgia. Two distinctly different regional management approaches have evolved in which culture, leadership, economics, water use, governance, geology, and hydrology have all influenced the resulting institutions and processes. The citizen-centered grassroots approach was most effective for the region with a rural culture. Because of its water-dependent, single-sector economy (i.e., based on irrigated agriculture), its limited governance infrastructure, and its dispersed and independent water use, the boundaries of this region are determined primarily by its geology, hydrology, and economy. In contrast, regions dominated by an urban culture will often foster a traditional business management approach. Such regions tend to have multifaceted economies not directly dependent on water, and their highly structured governments manage and allocate water use. Demographics and political boundaries determine participation in the urban water management region. Such a participatory water management planning process has the greatest chance of bringing about the cultural changes necessary to achieve freshwater sustainability. It provides every citizen with the opportunity to become educated, empowered, responsible, and able to participate in the decision-making process, and it provides a means for building consensus, cooperation, and trust. The result is usually a realistic plan that reflects the region's culture and collective values. Citizens vested in the process have a stake in the outcome thereby increasing the likelihood of its long-term viability.

Chapter 13 adds another level of complexity by addressing the issue of shared management and use of water resources across regional and national boundaries. In such cases, participating countries must make an extra effort to identify and address the differences in cultures and values that might otherwise affect equal distribution of freshwater supplies. The authors evaluated international and regional agreements and instruments used to achieve equitable and environmentally sustainable freshwater resources and concluded that an integrated approach to policy formulation and water management will be required to meet the complex challenges of sustainability.

The chapters in this section show that to achieve freshwater sustainability we must first develop an integrated process that not only plans for several generations into the future but also embodies both the human and ecological dimensions of sustainability. Only by undergoing such a process, experimenting with innovative polices, and occasionally failing, will we eventually develop an adaptable and comprehensive plan for managing and sustaining our freshwater resources in perpetuity.

Chapter 11

Sustainability of Aquatic Systems and the Role of Culture and Values

Sara A. Davis, Lawrence R. Shaffer, and Julie H. Edmister

Changing the way we think about water and aquatic resources is a daunting task. Many of us are aware, at some level, that there are problems on the horizon. Water shortages are often in the news; there are groundwater and surface water disputes within counties, across state lines, and across international borders. Few of us are unaware of tragic cases of the effects of water pollution. Will there ever be agreement on a proper water management plan? Will someone tell us the right thing to do? Who will enforce the rules if and when they are determined?

The nature of sustainable solutions to aquatic natural resource problems precludes the concept of an authority telling us what to do and enforcing the rules. Until society as a whole undergoes a cultural shift, a move to a culture of sustainability, imposed "solutions" are not likely to be enduring. Truly sustainable solutions will require the cooperation of disparate stakeholder groups, many of which are currently in competition for water resources.

For the purpose of this chapter, sustainability is used synonymously with the definition in the publication, *Our Common Future*, in which sustainability was defined as meeting the needs of the present without compromising the ability of future generations to meet their own needs (World Commission on Environment and Development 1987). The goal of this chapter is to discuss the ways in which culture influences our ability to achieve sustainable use of water and to examine key components that should be incorporated into implementing concepts of sustainability. The challenge lies in prioritizing the needs of humans and the needs of the biosphere. The relationship between humans and the environment is constantly evolving, making sustainable policies difficult to formulate. To successfully achieve sustainability we will need to shift to a holistic view of our world rather than the current atomistic view of individual actions and their consequences.

Contributions That Have Defined Sustainability

The concept of sustainability has its roots in ecological sustainability. A concern for this issue arose in the early seventies as growing numbers of people realized the degradation of the environment would seriously undermine the ability to ensure expanding prosperity and economic justice. Over the past thirty years academia, policy-makers, and civic organizations have wrestled with the nature and urgency of sustainability and the implications for society, economics, and education. The inadequacy of knowledge concerning sustainability in the United States is obvious when examining the public's understanding of aquatic ecosystems (Bjorkland and Pringle 2001). In 1972, the United Nations Stockholm Conference on the Human Environment developed a set of principles for ecological security (Clugston 1999). Since then, many groups and coalitions have made valuable contributions to the articulation of principles and values that define sustainability.

In 1987, the United Nations General Assembly formed the Brundtland Commission, comprising twenty-one individuals, and asked them to take an in-depth look at the planet's people and its resources. Developing long-term strategies for achieving sustainable development, finding ways of cooperation between nations, and considering ways the international community can deal more effectively with environmental issues were among the Commission's tasks. After more than three years of work, based on scientific advice and public hearings, the Commission, under the chair of former Norwegian Prime Minister Gro Harlem Brundtland, published its report, *Our Common Future*.

In 1991, The Ecological Society of America proposed the Sustainable Biosphere Initiative (SBI) in response to demands from the scientific community and policy-makers to set overarching priorities for ecological research. The SBI provided a framework for the acquisition, dissemination, and utilization of ecological knowledge (Lubchenco et al. 1991). SBI objectives included synthesizing existing knowledge on the ecological impacts of resource uses, linking policy options to their ecological consequences, identifying practical strategies for implementing sustainable policies and practices, and guiding future research toward unanswered management questions. The SBI project differed from other initiatives in its focus on the human use of whole ecosystems, its breadth of participants and regions, and the linkage of basic ecology to practical management. Between 1990 and 1992, nongovernmental organizations and governmental delegations from around the world worked on elements of an Earth Charter. This work culminated at the 1992 Earth Summit in Rio de Janeiro. Although no consensus was reached on an Earth Charter, Earth Summit participants did agree to endorse the Rio Declaration on Environment and Development. The goals of this declaration were to establish global partnerships through cooperation among countries, to work toward international agreements that respect the interests of all people, to protect the integrity of the global environment, and to recognize the integral and interdependent nature of the Earth (Earth Charter Commission 2000).

Worldwide consultation over a period of six years led to a release by the Earth Charter Commission of a final version of the Earth Charter in 2000. It contains a preamble, sixteen major principles, forty-seven sub-principles, and a conclusion. The five central themes emphasized in this landmark document are listed below (Clugston 1999):

1. The Earth Charter recognizes that existence depends upon a living community of diverse subjects who deserve respect and care. The preamble and the principles of the Earth Charter affirm a sensibility about existence that includes an appreciation of the beauty, integrity, and interconnectedness of natural systems, and the recognition of the intrinsic value of nature.
2. In the Earth Charter, diversity is a central value. Protecting the diversity of life forms, cultures, and languages, as well as rights and opportunities for each individual is fundamental. When different expressions of life are lost, loss of sources of knowledge, wisdom, and technology will follow. Some deep level of ecological and ethical existence requires the enhancement of diversity to protect against both the violence of exploitation and the efficiency of monoculture.
3. The Earth Charter demands the creation of open, participatory processes that empower people to contribute at all levels of decision making.
4. The Earth Charter recognizes that humans must accept a world of material limits and live within a framework of ecological laws, exercising caution and preventing harm.
5. The Earth Charter demands a new bottom line. The dominant economic indicators of successful development fail to distinguish between destructive and constructive activities. The new bottom line must be able to discern the difference between healthy and harmful growth in the economic and social order, valuing both natural and social capital.

Multiple Dimensions of Sustainability

Prior to and during the formulation of the Earth Charter, multiple dimensions of the term "sustainability" began to emerge (Chiras 1998). For example, in the

1987 Brundtland Commission report, the concept of sustainability shifted from ecological sustainability to sustainable development. Thus, environmental problems were no longer viewed as only ecological, but included human value systems and expectations, education, and judgment. Further, ecologists publicly noted that they wanted to join with policy-makers, resource managers, and society as a whole to minimize destruction of the environment (Lubchenco et al. 1991).

However, some researchers contend that sustainable development has several problematic features and reinforces an anthropocentric stance. For example, Shiva (1992) argues that from the perspective of the market economy, sustainable development will inevitably be measured by the maximization of profits. Therefore, true sustainable development requires that development is not separated from conservation and requires that markets and production processes be reshaped according to the logic of nature's returns. Shiva further suggests that sustainable development requires recognition that it is nature's economy that is primary, not the logic of profits. Thus, for many environmental advocates, the concepts of ecological sustainability and sustainable development represent an oxymoron—meaning that a conflict exists between the two. For example, according to Ophulus (1977), development as we know it is doomed by ecological scarcity and needs a completely new political philosophy and set of institutions. Ophulus' view arises from the claim that there are certain fundamental ecological imperatives that derive from the fact that nature, as a closed system, cannot sustain endless economic growth.

According to Bonnett (1999), perhaps the most significant feature to arise from a discussion of sustainability is the recognition of the human value system inherent in the views of all who use the term. Not everything can be sustained, argues Bonnett, and as soon as one clarifies what is to be sustained, one is involved in a selection that reflects a particular value or cultural position. Thus, in the broadest sense, conflict exists in the area of environmental ethics between the issues of anthropocentrism versus biocentrism. Should priority be given to the satisfaction of human needs or the needs of the biosphere and by which should we measure policy? Bonnett generally uses the term sustainability in the anthropocentric sense assuming the desirability of sustaining natural systems conducive to human flourishing. Such application presents a set of epistemological problems raised by the idea of sustainability. Put briefly, the problem is that stable systems remain predictable for relatively short periods of time and evolution of the human-environment relationship makes prediction hazardous. Another problem, states Bonnett, is that sustainable policies invite a holistic view essential when dealing with a system's interrelationships rather than an atomistic view of consequences.

Sound science can provide a solid foundation for decisions concerning the use of our natural resources; however achieving long-term sustainable use of our aquatic resources will require more than science alone can contribute. Science may be able to tell us the "best" way to protect a given resource. But protect the resource for whom? Which needs served by the resource will be given highest priority? In a world where many parties share, and often compete for, aquatic resources, sustainable solutions cannot be handed down from an authority. Clearly, science tells us that we cannot continue to squander our aquatic resources, but the implementation of conservation and protection measures is a problem that must be solved by all members of society. Without broad-based support, natural resource policies may be established but long-term adherence to such policies is unlikely.

Characteristics of Culture That Affect Sustainable Solutions

Achieving sustainability often requires that we unite people with diverse backgrounds and perspectives, people whose views of the world may differ widely. An understanding of the cultures and the diverse values held by these stakeholders is essential to arriving at sustainable solutions.

Discussions in the literature of organization theory, and more specifically, organizational culture, are presented in a context of an "organization" like a corporation, agency, or office workspace. However, the concepts can be readily generalized to apply to communities or users of a particular resource. Schein (1996) defines culture as having deep-level, basic assumptions shared by members of the group that are taken for granted and thus "invisible" or "preconscious." Culture is invented, discovered, or developed by the group as a successful coping strategy. It is taught to and learned by members of the group, thus implicit in the definition of the culture of a group is the idea that the group has been in existence for a substantial time period and that the members have a common, shared history. The term *culture* can be applied to any size social group that meets these criteria, leaving the possibility that there can be cultures within cultures. Within civilizations are national cultures; within these are ethnic groups with their own culture, and so on, down to levels such as surfers and snowboarders.

Levels of Culture

Schein (1996) defines three "levels of culture": artifacts, values, and basic assumptions. These definitions name and place in a context many of the terms we hear when discussing sustainable solutions. The visible expressions of a culture are referred to as its *artifacts*. Examples would include language, technology, and overt behaviors. Almost all aspects of a group give rise to some sort of artifact, making artifacts less valuable when seeking insights into a particular culture.

Values are defined as reflecting a sense of "what ought to be" as distinct from what is. An example of this might be the belief that groundwater is limitless. Another might be that because agricultural practices haven't changed much over the years there should be no problem, often phrased, as "this is how we've always done it." Often, it is the founder or an elder in the group that has a conviction about the nature of reality. This notion does not necessarily have any basis in fact. Sometimes solutions that are based on values are offered to a given problem. Such solutions are often not held by the group with the same degree of conviction as the proposer because the problem is novel and facts and experience by the group are lacking. When proposed solutions work, they are accepted as "correct" in a larger sense and undergo a transformation process, eventually dropping from visibility and joining the realm of *basic assumptions*. Obviously, not all values undergo a transformation.

Values are subject to physical validation. And there are some value domains that preclude physical validation, such as aesthetics. Social validation is a possibility, but not an eventuality. Consensus would be considered social validation. Values often remain visible and articulated because they serve as guidelines to be used in dealing with unusual circumstances. In the state of Mississippi, for example, many leaders consider economic development to be one of our most important values. Thus, when the merits of a particular new project (the unusual circumstance) are evaluated, its impact on economic development is given much consideration. This is an example of a cultural value being offered as a solution to a novel problem.

Basic assumptions within a cultural unit have become so taken for granted that there is little variation among members. Successful solutions to problems, which may have arisen as hunches, or even accidents, eventually become treated as reality. These unconscious assumptions are difficult to detect, yet they have a clear influence on decisions and actions of and within a group. As an example from the workplace, if we assume an employee will take advantage of the employer when given a chance, and we then observe an individual sitting quietly at his desk, we assume him to be loafing as opposed to perhaps contemplating a complex issue (Schein 1996). In isolated rural communities, actions of others from outside the community, or new to the community, have often disrupted the status quo. So often in fact, that suppressing the actions of those perceived as "outsiders" has become a successful strategy. The *value* in this case would be that strangers bring trouble, and this value has become so taken for granted and so pervasive that it can be considered a *basic assumption* of the culture. Because this fundamental assumption is held by the large cultural group that encompasses many of the subcultures involved in water-use issues (i.e., the farmers, the long-term residents of the town, the owner of the industry that employs a lot of the townspeople, etc.) it makes the introduction of new ideas such as an awareness of a water resource problem, very difficult. Furthermore, the watershed or aquifer may be large enough that people with common interests (a shared aquatic resource) may treat each other with suspicion and mistrust. One of western culture's most common basic assumptions is that a person has a right to make a profit. It doesn't seem to matter which subculture is being discussed, rural, agricultural, the business community, a person is *expected* to act in a manner that maximizes profit. Members of a culture that take a profit motive for granted will be confused by an environmentalist's message that the resource needs to be preserved for all living things. Mistrust of the conservationist's or environmentalist's message is a result of the deep-rooted nature of basic assumptions. Often the functions of wetlands and other water resources have to be explained in terms of economic benefit to appeal to cultures who hold profit motive to be a basic assumption.

Cultural Change and Its Characteristics

Cultures are maintained through rites of passage, by the use of values as guidelines, and by the common use of the artifacts of the culture. Cultures can also be changed and created. Although the concepts of changing and maintaining are analyzed in the context of the business community, they can be extended to other situations. It is unlikely that the culture of an ethnic group or western civilization will be destroyed and a new culture erected in its place; however, cultures do change.

In the business world, cultural change is desired by management as a means of coping with a changing environment (diminished sales revenues, loss of key markets, increased competition, etc.). Such a cultural change or replacement is analogous to the cultural changes that will be necessary to achieve sustainable solutions to our environmental problems. The amount of change envisioned can be described in four dimensions: pervasiveness, magnitude, innovativeness, and duration.

The *pervasiveness* of a change is the proportion of the activities of a group that will be affected. How many members will have to change the basic assumptions under which they operate and how frequently will they be changing what they do?

The *magnitude* of a cultural change has to do with the distance between the old way and the new way. How much will the status quo be disturbed?

The *innovativeness* of a cultural change reflects the degree to which other cultures have already undergone such a shift. It may be easier to effect a high-magnitude, highly pervasive cultural change if such a change is similar to what other cultures have gone through. For example, the Upper Suwanee Initiative resulted in large part from the success of the Southwest Georgia Water Resources

Task Force (see Chap. 12). Another way in which a cultural change may appear less innovative is if the basic assumptions of the new culture are similar to those of a subculture of the larger group.

It may take a significant amount of time to bring about a cultural change. *Duration* refers to this time as well as the expected lifetime of the new culture. Magnitude, pervasiveness, and duration can be related. Cultural changes of small magnitude that affect few people directly, such as a proper understanding of the use of storm sewers, may be brought about more rapidly than those of large magnitude, such as a reduction in the dependence on water use for irrigation.

The Process of Cultural Change

Actively changing cultures seems to be an important part of achieving sustainable solutions. Trice and Beyer (1996) offer some considerations. Cultural change is most likely to be successful when there is some obvious emergency or change in circumstances. This makes being proactive difficult. If we wait for an absolute persistent drought, action may come too late. Even in the face of what appears to be an obvious need for a change, some members of the group may be reluctant or may not see the need for the cultural change. For instance, ecologists may see, today, a pressing need for a change in the way water policy is formed. Ecologists may feel that their efforts are somewhat proactive, a response to indicators. The necessary cultural change that is needed *right now* may not be possible until the general public is very thirsty. Proponents of a cultural change often have to demonstrate to stakeholders that things are getting bad. This may involve identifying responsible parties or a specific environmental change beyond the control of humans. By the spring of 2002, the drought in the eastern United States had everyone thinking about water, and thus the drought qualified as an environmental change that could be pointed at as an impetus. The problem with citing this type of environmental change as a reason for cultural reassessment is that droughts go away. The temporary nature of a drought allows people to hold onto their notions that the overall plan for water use is okay when in fact it is likely that certain parties overuse available water supplies and some regulators allow them to.

The implementation stage of a cultural change is critical. Many attempts at cultural changes do not succeed because of a lack of institutionalization. There needs to be persistent incorporation of the change into the daily routine and culture of the group. An example of such an institutional arrangement is the creation in Massachusetts of the Water Supply Citizens Advisory Committee (WSCAC). Formed in 1978 through a memorandum of understanding between the Massachusetts Metropolitan District Commission (a state agency) and a local consortium of elected officials, the WSCAC consisted of representatives of thirty-five stakeholder groups including industry, nongovernmental organizations, academic and scientific communities, and others. The WSCAC advises state agencies on water conservation and watershed protection strategies and continues to function effectively today (Holland 1996).

Changing cultures requires leadership. An innovative cultural leader is able to convince members of the group to follow new visions. This new leader must find ways to destroy parts of the old culture, which, in the corporate world often involves discrediting or removing the persons representing the old way of doing things. This action is symbolic and metaphorical—it lets people see what the group now values, and it is practical—the old guard can persist and create resistance to change. Changing ideas about water resources requires a more inclusive approach than is available in the workplace. Achieving sustainability of water resources will necessitate changes in culture of large magnitude and duration. The complex relationships among the stakeholders make a plan of discrediting some individuals likely to be counterproductive. Often there is not a clear choice of a person or even an agency to blame and replace. We cannot "fire" the old guard. A more appropriate and effective strategy is one of education, leadership, and vision creating. No more elements of a culture should be changed than necessary to achieve the specific goals. Identifying the principles that will remain constant will help make the transition smoother and maintain continuity. This goes back to the idea of magnitude of the proposed cultural change and its potential effect on the success of the change. Resistance to cultural change occurs for many reasons, which are tabulated by Trice and Beyer (1996). There are individual and group levels of resistance (Table 11.1).

The dynamic nature of the relationship between humans and the environment becomes more apparent as our ability to detect the impact of humans on natural ecosystems increases. Although changing the culture of a group is an important aspect of a response to emerging environmental issues, the culture,

Table 11.1. Factors influencing resistance to cultural change at individual and group levels

Individual	Group
Fear of unknown	Threats to power and influence
Self-interest	Lack of trust
Selective attention and retention	Different perceptions and goals
Habit	Social disruption
Dependence	Resource limitations
Need for security	Fixed investments
	Interorganizational agreements

Source: Trice and Beyer (1996).

with its values and basic assumptions, should not be viewed as otherwise static. Cultural changes in a region can occur for a variety of reasons, such as immigration, emigration, changing age structure, or the influences of television and the Internet. Such changes can impact the use and treatment of aquatic resources. Rural cooperative water associations have been formed in many areas of the United States, and many systems are over fifty years old (Phoenix 2002). These associations have delivered safe and reliable drinking water to the community. Typically administered by volunteer board members, these associations delivered water at cost to their members who would previously have contended with well drilling and pump maintenance as independent individuals. As rural demographics change, these communities are composed more and more of suburban and urban water users who add their service demands, which may be quite different than preexisting demands of long-time locals (Phoenix 2002). Often these people are more than one generation removed from the days of having their own wells (and the problems associated with them). Small water associations are often absorbed by municipal water systems of neighboring cities with paid personnel. Thus, the basic cultural assumptions of the people now using the water have shifted. Seeking, treating, and delivering potable water has gone from an individual responsibility to a function of paid providers, and water has become like other commodities, expected to be available if the bill is paid.

Recommendations

Basic assumptions and values associated with divergent cultures should be considered in any efforts toward achieving sustainability. The changes in world view that are essential to sustainability will necessitate such considerations. Efforts to incorporate the concepts of sustainability will need to include a strong commitment to a sustainability philosophy, by the incorporation of the concepts of sustainability into key institutional mission statements, goals, objectives, and policies. Second, leaders must demonstrate a personal belief in and commitment to the deployment of the concepts of sustainability. Senior leaders can take an active role in helping incorporate sustainability concepts into their work responsibilities by serving as role models and by providing developmental training. Third, the development of a sustainability knowledge base requires a combination of vision, personal commitment, leadership, and involvement in and understanding of community initiatives.

References

Bjorkland, R., and C. Pringle. 2001. Educating our communities and ourselves about conservation of aquatic resources through environmental outreach. *BioScience* 51:279–282.

Bonnett, M. 1999. Education for sustainable development: A coherent philosophy for environmental education? *Cambridge Journal of Education* 29:12–17.

Chiras, D. D. 1998. *Environmental science: A systems approach to sustainable development.* Albany, N.Y.: Wadsworth Publishing.

Clugston, R. 1999. Introduction. Pp. 11–18 in *Sustainability and university life,* edited by W. Filho. New York: Peter Lang.

Earth Charter Commission. 2000. *Introduction to the Earth Charter Initiative and benchmark.* Accessed 11/25/02: www.earthcharter.org/.

Holland, M. M. 1996. Ensuring sustainability of natural resources: Focus on institutional arrangements. *Canadian Journal of Fisheries and Aquatic Science* 53 (Supplement 1):432–439.

Lubchenco, J., A. M. Olson, L. B. Brubaker, S. R. Carpenter, M. M. Holland, S. P. Hubbell, S. A. Levin, J. A. MacMahon, P. A. Matson, J. M. Melillo, H. A. Mooney, C. H. Peterson, H. R. Pulliam, L. A. Real, P. J. Regal, and P. G. Risser. 1991. The Sustainable Biosphere Initiative: An ecological research agenda. *Ecology* 72 (2):371–412.

Ophulus, W. 1977. *Ecology and the politics of scarcity.* W. H. Freeman. San Francisco.

Phoenix, L. E. 2002. Rural municipal water supply problems: How do rural governments cope? *Water Resources Impact* 4(2):20–26.

Schein, E. H. 1996. Defining organizational culture. Pp. 430–441 in *Classics of organization theory.* 4th ed. Edited by J. M. Shafritz and J. S. Ott. Fort Worth, Texas: Harcourt Brace College Publishers.

Shiva, V. 1992. Recovering the real meaning of sustainability. Pp. 187–193 in *The environment in question,* edited by D. Cooper and J. Palmer. London: Routledge.

Trice, H. M., and J. M. Beyer. 1996. Changing organizational cultures. Pp. 473–484 in *Classics of organization theory* edited by J. M. Shafritz and J. S. Ott. 4th ed. Fort Worth, Texas: Harcourt Brace College Publishers.

World Commission on Environment and Development. 1987. *Our common future.* New York: Oxford University Press.

Chapter 12

Regional Water Strategies

Elizabeth R. Blood

Even in the water-rich southeastern United States, societal thirst for water is running into direct conflict with the water requirements necessary to sustain natural resources (Kundell et al. 2001). The complexity of the scientific and societal issues, the intricate interactions within and between society and the natural resource, and the dynamic nature of both social and ecological systems make determining and balancing competing needs challenging (Likens 2001; Ludwig 2001). Government-funded engineering and administered regulations are not effective or efficient in addressing the spatial complexity and highly variable nature of these water resource problems (Adler et al. 1993; NAPA 1997). To achieve sustainability, a holistic systems approach is needed to evaluate, manage, restore, and sustain water resources (Likens 1998). Only when we understand the intrinsic links between the natural and human systems can sustainability of freshwater systems be achieved. Adaptive management, ecosystem management, and place-based management are holistic systems approaches that encompass the interactions and interdependencies of biological-chemical-physical, sociological, economic, health, and cultural characteristics of a region for development of appropriate and effective solutions (U.S. EPA 1996; Berkes and Folke 1998; National Research Council 1999). Watershed initiatives, community-based initiatives, and state comprehensive water management protocols are examples of policy approaches based on these management frameworks (Kenney 2000; Kundell et al. 2001). Other management protocols exist in the United States (e.g., in Massachusetts, Oregon); however, for these there is little documentation of the process and framework by which they evolved (Holland 1996).

In 1998, Georgia experienced a severe (and what has turned out to be a prolonged) drought, which prompted an enlightened governor and elected officials to begin developing a comprehensive water management planning framework for Georgia's water resources. The state of Georgia is in the process of developing a sustainable management framework and translating it into a public-policy process. Regional differences in geology, hydrology, land use, population, culture, economics, governance, and natural resources have necessitated different public-policy strategies to develop comprehensive planning and management (Couch et al. 1996; Torak et al. 1996; Mayer 1997; U.S. Army Corps of Engineers 1998). The Flint River basin exemplifies the complex issues and management challenges that must be addressed before long-term water resources sustainability can be achieved. Two distinctly different public policy strategies for implementing this framework are evolving in the Flint River basin in Georgia (Fig. 12.1). In the upper Flint River region, urban water quantity and quality associated with metropolitan Atlanta were the issues to be addressed. Municipal and county governments through their regulation of water and wastewater treatment facilities or stormwater ordinances were given responsibility. An

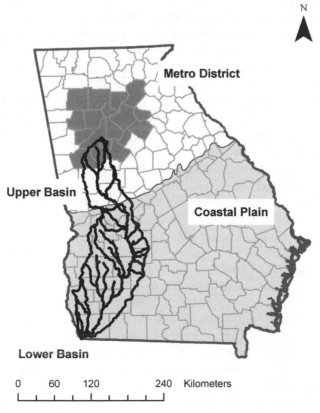

Figure 12.1. Location of the Flint River Basin within the state of Georgia, United States

appointed board oversees a traditional planning process that is implemented through county and municipal governance approaches and regulated by the Environmental Protection Division (EPD) of the Georgia Department of Natural Resources (DNR). In the lower Flint River region the largest water resource issue was irrigation withdrawals, with water use decisions residing with individual farmers. The region developed a grassroots process for planning and management to address water quantity issues in rural communities dependent on irrigated agriculture. The stakeholder-led process facilitated the emergence of citizen-based water resource management in Georgia. The lower Flint River basin process allowed multiple approaches to the development of management strategies and used effective networks to promote action. The evolution of the Flint River basin water policy will be used as a case study to examine how regional culture, governance, and leadership can lead to differing approaches to regional comprehensive water management.

Background

The Flint River is one of only forty remaining rivers in the United States with greater than 125 miles without impoundments (Benke 1990). The unimpaired flows are critical to maintaining a remarkable diversity of plant and animal species, including federally listed fish and mussel populations (Ziewitz 1997; Ziewitz et al. 1997). The Flint, Chattahoochee, and Apalachicola (ACF) river system, which originates in north Georgia, has been identified as "one of the most endangered rivers in the U.S." by the American Rivers Conservation Group (American Rivers 2000). Water use, altered stream flows, natural resource impacts, interstate water allocation negotiations, and evolving water policy were factors contributing to this designation. The upper Flint River basin provides water for municipal, industrial, recreation, and hydropower uses for the Atlanta metropolitan area; in the mid- to lower portion of the basin, agricultural irrigation is the main water use. Rapid population and economic growth in Atlanta and the resulting increased water demands, sewage discharges, and storm water runoff raised serious concerns about the long-term sustainability of the upper reaches of this river system (Clean Water Initiative 2000). The ecological integrity of the upper Flint River was further threatened by the proposed policy of assuring a reliable and adequate water supply for the Atlanta growth areas through developing community and multi-jurisdictional reservoirs (EPD 2001a). In the mid- to lower Flint River, concerns were raised by the rapid growth of irrigated agriculture since the 1970s and the impact on river flows from increased surface and groundwater withdrawals (Miller 1990; Harrison and Tyson 1999). Hydrologic models predicted that by 2010 permitted agricultural withdrawals would exceed the groundwater's capacity to sustain the Flint River's flow (EPD 2001b).

Beyond the inherent societal and ecological complexity, the development of effective strategies for the Flint River was complicated by a fragmented water policy environment in 2001. Rapid evolution of water policy, management, and regulatory options were resulting in multiple layers of oversight, authority, decision making, planning, and implementation. Federal, interstate, state, and regional activities were emerging independently. The following are illustrative of this fragmentation. A federal judge imposed an accelerated three-year (2000–2003) implementation of the total maximum daily load (TMDL) process for streams in Georgia not meeting federal water-quality criteria. Local and county governments must comply with the TMDL load reductions or be subject to state or federal intervention. In 2002, Georgia, Florida, and Alabama were negotiating an interstate water compact to allocate waters in the ACF rivers. The intent was adequate water supplies to ensure economic viability for all three states while maintaining sufficient river flows to maintain estuarine and freshwater habitat for aquatic resources and minimize declines in cold-water refugia (Light et al. 1998). A tri-state and federal commission (Tri-state Commission) was appointed and given responsibility for implementation of the compact. At the state level, Georgia DNR shifted from dilution-based minimum flow policy (e.g., 7Q10) to an interim flow policy that uses natural resource criteria to set limits on flow reductions. A statewide Drought Management Plan gave EPD broad regulatory authority to set additional constraints on water use, water use priorities, and minimum flow variances during extreme droughts. In 2002, no mechanism existed to reconcile DNR, EPD, and the Tri-state Commission's role in setting flow regimes.

Water resource management strategies were emerging without understanding the potential unintended consequences to other regions or citizens. As an example, a multi-county regional reservoir strategy was proposed to meet the anticipated growth in water use in the upper Flint River. During droughts, water retained in the proposed reservoirs for residential use by the upper basin citizens and communities had the potential to limit water available for downstream natural resource and human needs. During periods of water shortages like the 2002 drought, the Flint River Drought Protection Act required reductions in irrigation withdrawals from the lower Flint River region to maintain river flows. The reservoir strategy would meet the needs of the upper basin; however, no mechanism or policy was in place to assess either the impacts on lower basin flows or the fairness and equity in maintaining flows in the Flint River between the upper and lower regions.

Flint River Basin Water Strategy

The need for a flexible regional management strategy was demonstrated in the Flint River basin. The Flint River basin water policy development was four years ahead of the state comprehensive planning effort. The ACF Compact water allocation negotiations and the 1998–2002 drought had heightened the urgency to begin a management and planning dialog. Visionary and motivated leaders formed committees and organizations in the lower Flint River basin to raise awareness of the drought and policy negotiations and their impacts on rural Georgia health, communities, economics, and natural resources. Through the efforts of the lower Flint River organizations, awareness spread to the business community, conservation organizations, and elected officials in the Atlanta metropolitan area. A coalition of leaders from the Atlanta area took the lead to form a regional strategy for the Atlanta metropolitan area that included the upper Flint River basin.

The Upper Basin

From 1990 to 2000, a multifaceted economic boom, driven largely by factors other than direct access to water, fueled rapid urban growth in the Piedmont region of the state (Clean Water Initiative 2000; U.S. Census Bureau 2000). The population growth accompanying the economic expansion increased domestic water use and placed a strain on water resources. The state's population doubled between 1950 and 2000; the 39.5 percent growth in the ten-county Atlanta metropolitan area from 1990 to 2000 added over 1.2 million people. The Atlanta region domestic water need was 445 million gallons per day in 1995, and it was projected to increase by 50 percent in twenty years (Atlanta Regional Commission 1997). Over 98 percent of the drinking water needs in the Atlanta metropolitan area were obtained from surface waters. For metropolitan Atlanta residents of the Flint River basin, 88 percent of the domestic supply came from surface water (Marella et al. 1993). Over thirty public systems provided water to 254,000 residents. Approximately 85,000 residents were dependent on private wells for domestic supply. In addition, commercial and industrial sources were exclusively from surface water in the upper Flint River.

The urban development associated with the population growth and changing land-use patterns threatened water quality and stream functioning in the upper Flint River. Construction was the fastest-growing industry in suburban counties like Fayette County of the upper Flint River region (Bureau of Economic Analysis 1999). Land clearing for urban development increased sediment loads to receiving streams, impairing water quality with storm runoff and altered chemical processing between storms (Couch et al. 1995). Urban storm-water runoff and wastewater discharges (400 million gallons per day) from the Atlanta region were rapidly approaching the wastewater discharge capacity of the region's rivers (533 million gallons per day during low flow) (Clean Water Initiative 2000). Based on the twenty-year projected population growth, the region would need to treat and discharge 700 to 1,000 million gallons per day.

Of particular significance was the region's location in the headwaters of five major river basins that were among the most biologically diverse in the state. The projected wastewater loads would violate Georgia water quality standards and significantly impair the biological resource occurring in the river basins.

In response, a task force of business leaders, state and local officials, the Metro Atlanta Chamber of Commerce and the Regional Business Coalition, downstream representatives, and conservation leaders convened in April 2000 to formulate a response to Atlanta's growing water problem. The Boston Group (a business consulting group) facilitated the task force in developing concepts, options, and final recommendations. The Boston Group researched the water issues, provided briefings, and guided and distilled three potential frameworks that arose from the task force. Task force consensus and cooperation occurred between task force meetings. Given the short timetable for water plan development, a limited number of technically trained and policy savvy individuals were involved in the plan formulation. Engineering consultants and technical committees developed the plans, databases, and models (see Metropolitan North Georgia Water Planning District 2002a).

The task force, known as the Clean Water Initiative, recommended Georgia's first water-planning district. Through Georgia Senate Bill 130, the Metropolitan North Georgia Water Planning District (the Metro District) was established in November 2001 as a planning entity. A county governance and business organizational structure was used to create the Metro District (Fig. 12.2). Demographics and political boundaries were used to define the region: population size of greater than 200,000 was used to determine a county's inclusion in the district. An aggressive planning effort was legally defined in the bill requiring that the district complete its major planning efforts by May 2003. The Metro District developed a formal governing board, water authority, and several components of the water management plan as of 2002 (Fig. 12.2). Broader participation by citizens in the plan formulation was accomplished through commentary by appointees to the Basin advisory councils or public comment at Metro District meetings.

The Metro District established policy, created plans, and promoted intergovernmental coordination. Policy goals to guide the development and implementation of these water resource plans included supporting sustainable economic development; improving and protecting water quality to ensure streams meet designated uses; equitably distributing benefits, responsibilities, and costs; defining practical, integrated measures for local jurisdictions; and promoting public education and awareness. Comprehensive regional and watershed-specific water resources plans were developed to protect water quality and public water supplies, protect recreational values of the waters, and minimize potential adverse impacts of development on waters in and downstream of the region (see Metropolitan North Georgia Water Planning District 2002b). Future water

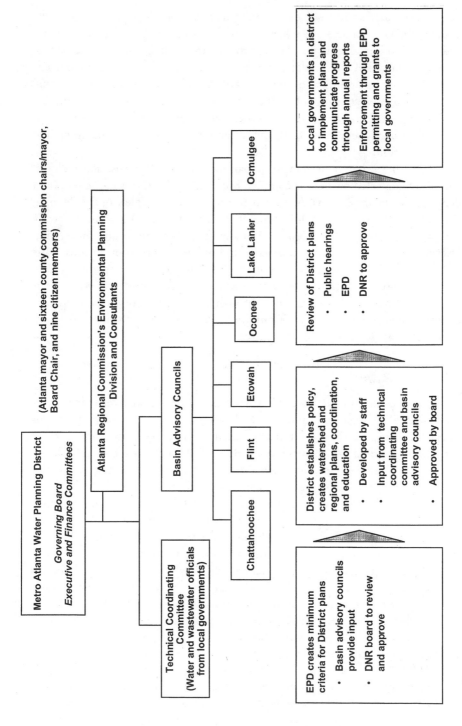

Figure 12.2. Established Metropolitan North Georgia Water Planning District

permitting, such as renewal of permits, modification or expansion of withdrawals, and new application evaluation, was used to assure compliance of county and municipal implementation. The Metro District has additional responsibilities, including education and public awareness for watershed protection; total maximum daily load planning and implementation; facilitating multi-jurisdictional water-related projects; and enhancing access to funding for water-related projects among local governments. The governing board of the district was given funding authority and strict time lines to accomplish the initial planning and implementation.

Under this water management scenario, concerned citizens, stakeholders, and other interested parties have limited opportunity for direct participation in development of these plans, management options or strategies, or for defining their role in the solutions. Only appointed advisory council members directly participated. Citizen interaction was initially limited to education, information briefings, public service announcements, and public comment on various drafts of the plan. Citizens options for participation in the process, planning, and implementation were through collective actions of the representatives of their county and municipal governments; through development of, or participation in, organizations that have lobbying or litigation options; and through assistance from their state legislative representatives.

The Lower Basin

Economic viability in the lower Flint River basin was directly related to water availability. The region's economy was largely dependent on agriculture for direct revenue, supporting industry revenue, and revenue from services surrounding agriculture (Boatright and Bachtel 2000). Outside of the Albany metropolitan area, 1999 county income from agriculture was the first- or second-largest source of income (Bureau of Economic Analysis 1999). Over 600 million dollars was added to the regional economy in 1999 directly from irrigation-enhanced agricultural profits (Hook 2000). Services, wholesale trade, and non-durable goods manufacturing were the next largest sources of income. Water to supply these commercial and industrial withdrawals came from one or several groundwater aquifers. Over 60 percent of the total water withdrawals in the Flint River basin were from groundwater and 82 percent of that groundwater was withdrawn in the lower basin. Agricultural groundwater withdrawals from the Floridan aquifer averaged 70 percent of the groundwater used in the lower region (Hook and Blood unpublished data). For many of the southernmost counties, irrigation water use was 90–95 percent of the total water used (Blood et al. 1999).

Regionally there were distinct demographics and domestic water use in the Flint River basin. In 2000, 49 percent of the population of the Flint River basin resided in the upper region; the population density was four times higher in the upper region (69 per square kilometer) than the lower region (17 per square kilometer) (U.S. Census Bureau 2000). From 1990 to 2000, the population in the upper region increased sevenfold compared to that of the lower region (35 percent versus 5 percent). All counties in the upper region experienced large population increases. In contrast, many rural counties in the lower region lost population during that ten-year period. Self-supplied domestic water withdrawals provided 60 percent of this lower region's population with water from the Floridan aquifer. Fifty-four public facilities provided domestic water from several aquifers to homes in the lower basin.

The regional differences in demographics and economics led to a fundamentally different approach to resolving regional water-resource issues in the lower Flint River. Scientists, resource professionals, farmers, federal and state agency representatives, business and industry professionals, legislators, governmental leaders, stakeholders, and interested citizens developed several water resource initiatives to address emerging water policy issues. The Southwest Georgia Health and Water Resources Initiative, the Southwest Georgia Agribusiness Association, and the Southwest Georgia Water Resources Task Force were ad hoc committees and associations formed by regional leaders and concerned citizens in the lower Flint River basin. Each organization had a different focus but had many similar underlying principles, goals, strategies, and philosophies. Education, dialog and knowledge exchange, networking, cooperative and collaborative problem solving, open participation by interested citizens, and trust building were common among these groups. Even established organizations such as the region's Farm Bureau formed water committees to engage in the water policy process.

Southwest Georgia Health and Water Resources Initiative

The Southwest Georgia Health and Water Resources Initiative (SWGHWRI) was formed in 1996 by water resource researchers, public health officials, and natural resource professionals to become informed and knowledgeable about health, natural resource, and water issues in rural Georgia. This group arose in response to an inadequate public process during the discovery of nitrate health risks in rural drinking water. The process of detecting, reporting, and responding to the public concerns surrounding the problem was unsatisfactory, and it became clear that a new mechanism for communication, knowledge exchange, and trust building was needed. The vision of the SWGHWRI was to ensure that healthy and vital regional systems were critically linked to the availability and sustainability of high-quality water resources. The principles and goals that guided this group were stewardship; providing leadership for the state by modeling an effective regional approach; reaching solutions through communication and networking among stakeholders; increasing regional knowledge concerning water resources; providing and supporting education for citizens and decision makers; developing water resources partnerships; ensuring regional input to water resources decisions and policy at all levels; and developing a long-term regional agenda for water resources and public health. Since the onset of the current drought in 1998, the SWGHWRI has focused on rural health impacts associated with the prolonged drought.

The 1998–2002 drought brought to light the vulnerability of the Flint River citizens to accessing drinking water. In 2000, the SWGHWRI and Georgia District 8 Public Health Department began the first survey of private drinking water well failures during extreme drought conditions. Following this group's lead, the Environmental Protection Division began the first statewide assessment of water security (days of available water) during drought. During that period, municipal reservoirs were below sustainable levels, public water supplies failed or had limited capacity, and domestic well failures were common (EPD 2001a). Twenty-three cities and five counties had less than a thirty-day drinking-water supply available during the summer of 2000. Citizens with self-supplied wells were at the greatest risk. Over 1,600 private domestic wells in forty counties had run dry for days to months during 2000 (EPD 2001a). Over half of those domestic well failures occurred in the lower Flint River basin (M. Jones, Southwest Georgia Health District Environmentalist, personal communication). In response, the Regional Development Council, the Georgia Department of Community Affairs, and the District Public Health secured emergency grant funds to provide $50,000 per county for low-income families to have their wells restored.

In 2001, a national conference on Public Health Impacts of Prolonged Drought in Rural America was convened to evaluate and anticipate potential adverse health effects of prolonged drought on human populations, develop surveillance tools to quantify impacts, and develop interventions to prevent or mitigate those effects. Three important contributions were made by this initiative: (1) public health was defined as physical, mental, social, environmental, and economic; (2) water security and public health were linked; and (3) public health was an explicit determinant of water resource sustainability.

Southwest Georgia Agribusiness Association

The Southwest Georgia Agribusiness Association (SWGAA) was seminal in developing collaborative approaches to problem solving and using facilitation and mediation as tools to solve complex water issues in rural Georgia. The association was formed by farmers, bankers, farm suppliers, and farm industry members in 1996 to identify limits and problems that could hinder the economic strength of the agribusiness community. The Association was the first Georgia agricultural organization to acknowledge the importance of water resources to agricultural productivity. This organization provided a forum for frank discussions on water issues, including options and policies for wise use of available water resources, and began a trust-building process among regulators, researchers, and the regulated farm community. The farmers in this association voluntarily provided measured irrigation quantities for crops in Georgia. This was the first direct participation by citizens in research relevant to ongoing policy negotiations. The SWGAA convened and facilitated the first meetings between state regulators and the farm community in southwest Georgia. In doing so, the SWGAA moderated a potentially politically volatile and divisive issue between Georgia's regulatory agencies and southwest Georgia agriculture. They initiated an ongoing dialog that resulted in legislation to protect agricultural water access and the water resources of southwest Georgia. The atmosphere of trust and cooperation that was created has encouraged farmers and water regulators to work together to solve the region's problems.

Southwest Georgia Water Resources Task Force and Water Summits

The Southwest Georgia Water Resources Task Force (Water Task Force) began in 1998 as a water committee of the Albany Chamber of Commerce with the mission to address water issues important to the region's economy and business community (see Southwest Georgia Water Resources Task Force 1998). A self-appointed group of concerned leaders, they expanded the participation of stakeholders in the regional process to include business, industry, natural resources, agriculture, public health, municipal government, and water supply. The Water Task Force broadened the regional process by aiding citizens of southwest Georgia in developing the leadership, knowledge, focus, voice, mechanisms, and processes necessary to understand the evolving water policy issues. In 2000, the Water Task Force became a 501(c)3 nonprofit organization. Its objective was to provide a forum for dialog among regional stakeholders and to encourage citizens and groups to participate in open discussion on water supply and water quality in southwest Georgia. The goal was to educate the region's citizens and stakeholders on water issues, develop an educated leadership, support and strengthen the stewardship and conservation ethic of the region, and develop a sustainable regional economy, society, and ecosystem. These goals guided the formulation of a regional identity, water strategy, policy, and management framework.

Leadership development was a cornerstone of the Water Task Force efforts. Leaders in agriculture, industry, commerce, health, municipal and county governments, conservation, and recreation from a thirty-county region of southwest Georgia as well as representatives from other regions in the state, state and federal agencies, nongovernmental organizations, and other interested parties were invited to participate in regional water leadership summits. Seven summits were conducted between January 1999 and November 2001, with summit attendance averaging 150 (100–300). These summits were a neutral forum with an atmosphere of trust and cooperation for all stakeholders to gain knowledge, develop their voice and vision, and express their concerns and opinions. At each summit, noted academic and natural resource experts, public officials, agencies, and citizens provided information, knowledge, and perspectives on the specific focus of the summit. Following the presentations, a series of questions and responses were solicited through a facilitated discussion to assess the stakeholders' concerns, issues, and desires in evolving a regional dialog.

The first three summits were focused on regionalism and defining a regional vision. During these initial summits, the leaders began the formulation of a regional strategy and water management framework. Summits four through seven were focused on specific emerging water policy issues that affected the region. The summits covered the following issues:

- Stakeholder concerns and the evolution of an integrated regional focus
- Implications for water and water use, and trends, events, or beliefs most important to the future of the region and the evolution of a regional water strategy
- Elements of strategy and underlying philosophy of a water authority that can lead to a regional water authority
- Protecting flows in the Flint River while balancing needs, uses, and environmental variation
- Water policy options for resolving water conflicts, including the Public Trust doctrine, water markets, and water rights
- Land-use strategies for maintaining water quantity and quality
- Regional reservoirs as challenges and opportunities for the Flint River.

The lower Flint River basin stakeholders clearly articulated a desire for a regional water-management strategy that was stakeholder initiated, developed, and managed rather than the planning district model that was developed for Atlanta. During the first three summits, major steps were taken toward embracing this "watershed initiative" approach to water management. The stakeholders identified as desirable a plan that:

- was regionally and issue focused
- used the leadership model for development and implementation
- was self-directed through partnerships with government, private, and nongovernmental organizations
- was based on the best knowledge
- had adequate resources
- was process focused
- was collaborative with open debate
- defined and used flexible and creative solutions

- met challenges through consensus and alternative dispute resolution
- had the ownership and citizen responsibility necessary for implementation.

Many of the elements articulated by these stakeholders were embodied in the definition of a regional/watershed initiative: A primarily self-directed and locally focused collection of parties, usually featuring both private and intergovernmental representatives, organized to address water-related issues at the watershed level or a similarly relevant physical scale, normally operating outside of traditional governmental processes or forums, and typically reliant on collaborative mechanisms of group interaction characterized by open debate, creativity in problem and solution definition, consensus decision-making, and voluntary action (Kenney et al. 2000). The general sentiment was strong for such an approach but entered into with caution, careful research and planning, drawing from the "best" of other programs, and integration with other authorities and planning entities in the region. During 2002 and 2003, summits will be employed to formalize a grassroots regional water management and planning framework based on these principles for other rural regions like the lower Flint River basin.

For Georgia, and particularly southwest Georgia, the drought that began in 1998 was the worst drought on record (EPD 2001a). This drought had a significant impact on the evolving regional process in the lower Flint River region. A hydrologic drought was occurring with record low flows and groundwater levels. Coincident with the climatic drought was an agricultural drought that increased dependence on irrigation. The ACF negotiation modeling efforts indicated that additional irrigation expansion would result in little or no flow in the Flint River if the drought persisted. With the heightened sensitivity of potential natural resource impacts from permitted agricultural water use, EPD placed a moratorium on additional irrigation withdrawal permits in a subarea of the lower Flint River region. Caught in this moratorium were approximately 2,000 irrigation permits already submitted to EPD for approval. In response, the Water Task Force convened a drought committee to define goals and objectives for a regional drought strategy. The committee developed regional stakeholder perspectives on drought concerns, issues, and strategies that would be effective for the region's economy, culture, and natural resources.

Many of the participants involved in the initial workshop represented the lower Flint region on the state drought study committee, and many of the ideas developed by southwest Georgia stakeholders were incorporated into the state drought planning process. The most significant outcome of the drought workshop was a smaller agricultural committee that developed a legislative approach to addressing drought irrigation water needs and protecting flows in the Flint River, and devised a strategy to allow the pending irrigation permits to be released. The Flint River Drought Protection Act (2000) outlined a process for protecting flows in the Flint River during drought. Summit four focused on understanding the concept of "protecting flows in the Flint River" and the ecological basis for determining what flows were appropriate for protection of the natural resources. When enforcement rules were written to implement the law, several key drought indicators and criteria defining severe drought were derived by the Environmental Protection Division. These would be the criteria used by the director of EPD to declare an eminent drought. During such droughts, agricultural irrigation demand would be voluntarily reduced and farmers would be compensated (using an auction process) for infrastructure maintained during the year that irrigation was halted. This was the first incentive-based law implemented in Georgia that linked climate, water use, flows in the river, and the need to protect natural resources. In addition, this was the first negotiated regional resolution and partnership with EPD and a regulated community to benefit the natural resources.

In 2001, a severe drought was declared, the law was implemented, and an auction was held to determine a fair compensation for providing the public service of protecting the flows. From the 194 participants, 209 irrigation withdrawal permits were suspended. Over 33,000 acres of land irrigated from the lower Flint River were withdrawn and 130 million gallons per day in stream flow was retained in the river. The 2001 iterative bid auction process netted $135.85 per acre. The 2002 auction suspended over 40,000 acres of surface-water-irrigated lands in the lower Flint River basin. The average bid price was $127.97. The total cost of the 2002 auction was $5.2 million, versus $4.5 million in 2001. Georgia State University and the Flint River Water Policy and Planning Center partnered with EPD to develop and implement the irrigation auction used in the implementation of the Flint River Drought Protection Act.

The Flint River Drought Protection Act and the permit moratorium raised significant concerns among the agricultural and rural communities in the lower Flint River basin. For a five-year period, water use options for economic development were frozen. The impact of these two policy decisions forever changed the value of water. A resource once viewed as unlimited became the determining factor in economic opportunity in the lower Flint River basin. Land values, land sales, investment interests, the ability to get capital, loan rates, and insurance rates were bound to the ownership of irrigation permits. Water was then viewed as a strategic commodity and the economic concept of water marketing became a topic of public debate. Prior to this, water was viewed as a public resource managed by the state in trust for all of Georgia's citizens. Reasonable use for economic gain was allowed through agricultural permits. These widely differing philosophical approaches to water management became the most contentious and hotly debated public policy issue in the state. As a result, summit five focused on the various policy options that were available to share the water resources of the state, manage water use demands, and provide for effective protection of surface- and groundwater resources.

Summit six focused on broadly educating the region on regional differences in water use, land use, and resultant water quantity and quality. Under a federal court order, Georgia EPD was tasked with developing total maximum daily load (TMDL) for watersheds with impaired water quality (EPD 2001b). In the lower Flint River basin, few point sources of pollutants occur; the watersheds designated with impaired water quality receive the greatest pollutant loads from nonpoint source runoff from agricultural lands, forest harvested lands, unpaved rural roads, denuded highway drainage ditches, and widely dispersed urban lands. Cooperative and voluntary land management was the only option for addressing this problem. An experiential learning approach was taken to educate the region. Two field tours were conducted to view the upper and lower areas of the lower Flint River basin. This summit provided stakeholders with an appreciation of the TMDL issue and a broad view of the suite of issues, options, opportunities, and activities available for this region in developing effective TMDLs.

Multiple regional and municipal reservoirs emerged as a critical component of "drought-proofing" the upper Flint River basin and providing future economic opportunity for the Atlanta metropolitan area. Summit seven focused on the concerns raised by southwest Georgia stakeholders over downstream impacts of the reservoirs on the flows in the Flint River—the very flows they were protecting by giving up their own economic potential. Overviews were given on the status of possible reservoir locations, applications, permitting, impacts, and opportunities for the upper basin. A major outgrowth of this summit was increasing awareness that future water management of the lower Flint River was not independent of management activities in the upper basin. The summit provided an opportunity for citizens of the lower Flint River to understand the challenges citizens in the upper basin face in securing water for their future. It clearly highlighted the need for constructing a mechanism to link water management decisions and strategies in the upper basin with water management in the lower basin and for doing so using a holistic approach to watershed management.

While the grassroots regional initiative was building momentum for a formal regional management framework, many collaborative efforts were underway to creatively build the scientific knowledge needed to address the emerging water resource issues in the lower Flint River basin. It became clear that the scientific knowledge needed to formulate effective management strategies was inadequate. Even basic information—the number of irrigated acres, irrigation water use, groundwater variation, groundwater inflow to the Flint River and tributaries, capacity of the groundwater to sustain use in 2002, variation in river flows with groundwater variation, status of the critical species, and flows needed to protect the natural resources—was not known. Regional institutions developed partnerships in research and management, policy and management-relevant research programs, policy and management tools, programs in education and outreach, and programs in water resource conservation. New research and policy centers were created to address water conservation and economic and policy issues facing the lower Flint River region. Two academic centers were formed at regional universities to develop education, research, and policy-evaluation programs. An irrigation research center was established for field investigations focused on conservation. A center for federal and state agency partnerships was formed to focus on rural water issues and conservation.

A major component of the success of the lower Flint River basin initiatives was building regional strengths and knowledge. Two research institutions, the Joseph W. Jones Ecological Research Center at Ichauway, in Newton, Georgia (Boring 2001) and the National Environmentally Sound Production Agriculture Laboratory, at the University of Georgia, in Tifton (established in 1988, see NESPAL 2002) were important technical resources for the lower Flint River. These regional institutions had water and natural resources conservation programs, public education, and extension focus, and conducted water-related research to determine sustainable use (irrigation water use, irrigation efficiency, impacts on resources, relationship between natural resources and flows, and ecological context such as environmental variation and natural resources response). The two institutions partnered in regionally relevant research (e.g., water quality, irrigation water use, stream biology), modeling, and management-tool development. Professionals at both institutions had interests and pursuits in the science, management, and policy interface; were developing research approaches that involve public participation; and had staff with the ability to translate complex, technical information into useable knowledge accessible to management professionals, policy makers, and general citizens. Both institutions contributed to the regional knowledge by providing technical assessments, conducting training, providing educational experiences, facilitating dialog, and capturing and incorporating local knowledge. As an example, a significant management tool (GIS-based permitting system for Georgia EPD) was co-developed by the research institutions, regulatory agency staff, and the farm community of the lower Flint River (Hook and Blood 2001). Over 3,000 farmers contributed local knowledge through mapping and documenting their irrigation water use.

New approaches to resolving conflict arose through collaboration among the regional leadership, agencies, and key resource professionals in the lower Flint River basin. Innovative partnerships were formed with state and federal agencies with responsibility for water and natural resource conservation to develop incentive-based solutions. Regional experiential education activities were developed for elected officials and outreach professionals (e.g., briefing the governor and congressional and state legislators on emerging water-policy issues; training agricultural cooperative extension agents on instream flow protection). Facilitation and mediation strategies were developed to resolve conflicts between agencies and the regulated community. Water policy and regulations were developed from negotiated resolutions between agencies and the regulated community. Conflicts did occur, but these occurred with groups and organizations from outside the lower Flint River basin and generally resulted from a lack of understanding of the regional culture and issues the rural citizens faced. Innovative and nontraditional educational efforts were initiated to inform elected officials, agencies, special interest groups, and citizens and organizations outside of rural Georgia of the issues and challenges facing the lower Flint basin and the values, approaches, and strategies being used to resolve them.

The purpose of the Water Task Force and the leadership water summits was not to formulate a regional policy or directive but to facilitate the process by which the regions' leaders evolve the strategy and agenda for themselves. The regional leadership that emerged from this process was from the agricultural community. Through funding and partnerships, the farm community, scholars, legislators, state officials, and community leaders conducted irrigation technology research (irrigation efficiency, irrigation audits and retrofitting); expanded capabilities of state agencies (Georgia Soil and Water Conservation Commission and Georgia Rural Water Users Association) to assist in conservation efforts; expanded research in regional universities; reduced direct withdrawals from surface waters; evaluated options for on-farm storage and regional reservoirs; created partnerships with natural resources agencies to find solutions to aquatic species issues resulting from water use; and formulated effective water policy. These efforts were institutionalized through the formation of Hooks and Hanner Center for natural resource partnering in Dawson, Georgia; (see Hooks and Hanner Center 2002), C. W. Stripling Irrigation Research Park for irrigation technology development and assessment, in Newton, Georgia (see Stripling Irrigation Research Park 2000), The Flint River Policy and Planning Center in Albany, Georgia, (see Flint River Water Planning and Policy Center 2002), and the Coastal Policy and Planning Center in Statesboro, Georgia (see Coastal Policy and Planning Center 2002) for economics and policy evaluation.

State Water Management

The state of Georgia initiated in 2001 a comprehensive planning process that provided the vision and framework for sustaining societal and natural resource needs for all water resources in Georgia (Georgia Joint Comprehensive Water Plan Study Committee 2002). The process was begun via Georgia Senate Resolution 142, which created the twenty-three-member Joint Comprehensive Water Plan Study Committee and the fifty-member Water Plan Advisory Committee. The Advisory Committee provided technical advice and stakeholder perspectives that aided the Study Committee in developing a comprehensive water planning framework for creating a comprehensive plan and management strategy. The Study Committee considered existing policy, laws, rules, and programs governing management of water resources; recommended a process and schedule for preparing a comprehensive water plan; formulated principles of a comprehensive water plan; studied the water resources issues (including water quality and quantity) facing Georgia, and recommended actions or legislation necessary to develop the plan. Because sustainability was the critical focus of the plan, a fifty-year vision was developed to ensure stewardship responsibilities through a multigenerational perspective. The vision stated: "Georgia manages water resources in a sustainable manner to support the state's economy, to protect public health and natural systems, and to enhance the quality of life for all citizens."

An important component of the water management framework was substate water management options. A flexible "regional" strategy was recommended in which geology, hydrology, water resource issues, socioeconomics, and governance could be used to define potential management entities and regional boundaries. The Metro District, created in 2001 and centered on the metropolitan region of Atlanta, was the only formal substate management structure in Georgia in 2002. The Metro District, as noted previously, was defined by county boundaries and a county's inclusion was based on population size. This designation provided a commonality in water resource issues, potential strategies, and implementation mechanisms.

This model did not apply across the remainder of Georgia or to the lower Flint River region. Approximately two-thirds of Georgia is in the coastal plain physiographic region where the major water source is underground aquifers. The hydrology of these aquifers is not constrained by surface watersheds; therefore, watershed management districts were not applicable. In addition, most water use decisions were not made by county or municipal governments but by stakeholder groups with differing cultural and socioeconomic interests. A commonality in culture, governance, and socioeconomic characteristics, opportunity for innovation, and increased creativity in problem solving as well as a regional delineation was needed to integrate human and biophysical systems and aid in addressing emerging water-resource issues.

Conclusion

Regional culture played a critical role in perceived resource values, resource use, defining management options, and achieving implementation. The lower Flint River basin was a rural landscape with agriculture as the primary economic support. Rural values are centered on families, community, religious morals and ethics, and traditions of self-reliance and self-sufficiency (Kellogg Foundation 2001). The multigenerational family ownership of the land and desire to pass it to future generations created a strong sense of place and a deeply held stewardship ethic. Common values and daily associations aided in the formation of a sense of community. The strong community values created an environment of trust, cooperation, and communication that aided in forming consensus, partnerships, and networks. Respect for the natural resources was a natural outgrowth of rural religious ethics. Hard work, self-reliance, and self-sufficiency motivated rural individuals to solve their own problems. They were highly motivated to obtain the resources, knowledge, partnerships, and alliances needed to manage complex problems, and they preferred minimal assistance from outside organizations, institutions, or government in problem solving.

Because of their close association with the land and water, rural Georgians have strong ties to natural resources, and high cultural values were placed on these for hunting, fishing, swimming, and boating. Agriculture productivity in the lower Flint River basin is dependent on weather and supplemental irrigation, and farmers are keenly aware of the variation in rain, streams, ponds, and more recently in the groundwater. Farmers who depend on surface water from streams and ponds know their use has limits.

Although many individuals in suburban and urban areas have the same values and morals as rural citizens, the collective culture of urban and suburban communities is different than that of rural communities. The sense of place was weakened by the short residence time of individuals, neighborhoods, subdivisions, or communities on a specific tract of land. Residents in urban areas have little direct contact with land, water, or other natural resources, and many individuals are transient. They do not have a sense of place in the larger landscape. The density and diversity of individuals make it hard to form a sense of community. Because major decisions about water quantity and quality or the natural resources were made by institutions in urban and suburban environments, there was little sense of personal responsibility for conservation and stewardship. There was a greater reliance on professionals, institutions, governments, and other entities to manage water resources and solve water resource problems.

The rural and urban public policy processes taken to achieve sustainability of the freshwater resources in the Flint River were similar in the initial stages, but two distinctly different societal approaches evolved to formulate and implement the management plans. The similarities included an initial visionary leadership, task force of leaders, stakeholder representation, a facilitated visioning process, and a cooperative and consensus approach to formulate the management framework. The processes differed in stakeholder participation, management framework development, planning structure and formulation, management approaches to achieve sustainability, implementation strategies, accountability, citizen involvement and education, and timing from crisis identification to management plan development and proposed implementation. Regional differences in culture, traditions, demographics, human system dominance, institutions, and economics were important human system factors in the evolution of strategies devised to achieve ecological system sustainability. Management options to achieve sustainability were related to regional differences in freshwater systems, their use, and ecological system integrity.

The leadership model, task force composition, stakeholder representation, and framework development reflected the immediacy of the water "crisis" and cultural approaches to problem solving in the regions. In 2000, the water "crisis" that motivated cultural change was the imminent federal intervention over degraded water quality in the Chattahoochee River from excessive storm water and wastewater discharges, and the adverse effects on continued economic development in the rapidly developing Atlanta metro area (Clean Water Initiative 2000). Two business leaders formed the initial vision for a regional response and a corporate or business leadership model evolved. The Metro Atlanta Chamber and the Regional Business Coalition appointed a task force, the Clean Water Initiative, to function as an executive committee. Education on regional water quality and quantity issues was limited to the task force and meeting observers. Regional representation and education opportunities were limited because of time constraints but were key to getting critical stakeholder buy-in. Regional interests were largely represented by the business and economic development stakeholders, local governments, elected officials, and environmental groups and attorneys (see Clean Water Initiative 2000). Concerned citizens and other stakeholder opinions and expertise were gathered through written submissions to Web pages, traditional public meetings, or other commentary approaches. The Clean Water Initiative recommendations were rapidly translated into state legislation and within six months the planning district was implemented. The entire process took about one year to complete from conception to implementation of the planning process.

The resulting Metro District structure and planning process reflected the business leadership model. A largely regulatory accountability and county governance strategy was proposed in the water management plan implementation. This planning and management strategy can work for urban regions where the collective water use and treatment options were made by local elected officials. In urban and suburban areas, local government fiscal and infrastructure decisions and the development of storm-water ordinances have significantly greater impact on water quantity and quality than individual management decisions by residents, commercial establishments, or industry.

Because institutions made major decisions about water quantity and quality or the natural resources in urban and suburban environments, there was little sense of personal responsibility for conservation and stewardship. These collective decisions by the elected officials resulted in limited participation of the residential, commercial, and industrial water users in the initial implementation. There was a greater reliance on professionals, institutions, governments, or other entities to manage water resources and solve water resource problems. As an example, during the extreme drought of 2001–2002, individual participation in water management was limited to EPD-mandated outdoor watering bans. Citizens were encouraged to reduce water use further through public information campaigns by a number of public and private organizations.

Rural regions, such as the lower Flint River basin, had time to develop a different leadership and regional consensus process that focused on leadership education, individual accountability, the formation of loosely knit collectives or networks, and the development of citizen leaders (Fig.12.3). In the lower Flint River basin, the perception of a water "crisis" arose over several years. Citizen education by regional experts, through the water summits, and among stakeholder groups; evolving policy (ACF Compact negations, permitting moratoriums); and an extreme and persistent four-year drought combined to create the regional perception of a regional "water crisis." Citizen education occurred through civic presentations, regional professional initiatives, media coverage, and professional organizations (e.g., Farm Bureau). The regional leadership education that occurred via the summits was critical in motivating grassroots leaders to get involved in water issues before an actual crisis occurred. Although the initial task force was smaller than the Clean Water Initiative task force, the summits increased the number of participants in the consensus process to between 100 and 300 individuals at any given meeting. The citizen leaders were educators and conduits of knowledge for other organizations and groups and motivated their members to participate in the evolving public process. The citizen leadership development and citizen awareness evolved over a longer period and allowed for greater individual participation.

In the lower Flint River region, the broad citizen and citizen leadership participation was necessary because the water issues and water-use decisions and responsibilities were dispersed among many water users throughout a large region. Individuals made the largest water-use decisions—irrigation withdrawals—and these were dispersed throughout the basin. Even residential water use was primarily from private domestic wells. In 2002, there was no monitoring of this water use or centralized measurement; therefore, accountability for that use was based on each individual's knowledge, economics, responsibility, and stewardship ethic. When concerns were raised about overallocation of surface and groundwater withdrawals for irrigation and the potential harm to the natural resources, the individual water users formed partnerships and networks to collectively define ad hoc management solutions. A suite of incentive-based options was developed in the lower Flint River basin to promote water conservation as a first approach to water management.

The grassroots approach that evolved in the lower Flint River regional initiative possessed many of the characteristics of other citizen-led watershed initiatives, watershed groups, or watershed councils that have emerged in the United States (Kenney 1999; Lant 1999). These approaches were organized at physically

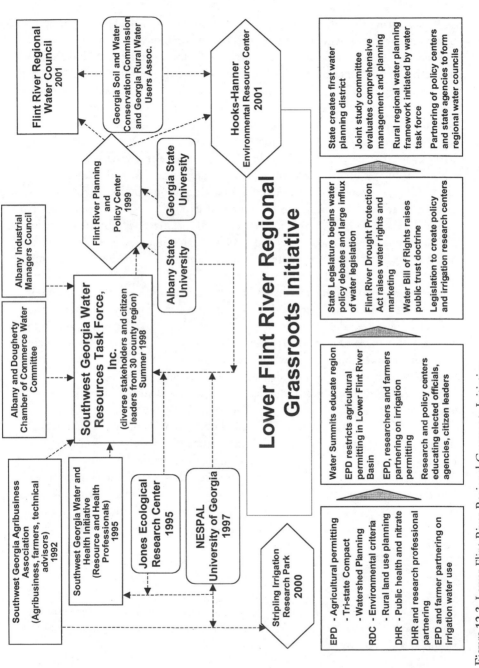

Figure 12.3. Lower Flint River Regional Grassroots Initiative

relevant regional scales, such as watersheds, and have taken an integrated resource management approach (Kenney and Lord 1999). As with the lower Flint River regional initiative, these initiatives were ad hoc, bottom-up associations of citizens, technical advisors, governmental, and nongovernmental participants. The citizens of the lower Flint River broadened their defined region beyond the physical watershed boundaries to include counties with similar rural culture, coastal plain geology, and agricultural economy. It was the region's shared values, rural culture, agricultural economics, public health issues, and natural resources that aided the citizens in overcoming self-interest and distrust and provided the basis for the evolving regional water management vision.

Over the four-year period from 1998 to 2002, the emergence of citizen leaders was the single most important success measure of the lower Flint River basin management process. The citizen leaders of the Flint River region exhibited "collaboration, common good, global concern, diversity and pluralism in structures and participation, client orientation, civic virtues, freedom of expression in all organizations, critical dialogue, qualitative language and methodologies, substantive justice, and consensus-oriented policy-making process" (Rost 1993). The regional leadership was involved in the basin's and the state's policy issues because of demonstrated knowledge gained, commitment of responsibility perceived, and experience of participation in the resource professional initiatives (e.g., SWGAA), organizations, partnerships, education, and negotiations that occurred in the lower Flint River basin. Accountability was dispersed throughout many levels from the individual citizen, to the county, to an evolving regional level as described in the Introduction (see Figure I.2).

The summits provided an opportunity for the Flint River regional initiative citizens and citizen leaders to fully participate in regional policy formulation, assessment, implementation, resolution, visioning, and goal setting. Tools used by the initiative groups included alternative dispute-resolution techniques, negotiated rule making, positive mechanisms to establish and implement policy, and collaborative processes for decision making and problem solving (Kenney 2000). The approach of partnering, consensus, alternative strategies for problem solving, and mutual support were key elements in forming workable strategies in the lower Flint River region that were "win-win" for all involved. Since many rural areas were losing population and thus legislative representation, efforts such as the lower Flint River regional initiative were critical for allowing stakeholders greater opportunity for self-determination.

What evolved in the lower Flint River region was a participatory democratic process that incorporated many of the fundamental principles of sustainability and equity (Gleick 1998). The lower Flint River basin citizens developed a grassroots process of building knowledge, trust, infrastructure, resources, support, consensus, negotiated solutions, and a collective regional vision rather than a county governance infrastructure that relied on regulatory constraints. The regional citizens were actively involved in the development of knowledge and tools for management. Local knowledge of irrigation water management, irrigation practices, and agricultural practices was critical in developing regional water conservation incentives, irrigation permit management tools, and irrigation research centers. Increased regional awareness of the interdependence and interconnection among all stakeholders (agriculture, industry, residential, and natural resources) and water led to consensus-based methods of problem solving and collaborative decision making (Ozawa 1991; Cortner and Moore 1999). However, after four years (1998–2002), the lower Flint River regional grassroots process had not developed a formal regional plan or water management infrastructure. It is not uncommon for a lasting, self-sustaining water management plan using a grassroots stakeholder process to take a decade or more to evolve (Mullen and Allison 1999). In fact, a slow process allows the coevolution of the social system, technical knowledge, and its incorporation into individual and collective behaviors and norms (Hollings 2001). A grassroots process maintains social flexibility as leaders, groups, and networks experiment in the management of the natural systems.

Citizen initiatives and the grassroots regional process developed by southwest Georgia had a ripple effect throughout Georgia. Two additional regional efforts were initiated by citizen leaders who participated in the Water Task Force summits. The Upper Suwannee River Watershed Initiative was a citizen-led organization that sought to improve and protect the natural and economic resources of the Alapaha, Little, Withlacoochee, and Suwannee Rivers in Georgia. The initiative emulated the summit and leadership approach of the Water Task Force. It became a 501(c)3 corporation in 2002 and began the grassroots process of developing a regional water management plan.

A proactive multistate watershed initiative process for the Savannah River watershed was begun in 2002 by citizens, elected officials, and state agency representatives of Georgia and South Carolina. The key visionary leaders of the Savannah River initiative were educated and inspired by the Water Task Force. Citizen leaders and elected officials from Georgia proposed a grassroots regional process for the basin. South Carolina elected officials proposed the creation of the Savannah River Basin Compact to ensure that Georgia and South Carolina had equal authority over and equitable use of the waters and resources of the basin. This compact was the first multistate effort proposed that was anticipatory and not reactionary to a crisis or litigation. The two states agreed to continue a dialog to form a mutually acceptable Savannah River interstate management process.

While the water policy process in Georgia and specifically the Flint River basin was in the formative stages in 2002, there were successes, accomplishments, and changes in water resources management, planning, regulation, and policy that moved the state clearly in the direction of a sustainable resource. The fifty-year vision for Georgia's comprehensive management plan is multigenerational, has sustainability as the ultimate objective, and balances human and natural resource needs. A greater emphasis has been placed on policy based on sound science, integrated approaches, regional-scale assessments, finding equitable solutions, stakeholder and citizen involvement, partnering, inclusive processes, negotiated resolutions, and planning. As an example of the influence of the lower Flint River basin on state policy, public dialog over fundamental principles underpinning the state's view and management of water resources arose during the fifth summit. When the leadership evaluated water policy options for regulating water use and resolving water conflicts, a public dialog ensued over water as a strategic commodity, and the potential for water management through market strategies versus water held in public trust and managed through permitted reasonable use. It was one of the three major policy discussions during the formulation of the state water-planning framework. The Flint River Drought Protection Act (2000) developed by stakeholders from this region raised the issue and potential for water markets and water rights. The Water Bill of Rights (pending 2003) developed by the environmental community in response to discussions from this region, asserted that all water, including groundwater, was held in trust by the state (public trust doctrine).

The grassroots process in the lower Flint River region influenced several state-level water policy efforts in Georgia. The need for a comprehensive water management plan for Georgia, several critical water policy issues identified by the Joint Comprehensive Water Plan Study Committee, and key plan components resulted, in part, from the issues, debates, approaches, and legislative proposals initiated by citizens in the lower Flint River region (see Georgia Joint Comprehensive Water Plan Study Committee 2002). Key leaders from the lower Flint River region were appointed by the governor, lieutenant governor, or legislature to the Joint Study Committee or Advisory Committee. Education and leadership training were institutionalized as requisite for future water management. Governor Roy Barnes's Environmental Advisory Council and the University of Georgia J. W. Fanning Institute for Leadership created the Institute for Georgia Environmental Leadership (IGEL) (see IGEL 2002). IGEL was designed for Georgians who had a commitment to addressing environmental issues in the state. The goals of the program were education on regional and state environmental issues, providing a forum for participants to develop an understanding of each other's views, and engaging participants in key aspects of leadership. Several key leaders from the lower Flint River basin are members of the council (see Environmental Advisory Council 2002).

Regional management and planning is a political, social, economic, and cultural entity as well as a technical and scientific process (Policansky 1998). For citizens to participate in management formulation and implementation, they must interact with current governance structures or create new ones (Ludwig

2001). In the upper Flint River region, citizens were represented through appointees to the Metro District boards or advisory councils or by their elected officials and county governance structures. Although citizen/governance relationships changed little, the sixteen-county partnering and joint planning process formed a new governance structure (the Metro District) to collectively plan and manage the water resources. New informal governance structures emerged in the lower Flint River region that increased citizen participation. New institutions, organizations, and relationships with regulatory and management institutions arose that facilitated collaborative, cooperative consensus, and partnership approaches to water resource problem solving. During 2002, the leadership summits provided the forums to develop a rural regional planning and management framework.

Recommendations

Each region, state, or country has unique water issues, resource challenges, and the human and economic capital to resolve those challenges. Other models for participatory approaches to water management and watershed experiments are evolving (Ewing 1999; Porto et al. 1999; Rhodes 2000) from which we can learn. Several lessons emerge from the different management processes that evolved in the Flint River basin. Sustainable water resource management must form flexible management systems (Olsson and Folke 2001). The management system should be place-based and in a context that makes sense to the participants so that effective implementation can occur. Rather than a geologically defined area such as a watershed, using a more flexible concept like regionalism creates greater opportunity for commonality among citizens, citizen understanding, and citizen participation. Regions should be defined using several factors such as the issue, hydrology, water use, culture and population, enterprise (economics), governance, physical boundaries, political (county), or other relevant criteria that make sense for effectively formulating management strategies and implementing them.

In this era of management transition, an adaptive co-management process that permits policy experimentation provides the best opportunity for humans, economies, and nature to cope with change (Gadgil et al. 1993; Hollings 2001). Because complex interactions of human and natural systems are not well understood, an emphasis on process rather than on ultimate management structure will encourage greater citizen participation in that transition. The stakeholders, concerned citizens, and citizen leaders must be empowered through education and opportunity to participate. The effort must have a visionary leadership group that is not constrained by current institutions or policy, is open to creative solutions based on local knowledge, and can provide the educational opportunities for developing additional regional leadership. Multiple educational approaches are needed such as experiential education, tours, facilitated dialog, workshops, civic presentations, presentations to special interest groups, conferences, and summits on specific planning and management topics. Opportunities for facilitated dialog during planning and management summits are critical to building a regional vision because mutual education promotes understanding and empathy for other's views, values, and perspectives.

An increased opportunity for effective implementation and sustainability of the resources was gained from a regional, grassroots, leadership, and citizen-centered approach to water resource planning and management. A grassroots approach increases the adaptive capacity and institutional flexibility necessary to be more in tune with evolving social arrangements and local natural resource dynamics (Olsson and Folke 2001). Consensus, cooperation, and partnerships build trust and opportunity for effective problem solving. The process is success oriented because it enhances and fosters positive human behavior through education, leadership development, and incentive-based management strategies. It employs a leadership model to educate, enable, and empower citizens. There is a focus on incentives rather than on punitive regulations. The citizens are motivated and invest their time and energy into the process. Citizens are vested in the process and, therefore, have ownership in its outcome. The resulting process is fair and equitable and reflects the region's collective values, beliefs, and culture.

Formulation of adaptive co-management strategies for the Flint River basin that foster both the vitality and sustainability of its intrinsically linked human and ecological systems typifies the complexity, challenges, and opportunities society faces in achieving sustainable freshwater resources. Regional differences in freshwater systems, human systems, their interdependence, their dynamics, drivers of change, and resource use trajectories challenges the notion of only using a watershed (i.e., geologically and hydrologically defined boundaries) approach to planning and management. This requires we maintain social flexibility and adaptive capability in facilitating constructive change through new freshwater resource management approaches. Finding the appropriate balance in sustaining culture, economics, and the natural resources will require that all concerned citizens, stakeholders, citizen leaders, elected officials, regulators, and decision makers participate in the adaptive co-management process. Their planning and management options must be based on the best technical, scientific, experiential, and professional knowledge and judgment available. New social and institutional partnerships will be needed to effectively translate and integrate knowledge into societal beliefs and norms. Through communication, adaptation, and transformation, citizens can tackle the issues, construct a sustainable vision and knowledge, define the appropriate management prescriptions, and assess their effectiveness.

Many federal (e.g., U.S. Environmental Protection Agency, Natural Resources Conservation Service), regional (Western Governors Association), and western state (e.g., Oregon, Washington, California) agencies support these citizen-based, place-based, or watershed initiatives. The Western Governors Association has incorporated this consensus, empowering, incentive-based approach into their guiding policy framework entitled Enlibra (Policy Resolution 02–07 June 2002, see Enlibra 2002). Embedded within the watershed initiative paradigm is an integrated systems approach that can provide the framework necessary to address the complex interlinking of human and ecological systems. Although there are many critics of this approach (Kenney et al. 2000), it offers some intriguing opportunities to resolve competing, conflicting, complicated, and intractable issues. Summaries of other initiatives have been described by the Natural Resources Law Center in *The Watershed Source Book* (1996 and revised in 2000), the U.S. EPA's Surf Your Watershed database (U.S. EPA 2002), and the National Watershed Network within the Know Your Watershed site of Purdue University Conservation Technology Information Center (PUCTIC 2000).

Acknowledgements

It has been my privilege to observe, be educated, be empowered, and be enabled by visionary leaders who "think outside of the box," understand the power of knowledge, seek balanced solutions to complex challenges, and focus on the process of creating leadership. This chapter is their story. The members of the Water Task Force, SWGHWRI, SWGAA, and 9th District of the Georgia Farm Bureau helped me understand the value of partnerships, networks, and trust. Dr. Jim Hook, Dr. Gail Cowie, Mr. Paul Deloach, Dr. Lindsay Boring, Dr. Stephen Draper, Ms. Lucy Draper, Mr. Harold Reheis, Mr. Ralph Powell, Mr. Morgan Murphy, Ms. Susan Reyher, Dr. Paul Newell, Mr. Pete McTier, Mr. Bob Kerr, Mr. Murray Campbell, Mr. Hal Haddock, and Dr. Ron Cummings provided insights to personal responsibility, leadership, and the many "shades of gray." Governor Roy Barnes, Lt. Governor Mark Taylor, Representative Bob Hanner, Representative Richard Royal, and Representative Tom McCall provided unique opportunities to understand the interface of science and policy. My Jones Center colleagues (Mr. Steve Golladay, Mr. Steve Opsahl, and Mr. Woody Hicks) reviewed the chapter and provided valuable insights. Ms. Anne Miller reviewed and edited the final manuscript.

References

Adler, R. W., J. C. Landman, and D. M. Cameron. 1993. *The Clean Water Act: Twenty years later.* Washington, D.C.: Island Press; Washington, D.C.; Natural Resources Defense Council.

American Rivers. 2000. *Americas' most endangered rivers of 2000.* Report by American Rivers Organization, Washington, D.C.

Atlanta Regional Commission. 1997. *Regional water supply plan.* Accessed 11/15/02: www.atlantaregional.com/.

Benke, A. C. 1990. A perspective on America's vanishing streams. *Journal of the North American Bethological Society* 9(1):77–88.

Berkes, F., and C. Folke, eds. 1998. *Linking social and ecological systems: Management practices and social mechanisms for building resilience.* Cambridge, U.K.: Cambridge University Press.

Blood, E. R., J. E. Hook, and K. A. Harrison. 1999. Agricultural water consumption in the ACT/ACF River basins: Approaches for projecting irrigated acreage. Pp. 433–438 in *Proceedings of the 1999 Georgia Water Resources Conference,* edited by K. J. Hatcher. University of Georgia Institute of Ecology, Athens, Ga.

Boatright, S. A., and D. Bachtel. 2000. *The Georgia county guide.* 19th ed. Accessed 11/15/02: www.fcs.uga.edu/hace/gafacts/index.html.

Boring, Lindsay R. 2001. The Joseph W. Jones Ecological Research Center: co-directed applied and basic research in the private sector. Pp. 233–258 in *Holistic Science: The evolution of the Georgia Institute of Ecology,* Garry W. Barrett and Terry L. Barrett, editors. *(1940–2000),* New York: Taylor & Francis.

Bureau of Economic Analysis. 1999. *County bearfacts for Georgia 1999–2000.* Accessed 11/15/02: www.bea.doc.gov/bea/regional/bearfacts/.

Clean Water Initiative. 2000. *Final report of the Clean Water Initiative.* A project of the Metro Atlanta Chamber of Commerce and Regional Business Coalition. Report prepared by the Boston Consulting Group. Atlanta, Ga.

Coastal Policy and Planning Center. 2002. Georgia Southern Expands Water Center Team. Accessed 11/27/02: www.waterstewards.com/gasouthern_expands.htm.

Cortner, J. J., and M. A. Moore. 1999. *Politics of ecosystems management.* Washington, D.C.: Island Press.

Couch, C. A., J. C. DeVivo, and B. J. Freeman. 1995. *What fish live in the streams of metropolitan Atlanta?* U.S. Geological Survey Fact Sheet FS-091-95. U.S. Geological Survey, Atlanta, Ga.

Couch, C. A., E. H. Hopkins, and P. S. Hardy. 1996. *Influences of environmental settings on aquatic ecosystems in the Apalachicola-Chattahoochee-Flint River basin.* U.S. Geological Survey Water Resources Investigations Report 95-4278. U.S. Geological Survey, Atlanta, Ga.

Enlibra. 2002. Principles for environmental management in the West: Policy Resolution 02–07 of the Western Governors Association. June 25, 2002 annual meeting. Phoenix, Ariz. Accessed 11/15/02: http://www.westgov.org/wga/policy/02/enlibra_07.pdf.

Environmental Advisory Council. 2002. Accessed 11/15/02: www.ganet.org/dnr/eac.html.

EPD (Environmental Protection Division). 2001a. *1998–2000 Georgia drought report.* Georgia Department of Natural Resources, Atlanta, Ga.

————. 2001b. *Georgia's environment* Department of Natural Resources. Atlanta, Ga. Accessed 11/27/02: www.dnr.state.ga.us/dnr/environ/gaenviron-files/annlrpt-files/gaenv00_01.html.

Ewing, S. 1999. Landcare and community-led watershed management in Victoria, Australia. *Journal of the American Water Resources Association* 35(3):663–674.

Flint River Water Planning and Policy Center. 2002. Accessed 11/27/02: www.h2opolicycenter.org.

Gadgil, M., F. Berkes, and J. Colding. 1993. Indigenous knowledge for biodiversity conservation. *Ambio* 22:151–156.

Gleick, P. H. 1998. Water in crisis: Paths to sustainable water use. *Ecological Applications* 8(3):571–579.

Harrison, K. A., and A. Tyson. 1999. Agricultural irrigation trends in Georgia. Pp. 421–424 in *Proceedings of the 1999 Georgia Water Resources Conference*, edited by K. J. Hatcher. University of Georgia Institute of Ecology, Athens, Ga.

Holland, M. M. 1996. Ensuring sustainability of natural resources: Focus on institutional arrangements. *Canadian Journal of Fisheries and Aquatic Science* 53:432–439.

Hollings, C. S. 2001. Understanding the complexity of economic, ecological, and social systems. *Ecosystems* 4:390–405.

Hook, J. E. 2000. Irrigation sustains the economies of rural farm communities. Presentation at the *Conference on Sustainability of Wetlands and Water Resources: Achieving Sustainable Systems in the 21st Century.* University of Mississippi, Oxford, Miss. May 23–25, 2000.

Hook, J. E., and E. R. Blood. 2001. Mapping agricultural withdrawal permits and irrigated area in the lower Flint basin. Pp. 105–109 in *Proceedings of the 2001 Georgia Water Resources Conference*, edited by K. J. Hatcher. University of Georgia, Athens, Ga.

Hooks and Hanner Center. 2002. From peanut company to research facility: A tale of two lawyers. Accessed 11/27/02: www.waterstewards.com/Tale_lawyers.htm.

IGEL. 2002. Institute for Georgia Environmental Leadership. Accessed 11/27/02: www.dnr.state.ga.us/igel.pdf.

Joint Comprehensive Water Plan Study Committee. 2002. *Final Report of the Georgia Joint Comprehensive Water Plan Study Committee.* A report to the Governor and the General Assembly. Carl Vinson Institute of Government. University of Georgia, Athens, Ga.

Kellogg Foundation. 2001. *Grassroots leaders: Growing healthy and sustainable communities.* Kellogg Foundation, Battle Creek, Mich.

Kenney, D. S. 1999. Historical and sociopolitical context of the Western Watersheds Movement. *Journal of the American Water Resources Association* 35(3):493–503.

————. 2000. *Arguing about consensus: Examining the case against western watershed initiatives and other collaborative groups active in natural resources management.* University of Colorado School of Law, Natural Resources Law Center. Boulder, Colo.

Kenney, D. S., and W. B. Lord. 1999. *Analysis of institutional innovation in the natural resources and environmental realm.* University of Colorado School of Law, Natural Resources Law Center, Boulder, Colo.

Kenney, D. S., S. T. McAllister, W. H. Caile, and J. S. Peckham. 2000. *The new watershed source book: A directory and review of watershed initiatives in the western United*

States. University of Colorado School of Law, Natural Resources Law Center, Boulder, Colo.

Kundell, J. A., T. A. DeMeo, and M. Myszewski. 2001. Developing a comprehensive state water management plan: A framework for managing Georgia's water resources. Research Atlanta, Inc. Atlanta, Ga., and Carl Vinson Institute of Government, Athens, Ga.

Lant, C. L. 1999. Introduction human dimensions of watershed management. *Journal of the America Water Resources Association* 35:483–486.

Light, H. M., M. R. Darst, and J. W. Grubbs. 1998. *Aquatic habitats in relation to river flow in the Apalachicola River floodplain, Florida*. United States Geological Survey Professional Paper 1594. Denver, Colo.

Likens, G. E. 1998. Limitations to intellectual progress in ecosystems science. Pp. 247–271 in *Successes, limitations, and frontiers in ecosystem science*, edited by M. Pace, and P. Groffman. New York: Springer-Verlag.

———. 2001. Ecosystems energetics and biogeochemistry. Pp. 53–88 in *A new century of biology*, edited by W. J. Kress and G. W. Garrett. Washington, D.C.: Smithsonian Institution Press.

Ludwig, D. 2001. The era of management is over. *Ecosystems* 4:758–764.

Marella, R. L., J. L. Fanning, and W. S. Mooty. 1993. *Estimated use of water in the ACF River basin during 1990 with state summaries from 1970 to 1990*. U.S. Geological Survey Water Resources Investigation Report 93-4-84. Tallahassee, Fla.

Mayer, G. C. 1997. *Ground-water resources of the lower-middle Chattahoochee River basin in Georgia and Alabama, and middle Flint River basin in Georgia, Subarea 3 of the Apalachicola-Chattahoochee-Flint and Alabama-Coosa-Tallapoosa River basins*. U.S. Geological Survey Open-File Report 96-483. Atlanta, Ga.

Metropolitan North Georgia Water Planning District. 2002a. Accessed 11/27/02: www.northgeorgiawater.org.

———. 2002b. *Bylaws of the Metropolitan North Georgia Water Planning District*. Accessed 11/27/02: www.northgeorgiawater.org/pdfs/bylaws.pdf.

Miller, J. A. 1990. *Ground water atlas of the United States, Alabama, Florida, Georgia, and South Carolina*. U.S. Geological Survey Professional Paper HA 730-G. Denver, Colo.

Mullen, M. W., and B. E. Allison. 1999. Stakeholder involvement and social capital: Keys to watershed management success in Alabama. *Journal of the America Water Resources Association* 35:655–662.

NAPA (National Academy of Public Administration). 1997. *Resolving the paradox of environmental protection: An agenda for Congress, EPA, and the states*. Washington, D.C.

National Research Council. 1999. *New strategies for America's watersheds*. Washington, D.C.: National Academy Press.

NESPAL. 2002. Accessed 11/15/02: www.nespal.org.

Olsson, P., and C. Folke. 2001. Local ecological knowledge and institutional dynamics for ecosystem management: A study of Lake Racken Watershed, Sweden. *Ecosystems* 4:85–104.

Ozawa, C. P. 1991. *Recasting science consensual procedures in public policy making*. Boulder, Colo.: Westview Press.

Policansky, D. 1998. Science and decision making for water resources. *Ecological Applications* 8(3):610–618.

Porto, M., R. Lal, L. Porto, and L. G. T. Azevedo. 1999. A participatory approach to watershed management: The Brazilian system. *Journal of the America Water Resources Association* 35:675–683.

PUCTIC (Purdue University Conservation Technology Information Center). 2000. National Watershed Network. Accessed 11/27/02: www.ctic.purdue.edu/KYWI.

Rhodes, R. E. 2000. The participatory multipurpose watershed project: Nature's salvation or Schumacher's nightmare. Pp. 327–343 in *Integrated watershed management in the global ecosystem*, edited by R. Lal. Washington, D.C.: CRC Press.

Rost, J. 1993. *Leadership for the twenty-first century*. Westport, Conn.: Praeger Publishers.

Southwest Georgia Water Resources Task Force. 1998. Accessed 11/27/02: www.nespal.org/summit.

Stripling Irrigation Research Park. 2000. Accessed 11/27/02: www.nespal.org/agwateruse/initiative/park.asp.

Torak, L. J., G. S. Davis, G. A. Strain, and J. G. Herdon. 1996. *Geohydrology and evaluation of the stream-aquifer relations in the ACF River Basin, southeast Alabama, northwestern Florida and southwest Georgia*. U.S. Geological Survey Water-Supply Paper 2460. Atlanta, Ga.

U.S. Army Corps of Engineers. 1998. *Water allocation for the ACF River Basin*. Draft Environmental Impact Statement. Main Report. Alabama, Florida, and Georgia. U.S. Army Corps of Engineers Mobile District, Mobile, Ala.

U.S. Census Bureau. 2000. *State and metropolitan area data book 1997–1998. A statistical abstract supplement*. Accessed 11/27/02: www.census.gov/statab/smadb/smaguide.pdf.

U.S. EPA (United States Environmental Protection Agency). 1996. *Watershed approach framework*. EPA840-S-96-001. U.S. Environmental Protection Agency, Office of Water, Washington, D.C.

———. 2002. Surf your watershed. Accessed 10/10/02: www.epa.gov/surf/.

Ziewitz, J. W. 1997. *Anadromous fish habitat in the ACT and ACF River Basins*. Fish and Wildlife Service, Panama City, Fla.

Ziewitz, J. W., B. K. Luprek, and J. W. Kasbohm. 1997. Protected species inventory and identification in the ACT and ACF River Basins. Vol. 1. Fish and Wildlife Service, Panama City, Fla.

Chapter 13

Sustainable Freshwater Resources: Achieving Secure Water Supplies

Walter Rast and Marjorie M. Holland

As stated in Chapter 1, all governments typically embrace the goal of economic development as the primary means of improving the well-being and living standards of their citizens. A reality of economic development, however, is that it cannot usually be sustained without proper regard for the environmentally sound management and use of natural resources, a goal embodied in the concept of "sustainable development" (Laszlo et al. 1988). This concept highlights the reality that if humanity continues to engage in unbridled exploitation of natural resources, or continues to exhibit uncontrolled pollution, it can eventually overwhelm nature's ability to provide the needed resource base and pollutant assimilative capacity needed for economic growth. This fact will ensure that, although temporary economic gains may be realized, the desired economic development cannot be maintained over the long term, and will usually have direct environmental or economic consequences.

Chapters 11 and 12 discussed cultural perspectives for natural resource use, highlighting interstate or regional approaches within the United States used to facilitate the goal of sustainable use of freshwater resources. In contrast, this chapter focuses on the shared management and water resources across regional and national boundaries. It is noted that the principles and examples highlighted in this chapter have general utility on the scale of the river basin or groundwater aquifer, whether applied at the local, state, national, or international level. Further, since the tragic events of September 11, 2001, in New York City, the notion of "water security" has been defined by some as concern about public health threats to national water resources. As used in this chapter, however, the notion of water security denotes the management and use of shared water resources in the absence of conflict, be it litigation or warfare. It necessarily includes discussion of tools and techniques for identifying, analyzing, and accepting cultural differences that may exist in regard to ensuring equitable access to sustainable supplies of freshwater, as well as the process of planning and preparing within regional groups to assure sustainable freshwater supplies over the long term, and particularly during periods of drought.

Causes of Environmentally Unsustainable Use of Water Resources

As introduced in Chapter 1, water security is related directly to the goal of environmentally sustainable use of water resources. This chapter describes the use of tools and techniques for achieving the latter goal. Environmentally unsustainable water use denotes human water use for beneficial purposes at a rate faster than it can be naturally replenished by rivers, lakes, and underground aquifers. It also incorporates the pollution of water to the extent that its decreased quality can cause serious illness or death when used for a drinking-water supply. Howe (1995) has suggested that achieving environmentally sustainable management of freshwater resources is not so much a problem of a lack of appropriate tools or techniques, or even guidance in using them, as it is a failure to use them in an integrated manner on a drainage-basin scale.

Experience around the world highlights the fact that the unsustainable use of freshwater resources is a continuing problem in both developed and developing countries. If allowed to continue, there is ample evidence this situation will lead to increasing social conflict, individual misery, and both economic and environmental costs over the long term. A senior official of the World Bank stated, "Current water management practices and policies have resulted in stark and terrible failures. But the problems we witness today are only an indication of what may lie ahead" (Serageldin 1995).

As noted by Smith and Rast (1998), the reasons that humans use freshwater resources in an unsustainable manner include the following:

• Water is not a priority issue on most political agendas
• Authority for different water uses and allocations is typically fragmented among a number of agencies and organizations, sometimes with conflicting missions or goals
• Available assessment tools and techniques for sustainable water management are applied in an incomplete or un-integrated manner
• Many areas are experiencing uncontrolled human population growth and urbanization, and associated increased water needs
• Many governments have difficulty identifying and addressing the myriad related social, technical, legal, institutional, economic, and political factors.

One of the most compelling reasons that environmentally sustainable use of freshwater resources does not have a high priority on national agendas is the lack of recognition of the environment as a fundamental component of sustainable development. Stated another way, because the natural environment is the source of the natural resources needed for economic development, it is the entity that makes development *sustainable* in the first place; thus, the environment *is* the fundamental resource.

Equally compelling is the fact that freshwater resources are both finite and irreplaceable. Although the quantity of available water in different parts of the world can vary significantly, there is only a fixed volume of water on Earth. We have no way to increase the total volume, and there is no substitute for water for virtually any of its uses. One cannot, for example, make steel with milk, nor paper with orange juice. Indeed, humans cannot even make the milk or orange juice without water!

Because the global volume of water remains constant even as the global population continues to increase, the quantity of water available per capita also is decreasing in many regions. Humans will continue their current cycle of water withdrawal: use, pollute, discharge, withdraw, pretreat, use, pollute, discharge, and so forth. Using water in an environmentally sustainable manner, however, facilitates its reuse and with less pretreatment than would otherwise be necessary.

Costs of Environmentally Unsustainable Use of Water Resources

A major impediment to sustainable freshwater resources is that the range of significant environmental, economic, and social costs of not using it sustainably is not adequately considered in the design and implementation of most water projects (Smith and Rast 1998). Experience indicates, however, that these costs can be sufficiently large to render many water projects and policies uneconomical over the long term. A large irrigation project in West Africa provided ample proof of this reality; upon its completion, the project's downstream "costs" were found to exceed the total estimated economic benefits. Not considering all significant economic costs and benefits *before* its completion ensured the project would fail on both economic and environmental grounds (Barbier et al. 1993).

Long-term Costs

The economic costs of unsustainable water use can vary greatly, only becoming apparent over the long term, and can include lost production and underutilized investments. The environmentally unsustainable use of water resources in the Aral Sea drainage basin, for example, decreased the lake's water levels and quality to the extent that the previously robust fishing industry completely collapsed. As a result, nearly all previous investment in this industry now lies idle. Inefficient irrigation practices in this semiarid region also led to increased soil salinization, causing subsequent decreases in agricultural productivity and, ironically, negating the very purpose of the water diversions in the first place (UNEP 1993). Some may argue that the water needs in some situations are so urgent that its unsustainable withdrawal and use is justified. Nevertheless, policy-makers must not ignore the long-term costs of such expedient actions. If efforts are made to identify the major consequences of unsustainable water use *before* negative impacts occur, comprehensive water planning and incentive schemes can be more readily justified and implemented.

Subsidies

The long-term costs imposed on society for supplying water at subsidized prices also can contribute to unsustainable water use. If viewed in the short term, supplying irrigation water at subsidized rates, for example, may appear to be beneficial and reduce the costs for agricultural products. However, subsidies typically lead to inefficient water use and, in many cases, ultimately to soil salinization and waterlogging. Further, in many regions, the water also could be used for more highly valued purposes. Thus, this practice ultimately imposes economic costs on the sector of society paying the subsidy, including the general public.

Restrictions on Other Water Uses

Using water resources for one activity so that it restricts other uses also can impose economic costs. Building a dam to provide general hydropower, for example, can restrict use of the water resources for fish spawning, or for the periodic inundation of fertile silt on low-lying farmland.

Pollution

Water pollution can impose significant social and health costs on water use. For example, although agriculture is necessary for food production, it both uses and generates numerous water pollutants, including sewage, nutrients, and persistent organic compounds. In addition to direct human health impacts, pollutants can cause lost economic production due to absentee workers. Equally important is the fact that once a waterbody is significantly polluted, restoring its water quality to a usable condition can be prohibitively expensive or technically difficult. Management of the water for its sustainable use can minimize such problems.

Ecosystem Damage

The costs of unsustainable water use on natural ecosystems can be difficult to identify. Nevertheless, factors such as pollution, siltation, salinization, and water depletion can significantly disrupt balanced and properly functioning ecosystems. Unfortunately, however, such damage is often difficult to quantify in monetary terms, making it easy to dismiss them as unimportant when assessing the potential environmental impacts of economic development projects.

Misallocation of Water for Different Uses

Unsustainable water use can cause large-scale misallocation of water resources. Using water subsidies as an example, not considering the full costs of water at the beginning of irrigation projects can ultimately result in higher levels of economic investment being necessary to correct environmental damages. This represents a misallocation in that the additional funds ultimately required to correct the problems of unsustainable water use could have been used elsewhere in the economy for higher-value purposes.

Tools and Techniques for Environmentally Sustainable Water Management and Use

A large number of tools and techniques are available to facilitate the goal of environmentally sustainable management and use of freshwater resources, including diagnostic studies, water quality assessments, hydrologic models, cost-benefit analysis, and environmental impact assessments (Smith and Rast 1998). In fact, even though most of these tools and techniques actually have been available for many years, they typically have not been applied in a coherent and integrated manner.

Further, integrated, environmentally sustainable water management is more than simply carrying out environmental impact assessments. Rather, it requires integration of such factors as water policy formulation, project appraisal, water management institutions, and law across the breadth and depth of the decision-making process regarding water resources, as discussed in the following sections.

Building Consensus

Building consensus among competing factions is most rapidly achieved when a highly visible problem impacts a large group of people. Living through a serious drought, for example, can bring diverse groups of people together to develop and agree on approaches to tackle common problems. A late-1960s drought in New England illustrated this observation (Platt 1995). The agency responsible for water distribution in the Boston metropolitan area proposed water diversion from the Connecticut River to solve future anticipated regional droughts. To review this proposed water diversion, the Water Supply Citizens Advisory Committee (WSCAC) was created in 1977 by an agreement between a Massachusetts state agency and a local consortium of elected officials. Comprising representatives of thirty-five major stakeholders, including representatives of industry, local government, nongovernmental organizations, Connecticut and Massachusetts state governments, watershed associations, and the academic community, WSCAC developed an ecosystem management agreement to address the Connecticut River water diversion (Holland 1993). The multidisciplinary expertise of the individuals serving on WSCAC included ecologists, farmers, land-use planners, industrial water engineers, environmental lawyers, municipal water managers, state agency scientists, and elected officials.

In addition to providing a forum for interdisciplinary cooperation, WSCAC committee members and the agencies working with them came to view citizen participation as a good investment, facilitating public support for cost-effective and environmentally sound solutions to common water-related problems. The WSCAC mechanism also provided needed expertise, continuity, coordination of efforts, and a single point of contact with state officials and water planners (Platt 1995). Other factors facilitating WSCAC's effectiveness included (1) a vision for the future and the ability to explain it to high-level government officials, (2) a transparent and inclusive consultation process, and (3) trust and respect among all WSCAC representatives. The WSCAC effort also highlighted the value of having a citizens committee engage in thoughtful critiques of agency proposals and policies, which, in turn, facilitated receptive and professional responses by agency officials to WSCAC inputs. It demonstrated that not only was reaching a consensus important but also that the professionalism which developed between the citizens committee and funding agency officials facilitated WSCAC's effective functioning. Even though the Memorandum of Understanding creating WSCAC was signed in 1978, it continues to function effectively to the present time (Holland 1993, 1996).

Drainage Basin Diagnostic Studies

Another fundamental requirement is a drainage-basin scale-inventory of available freshwater resources, including water quantity and quality, and the relevant scientific, technical, and socioeconomic factors affecting these and related components.

Incorporating Environmental Aspects of Freshwater Resources in Policy Formulation

Although freshwater resources policies and projects are typically formulated by governmental agencies, national environmental agencies often do not have an opportunity to provide relevant input at early design stages. A logical solution is to require relevant government departments to widely circulate water-relevant policy and project proposals at the earliest possible stage. Even more appropriate is formation of interdepartmental committees (including environmental department heads) to finalize policy and project design prior to its submission to government decision-makers. An alternative would be a high-level central screening agency whose responsibility it would be to ensure all relevant views are adequately incorporated into government recommendations regarding water resources and socioeconomic development.

Integrated Economic, Environmental, and Social Policy and Project Appraisals

Environmentally sustainable water resources also require integrated economic and environmental appraisals of policy and project proposals. This requirement reflects the reality that society often has multiple objectives but inadequate resources to meet all of them. Thus, decision makers typically face the difficult task of trying to balance often-competing societal demands for water and other key resources. This task requires multiple-objective planning, with key decisions based on transparent, systematic, and integrated appraisals of all relevant environmental, economic, and social factors. The elements of an integrated assessment should include (1) cost-benefit analyses from the national and regional perspectives, (2) environmental impact analysis, and (3) social impact analysis (Howe 1995). Although our knowledge is not sufficient to ensure accurate monetary values for all costs and benefits of freshwater resources, this approach will work to at least ensure their identification and consideration. Establishing the relative importance of the different costs and benefits of these resources then becomes a political decision (Smith and Rast 1998).

Environmental Impact Assessments and Strategic Environmental Assessments

The process of environmental impact assessments was initially designed to identify negative impacts of activities and projects affecting the environment and to make it easier to identify solutions. Although such assessments have been carried out for decades in some cases, the environmental impacts of economic policies and projects are still not being adequately addressed in many cases. A primary reason is the lack of comprehensive integration of environmental impact assessments with project appraisal and implementation (World Bank 1996). Carrying out integrated economic and environmental policy and project appraisals comprises a number of fundamental steps, and environmental impact assessments should be carried out at both the policy and the project level. In contrast to environmental impact assessments at the project level, policy-level assessments are often referred to as strategic environmental assessments.

A fundamental problem with using environmental impact assessments, however, is that in many cases they often are poorly carried out because of inadequate facilities, data, or trained personnel. Further, environmental conservation and protection of freshwater resources often are not high-profile issues in national developmental agendas, resulting in a vicious circle. On the one hand, environmental impact assessments may not be carried out because environmental protection and conservation are not necessarily viewed as important elements in economic development. On the other hand, it is for this very reason that environmental impact assessments are needed to highlight *all* the major costs of environmentally unsustainable freshwater use. An environmental impact assessment during the policy or project-formulation stage also can assist policy-makers to narrow their options, helping to steer project options toward more environmentally sustainable development activities and ultimately reducing environmental impacts and costs at a later date.

Assessing Environmental Impacts

Environmental impact assessments must be carried out sufficiently early to ensure they are an integral part of the project or policy appraisal cycle and can actually influence policy choices. An unfortunate reality of many planning efforts, however, is that the proposing department often does not discuss its projects with the departments responsible for environmental protection and conservation until key decisions have already been made, thereby reducing the utility of subsequently conducted environmental impact assessments. Equally important is the need to identify and compare project and policy options, facilitating formulation of equivalent end products at lower cost and/or reduced environmental impacts.

Comparison of Economic Costs and Benefits of Environmental Impact Assessment Recommendations

Comparing the environmental impact assessment economic costs and benefits can improve the environmental sustainability of water use. An assessment of a proposed irrigation project, for example, may result in a recommendation for less groundwater withdrawal and use. Without adequate explanation, this recommendation could result in public or governmental protests. However, the assessment also can highlight the economic and environmental costs of unsustainable water withdrawals from aquifers thereby facilitating its acceptance as a rational policy decision. Unfortunately, water analysts often do not consider these types of costs and benefits because they lack the necessary background or skills to calculate such costs. Thus, environmental assessment analysts must work closely with economists and engineers to identify and calculate accurate environmental costs and benefits, including them with other project costs and benefits.

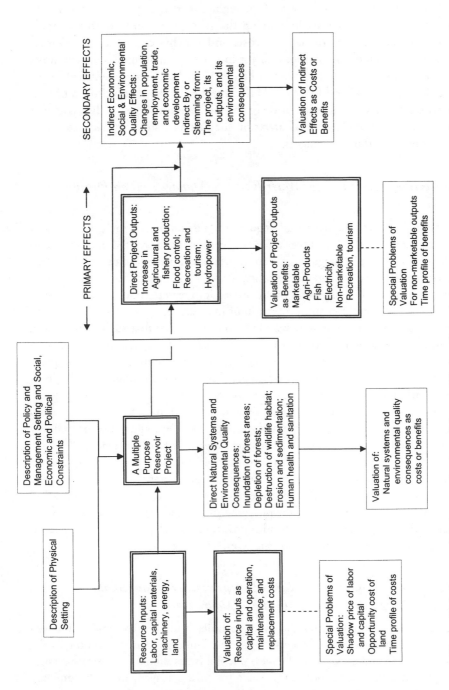

Figure 13.1. A comprehensive examination of the possible benefits and costs of a hypothetical development project (Hufschmidt et al. 1993)

Although the tools and methodologies for calculating environmental costs and benefits are admittedly imperfect, environmental impact assessments do provide a means of at least identifying the major costs and benefits in most situations. Calculations of detailed costs and benefits can be a second-order priority. An example of an approach for integrating environmental, economic, and social assessments is provided in Figure 13.1. The factors identified in the double-lined boxes (modified from Hufschmidt et al. 1993) constitute a narrow benefit-cost analysis, while inclusion of the factors in the boxes with single lines incorporates the whole array of effects on the natural system, the receptors, and the economy within the analysis.

Institutional Structures for Water Resource Management on Drainage-Basin Scale

Sustainable water resources also require an institutional structure for water management capable of integrating the various water-related concerns and issues. Howe (1995) suggested an appropriate institutional framework should ensure coordinated management of surface water and groundwater and of water quantity and quality, provision of incentives for greater economic and physical efficiencies in water use, and protection of instream flow values and other public values related to water systems. He further suggested that such a framework should (1) be capable of coordinating water plans and management procedures with other functional agencies (e.g., agriculture, environment, economic planning, industry); (2) consider a wide range of alternative solutions to water problems, including nonstructural measures and economic instruments (e.g., pricing, taxes, subsidies); (3) be capable of separating planning and evaluation from construction and management functions (e.g., agencies responsible for building dams should not necessarily be responsible for watershed management); (4) have multidisciplinary expertise to carry out multiple-objective planning and evaluation; (5) observe the "subsidiary principle" in assigning responsibilities to agencies at the lowest level consistent with the scale of the water issue; (6) include all stakeholders from the onset of the planning phase; and (7) incorporate a reward system that stimulates creativity and innovation, as well as emphasizing lessons learned through post-construction analyses.

Developing Legislation to Address Environmentally Sustainable Management and Use of Freshwater Resources

Another requirement for using these various available tools and techniques is development and enforcement of relevant laws. Based on experience around the world, laws meant to address water and environmental issues should incorporate a range of relevant elements, including (1) water resource management at the drainage basin and groundwater aquifer level, (2) incorporation of sustainable water management and use principles, (3) integrated management of water and environmental issues, (4) prevention of fragmentation of water allocation and use decisions among multiple government departments, (5) integrated economic and environmental policy and project appraisals, (6) establishment of relevant water management institutions, and (7) establishment of enforceable incentives for environmentally sustainable management and use of water resources. Developing and enforcing laws incorporating such elements also provides an indication of a government's committment to achieve sustainable water resources (Smith and Rast 1998).

Conflict Resolution

Conflict resolution, or dispute mediation, has become a more widely understood and practiced profession in many locations over the last several decades. In 1998, for example, the U.S. Congress established the U.S. Institute for Environmental Conflict Resolution at the Morris K. Udall Foundation in Tucson, Arizona, to assist it to resolve environmental, public land and natural resources disputes. The establishing legislation directed the Institute to develop a national roster of environmental conflict resolution and consensus building professionals to provide needed expertise in given situations, reflecting the fact that the use of alternative dispute resolution (ADR) in the environmental and public policy arena has grown markedly over the last two decades. ADR techniques range from conflict prevention (e.g., consensus building) and facilitation of public policy dialogues, to assisted negotiations and mediation to resolve specific disputes. The number of environmental conflict resolution practitioners in the United States and elsewhere has grown as this issue has gained prominence, with professionals from a variety of disciplines becoming attracted to its advantages and opportunities.

Other conflict-resolution centers and institutes have subsequently been established in other states. The Florida Conflict Resolution Consortium at Florida State University, for example, has successfully used ADR in land-use and environmental disputes. A partnership between the New York School of Industrial and Labor Relations at Cornell University and the Foundation for the Prevention and Early Resolution of Conflict resulted in the development of an Internet-based, distance-learning program on conflict resolution. As such centers become more widely established in the United States and elsewhere, they will likely be utilized with increasing frequency to mediate regional water disputes.

Sharing Environmental and Economic Benefits

The principles, tools, and techniques discussed in this chapter generally apply equally well at local, national, and international levels (Fig. 13.2). Their consideration at the international level, however, involves integration of national developmental and environmental concerns of multiple riparian countries in a drainage basin. This goal is most easily achieved between riparian countries characterized by a history of amiable relations, similar cultural values, and comparable economic standards. It is obviously more difficult between riparian countries with a history of strained relations, differing or conflicting economic goals and cultural values. In both situations, however, developing and implementing binding international agreements, clearly outlining the commitments and obligations of all involved riparian governments, can be of major value in achieving environmentally sustainable freshwater resources (Rast 1996). The previously described cost-benefit analyses and environmental impact assessments can assist riparian governments in deciding how to equitably share the environmental and economic costs and benefits of sustainable water resources. Diplomacy is also a necessary ingredient in such activities, experience suggesting that a major factor in such situations is the commitment of all the riparian governments involved in such agreements. The experience with a range of international agreements and instruments is discussed further in the following sections.

Regional Instruments

Although this chapter focuses on international agreements and instruments, it is instructive to touch briefly on regional water resources agreements. The regional agreements in effect around the world range from U.S. interstate compacts to regional groupings involving multiple administrative and governmental entities. Most can be characterized as political agreements between two or more governmental entities meant to achieve specific objectives in the most expeditious manner. For purposes of illustration, this section focuses on a few examples that address regional water issues and goals.

Chesapeake Bay Commission

One major cooperative regional effort in the United States focuses on Chesapeake Bay, on its eastern coast. The quality of the bay has decreased over time, and its indigenous biological communities impacted, because of increasing pollutant loads entering the bay, especially nutrients from point (municipal wastewater effluents) and nonpoint (agricultural and urban runoff) sources in its drainage basin. Following a 1978 study by the joint Maryland-Virginia Chesapeake Bay Legislative Advisory Commission, the Chesapeake Bay Commission was established in 1980 to assist the two riparian states to cooperatively manage the bay. It was established as a bi-state commission primarily because (1) it did not involve any federal statutory limitations, (2) it highlighted state responsibility for cleaning up the bay, and (3) it strengthened interstate policy linkages. It also focused

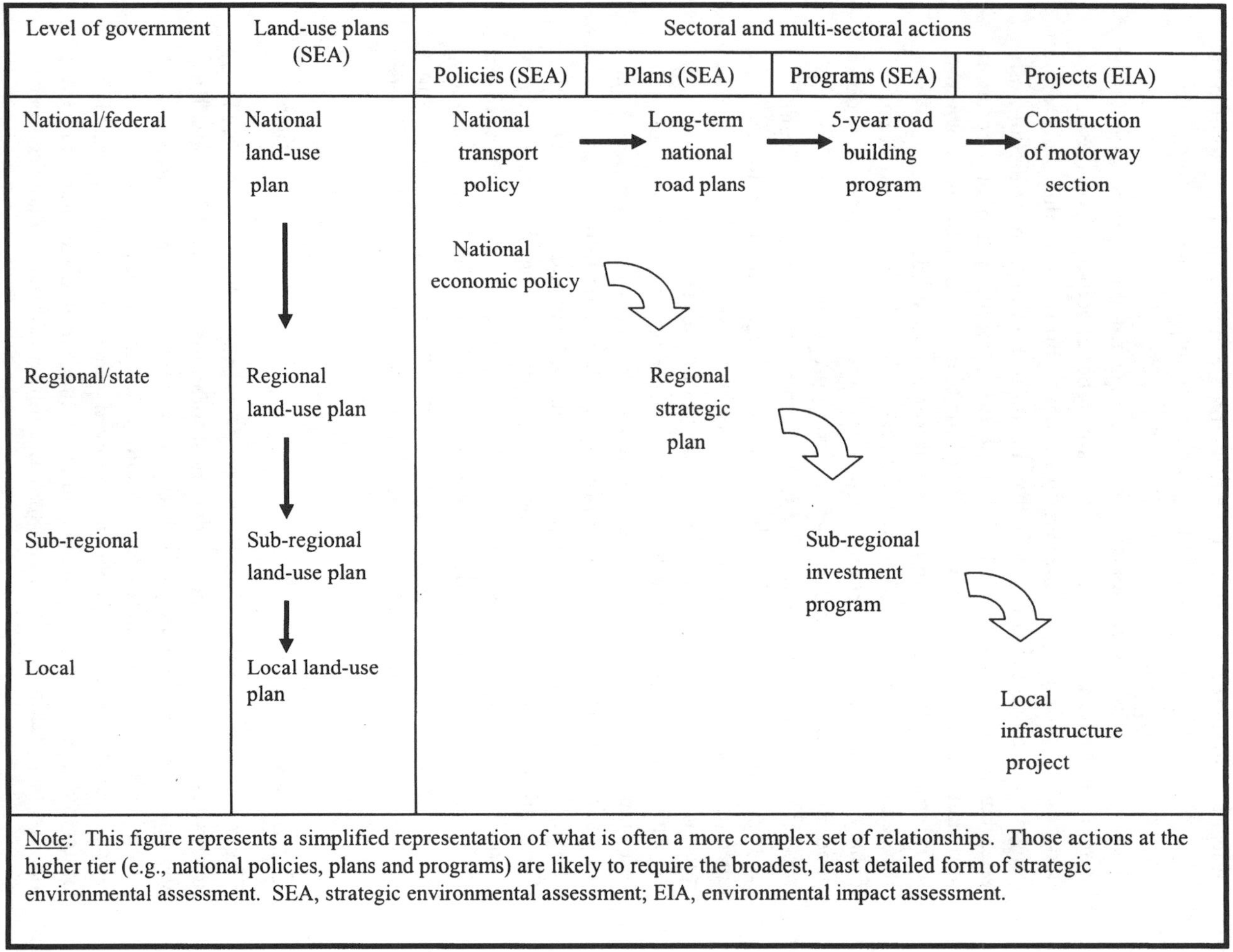

Level of government	Land-use plans (SEA)	Sectoral and multi-sectoral actions			
		Policies (SEA)	Plans (SEA)	Programs (SEA)	Projects (EIA)
National/federal	National land-use plan	National transport policy National economic policy	Long-term national road plans	5-year road building program	Construction of motorway section
Regional/state	Regional land-use plan		Regional strategic plan		
Sub-regional	Sub-regional land-use plan			Sub-regional investment program	
Local	Local land-use plan				Local infrastructure project

Note: This figure represents a simplified representation of what is often a more complex set of relationships. Those actions at the higher tier (e.g., national policies, plans and programs) are likely to require the broadest, least detailed form of strategic environmental assessment. SEA, strategic environmental assessment; EIA, environmental impact assessment.

Figure 13.2. Sequence of actions and assessments within a tiered planning system (modified from Smith and Rast 1998)

legislative attention on bay problems identified by the states' executive agencies by providing timely policy advice to state legislatures.

The Commission's tasks included (1) assisting the legislatures to evaluate and respond to mutual bay-related concerns, (2) promoting intergovernmental cooperation and coordination for resource planning, (3) promoting uniformity of legislation where appropriate, (4) enhancing the function and powers of existing offices and agencies, and (5) recommending improvements in the management of the bay's resources.

The Commission's membership was subsequently increased to include the state of Pennsylvania. It has undertaken a number of activities over the last two decades, including bay-wide environmental protection and restoration programs. It promoted policy initiatives in the areas of nutrient reduction, fisheries management, toxics remediation, pollution prevention, habitat restoration, and land management. During the 1980s, the Commission was instrumental in working with state agencies and federal partners to establish a bay-wide ban on threatened striped-bass stocks, which facilitated the subsequent recovery of this fishery. It was involved in a coordinated effort to ban the use of phosphate detergents in the drainage basin and was a strong proponent of key land-use laws protecting the bay's shorelines. The Commission also has sponsored legislation in the various riparian counties for nutrient management plans for livestock operations, maintenance of riparian forest buffers, prevention of non-indigenous aquatic species, and reduction of sediment and erosion impacts.

Although the Chesapeake Bay Commission represents a good example of interstate cooperation in the pursuit of ecosystem management, it nevertheless suffers from the lack of a comprehensive ecosystem approach to environmentally sustainable economic development of Chesapeake Bay and its drainage basin. Consequently, after two decades the bay still suffers in varying degrees from virtually all the water-related problems that facilitated its establishment in the first place. Lack of a comprehensive ecosystem approach will likely continue to hinder timely achievement of this goal, although future cooperative efforts may ultimately bring some or all of the problems of the bay and its drainage basin under control.

Colorado River Compact

There are many interstate river-basin compacts in the United States, involving numerous river basins. One of the most prominent is the Colorado River Compact, which addresses the allocation of the river between its riparian states as well as its role as an international resource. It was meant to address common water-related concerns between the involved states, and between the United States and Mexico, in an expeditious manner. Since its implementation in 1922, the compact has been revised and updated numerous times to address specific

Table 13.1. Summary of Colorado River Compact components

Name of component	Relevant actions
Colorado River Compact (1922)	Divided Colorado River into Upper and Lower Basins in allocating its water resources
Boulder Canyon Project Act (1928)	Authorized construction of Hoover Dam and All-American Canal to Imperial Valley in California, effectively apportioning Lower Basin states' allocation under 1922 Colorado River Compact
Rio Grande Compact (1938)	Apportioned waters of the Rio Grande Basin between Colorado, New Mexico, and Texas
Mexico Treaty (1944)	Allocated waters of certain international rivers, including Colorado River
Upper Colorado River Compact (1948)	Apportioned the waters of the Colorado River among the Upper Basin states available to them under 1922 Colorado River Compact
Colorado River Storage Project Act (1956)	Authorized construction of the Glen Canyon, Flaming Gorge, Aspinall Units (Curecanti), and Navajo dams on Colorado River
Arizona vs. California 373 U.S. 546 (1963)	Arizona brought suit in U.S. Supreme Court to resolve dispute with California over rights to use water apportionment of Lower Basin states; the Court held that by passing the Boulder Canyon Project Act the Congress had apportioned the main stem of Colorado River
Colorado River Basin Project Act (1968)	Authorized Central Arizona Project
Coordinated Long Range Operating Criteria— Colorado River Reservoir (1970)	Promulgated criteria to control coordinated long-range operation of storage reservoirs and projects in the Colorado River Basin
Colorado River Basin Salinity Control Act (1974)	Committed the United States to deliver water containing no more than 115 parts per million of salt more than the salt content of water diverted to All-American Canal at Imperial Dam, California, to Mexico from Colorado River

concerns considered urgent at the time its various components were implemented. Focusing on water apportionments and allocations, the primary components of the Colorado River Compact are summarized in Table 13.1.

The Colorado River compacts, acts, and criteria address various water apportionment, allocation, and quality problems. As with virtually all interstate compacts in the United States, however, the Colorado River Compact does not employ an ecosystem approach directed to sustainable management and use of the waters of the Colorado River. This is doubtless due partly to the fact that the notion of an ecosystem approach for sustainable environmental management was unknown when most of these components were developed. Thus, although these various components were meant to alleviate specific problems common to two or more entities using Colorado River waters, it nevertheless represents a piecemeal approach, unable to ensure environmentally sustainable water use as evidenced by continuing water-quantity and quality problems throughout the Colorado River drainage basin.

International Agreements

Given that water resources are likely to be the most pressing environmental concern of the twenty-first century, the problems associated with environmentally sustainable water resources are exacerbated in the case of transboundary water systems. Transboundary waters comprise a major regional and global water resource. It is estimated, for example, that there are 261 international rivers around the world, which cover about 45 percent of the Earth's land surface (Wolf et al. 1999).

Ironically, there are currently a myriad of multilateral environmental treaties in effect around the world. The United Nations Environment Programme (UNEP 1997) developed an index of environmental treaties as of December 31, 1995. This index identified 216 treaties covering a range of environmental issues, including conservation of nature and natural resources; biological diversity; trade in endangered species; plant protection; animal protection; marine living resources; marine pollution; exploration and exploitation of the sea; law of the sea; international fresh waters; mountain environment; drought and desertification; forestry; Antarctica; outer space; natural and cultural heritage; air pollution; ozone layer; climate change; energy; chemicals; transboundary movement of hazardous wastes; nuclear material and safety; environment impact assessment; industrial accidents; working environment; military activities and the environment; general regional environmental protection; and liability and compensation.

As with interstate compacts and regional agreements, however, there are few examples of international treaties addressing environmentally sustainable water resources. The environmental treaties implemented over the last two decades nevertheless offer the best examples of attempts to incorporate an ecosystem approach to management of water resources for their sustainable use. Interestingly, relevant elements for the environmental management of the waters of large international river basins for their sustainable use were previously identified and promulgated by the UNEP in 1986, fully six years before the same notion was incorporated into Agenda 21 as an essential component of sustainable development (Laszlo et al 1988; United Nations 1992; also see Chap. 1). The following sections provide examples of international agreements addressing transboundary water resources shared by both developed and developing countries.

Rio Grande

The Rio Grande (also known as the Rio Bravo in Mexico) flows approximately 3,000 kilometers from its headwaters in the state of Colorado in the United States to the Gulf of Mexico. Enroute to the Gulf, the river receives surface water runoff from, and experiences water withdrawals from, three U.S. states and five Mexican states. It also forms the international boundary between the United States and Mexico along its lower 2,053 kilometer-stretch. Approximately half of its 862,000-square-kilometer drainage basin consists of closed-basin areas that contribute little or no water to the river's flow. However, there are numerous tributary streams and rivers along its international reach between Texas and Mexico that contribute surface water runoff, with the Conchos, Pecos, San Diego, San Rodrigo, Salado, and San Juan Rivers being the most important. Overall, the two countries each contribute approximately half of the river's flow along its international stretch, which also contains two major international reservoirs.

Other relevant drainage-basin characteristics include the international stretch's location in a highly arid region, the utilization of approximately 80 percent of the river's water supply for agriculture, and the environmental impacts of seven pairs of twin cities and numerous small communities along the Texas-Mexico border (Brown and Mumme 2000). The Convention of 1906 between the United States and Mexico allocated the waters of the Rio Grande above Fort Quitman, Texas, for the 143-kilometer (89-mile) international reach of the river through the El Paso (Texas)–Juarez (Mexico) valley. The convention is managed by the International Boundary Commission (later changed to the International Boundary and Water Commission), previously established by the Convention of 1889 between the two countries.

The subsequent Treaty of 1944 ("Utilization of Waters of the Colorado and Tijuana Rivers and of the Rio Grande") allocated the waters of the Rio Grande from Fort Quitman, Texas, to the Gulf of Mexico, thereby being the primary agreement for water allocation in the international stretch of the river. It is noted that the goals of the subsequently signed North American Free Trade Agreement provide elements that must be considered in pursuit of the environmental management of the Rio Grande for its sustainable use.

The river has several characteristics that must be considered in evaluating the value of the 1944 Treaty. The first is the differing flow regime of the Rio Grande

River upstream and downstream of the Rio Conchos, which provides the bulk of the Mexican water allocation under the treaty. The river flow upstream of the Rio Conchos is dominated by melting snow in the Rocky Mountains of Colorado in the United States, with the bulk of the water being allocated to urban and agricultural water use in New Mexico and to agricultural water use in Mexico. In contrast, the river flow downstream of the Rio Conchos is dominated by late summer rains, when they occur, of the North American monsoon.

A second factor complicating the environmentally sustainable management and use of the Rio Grande is the numerous water rights and uses that have been parceled out within a myriad of water rights, contracts, reclamation projects, interstate compacts, and binational treaties. These water rights and uses have promoted localized planning over drainage-basin-scale management for sustainable use. They also tend to focus management attention on historic water allocations rather than on future priorities. A tradition of multistakeholder problem-solving across segments, sectors, and borders also has not developed along the border, further hindering the environmentally sustainable management and use of the Rio Grande.

The 1944 Treaty was meant primarily to allocate the waters of the international portion of the Rio Grande in an equitable manner between the United States and Mexico. It is generally lacking in regard to environmental sustainability and the use of an ecosystem approach to manage it. This is evident in the increasing sensitivities between the two countries regarding Mexico's current water debt of approximately 1.5 million acre-feet owed to the United States under the 1944 Treaty. As noted in the New York Times in the May 24, 2002, issue, "What started as a local dispute along the Rio Grande has turned into an international imbroglio, a question of national security for Mexico and a matter of survival for several million Texans and Mexicans. The crisis is shocking people on both sides of the border into seeing that there may be limits to growth." This surprisingly insightful observation highlights the urgent need for environmental management of the water of the Rio Grande as a fundamental requirement for its sustainable use. Indeed, it is difficult to see how this important international river can survive without increased attention being paid to environmental management.

Zambezi River

The Zambezi River and its tributaries comprise the fourth-largest river basin in Africa, draining almost its entire south-central region (Angola, Botswana, Malawi, Mozambique, Tanzania, Zambia, Zimbabwe). It flows east about 3,000 kilometers from its source on the Central African Plateau to the Indian Ocean. With a drainage basin area of about 1.3 million square kilometers, it encompasses territories of eight countries, with a basin population of about 20 million people.

The river's historically significant lower course provided a trade artery for Arabs to the African interior in the tenth century and for the Portuguese from the sixteenth century (Laszlo et al. 1988).

The economic and social development of the Zambezi River Basin over past decades has tended to deplete its natural resources and increase its environmental stresses. The drainage basin is largely rural in character, with its land dominated by agricultural activities. It suffers from a number of environmental problems, including the physical planning to coordinate its development within its available resources being largely confined to the basin's major cities. Even this planning has been limited to infrastructure concerns, thereby not addressing the haphazard and environmentally unsustainable developmental patterns characterizing the drainage basin.

It is noted that the Zambezi River Basin is the first basin in which UNEP assisted riparian governments to apply UNEP's program for the environmentally sound management of inland waters (EMINWA). UNEP's focus was on the transboundary Zambezi River water system, emphasizing the goal of sustainable water use as a guiding principle (Laszlo 1988). As outlined by Laszlo et al. (1988) and Smith and Rast (1998), the EMINWA process involves a two-step program of diagnosis and action. The EMINWA process typically comprises an initial diagnostic study of the present state of the ecology and the environmental management of a river basin, including the environmental, scientific, technical, social, economic, institutional, legal, and political factors affecting these issues. The diagnostic study is followed by development and implementation of a basinwide action plan designed to address problems identified in the diagnostic phase and to facilitate achievement of environmentally sustainable use of transboundary water systems.

During 1985–1987 the Zambezi Working Group of Experts identified the following major problems to be addressed through selected activities within the Zambezi Action Plan (ZACPLAN) (UNEP 1987a; Laszlo et al. 1988), as follows:

- Inadequate monitoring and exchange of information regarding climate, water quantity and quality, and pollution control
- Soil erosion, inadequate soil and water conservation, and inadequate flood plain management
- Deforestation due to population growth and pressure on land resources
- Lack of adequate drinking-water supply and proper sanitation facilities
- Insufficient community participation in planning, construction, and maintenance of water supply and sanitation systems, particularly on the part of women as "end users" of water
- Inadequate health education for the public, especially for women
- Inadequate land use and river basin planning
- Inadequate human resources development
- Inadequate coordination and consultation at the national and river basin levels

- Degradation of the natural resources base
- Degradation of flora and fauna
- Inadequate information on environmental impacts of water resources and related development projects (e.g., hydropower, irrigation)
- Inadequate dissemination of information to the public
- Inadequate protection of wetlands.

With the objective of overcoming these problems and promoting environmentally sound management and use of the basin's water resources, the riparian countries subsequently developed a basinwide action plan called ZACPLAN. Comprising a series of short-term (Category I) and long-term (Category II) activities directed to alleviating the above-noted problems, ZACPLAN was approved by the riparian governments in May 1987 (UNEP 1987b), with its activities directed to the main areas of environmental assessment, management, and legislation (Table 13.2).

Table 13.2. Overview of components of ZACPLAN

Category of project	Category project components
Category I	Up-to-date compilation of all completed, ongoing, and planned development projects related to ZACPLAN
	Up-to-date compilation of national and international laws related to utilization and protection of water and the environment
	Survey of national capabilities and means to respond to environmental problems
	Development/strengthening of national research laboratories and institutions to develop water-related environmental research and training policies and priorities
	Basinwide, unified monitoring system related to water quality and quantity
	Development of integrated water management plan for Zambezi River Basin, based on Category I sub-basin plans
	Promotion campaigns to persuade communities, schools, and individuals to provide themselves with sufficient drinking water of acceptable quality, good sanitary facilities, soil conservation measures, and forest protection and fuel-wood plantations
	Development of unified water engineering planning and design criteria/manuals for nonpiped and piped drinking-water supply and sanitation schemes

Category of project	Category project components
Category II	Basinwide harmonization of methodologies on environmentally sound water resources management and their application in water-related decision making
	Development and strengthening of riparian abilities to prepare environmental impact analysis of major economic development projects and plans
	Increased technical and financial support for environmentally sound management practices within ongoing economic development activities for demonstration effects
	Implementation of energy projects in close cooperation with South African Development Coordination Conference (SADCC) Energy Sector
	Adoption of watershed management guidelines based on introducing environmental planning concepts in catchment area management
	Prevention and control of waterborne diseases in Zambezi River Basin
	Limnological studies of Lake Malawi (formerly Lake Nyasa), Lake Kariba, Lake Cabora Bassa, and Lake Chilwa, focusing on fisheries resources
	Application of ecologically sound elements into vector control programs in Zambezi River Basin
	Studies of interbasin water transfer possibilities and impacts
	Establishment of living resource conservation programs within the river basin
	Research on the eradication and prevention of the spread of harmful flora

Source: UNEP 1987b.

In spite of the comprehensive nature of ZACPLAN and the benefits its implementation would provide the riparian countries and their inhabitants, progress in its implementation has been disappointedly slow. Although most of the Category I program elements have been addressed to varying degrees, there has been little implementation of the more comprehensive Category II activities. This situation exists not because of fundamental faults in the components of ZACPLAN, however, but rather because of inadequate financial and human resources in the riparian countries for implementing its many complementary elements. It is noted that SADCC has been involved in implementing ZACPLAN since its development. However, because its members comprise essentially the same riparian countries as those that developed ZACPLAN in the first place, it suffers from the same constraints. Ideally, the riparian countries of the Zambezi River Basin will eventually acquire the necessary financial and human resources needed to implement all Category I and II activities comprising ZACPLAN, thereby demonstrating its soundness in managing the water resources of the basin for their sustainable use and within the context of sustainable economic development.

Lake Chad

Lake Chad is located in the arid zone of north-central Africa. It is a terminal lake within a closed lake basin, thereby having no outlets to the sea. The Lake Chad drainage basin covers approximately 2.5 million square kilometers, including parts of Cameroon, Chad, Niger, Nigeria, and the Central African Republic. The basin population in 1987 was approximately 8.5 million persons, and it was estimated the population would reach 11.5 million persons by the year 2000. The major socioeconomic activities in the Lake Chad basin are primarily traditional agriculture, animal husbandry, and fishing. Major urban centers in the drainage basin in 1989 were N'Djamena, Chad (population of 0.5 million), Maiduguri, Nigeria (population of 0.6 million), and Maroua, Cameroon (population of 0.1 million).

The region is arid in nature, with continuing, serious water shortages. The back-to-back droughts of the 1970s and 1980s produced dramatic changes in the environmental conditions of Lake Chad. The decline of agriculture, livestock, and fisheries also has had significant socioeconomic impacts on the drainage basin inhabitants. In fact, the first African Ministerial Conference on the Environment, held in Cairo in December 1985, decided to support the Lake Chad Basin Commission for the integrated development of the Lake Chad Basin as one of the "priority subregional activities."

A diagnostic study of the Lake Chad drainage basin was conducted in 1990, identifying significant water-related environmental problems, including (1) erosion of formerly productive lands, (2) excessive withdrawal of groundwater resources, (3) loss of wildlife species, and (4) forced migration of humans during periods of famine and drought. Based on these identified problems, the riparian countries proposed projects dealing with the following issues relevant to the goal of sustainable water resources in the Lake Chad drainage basin (UNEP 1990):

• Prevention of soil erosion, and improvement of soil fertility, infiltration, and water-holding capacity
• Improvement of water conservation, promotion of equitable water use, and prevention of water-quality degradation

- Maintenance of vegetative cover, improvement of nutritive value of pasture-lands, restoration of denuded landscapes, balancing regeneration of wood biomass with harvest, and sustained yield management for hardwoods
- Improvement of protection and maintenance of biodiversity, collection, and testing of cultivars for farmers and agroforestry, and preservation of unique ecosystems and species of special concern
- Reorganization and enhancement of human energies and productivity, to provide individuals and communities with more time and income to participate in natural resource management activities
- Reorganization of government and international assistance, to assign high priority to the long-term conservation of natural resources in development projects.

These major areas of concern are discussed in greater detail in the Lake Chad diagnostic study (UNEP 1990). Based on the study, the riparian countries agreed on a master plan to address these concerns within the context of sustainable water use within the Lake Chad drainage basin, comprising approximately thirty-six projects (Table 13.3) relating to water resources, agriculture, forestry, biodiversity management, livestock, and fishery development (UNEP 1991).

Table 13.3. Components of Lake Chad Action Plan

Name of project	Project components
Lake Chad multipurpose project	Technical review of all aspects of Lake Chad diagnostic study, to develop capacity for environmentally sound planning, development, and management of lake region
Upper Ubangi-Chari water transfer investigations	Examination of feasibility of augmenting water resources by long-range water transfer from Upper Ubangi River
Chari/Logone multipurpose project	Technical review of all aspects of Lower Chari and floodplains of Logone sub-basins, which contribute over 95 percent of water inflow to Lake Chad
Komadougou-Yobe multipurpose project	Formulation of recommendations for environmentally sound, conjunctive use of surface and groundwater resources of Komadougou-Yobe sub-basins
Borno Drainages multi-purpose project	Technical design of regional water supply system based on conjunctive utilization of local surface and groundwater resources
Mayo Kebbi investigations	Establish stage-discharge relationship for Mayo Kebbi floodwaters, and development of sub-basin water resources management plan

(continues)

Table 13.3. Continued

Name of project	Project components
Groundwater investigations	Determination of aquifer characteristics for lower geographical formations in drainage basin
Improvement of meteorological and hydrological network stations	Review of meteorological and hydrologic networks and development of basinwide, unified hydrometeorological information system
Food security preparedness scheme	Combined irrigated agriculture and food processing, preservation, and storage needs throughout drainage basin, to address food shortages
Environmental and socioeconomic assessment of water projects	Assessment of water projects to ensure they contribute to environmentally sustainable economic and social development in drainage basin
Comparative watershed management and research program	Research, monitoring, and management to improve baseline data within drainage basin
Basinwide library	Centralized bank of information on Lake Chad drainage basin
Waza National Park environmental review	Examination of water-related environmental impacts on ecosystem resources of Waza National Park
Hadejia-Nguru wetlands project	Long-term water management plans for Kano and Borno states
Sambissa Wetlands project	Determination of waterflow needs, and establishment of rights and boundaries for protected areas
International fisheries research and monitoring center	Research, monitoring and conservation efforts to reestablish sustained yield fisheries in drainage basin
Development and harmonization of natural resources management codes	Review national rules and regulations with transboundary environmental impacts
Biosphere reserve at Lake Fitri	Establish multiple-resource use zone around Lake Fitri wetlands
Biosphere reserve at Lake Lere	Establish multiple-resource use zone around Lake Lere wetlands
Revegetation of northern diagnostic basin	Facilitate revegetation, dune stabilization, pasture improvements, and erosion control
Research project for vegetation recovery in Lake Chad drainage basin	Facilitate return of vegetative cover, biomass productivity and harvestable wood, shrub, and grass products
Basin-wide environmental education program	Promote environmental awareness in primary and secondary school curricula

Name of project	Project components
Early warning systems	Improve dissemination of information about rainfall and flood patterns, expected droughts, crop pests, livestock disease, food insecurity, and human epidemics in the drainage basin
Basinwide microwave communications	Create operational microwave transmission links between riparian countries
Basinwide transportation network	Improve roads and bridges to facilitate basinwide social and economic integration and reduce soil erosion
Inventory and protection of endangered fauna	Inventory and design of protective measures for endangered faunal species

Source: UNEP 1991.

A major constraint to timely implementation of this comprehensive master plan is one that continues to plague developing riparian countries; namely inadequate financial and human resources. Further, the intention of the riparian countries was that the Lake Chad Basin Commission would oversee implementation of the master plan. Unfortunately, the capabilities of the Commission have fallen far short of its mandate, largely because of the same reasons that constrain the ability of the riparian countries to implement the master plan. As stated in the diagnostic study (UNEP 1990), "Evidence of the Commission's presence is virtually invisible in the conventional basin apart from some scattered infrastructure." Although some efforts have been made by donor and developmental organizations in recent years to strengthen the institutional framework and capabilities of the Lake Chad Basin Commission, including development of a mathematical model for the basin's surface water resources, the water-related problems of the Lake Chad drainage basin have continued to worsen over time, attesting to the urgent need to fund and implement the Lake Chad Master Plan. A recently outlined project on the integrated management of Lake Chad, funded by the Global Environment Facility, may work to assist the Lake Chad Basin Commission and the Lake Chad riparian countries to focus more effectively on the environmentally sustainable management and use of Lake Chad and its water-related resources.

Mediterranean Regional Seas Programme

Environmental protection has proved to be a unifying issue in regard to sustainable use of the Mediterranean Sea, particularly within the concept of UNEP's Regional Seas Programme. First launched in 1974 to tie coastal nations (i.e., Albania, Algeria, Bosnia and Herzegovina, Croatia, Cyprus, Egypt, France, Greece, Israel, Italy, Lebanon, Libya, Malta, Monaco, Morocco, Slovenia, Spain, Syria, Tunisia, Turkey, and the European Union) together in a common commitment to mitigate degradation of the world's coastal areas, inland waters, and the open oceans, thirteen regional conventions and action plans have been established under the Regional Seas Programme. Four similar agreements have been established among developed countries, though not as part of UNEP-mediated programs.

Although international in scope, regional seas conventions provide a legal framework for regional action plans directed to sustainable development, expressing the legal commitment and political will of the involved riparian countries to tackle common environmental problems. The UNEP Regional Seas Programme is a regional approach primarily because every regional sea has its own environmental problems and needs. Each of the regional seas programs represents a patchwork of different cultures and economic structures as well as contrasting physical environments. Thus, regional conventions recognizing these differences in proposing solutions to environmental problems are more likely than global conventions to attract the full interest and commitment of the governments signing it.

Similar in concept to the UNEP EMINWA process (Laszlo et al. 1988), regional seas programs typically comprise (1) an action plan for cooperation on the management, protection, rehabilitation, monitoring, and research of coastal and marine resources; (2) an intergovernmental agreement for a framework convention, embodying general obligations of the riparian countries; and (3) detailed protocols outlining specific steps to address regional environmental problems (e.g., oil spills, pollution from land-based sources, habitat conservation). The primary elements of the action plans are identified in Table 13.4.

The Mediterranean Regional Seas Programme arose from the Barcelona Convention for the Mediterranean, signed by the riparian countries in 1976. It was subsequently revised in 1995 as part of the restructuring of the Mediterranean Action Plan. The Mediterranean Sea, a virtually enclosed miniature ocean occasionally referred to as "the cradle of civilization," has been the well-beaten crossroads of European, Asian, and African civilizations for many centuries. Major concern over the quality and sustainability of the Mediterranean Sea arose during the 1960s, when pollution from land-based sources, as well as oil from heavy tanker traffic and ill-managed coastal development, were identified as the most significant problems.

Governments of the Mediterranean states and the European community subsequently adopted the Mediterranean Action Plan to address these problems in 1975, even before the above-noted Barcelona Convention was convened. Interagency cooperation in implementing the plan began with development of the pollution monitoring and assessment program (MEDPOL) in the mid-1970s.

Table 13.4. Primary elements of UNEP regional seas action plans

Type of activity	Activity components
Environmental assessment	Monitoring and assessment activities to provide a scientific basis for setting regional priorities and policies, including identification of most urgent environmental problems
Environmental management	Activities to address existing environmental problems and prevent new ones
Environmental legislation	Umbrella convention to provide legal framework for cooperative regional and national action, and elaborated by specific technical protocols
Institutional arrangements	Agreement by riparian governments on an organization to function as permanent or interim secretariat for implementation of action plan
Financial arrangements	UNEP and selected United Nations and other organizations to provide catalytic funding ("seed money") in early stages of regional programs, with the expectation the riparian governments will progressively assume full financial responsibility for programs

Involving a range of international agencies and government-appointed and regional institution scientists, the MEDPOL program quickly became a model of scientific cooperation. In cooperation with the Food and Agriculture Organization; United Nations Educational, Scientific, and Cultural Organization; International Maritime Organization; World Health Organization; International Atomic Energy Agency; United Nations Industrial Development Organization; Economic Commission for Europe; and the General Fisheries Council for the Mediterranean, it implemented eleven projects during its five-year first stage, focusing on initial assessments of the environmental conditions of the Mediterranean Sea. The projects included baseline studies and monitoring of oil and petroleum hydrocarbons in marine waters; baseline studies and monitoring of metals, DDT, PCBs, and other chlorinated hydrocarbons in marine organisms; effects of pollutants on marine organisms, populations, communities and ecosystems; problems of coastal transport of pollutants; coastal water quality control; biogeochemical studies of selected pollutants in the open waters of the Mediterranean Sea; role of sedimentation in pollution of the Mediterranean Sea; pollution from land-based activities; and intercalibration of analytical techniques.

Since its inception, the Mediterranean Regional Seas Programme has been effective in engaging the riparian governments to protect the coastal environment.

A key element of the program's success has been its focus on cooperation and inclusion. This is a critical element, given that nearly half of the world's population currently lives within 100 kilometers of a coastline (with predictions of increasing proportions in the future), and because rivers flowing into the coastal areas contribute an estimated 80 percent or more of the pollutant load to the oceans. Thus, although the primary focus of the Mediterranean and other regional seas programs is on protection of the quality, habitats, and living resources of the coastal regions for their sustainable use, the bulk of the activities designed to protect these entities actually will be implemented in the river basins that drain into them.

Although some of the other regional seas programs continue to struggle with funding problems and the difficulty of establishing high-priority status for addressing environmental issues in governmental economic development agendas, this regional mechanism demonstrates how countries with diverse backgrounds, objectives, and capabilities can be unified in their desire to protect shared water resources. This mechanism also provides a forum for the countries to bring together often-divided and diverse fields and sectors of interest, including basic science, maritime transport, human health, cultural heritage, energy production, agriculture, fisheries, environmental law, and species conservation, within the context of environmental management for sustainable water use.

The Boundary Waters Treaty of 1909 and the North American Great Lakes

One of the most successful examples of international cooperation in environmental management of a water system for its sustainable use is provided by the North American Great Lakes of North America, a transboundary water system shared by the United States and Canada. The two countries established the Boundary Waters Treaty in 1909 for the purpose of preventing disputes with the use of boundary waters and for assisting them in settling questions involving the rights, obligations, and interests of either country in relation to the other along their common border (IJC 1998). The Treaty also established the International Joint Commission (IJC) as the primary vehicle for assisting the two countries to carry out their binational obligations under the Treaty.

Under the Boundary Waters Treaty, the water quality of the Great Lakes continues to be a primary concern of the International Joint Commission. The Great Lakes contain approximately 23,000 cubic kilometers of water—about one-fifth of the liquid freshwater on the Earth's surface. The Great Lakes drainage basin covers about 767,000 square kilometers, including all or part of the U.S. states of Illinois, Indiana, Michigan, Minnesota, New York, Ohio, Pennsylvania, and Wisconsin, and the Canadian provinces of Ontario and Quebec. The drainage basin contains approximately 33 million people and generates a significant portion of the gross national products of the two countries.

Even though they possess an enormous water volume, the Great Lakes are nevertheless sensitive to a wide range of water pollutants, including effluent from industrial factories and municipal plants, storm-generated water runoff, seepage from waste disposal sites, and atmospheric deposition. Because the outflow from the Great Lakes is relatively small compared to their total water volume, some pollutants entering the lakes are retained in them, becoming more concentrated over time.

The binational concern with Great Lakes water quality is based on IJC studies conducted in the late-1960s, which concluded that the degraded water quality observed in the Great Lakes at that time was not entirely attributable to pollutant loads from point sources. Rather, a significant pollutant load entered the Great Lakes from nonpoint source runoff from agricultural activities, urban drainage, forestry, transportation corridors, and waste disposal operations in its drainage basin (IJC 1969; PLUARG 1978).

To address these findings, the U.S. and Canadian governments signed the Great Lakes Water Quality Agreement in 1972 (IJC 1994), with the purpose being "to restore and maintain the chemical, physical, and biological integrity of the Great Lakes Basin Ecosystem." The Agreement was also perhaps the first international water agreement that specifically identified the benefits of employing an ecosystem approach for the sustainable management and use of aquatic ecosystems, mandating its use to the maximum extent in addressing Great Lakes Basin Ecosystem water-quality issues (PLUARG 1978; IJC 1998).

Originally signed in 1972, the Agreement was revised in 1978 and subsequently amended in 1982 and 1987, identifying additional binational concerns and refining the goals of earlier versions of the Agreement. The Agreement currently contains annexes addressing general and specific water-quality objectives, phosphorus, vessel discharges of solid wastes, oil and hazardous polluting substances, dredging, discharges from onshore and offshore facilities, hazardous polluting and persistent toxic substances, nonpoint-source pollution, contaminated sediments, airborne toxic substances, and contaminated groundwater. It also contains annexes dealing with surveillance and monitoring, contingency plans for spills or accidental discharges of hazardous polluting substances, and research needs.

In facilitating an ecosystem approach to address water-quality degradation in the Great Lakes Basin Ecosystem, the Agreement calls for comprehensive management plans to restore beneficial water uses, including unimpaired use of the ecosystem by all living components. The Agreement required the two governments to develop Remedial Action Plans for forty-seven Areas of Concern exhibiting significant local impairment of beneficial water uses. Further, it mandated lakewide management plans to deal with critical or hazardous pollutants affecting whole lakes or large portions thereof, including identification of key steps for restoring and protecting them. It also called for development of ecosystem objectives to measure the restoration of lake ecosystem integrity (IJC 1994).

The Great Lakes' water-quality problems involve two nations, two Canadian provinces, and eight U.S. states, as well as local, regional, and special-purpose bodies, thereby requiring binational cooperation in addressing these problems. The Agreement also encouraged cooperation, in the form of IJC public consultations, as an essential component of the transboundary decision-making process for the Great Lakes Basin Ecosystem.

International Joint Commission annual reports over the past two decades suggest the water and living resources of the Great Lakes Basin Ecosystem have significantly improved in some areas since the Agreement went into effect, attesting to the utility of using an ecosystem approach to sustainable use of freshwater resources. Thus, the Agreement, implemented within the structure of a transboundary organization such as the International Joint Commission, provides a model to emulate in addressing similar problems. The inhabitants of the Great Lakes Basin and its ecosystems have clearly benefited from this approach. In making this observation, however, it is noted that the United States and Canada have similar cultural and environmental values, as well as significant financial and intellectual resources at their disposal, thereby facilitating their binational actions. Successful transfer of the IJC model and experience to other international water resources will require concerted and cooperative efforts involving governments, the public and the media, as well as adequate technical and financial resources. Such efforts may be difficult for developing nations, which typically have a limited financial and human resource base upon which to draw. Nevertheless, such international organizations as the UNEP, the Ramsar Convention (The Convention on Wetlands of International Importance, especially as Waterfowl Habitat), the International Union for the Conservation of Nature and Natural Resources, World Wildlife Fund, the World Water Forum, and the Global Water Partnership can facilitate discussions and collaborative actions between developing nations sharing a transboundary water system.

Recommendations for the Future

As discussed in the examples provided in this chapter, the concept of integrated environmental management of water resources for their sustainable use is being applied to varying degrees in different hydrologic and geographic settings, with mixed results. In some quarters, even an appropriate definition for this approach is still under discussion. Thus, no unequivocal example of its successful application yet exists. Accordingly, achievement of this goal continues to be both elusive and difficult for most riparian governments. In recognition of this fundamental deficiency, it is crucial that governments, agencies, and other major water stakeholders continue to define and refine this concept as the logical basis for addressing the complex issue of sustainable water resources, whether on the local, regional, or international level.

As noted in the introduction to this chapter, the notion of water security denotes the management and use of shared water resources in the absence of conflict. This goal is difficult to achieve fully without development and implementation of integrated management of water resources for their sustainable use. It also is a cornerstone of natural resource conservation within the context of sustainable development. Unfortunately, most regional and international agreements were developed and implemented prior to recognition of the fact that management of water systems for their sustainable use is fundamental to long-term social and economic development. The notion of an ecosystem approach also is alien to most such agreements, although the United States and Canada provide an example, with the North American Great Lakes Water Quality Agreement, of how this concept can be applied in the pursuit of sustainable development (IJC 1994). The continuing deterioration of the natural environment on a global scale, and the increasing demand for natural resources to service a growing human population, provide considerable impetus for more general and widespread use of this approach.

Ironically, most, if not all, of the tools and techniques for developing management policies and programs for the sustainable use of water resources already exist, including consensus building, drainage-basin-scale diagnostic studies, inclusion of environmental aspects of sustainable water resources in policy formulation, integrated economic, environmental, and social policy and project appraisals, environmental impact assessments and strategic environmental assessments, and mechanisms for conflict resolution. A fundamental problem, however, is that they typically are not applied appropriately or at the proper time in the development of national and regional economic development plans and programs. Accordingly, it is surprising (and disappointing) that the reality that water is precious, finite, and irreplaceable, and that we have *no* substitutes for it, does not provide us with the appropriate impetus for a proactive approach to sustainable use of water resources, whether on the local, regional, or global scale. Continuing experiences around the world provide example after example of the need to ensure environmental management of water resources on a drainage basin or aquifer scale for their sustainable use, both within and between countries. At the same time, sustainable water resources remains a difficult and elusive goal, as demonstrated in the various chapters of this book that highlight the range of scientific, technical, economic, cultural, and political considerations that must be integrated appropriately into relevant programs and plans. Nevertheless, the judicious use of the tools and techniques outlined in this chapter provides readers with the potential for achieving these critical goals, based on realistic principles and guidelines. Development and successful implementation of agreements for various water systems around the world does demonstrate that effective collaboration can and does occur. Given the continuing degradation of our water resources at the global, national, and local level in many places, it would seem that such goals are not merely desirable—they are imperative.

Note: The opinions expressed in this chapter are those of the authors and do not necessarily represent the views or policy of any national, regional, or international organizations or governments identified herein.

References

Barbier, E. G., W. M. Adams, and K. Kimmage. 1993. An economic valuation of wetland benefits. Pp. 191–209 in *The Hadejia-Jama'are Wetlands: Environment, economic and sustainable development of a Shelina Floodplain wetlands*, edited by G. E. Hollis, W. M. Adams, and M. Aminu-Kano. International Union for the Conservation of Nature, Goland, Switzerland.

Brown, C. P., and S. Mumme. 2000. Applied and theoretical aspects of binational watershed councils (Consejos de Cuencas) in the U.S.-Mexico borderlands. *Natural Resources Journal* 40:895–929.

Holland, M. M. 1993. Management of land/inland water ecotones: Needs for regional approaches to achieve sustainable ecological systems. *Hydrobiologia* 251:331–340.

———. 1996. Ensuring sustainability of natural resources: Focus on institutional arrangements. *Canadian Journal of Fisheries and Aquatic Science* 53:432–439.

Howe, C. 1995. *Guidelines for the design of effective water management institutions utilizing economic instruments*. Report presented at Workshop on the Use of Economic Principles for the Integrated Management of Freshwater Resources, Economics Unit, United Nations Environment Programme (UNEP), Nairobi, Kenya, June.

Hufschmidt, M. M., D. E. James, A. D. Meister, B. T. Bower and J. A. Diaxon. 1993. *Environment, natural systems and development: An economic valuation guide*. Baltimore, Md.: Johns Hopkins University Press.

IJC (International Joint Commission). 1969. *Report to the International Joint Commission on the pollution of Lake Erie, Lake Ontario, and the international section of the St. Lawrence River*. International Joint Commission, Washington, D.C.

———. 1994. *Revised Great Lakes Water Quality Agreement of 1978*. International Joint Commission, Washington, D.C.

———. 1998. *The International Joint Commission and the Boundary Waters Treaty of 1909*. International Joint Commission, Washington, D.C.

Laszlo, J. D. 1988. Environmentally sound management of the Zambezi River Basin. *Water Resources Development* 4:80–102.

Laszlo, J. D., G. N. Golubev, and M. Nakayama. 1988. The environmental management of large international basins. The EMINWA Programme of UNEP. *Water Resources Development* 4:103–107.

Platt, R. H. 1995. The 2020 water supply study for metropolitan Boston: The demise of diversion. *Journal of the American Planning Association* 61:185–199.

PLUARG (Pollution from Land Use Activities Reference Group). 1978. *Environmental management strategy for the Great Lakes System*. Final Report of the International Reference Group on Great Lakes Pollution from Land Use Activities, International Joint Commission, Washington, D.C.

Rast, W. 1996. International cooperation for global water problems. Pp. 221–233 in *International Forum on Technology for Water Management in the Twenty-first Century*. November 25–27, 1996, International Environmental Technology Centre, United Nations Environment Programme, Shiga, Japan.

———. 1999. Overview of the status of implementation of the freshwater objectives of Agenda 21 on a regional basis. *Sustainable Development International* 1:53–57.

Serageldin, I. 1995. *Towards sustainable management of water resources.* Technical Report, World Bank, Washington, D.C.

Smith, D., and W. Rast. 1998. Environmentally sustainable management and use of internationally shared freshwater resources. Pp. 277–297 in *Watershed management: Practice, policies, and coordination*, edited by R. J. Reimold. New York: McGraw-Hill.

UNEP (United Nations Environment Programme). 1987a. Diagnostic study on the present state of ecology and the environmental management of the common Zambezi River system. EMINWA Programme. UNEP/IG.78/Background, Paper 1 (Conference of Plenipotentiaries on the Environmental Management of the Common Zambezi River system, Harare, 4–6 May, 1987), UNEP, Nairobi, Kenya.

———. 1987b. *Agreement on the action plan for the environmentally sound management of the common Zambezi River system.* Final Act. UNEP, Nairobi, Kenya.

———. 1990. *The Lake Chad Conventional Basin: A diagnostic study of environmental degradation.* UNEP, Nairobi, Kenya.

———. 1991. *Master plan for the development and environmentally sound management of the natural resources of the Lake Chad Conventional Basin.* UNEP, Nairobi, Kenya.

———. 1993. *Diagnostic study for the development of an action plan for the conservation of the Aral Sea.* Technical Report, Water Branch, UNEP, Nairobi, Kenya.

———. 1997. *Register of international treaties and other agreements in the field of the environment 1996.* United Nations Environment Programme, Nairobi, Kenya.

United Nations. 1992. Agenda 21. *The United Nations Programme of Action from Rio.* Development and Human Rights Section, United Nations, New York.

Wolf, A. T., J. A. Natharius, J. J. Danielson, B. S. Ward, and J. K. Pender. 1999. International river basins of the world. *Water Resources Development* 15:387–427.

World Bank. 1996. *African water resources: Challenges and opportunities for sustainable development.* Technical Report, World Bank, Washington, D.C.

Chapter 14

The State of Freshwater Resources: Conclusions and Recommendations

Marjorie M. Holland, Elizabeth R. Blood, and Lawrence R. Shaffer

Our purpose for this volume was to give an overview of the state of freshwater resource management today and to suggest ways in which practical steps can be taken to understand, conserve, and sustain those resources in ways that are valued by society. For example, several authors have made the point that it is in the best interest of human *and* natural communities to take a holistic approach to viewing freshwater resource issues, and they cite references that note the value of a holistic approach—an approach that was promulgated enthusiastically by countries throughout the world ten years ago at the Rio Summit (United Nations Convention on Environment and Development) as the logical basis for the sustainable use of natural resources, including freshwater, and as a fundamental requirement for uniting the goals of economic development and environmental protection and conservation within a single planning, policy, and management framework. As we look back on the seminal Rio Summit a decade ago and the World Summit on Sustainable Development held in August and September 2002 to review the results of the two Summits, the distressing reality is the relative lack of progress that has been made in achieving these goals. It also highlights the fact that what are most needed now are capable, educated, and motivated leaders to implement them.

Three themes have been emphasized in this book. The first is the need to understand the intrinsic links between human and natural systems that foster sustainable freshwater systems. The second urges adoption of a holistic systems approach to reach solutions to achieve sustainability of freshwater systems. The third urges promotion of action through effective networks. As stated in our Introduction, the editors have adopted an hourglass approach to organize the book's contents, moving from general, "big picture" topics to focus on examples from specific wetland types common in the Mid-South of the United States of America (USA), and back to a more global, "big picture" assemblage of topics.

In synthesizing the main points we make in this volume, first and foremost we would point out that effective leadership is fundamental to implementing these three themes. We call attention to what we call "the five E's" of successful leadership: (1) empathy—issues, perspectives, and values are understood; (2) education—including clear and effective dialog among all parties; (3) empower—suggesting each individual share knowledge, take advantage of opportunities, and participate in all ways possible; (4) enable—inclusion in initiatives, governance, partnerships, and finances; and (5) equity—suggesting collaboration, cooperation, and consensus.

In commenting on the need for leadership, we note that human and natural systems are inextricably linked to one another, and we urge acceptance of and collaboration among the social, economic, institutional, and scientific components of freshwater resource management. Although there are technical and scientific books that address freshwater ecosystems and books that address water resource management, this volume is unique in its recognition of cultural nuances that may hamper current leaders from effective implementation of those points and procedures that society already understands and accepts.

Humans need to recognize that water is precious, finite, and irreplaceable, that life would not be possible without it, and that we have no substitutes for it. In fact, the authors of Chapters 3 and 4 emphasize the relationship between public health issues and water quality. These chapters highlight the critical link between clean water and a high standard of living for both human and other forms of living organisms. Ecosystem sustainability necessitates understanding all significant—and, in particular, all harmful—interactions between hydrologic alterations and contaminant transport and proactively addressing resultant environmental problems on a scientific, technological, and societal level.

Fresh waters are biogeochemical systems, and understanding them requires consideration of the entire ecosystem, whether part of a drainage basin or an aquifer, as well as interactions between ecosystems and their living and nonliving components. Most interstate and international compacts and agreements were not written with a holistic, ecosystem approach in mind but rather were written to handle a specific institutional or political issue. However, an ecosystem approach to the integrated management of freshwater resources is fundamental to ensure their sustainable use. Appropriate institutional frameworks are needed to support integrated ecosystem management.

Our examination of specific wetland types focused on those common to the Mid-South region of the United States. Wetlands are very complicated and important ecosystems that remain relatively underexplored from the standpoints of biodiversity and ecology. Although some background scientific information is available, the relationship between nutrient sources and sinks in various freshwater wetlands, and the interactions between the sources and sinks in relation to the sustainable use of these wetlands, should be further explored and quantified. Still more information is needed. A survey of the chemical ecology (the way chemicals affect the operation of organisms in a field setting) of wetland organisms suggests that this relatively unexplored resource may be able to add future value to biotechnology markets and that the selective factors that have resulted in the elaboration of wetland natural products should not be disregarded as valueless.

Where wetlands were once intentionally drained, many landowners are now restoring them with the construction of "artificial" wetlands as a means of containing and remediating runoff. By implementing successfully constructed wetland remediation practices, agriculture can make significant progress in decreasing the effects of runoff contamination in rivers, streams, lakes, and reservoirs. Increased funding for incentive-based programs that encourage restoration on private lands has proved in some cases to be a successful strategy for increasing scientific understanding of the developing field of wetland restoration.

In those biomes where forests are common, healthy forests (whether upland or bottomland) are critical to sustaining freshwater ecosystems. Where streams flow through contaminated or degraded forests, stream water may pick up heavy metals or other contaminants that can degrade the downstream pond or lake where waters are discharged. If forests have become degraded due to human activities, a successful restoration effort should be designed to restore ecological functions as well as ecological structure, as quickly as possible. Both humans and wetland systems benefit from restoration of ecological services, but effective restoration of all aquatic ecosystems continues to be challenging.

Following the hourglass image, we now scale up again and return to the "big picture." As was suggested in the Introduction (Fig. I.2), sustainable management works best if those involved have a specific context in which to operate. Sustainable water resource management should be place-based, flexible, and operate in a context that makes sense to the participants in that place so that effective implementation can occur. A "place" (e.g., Fig. I.1) could encompass a local area (e.g., a stream bank) or a region (e.g., the Atlanta, Georgia, metropolitan area) or a large river drainage basin (e.g. the Amazon River Basin). A flexible management strategy that can adapt to new situations or challenges is strongly recommended. Consensus, cooperation, and partnerships build trust and opportunity for effective problem solving and decision making. For place-based management to function, it will be essential to develop regional strengths, institutions, and resources. Finding mechanisms to incorporate local knowledge, traditions, and norms will enhance stakeholder and citizen participation and ownership, thereby working to increase effective implementation.

Efforts to incorporate the concepts of sustainability will need to include a strong commitment on the part of all major stakeholders to a sustainability philosophy, including the incorporation of the concepts of sustainability into key institutional mission statements, goals, objectives, and policies (Gandy et al. 2002). The development of a sustainability knowledge base rests upon a foundation of a combination of vision, personal commitment, leadership, and involvement in and understanding of community initiatives (Fig. 14.1).

A multigenerational vision for water resource use is essential. In the state of Georgia, a fifty-year perspective has recently been adopted. This time frame forces Georgia residents to take a multigenerational perspective on sustainability. We urge other groups to use similar long-term time frames when considering sustainable use of freshwater and other natural resources. Water resource management must contain sufficient flexibility to adjust to changes (e.g. policy, climate, markets) occurring at scales outside the boundaries defined by the management plan. It is important to understand the drivers and trajectories of change occurring at higher scales, so that management strategies will be effective for multiple generations.

Civilized societies developed to provide social order as a means to equitably share common resources. To continue to develop, societies will have to consider sharing these resources in ways not imagined ten to twenty years ago. Successful models of collaboration can motivate groups to initiate their own functional partnerships. Often, it takes only one or two leaders to identify a working model, and subsequent models will be developed when they are needed. Leaders need to remember that the process is as important as the goal, and thus various ideas and perspectives that incorporate different viewpoints must also be considered. The final process should incorporate education, regional identity formulation, citizen participation, leadership development, knowledge building, problem-solving strategies, policy formation mechanisms, implementation strategy experimentation, evaluation capabilities, and the ability to look ahead to anticipate future opportunities. It is our firm belief that sustainability of our water and wetland resources is achievable when enabled and empowered citizens are motivated by stewardship and personal responsibility and guided by visionary leadership. There are no limits to the human potential in solving these problems when we partner to share the challenges.

References

Gandy, L., R. Roberson, and T. Foti. 2002. Little Cypress Creek Study: A watershed restoration case study. Pp. 65–74 in *Proceedings of a Conference on Sustainability of Wetlands and Water Resources*, edited by M. M. Holland, M. L. Warren Jr., and J. A. Stanturf. USDA Forest Service, General Technical Report SRS-50.

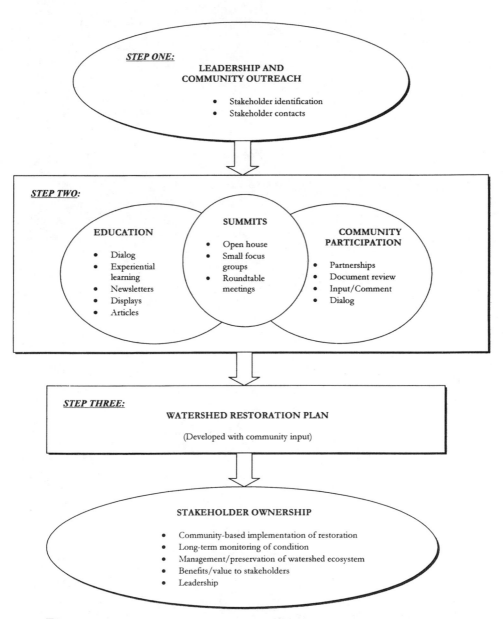

Figure 14.1. Three steps have been shown to lead to stakeholder ownership (modified from Gandy et al. 2002)

List of Reviewers

The editors gratefully acknowledge the following people, who reviewed part or all of the manuscript.

David W. Arnold
P.O. Box 103
Yazoo City, Mississippi 39194

Lindsay R. Boring
Director
Joseph W. Jones Ecological Research Center
Ichauway, Route 2, Box 2324
Newton, Georgia 31770

Eugene C. Bricklemyer Jr.
President
Aquatic Resource Conservation Group
3706 Southwest Hill Street
Seattle, Washington 98126-2034

Mark M. Brinson
Department of Biology
East Carolina University
Greenville, North Carolina 27858

Richard Buchholz
Assistant Professor of Biology
University of Mississippi
104 Shoemaker Hall
University, Mississippi 38677

Christopher Craft
Environmental Science Research Center
Indiana University
1315 East 10th Street
Room 410 J
Bloomington, Indiana 47401-1710

Richard Devereux
Research Microbiologist
United States Environmental Protection Agency
Gulf Ecology Division
Gulf Breeze, Florida 32561

Stephen D'Surney
Associate Professor of Biology
University of Mississippi
504 Shoemaker Hall
University, Mississippi 38677

Katherine C. Ewel
United States Department of Agriculture,
Natural Resources Conservation Service
Prince Kuhio Federal Building
Room 4-112
P.O. Box 50004
Honolulu, Hawaii 96850

Stuart Findlay
Institute of Ecosystem Studies
Box AB
Millbrook, New York 12545-0129

Barry Gillespie Jr.
Project Scientist
ENTRIX, Inc.
5252 West Chester, Suite 250
Houston, Texas 77005

Yaffa Grossman
Assistant Professor of Biology
Beloit College
700 College Street
Beloit, Wisconsin 53511

Lidija Halda-Alija
Assistant Professor of Biology
University of Mississippi
508 Shoemaker Hall
University, Mississippi 38677

Frank Harris
Oak Ridge National Laboratories
P.O. Box 2008
Oak Ridge, Tennessee 37831-6253

Richard Hauer
Flathead Lake Biological Station
University of Montana
311 Bio Station Lane
Polson, Montana 59860-9659

Vance Hughes
607 14th Street, Northwest
Suite 900
Washington, D.C. 20005

Bob Izler
Director
Administrative Center for Forest Business
School of Forest Resources
University of Georgia
Athens, Georgia 30602-2152

Nan Johnson
P.O. Box 167
Water Valley, Mississippi 38965

Sammy King
Department of Forestry, Wildlife, and Fisheries
University of Tennessee
278 Ellington Plant Sciences Building
P.O. Box 1071
Knoxville, Tennessee 37996

Barbara Kleiss
Wetlands Research Team (WESR-W)
United States Army Corps of Engineers
Water Ways Experiment Station
P.O. Box 631
Vicksburg, Mississippi 39181-0631

Bob Kochtitzky
The Mississippi 2020 Network
P.O. Box 13506
Jackson, Mississippi 39236

Lucile McCook
Assistant Professor of Biology
The University of Mississippi
406 Shoemaker Hall
University, Mississippi 38677

Bill Michener
LTER Network Office
801 University Boulevard, Southeast
Suite 104
Albuquerque, New Mexico 87131

Paul Newell
Director
District 8 Public Health Service
1109 North Jackson Street
Albany, Georgia 31707-2022

Steve Opsahl
Assistant Scientist
Joseph W. Jones Ecological Research Center
Route 2, Box 2324
Newton, Georgia 31770

Jamison Posey
Research Assistant, University of Mississippi Field Station
15 Road 2078
Abbeville, Mississippi 38601

Garth Redfield
Resource Assessment Division,
South Florida Water Management District
P.O. Box 24680
West Palm Beach, Florida 33416-4680

Paul Risser
Chancellor
Oklahoma State Regents for Higher Education
655 Research Parkway, Suite 200
Oklahoma City, Oklahoma 73104

Jean Shaw
Professor Emeritus
The University of Mississippi
207 St. Andrews Circle
Oxford, Mississippi 38655

Jeffrey Thornton
Principal Planner (Environment)
Southeastern Wisconsin Regional Planning Commission
P.O. Box 1607
Waukesha, WI 53187-1607

David White
Professor, Biological Sciences
Murray State University
Hancock Biological Station
561 Emma Drive
Murray, Kentucky 42071-6239

Linda Winfield
2280 Freetown Road
Vicksburg, Mississippi 39180

Joy Zedler
Department of Botany
University of Wisconsin
Birge Hall, 430 Lincoln Drive
Madison, Wisconsin 53706

List of Contributors

Elizabeth R. Blood: Dr. Elizabeth Blood is an ecologist at the Joseph W. Jones Ecological Research Center in Newton, Georgia, and an adjunct graduate professor at the Institute of Ecology, University of Georgia, Athens. She has published several books and many scientific articles on a variety of water-related topics, including regional water management, wetlands, watershed modeling, estuary conditions, agricultural water consumption, and nutrient cycling. Dr. Blood was appointed by Georgia Governor Roy Barnes to the Georgia Joint Comprehensive Water Plan Study Committee, and she is a member of the Georgia Drought Management Planning Committee, the Southwest Georgia Agribusiness Association, and a founding member of the Southwest Georgia Water Resources Task Force and Southwest Georgia Water Resource and Health Initiative. In 2000, she was named in *Georgia Trend* magazine's "One Hundred Most Influential Persons in Georgia."

Bryan W. Brooks: Dr. Bryan W. Brooks is an assistant professor in the Department of Environmental Studies at Baylor University. He completed a doctoral degree in environmental science at the Institute of Applied Sciences, University of North Texas, in 2002 and a master's degree in limnology at The University of Mississippi in 1998. His current research interests include risk assessment of pharmaceutical contaminants in surface waters and the relationship between ecotoxicological biomarkers and higher levels of biological organization.

W. James Catallo: Dr. W. James Catallo received his doctoral degree in marine sciences/chemistry in 1989 at the Virginia Institute of Marine Science, College of William and Mary, in Williamsburg, Virginia. Since then he has directed the Laboratory for Ecological Chemistry and Toxicology at Louisiana State University, Baton Rouge. His research interests include organic chemistry in high energy (supercritical water, sonochemical fields) and low energy (sediments, organisms) aqueous systems, biomass conversion to fuel

329

and petrochemical feedstocks (i.e., green chemistry of petrochemicals), and ecological systems modeling and restoration/recovery.

Alice M. Clark: Dr. Alice M. Clark is The University of Mississippi's vice chancellor for research and sponsored programs. The Frederick A. P. Barnard Distinguished Professor joined the faculty in 1979 as a postdoctoral research associate, and she has authored or contributed to more than ninety peer-reviewed research articles, numerous invited book chapters, non-refereed publications and presentations, and is an inventor on more than twenty patents. Clark's research interests include discovery and development of prototype antibiotics and use of microorganisms as tools in synthesis and metabolism studies.

Charles M. Cooper: Dr. Cooper is a supervisory research ecologist for the United States Department of Agriculture, Agricultural Research Service at the National Sedimentation Laboratory in Oxford, Mississippi. He received his M.S. and Ph.D. degrees from The University of Mississippi in Oxford. His research interests include investigation of basic sediment-biological-chemical interactions in aquatic ecosystems, documentation and explanation of the effects of agriculture and watershed conservation measures on stream and impoundment water quality and ecology, and stream corridor management and restoration.

Sara A. Davis: Dr. Sara Davis is the project coordinator for Remote Acoustic Hemostasis for the Jamie Whitten National Center for Physical Acoustics at The University of Mississippi. Her publications and projects focus on themes such as utilization of native plant species for constructed wetlands for wastewater treatment, integration of sustainability concepts into teaching at postsecondary educational institutions, and biomedical acoustics applications.

Ronald D. DeLaune: Dr. DeLaune is a professor in the Wetland Biogeochemistry Institute and an adjunct professor in the Agronomy Department at Louisiana State University. His research interests include biogeochemical cycling, remediation of oiled wetlands, coastal restoration, soil-plant interactions, coastal marsh stability, sediment processes, wetland plant ecology, degradation and bioremediation of toxic organics, heavy metal chemistry, ecotoxicology, and greenhouse gasses.

Julie H. Edmister: Dr. Edmister is Associate Professor of Educational Leadership at The University of Mississippi, where she teaches and conducts research in leadership and organizational effectiveness. Julie is the author of numerous articles on quality management theory and practices, and a contributing author of a two-volume book, *High Performing Colleges: The Malcolm*

Baldrige National Quality Award as a Framework for Improving Higher Education. She served as a Malcolm Baldrige National Quality Award Examiner for five years and was selected by the National Institute of Standards and Technology to serve as a member of the Baldrige Education Pilot Evaluation Team tasked with developing and refining the key elements that make up a rigorous and credible award system for education.

Kristen M. Fletcher: Dr. Fletcher received her B.A. degree from Auburn University, her J.D. degree from the University of Notre Dame Law School, and her L.L.M. degree in environmental and natural resources law from the Northwestern School of Law of Lewis and Clark College. Dr. Fletcher serves as the director of the Mississippi-Alabama Sea Grant Legal Program and the National Sea Grant Law Center. She advises Sea Grant constituents on national and regional ocean and coastal law issues, and she researches and publishes papers on natural resources, marine, and environmental law issues.

Christy M. Foran: Dr. Foran, currently an assistant professor of biology at West Virginia University, received her B.S. degree in May 1992 from the Department of Zoology at the University of Texas, Austin, and her Ph.D. in August 1998 in neurobiology and behavior from Cornell University. Her research focuses on the ways environmental stimuli impacts the development and expression of adult reproductive phenotypes.

Bruce Forsberg: Dr. Bruce Forsberg (B.S., Michigan State University; Ph.D., University of Minnesota; postdoctoral fellow, University of Washington) is a research scientist at the Instituto Nacional de Pesquisas da Amazonia, in Manaus, Brazil. Dr. Forsberg's two decades of research in the Amazon Basin has considered the limnology of floodplain lakes, the biogeochemistry of carbon in the river, and mercury contamination and trophic relations in lakes and rivers. He advises agencies and nongovernmental organizations on the conservation of aquatic resources in the Amazon River Basin.

Emile S. Gardiner: Dr. Gardiner is a research forester with the USDA Forest Service, Southern Research Station, and is based at the Center for Bottomland Hardwoods Research in Stoneville, Mississippi. He received his B.S. and M.S. degrees from Louisiana State University in Baton Rouge and his Ph.D. from Mississippi State University in Starkville. His research interests include the regeneration processes of bottomland hardwood tree species.

Laura Hess: Dr. Laura Hess (B.A., University of California, Berkeley; Ph.D., University of California, Santa Barbara) is a postdoctoral researcher at the Institute for Computational Earth System Science, University of California,

Santa Barbara. Dr. Hess's research concerns applications of microwave and optical remote sensing to the ecology and hydrology of wetlands. Her paper topics include analyses using synthetic aperture radar data obtained from the space shuttle, aircraft, and satellites, and using extensive digital videography coverage of the Amazon River Basin.

Marjorie M. Holland: Dr. Marjorie M. Holland has over a decade of experience in natural resource management and public policy at local, state, regional, national, and international levels. In June 1987, her background in wetland science led her to serve as the science representative from UNESCO (United Nations Educational, Scientific, and Cultural Organization) to the Third Meeting of the Conference of the Contracting Parties to the Convention on Wetlands of International Importance Especially as Waterfowl Habitat, held in Regina, Saskatchewan, Canada. Currently, Dr. Holland serves as director of The University of Mississippi Field Station and the Center for Water and Wetland Resources and is a professor in the Biology Department. In October 1999, she was awarded "Remarkable Woman" status by Smith College, in Northampton, Massachusetts, "for her pioneering work in environmental public policy and for her scholarship and teaching that helps protect our nation's waterways."

K. Erica Marsh: Erica Marsh is a student in the Department of Biology's M. Sc. program at The University of Mississippi. Her research interests focus on the evolution of sexual strategies in coral reef fishes and marine chemical ecology. Combining these two areas has led to her current project studying sex pheromones in gobies, which she is presently investigating in the Exuma Cays of the Bahamas.

John M. Melack: Dr. Melack is a professor of Biological Sciences at the University of California, Santa Barbara. His fields of expertise are limnology of tropical, saline, and alpine lakes; phytoplankton and zooplankton ecology; biogeochemistry; wetland ecology; and remote sensing. Professor Melack and his graduate students have successfully applied microwave remote sensing to delineate inundation and wetland vegetation in the Amazon and other tropical wetlands in Brazil and Australia.

Leal Mertes: Dr. Leal A. K. Mertes is a professor of geography at the University of California, Santa Barbara. She is an interdisciplinary scientist with B.S. degrees in both geology and biology from Stanford University and M.S. and Ph.D. degrees in geology from the University of Washington. Her research investigates the geomorphic and hydrologic processes responsible for the evolution of floodplains in large river systems and involves developing remote sensing techniques for analysis of wetlands and water properties.

Scott A. Milburn: Mr. Scott Milburn received his M.S. degree in biology from The University of Mississippi in 1999. He is currently employed as a wetland scientist with Peterson Environmental Consulting in Mendota Heights, Minnesota. He has served as project manager for wetland field surveys and as an investigator for threatened and endangered species on projects in the Great Lakes region.

Matthew T. Moore: Dr. Matthew Moore is an ecologist for the United States Department of Agriculture, Agricultural Research Service, at the National Sedimentation Laboratory in Oxford, Mississippi. He received his Ph.D. in biology and aquatic ecotoxicology from The University of Mississippi in 1999. His research interests include the use of constructed wetlands and other edge-of-field best management practices for water quality improvement, the impacts of agricultural storm-water runoff on aquatic ecosystems, TMDL (Total Maximum Daily Load) issues, water-quality criteria (primarily nutrients and sediments), and toxicology.

Dale G. Nagle: Dr. Nagle earned his Ph.D. in pharmacy in 1994 at the Oregon State University College of Pharmacy. Dr. Nagle was appointed Assistant Professor of Pharmacognosy and Research Assistant Professor of The Research Institute of Pharmaceutical Sciences at The University of Mississippi School of Pharmacy in 1997. His research combines chemistry and biology to discover new agents for use in agriculture and the treatment of human disease.

John A. Nyman: Dr. Nyman is an assistant professor in the School of Renewable Natural Resources at Louisiana State University Agricultural Center in Baton Rouge. Dr. Nyman's research interests usually explore the response of wetland ecosystems to hydrological alteration, global sea level rise, or pollution. Much of his research addresses vegetation.

Clifford A. Ochs: Dr. Ochs is an associate professor in the Department of Biology at The University of Mississippi in Oxford. His research interests include population dynamics and ecological interactions of aquatic microorganisms, the effects of the light and chemical environment on aquatic microbial community structure and function, and nutrient biogeochemistry in aquatic and terrestrial ecosystems.

S. Reza Pezeshki: Dr. Pezeshki is a professor in the Department of Biology at The University of Memphis and has served as principal/co-principal investigator of numerous research projects funded by agencies including the U.S. Forest Service, National Science Foundation, and the USDA Competitive Grants Program. He is the author or co-author of over 150 reports and technical papers including those published in scientific journals such as *Freshwater Ecology Management*, *Environmental and Experimental Botany*, and *Wetland Ecology and Management*. Dr. Pezeshki's areas of interest include basic and applied aspects of plant ecophysiology, wetland ecology, and restoration.

Catherine M. Pringle: Dr. Pringle is a professor for the Institute of Ecology at The University of Georgia, where she serves as chair of the Graduate Program in Conservation Ecology and Sustainable Development. Research interests include aquatic ecology, conservation biology, tropical ecology, and effects of environmental problems on the ecology of aquatic ecosystems. She is currently serving as president of the North American Benthological Society (2002–2003) and chair of the Ecological Society of America's Sustainable Biosphere Initiative, Steering Committee.

Walter Rast: Dr. Rast is the director of the Aquatic Station and Associate Professor of Biology at Southwest Texas State University in San Marcos. He served as Environmental Scientist and Secretary for the Great Lakes Water Quality Board at the Great Lakes Regional Office of the U.S.–Canada International Joint Commission in Windsor, Ontario, Canada. Prior to serving with the Commission, he served as deputy director of the Water Branch at the headquarters of UNEP (the United Nations Environment Programme) in Nairobi, Kenya. Dr. Rast's general research interests focus on the limnological similarities and differences between lakes and reservoirs, water quality, and the assessment and environmentally sound management of freshwater resources for their sustainable use in meeting human needs and for ecosystem maintenance, including international water systems.

Paul B. Rodrigue: Paul Rodrigue is a hydrologist for the Natural Resources Conservation Service (NRCS), Wetland Science Institute. Mr. Rodrigue's area of interest includes integrating hydrologic principles into Wetland Science Institute activities, including technical procedures for wetland hydrology determinations, improved methods for wetland hydrology restoration, and constructed wetlands for treatment of agricultural runoff. In addition, he serves as technical lead for the NRCS Hydrology Tools for Wetland Determination and Restoration Course.

Lawrence R. Shaffer: Dr. Shaffer is currently a professor at the Oxford, Mississippi, campus of Northwest Mississippi Community College. He received his Ph.D. in quantitative biology at the University of Texas, Arlington. Dr. Shaffer has served in such positions as research scientist for the Center for Water and Wetland Resources at The University of Mississippi, assistant professor for the Department of Biology for The University of Mississippi, and National

Research Council Research Associate for the Waterways Experiment Station in Vicksburg, Mississippi. His research interests include freshwater biology and behavioral ecology.

Marc Slattery: Dr. Slattery is an associate professor of pharmacognosy and a research associate professor at the Research Institute of Pharmaceutical Sciences. In 1994, he received his Ph.D. in biology from the University of Alabama, Birmingham, for chemical ecology research conducted in Antarctica. Dr. Slattery was awarded a Marine Biotechnology Fellowship from the National Science Foundation in 1994 to continue his research on the tropical Pacific reef systems at the University of Guam. Dr. Slattery's current research interests include the chemical ecology of marine invertebrates and bacteria, particularly those from extreme environments, and phenotypic plasticity of these chemical defenses.

John A. Stanturf: Dr. Stanturf, project leader for the Disturbance and Management of Southern Ecosystems Unit of the Southern Research Station, U.S. Forest Service, received his Ph.D. in forest soils in 1983 from Cornell University. His major research interests include ecology and sustainable management of forested ecosystems in the South. Dr. Stanturf's work fits into three broad categories: ecosystem renewal, ecosystem restoration, and intensive plantation culture.

Melvin L. Warren Jr.: Dr. Warren is a research biologist and team leader for the Ecology of Aquatic and Terrestrial Fauna Team for the U.S. Forest Service, Center for Bottomland Hardwoods Research. Dr. Warren's core area of research includes the biology and community ecology of native warm-water fishes and freshwater mussels, with emphasis on threatened, endangered, and sensitive species at scales encompassing habitat units within a reach to whole river basins.

Robert G. Wetzel: Dr. Wetzel is currently a professor at the University of North Carolina's Department of Environmental Sciences and Engineering. He has won numerous awards for his work and has held or is currently holding thirty-eight editorial positions with leading journals and professional organizations. He has authored, co-authored, and edited more than 20 books and 350 refereed journal publications, has published 227 abstracts, and has directed the work of 36 doctoral students and 30 postdoctoral associates. Dr. Wetzel's research interests include physiology and ecology of algae and higher aquatic plants, biogeochemical cycling in freshwater ecosystems, and functional roles of organic compounds and detritus in aquatic ecosystems.

Kristine L. Willett: Dr. Willett is an assistant professor of pharmacology and a member of the research faculty for the Environmental Toxicology Research Program in the Research Institute of Pharmaceutical Sciences, School of Pharmacy, The University of Mississippi, in Oxford. Her research involves understanding the mechanisms of action of environmental contaminants in fish.

Keith M. Wright: Mr. Wright is an educator, writer, and activist. He was formerly affiliated with The University of Mississippi's Center for Water and Wetland Resources, where he worked on editing and writing while beginning a second career as a wetlands scientist. He is currently finishing a master's degree in wetlands conservation at the University of Massachusetts in Amherst.

Index